Rediscovering Groups

The International Library of Group Analysis
Edited by Malcolm Pines, Institute of Group Analysis, London

The aim of this series is to represent innovative work in group psychotherapy, particularly but not exclusively group analysis. Group analysis, taught and practised widely in Europe, has developed from the work of S.H. Foulkes.

Other titles in the series

Circular Reflections
Selected Papers on Group Analysis and Psychoanalysis
Malcolm Pines
International Library of Group Analysis 1
ISBN 1 85302 492 9 paperback
ISBN 1 85302 493 7 hardback

Group Psychotherapy of the Psychoses
Concepts, Interventions and Context
Edited by Victor L. Schermer and Malcolm Pines
International Library of Group Analysis 2
ISBN 1 85302 584 4 paperback
ISBN 1 85302 583 6 hardback

Attachment and Interaction
Mario Marrone with a contribution by Nicola Diamond
International Library of Group Analysis 3
ISBN 1 85302 586 0 paperback
ISBN 1 85302 587 9 hardback

Self Experiences in Group
Intersubjective and Self Psychological Pathways to Human Understanding
Edited by Irene Harwood and Malcolm Pines
International Library of Group Analysis 4
ISBN 1 85302 610 7 paperback
ISBN 1 85302 596 8 hardback

Taking the Group Seriously
Towards an Post-Foulkesian Group Analytic Theory
Farhad Dalal
International Library of Group Analysis 5
ISBN 1 85302 642 5 paperback

Active Analytic Group Therapy for Adolescents
John Evans
International Library of Group Analysis 6
ISBN 1 85302 616 6 paperback
ISBN 1 85302 617 4 hardback

The Group Context
Sheila Thompson
International Library of Group Analysis 7
ISBN 1 85302 657 3 paperback

Group
Claudio Neri
International Library of Group Analysis 8
ISBN 1 85302 418 X paperback

INTERNATIONAL LIBRARY OF GROUP ANALYSIS 9

Rediscovering Groups

A Psychoanalyst's Journey Beyond Individual Psychology

Marshall Edelson and David N. Berg

Foreword by Robert M. Lipgar

Jessica Kingsley Publishers
London and Philadelphia

First published in the United Kingdom in 1999 by
Jessica Kingsley Publishers Ltd
116 Pentonville Road
London N1 9JB, England
and
325 Chestnut Street
Philadelphia, PA 19106, USA

www.jkp.com

Copyright © 1999 Marshall Edelson except
Chapters 5, 6, 7, 8, 10, 12, 15, 18, 21, 23, 26, 28 © 1999 David N. Berg

Library of Congress Cataloging-in-Publication Data
A CIP catalogue record for this book is available from the Library of Congress

British Library Cataloguing in Publication Data
Edelson, Marshall, 1928–
Rediscovering groups : a psychoanalyst's journey beyond individual psychology. –
(International library of group analysis ; 9)
1.Group psychotherapy
I.Title II.Berg, David N., 1949–
616.8'9152

ISBN 1 85302 726 X paperback
ISBN 1 85302 725 1 hardback

Printed and Bound in Great Britain by
Athenaeum Press, Gateshead, Tyne and Wear

In memory of Daniel J. Levinson

Books by Marshall Edelson

The Termination of Intensive Psychotherapy (1963)
Ego Psychology, Group Dynamics and the Therapeutic Community (1964)
Sociotherapy and Psychotherapy (1970)
The Practice of Sociotherapy: A Case Study (1970)
The Idea of Mental Illness (1971)
Language and Interpretation in Psychoanalysis (1975)
Hypothesis and Evidence in Psychoanalysis (1984)
Psychoanalysis: A Theory in Crisis (1988)

Books by David Berg

Failures in Organization Development and Change (with P.H. Mirvis) (1977)
Exploring Clinical Methods for Social Research (with K.K. Smith) (1985)
Paradoxes of Group Life: Understanding Conflict, Paralysis, and Movement in Group Dynamics (with K.K. Smith) (1988)
Keeping the Faith (1992)

I tell the truth, not as much as I would but as much as I dare –
and I dare more and more as I grow older.

Montaigne

The individual's apartness from the group is brought about
through splitting and projection, projection into an individual
group member or into the group as a whole. Hence we see the
development of a 'nothing to do with me' attitude and a group's
capacity to offer the individual opportunities for opting out.

Pierre M. Turquet

Contents

PART THREE: INDIVIDUAL VS. GROUP

PART FOUR: USING AND ABUSING AUTHORITY

PART FIVE: PERNICIOUS PROCESSES IN GROUPS

PART SIX: INTERGROUP RELATIONS

PART SEVEN: USING GROUPS TO HELP PEOPLE

Acknowledgments

I, Marshall Edelson, have shifted in my life from one way of looking at things to another – as a cinematographer changes from one kind of shot to another. I have chosen the frame, individual or group, as a cinematographer may choose the frame even while the camera remains pointed at the same phenomena.

Using a close-up, I have concentrated on – I have filled the frame with – the ineffable expressiveness of a human face. I have been drawn in, absorbed by, immersed in this face; nothing could distract me from the mystery of this person's psyche. I have imagined the thoughts and feelings those eyes and lips, the markings on that skin, the suggestion of bone, the light and shadows betray – even when the tongue is still. I have been moved to wonder – I have made up stories – about the motives, the plans, the obstacles faced and overcome by this individual.

But this same individual played a part in another kind of story. I have been interested in that story too. So, using a wide deep-focus shot, I have included in the frame a complex scene, entire, with all its details, props, characters, events, some in the foreground, some in the background, some in between. One conversation or action overlaps another. Different objects convey different information, raise different questions, have different possible significances. I have taken it all in, letting my eye and ear move unhurriedly from place to place. I have reflected on the patterns of relations between events, setting, and characters. I have wondered – I have made up stories – about the roles this individual and other individuals played in creating these patterns, about how the patterns remained the same or what might change them, about their consequences, about the participation of individuals in collective processes and the influence of situational and social-structural factors on these processes.

Who and what circumstances have influenced at various times which frame, group or individual, I favor?

As a graduate student in psychology at the University of Chicago in the late 1940s, I worked alongside Robert Lipgar and Dorothy Stock in the Group Relations Laboratory of Herbert Thelen. Our studies of groups were in the traditions both of Kurt Lewin and W. R. Bion. I also participated in a National Training Laboratory conference in group relations, Bethel, Maine; NTL was led largely by students of Kurt Lewin. While I later lost personal contact with Dorothy Stock Whitaker, I was to be influenced by her books, *Psychotherapy through the Group Process* (with Mort Lieberman) and *Using Groups to Help People*, and to use them in my teaching.

As I attempted (1961–1968) to develop therapeutic communities in residential treatment centers, struggling to understand what happened in such treatment centers, I immersed myself in the study of sociology, especially the work of Talcott Parsons and Robert Merton, and was also drawn to the writings of Fritz Redl. In the mid 1960s, I attended Group Relations Conferences at Mount Holyoke College, which were sponsored by the Tavistock Institute of Human Relations in England and the Washington School of Psychiatry and also by the Department of Psychiatry, Yale University School of Medicine. I attended the Tavistock Group Relations Conference at the University of Leicester in England. From 1966 to 1968, I was on the faculty of the Mount Holyoke Tavistock Conferences. I was deeply influenced by my work during this period with Pierre Turquet and A. K. Rice, and by the writings of such figures as Jacques Sutherland and Isabel Menzies.

I continued through the years, usually in extended phone conversations, to discuss group processes with Bob Lipgar, who followed me in participating in the Mount Holyoke Tavistock Conferences, and eventually became a leader of such conferences in the Chicago area, a major teacher and practitioner of group psychotherapy, and a prominent figure in the Illinois Group Psychotherapy Association. Bob read and commented in detail on an entire earlier draft of the book. It is not easy to find even a close friend who is willing to take on that job. My wife Zelda, a skilled editor, heroically has done this not once but with each of the many drafts that came along. Sue and Greer Allen repeatedly offered enthusiasm and encouragement; Sue read and helpfully commented 'as a lay reader' on a large portion of an early draft.

From 1968 on, I became relatively separated from a social system perspective in what I did, studied, and thought. I was learning psychoanalysis. At least one of my teachers in the institute in which I was enrolled questioned whether I was 'truly committed' to psychoanalysis when I missed a class in order to attend a Tavistock Conference. It was also not accidental, I believe, that Freud's works on the social – his *Group Psychology and the Analysis of the Ego, Civilization and Its Discontents,* and *Totem and Taboo* – were not part of the curriculum of the institute. I turned my attention from the social to the individual. Abandoning the dream of creating a therapeutic community, I began working primarily with problems of curriculum as an educator in a university department of psychiatry. I practiced psychoanalysis and taught individual psychotherapy in the department and psychoanalysis in the institute. I watched Hollywood movies, which represent and resolve social system problems in stories about individuals or couples.

However, as I struggled as a teacher with experiences in seminar groups, and experienced various dissatisfactions with the way in which groups in the organizations in which I worked functioned, I felt increasingly that a psychodynamic or psychoanalytic perspective, which focused on individuals and their motives and problems, was not sufficient to understand these experiences. I was fortunate to have two friends who brought me back to what I knew about groups and organizations and extended what I knew about them: Daniel Levinson and David N. Berg, one a social psychologist and the other an organizational psychologist. To both of them, in extended conversations, often at lunch, I talked of my life in organizations and groups (at work, as a faculty member, administrator and teacher, in committees and seminars, and also at home, as a husband and father). We told stories to each other, and learned from each others' stories. I think of Dan and David as my teachers in the most important sense of the word *educator;* they drew out of me what was in me, what I already knew but had forgotten or no longer knew that I knew.

A book born out of relationships

I need another word than 'Acknowledgments'. It is a cliché to say that this book would not have been written except for … , but what I want to say is that this book was born of two relationships, one between myself and Dan and the other between myself and David. Each of these pairs has some claim to be the book's progenitor. The child does not belong to one or the other member of either pair; this part of the child does not belong to one and that part to the other of either pair. The entire book is created out of these relationships and could not have come into being without them. The relationships were expressed in intimate, uninhibited, lively, and absorbing conversations, in which both listening and response were intense.

Dan was one of my few close friends who was neither a member of a much older or a much younger generation. I felt we were at about the same place in our lives. Both he and I, though we were peers, felt able and happy to learn from the other. He cared very much also about relationships across generations. He loved his sons and reflected a good deal about the ways in which he might be clumsy in his relationship with them. This sense of the next generation carried over into his professional life. He felt it was of major importance for a faculty member to be a mentor of someone younger, to assist that younger person in their career and in creating the structure of their lives. He had a gift for imagining how a particular situation would be experienced by another, a daughter, a son, a wife, a student, a woman in a world dominated by men. He accepted in himself and helped me to accept in myself what was masculine and feminine; that was liberating. He listened to my stories with an intense unwavering attention I have not often experienced. When we talked, I had no sense that time had any meaning for him. I felt an enveloping maternal concentration on what we were sharing. I existed completely in that moment of his complete attention. He saw the beginnings of this book, urged me to get on with it, and as a beneficiary of his caring, for all I owe him, I dedicate it to his memory.

Dan brought David, then in his thirties, and me, then in my fifties, together. Both David and I, though of different generations, were exhilarated to find that we could bridge that gap and, crossing it in both directions, learn from each other, surviving and indeed making use of diversity in our backgrounds, interests, and approaches, and the often angry disagreements that arose from it. That in my sixties I still wanted to learn, that I was open to learning from someone younger than myself, and that I in turn could connect with and affect someone across the divide of generational difference, was deeply meaningful to me. For me, to lose touch with the next generation is to lose life. So this book is testimony that such an intergenerational relationship is possible and that life continues.

The contributions of David Berg to this work

I, psychiatrist and psychoanalyst, in my sixties, told David Berg, organizational psychologist, in his forties, many stories about my experiences in groups and organizations. David responded, often by telling a story from his own life in groups and organizations. His response might remind me of still other stories, which through their relation to the story with which I began, changed my view of it. I would begin to reflect on my story. I would make use of some idea of David's that was new to me, or remember some idea I once held and used in years past when I had worked with and thought about social systems – an idea that had become lost to me as I became a psychoanalyst and focused more and more on individuals. The idea then would find its way into my story as I might later, for example, in writing this book, retell it. I would test the idea, what I thought I had learned (the 'moral' of the story), by trying out something different in a group setting, for example, in a seminar I was teaching. That experiment became a new story.

So any story I tell in this book has already been to some degree transformed by the exchanges between David and me. This process proved difficult, indeed impossible, to reproduce in this book as it had occurred, although we wish we could have found a way to represent it adequately. But it is this process that makes David and me co-authors of this book, although we did not literally *write* all of it together. Each of us kept in separately written sections his own voice and these sections are so marked. We continued engaging in lengthy conversations. The book only faintly represents those conversations, but it bears their mark. Sometimes what David writes is a commentary on – a reaction to – stories of my own experiences and my attempts to make sense of them. At other times, he brings to bear his experiences and reflections *ab initio* on a topic we are jointly considering or that he invites us to consider. Similarly, sometimes I write primarily about ideas I have found useful in understanding and dealing with particular experiences. At other times I react to or make use of some perspective or concept of David's that for me is a new way, or a rediscovery of a way, of thinking about these experiences.

During all of the five plus years I came up with one version after another, David acted as muse, inspiring and encouraging me to go on, to give birth to what he insisted was 'my' work. We came to agree that in a sense it was 'my' book – a distillation of experiences, skills, and ideas applicable to group and organizational life that I felt motivated now at this age to set down as a legacy. But David's stories, thoughts, experience, and expertise, and above all his affectionate and creatively turbulent interactions with me, exist throughout it. In both our minds, this book is the outcome of our relationship, in which we learned from and influenced each other.

There are things in the book that would not be there at all except that he gave them to me. My stories often have mental health settings. David's stories about his experiences in *other kinds of groups and organizations* provide grounds to continue to believe that the group and organizational dynamics about which we write are characteristic of more than one kind of group or organization.

I came to the writing of the book holding onto the idea of solidarity – what was shared and how widely and deeply it was shared – as the measure of what I valued and sought in group life. Before talking and working with David, I often regarded disagreements and conflicts in work groups as personally motivated or as symptomatic of a collective descent into irrationality, which in either case obstructed collective task-achievement. (I did recognize as inevitable and interesting, though problematic, those conflicts I understood as arising from a division of labor that led groups responsible for different kinds of subtasks to differ in the values they held or to compete for the same limited resources.) David, however, changed me, and the emerging book, by arguing for *the value of diversity and dissent* – and for the *potential creative consequences of conflict* – in group and organizational life.

I also came to the writing of this book with a much narrower view than David's of what kinds of experiences were subjects for stories about *intergroup* relations. He believed that looking at an unexpectedly wide range of group and organizational phenomena with *group identities* (gender, race, ethnicity, age, socioeconomic status, hierarchical position) and *the relations between these kinds of groups* in mind helps us to grasp the dynamics that produce this variety of phenomena. He saw that, however things seemed, many stories are best told as intergroup stories. His persistent focus on group identities and intergroup relations increasingly influenced my thinking.

And, finally, David's deep interest in exploring *the dynamics of two-person collaborations*, including collaborations *across generational lines* such as ours, is not only evident in the book itself, but got us through some difficult patches in writing it.

More acknowledgments

The sources of the epigraphs at the beginning of the book and preceding each of the seven parts of the book are as follows.

Before acknowledgments

Quotation by Montaigne, from: *The Concise Columbia Dictionary of Quotations.* Microsoft Bookshelf CD-ROM Reference Library. 1993 Multimedia PC edition. Quotation by Pierre M. Turquet, from: Turquet, Pierre M. (1978) 'Leadership: the individual and the group.' 349–371. In Graham Gibbard, John Hartman, and Richard Mann (eds) *Analysis of Groups.* San Francisco: Jossey-Bass, 369. Reprinted with the kind permission of Jossey-Bass.

Before part one

Quotation by Walter Benjamin, from: Benjamin, Walter (1968) 'The storyteller,' 83–110. In Hannah Arendt, (ed) *Illuminations: Essays and Reflections* by Walter Benjamin. New York: Schocken Books, 83, 89, 90. Excerpts from 'The Storyteller' in *Illuminations* by Walter Benjamin, copyright © 1955 by Suhrkamp Verlag, Frankfurt-am-Main, English translation by Harry Zohn, copyright 1968 and renewed 1966 by Harcourt-Brace and company, reprinted by permission of Harcourt-Brace and by permission of Suhrkamp Verlag.

Before part two

Quotation by Leroy Wells, from: Wells, L. (1980) 'The group-as-a-whole: a systemic socio-analytic perspective on interpersonal and group relations,' 54, 55, 64–65. In C. P. Alderfer and C. L.Cooper (eds) *Advances in Experiential Social Processes.* New York: John Wiley and Sons, 165–199. Copyright © John Wiley and Sons Limited, and reproduced with their kind permission.

Before part three

Quotations by Henry D. Thoreau from: Thoreau, H. D. (1937) *Walden.* New York: Modern Library. Quotation by Odell Sheppard from: Sheppard, O. (1937) *Pedlar's Progress.* Boston: Little, Brown and company publishers, 167–169. Quotation by V. F. Perkins, from: Perkins, V. F. (1972) *Film as Film: Understanding and Judging Movies.* New York: Penguin Paperback, 156. Copyright © V.F. Perkins 1972. Reprinted with the kind permission of Penguin Books Ltd.

Before part four

Quotation by David Rapaport, from: Rapaport, David 'The autonomy of the ego,' pp. 357–367. In: Merton Gill (ed) *The Collected Papers of David Rapaport.* New York: Basic Books, 357–358. Originally published in the *Bulletin of the Menninger Clinic, 15,*11, 3–123. © 1951 The Bulletin of the Menninger Clinic. Reprinted with permission.

Before part five

Quotation by James Baldwin, from: Baldwin, J. (1965) 'The American dream and the American Negro' *The New York Times Magazine,* March 7, 32–33, 87, 89. Copyright © 1965 The New York Times Company. Reprinted with permission. Poem by A. R. Ammons, 'No Tirement Like Retirement' (1977). In *The Snow Poems.* New York: W.W. Norton. Copyright © 1977 A.R. Ammons. Reprinted by permission W.W. Norton and company Inc.

Before part six

Quotation by Kenwyn Smith and David Berg, from: Smith, Kenwyn K. and Berg, David N. (1988) *Paradoxes of Group Life*. San Francisco: Jossey-Bass, 197–199. Reprinted with the kind permission of Jossey-Bass.

Before part seven

Quotation by D. S. Whitaker, from: Whitaker, D. S. (1985) *Using Groups to Help People*. London: Routledge & Kegan Paul, 32, 52–53. Reprinted with the kind permission of Routledge Ltd.

At the end of chapter thirteen

Excerpt from the poem 'The Ubiquitous Lout', in *Saint Suniti and the Dragon*. London: Virago Ltd., 1954. Reprinted with the kind permission of the author Suniti Namjoshi.

Foreword

Rediscovering Groups is an extraordinary achievement. It illuminates, through narrative and commentary, the complexities and contradictions of group and organizational life. Marshall Edelson and David N. Berg, by writing with uncommon intelligence, wisdom, frankness, and clarity about their own intensely felt experiences, give us observations and insights that are at once intimate and universal. The book is so carefully constructed and richly textured, with stories so well told and commentary so pertinent, that it should be required reading for all of us – whatever our role – who work with groups of any kind. It fills a need that no other book comes close to filling.

It happens to be Marshall Edelson's ninth book, and as I read it I was reminded of Beethoven's Ninth Symphony. In dialogue with David Berg, Edelson takes us on an exciting journey, exploring the most relevant and familiar group themes. Their dialogue is so varied and evocative that it is as if we were listening to an entire chorus. Edelson's previous books are scholarly and conceptual but here, in his ninth, he and his collaborator reach us directly through stories that sing, transport, and transform.

Rediscovering Groups is at once monumental in scale and comprehensiveness yet intimate and accessible, profound in its insights yet touchingly personal. Edelson's and Berg's voices sound from these pages with an immediacy and directness that compel our personal reflection and thoughtful responses. Their tales educate and enlighten us in ways that only time spent with good companions can. All of us – organizational consultants, teachers, clinicians, managers, executives, administrators, or committee and team members – who have tried to contribute to groups and organizations, to their productivity and meaning, will find ourselves in these tales. As the authors share their experiences, we revisit encounters and frustrations of our own and see new meanings in them. They narrate familiar scenarios of group life in ways that extend our vision, whether we look back or plan ahead.

Rediscovering Groups is a storehouse of insights into the interplay of intrapsychic, intragroup, intergroup and interorganizational dynamics. Edelson, in dialogue with Berg, explores scapegoating and gender stereotyping; the uses and abuses of authority; leadership and followership; power and influence; hierarchical and collaborative organizational structures; relations between groups; conflict and rebellion; shame and vulnerability; and mentors and mentoring – themes fundamental to group psychology. For me, exploring these themes with them was an enriching and rewarding adventure, one that has influenced the way I find myself working with patients, students, and colleagues.

This is a work that reaffirms my hopes for psychology – that our careful investigations of the human condition in clinical and educational settings will yield knowledge useful to those working in other settings.

Rediscovering Groups is unique in its field. It is the first book in fifty years to continue and extend the seminal work of Wilfred Bion's *Experiences in Groups*. Like Bion, Edelson and Berg share their experiences with us and, like Bion, they are very keen and wise observers in search of the fundamentals of group psychology. But their stories are more accessible than Bion's, more fully drawn, and taken from a wider range of group and organizational situations.

Edelson and Berg bring distinguished backgrounds and distinctive voices to their work. Their differences, perhaps even more than their similarities, enliven this book. Edelson, a respected professor and a scholar on the boundary between psychiatry/psychoanalysis and the social sciences, possesses broad clinical and administrative experience. He is a practicing psychoanalyst and psychotherapist, and is known to be a consummate teacher, generous, caring, and influential. In this volume, he takes us (and his collaborator) into his confidence and opens for us a great window on how to think, work and live in the complexities of social reality. Berg, a generation younger, brings to this collaboration a rare combination of organizational and clinical training and experience. Although he participates regularly in academia, he is primarily involved in an active independent consulting practice, working with a wide range of organizations and institutions as they confront the challenges of change, conflict, diversity, restructuring, and retraining.

The excitement of participating with Edelson and Berg as they work together was one of many surprises I found reading this book. Not only does *Rediscovering Groups* contain closely examined stories about their collaboration, but the book itself is an enactment of the changes and growth their work together required of them. It documents how they learned from each other. At the beginning of the book, Berg is in the role of a kind of alter-ego and consultant to Edelson, and then, by the end of the book, we find him as a co-worker, an active and interactive partner in teaching and consulting projects. This aspect of the book brings us into direct contact with the challenges of cooperating across boundaries of status, experience, areas of expertise, and generational differences – boundaries that so many of us have to negotiate daily at work and at home. This alone would be 'worth the price of admission'.

Rediscovering Groups concludes with a story about designing a boldly innovative group program. This story, like many others in the book, brings us to a deeper understanding of salient issues: how to consult to organizations; how to work collaboratively; how to initiate change within institutional settings; how to contend with our own aspirations, disappointments, and desires as these affect our work; and, most importantly perhaps, how to use our feelings as we think about what we're doing.

For all of us who may benefit from guideposts and beacons as we navigate the turbulent currents of contemporary group and organizational life, Edelson concludes with a succinct and powerful statement of his vision of the future of his own profession. Reading his prologue and conclusions may encourage the reader, struggling with difficult group experiences, to use the entire carefully constructed collection of stories and commentary as a consultant-in-residence. I believe many readers will recommend this book to others who want to understand better how to live in today's world of multiple, overlapping group identities, allegiances, and commitments.

This is not a book that offers abstract generalizations and general pre-scriptions. It is not a book of success stories. Rather it is a book that enacts the process of learning from experiences and from mistakes. Edelson and Berg have written a classic.

Robert M. Lipgar
Clinical Professor, Department of Psychiatry
University of Chicago Medical Center
November 15, 1998

Prologue

Marshall Edelson

This book is about understanding experiences in groups and organizations – no matter what kind of group or organization it is. Whenever there is a problem in a group or organization, its members in their attempts to solve it tend to become 'individual psychologists', each feeling 'it has nothing to do with me'. They identify *another* person who is or has 'the problem', who is to blame for it. They are satisfied that getting rid of or counseling this difficult, troublesome, or deviant individual will solve the group's or organization's problem. Making an individual the scapegoat and treating or replacing him[1] are simple 'solutions', but destructive of the individual and costly for the group or organization and its task.

But what if, instead, faced with a problem in a group or organization and wanting to understand it, its members were to consider characteristics of the group or organization itself: the kind of mission it exists to accomplish; the availability of resources required to accomplish that mission; the competition among different goals it pursues; the assignment of priorities to these goals? All pose quandaries. So also, paradoxically, the system's most highly prized procedures, arrangements, and norms and values, examined, turn out to have both work-enhancing and work-sabotaging consequences.

In addition, individual members of a group represent (wittingly or unwittingly), or are perceived as representing, other groups to which they also belong; that influences whether and how these individuals work together. The images that various groups or subgroups have of each other influence whether and how these groups make needed contributions to a joint endeavor. What bonds people together in groups are not only shared tasks, but also shared identities (for example, gender, race, socioeconomic class, ethnicity) that are not obviously relevant to a group's work but may enhance or interfere with it. Covert or informal groups also form around shared motives or attitudes people bring to a work situation (for example, sexual pursuits or rebellious dispositions) that are likely to prove inimical to work. Finally, pressures on a group or organization arise from changes in its current environment; these pressures, especially if their source or nature are ignored, are frequently translated maladaptively into intragroup tensions.

The approach to a problem in a group or organization suggested by these kinds of considerations is not easy to implement. It requires collecting masses of information from different sources. It involves putting together many apparently unrelated pieces, discovering links between many apparently unconnected events, and identifying many different contributions to the problem from different quarters. It not only implicates inimical conditions *external* to the group or organization to which members may not be paying attention, as well as integrative tensions attending value-conflicts and alienation *within* the group or organization, but – rather than just pointing to one person – it typically implicates a lot of people, each of whom contributes at least a little to the problem.

The understanding such an approach engenders is dauntingly complex. So, it is frustratingly slow in coming, and even slower in begetting a solution. But such solutions are likely to be more satisfactory in the long run than for members to join in disowning what belongs to the group-as-a-whole, instead blaming an individual for the problem. That individual, who is perceived as carrying what is disowned by others, becomes a casualty, at great cost to the group or organization and its work – and to no purpose. For, even when the scapegoated individual is extruded from the group or organization, the problem continues, and so someone else must inevitably be chosen to take the blame for it. Such a process may continue interminably, or may be terminated by the group's or organization's failure to survive. The more complex understanding, on the other hand, at the least helps us to keep our heads above water, to remain calm in the midst of turmoil, to retain perspective, to avoid taking what happens 'personally', and, above all, not to become totally immersed in collective, nothing-to-do-with-me, she-is-to-blame[2] persecutory processes.

I have never found theoretical talk about groups or organizations by itself draws people away from their preference for locating *the* problem person, or helps them to a better understanding of what is going on and what to do about it. Rather, telling and listening to stories has been my path to understanding experiences in groups and organizations. I have come to believe practical knowledge, our understanding of experiences in everyday life, is structured as stories rather than general theory. So, in this book, narrative is the method I use to represent or impart knowledge.

How does narrative participate in what we learn or know? As we attempt to understand a problem, and decide what to do about it, features of our current experience remind us of other similar or contrasting pieces of past experiences. These past experiences are encoded, stored in our minds, and reconstructed and recovered by us, as narratives, scripts, scenarios, scenes, or dramatic situations having or demanding resolution. One narrative reminds us of another because motifs, themes, constellations of characters, events, or relations between events in the one are similar to or contrast with those in the other. We remember how stories unfolded, what led to or caused what, what we did to achieve a goal or overcome an obstacle to achieving a goal, and to what effect. Remembering the moral of *that* story, we wonder if it might be applicable to *this* one in which we now find ourselves.

So, changing the way we think about groups and organizations requires access to stories about groups and organizations – *not* stories about an individual hero or villain, and in the main *not* general theory. This book contains lots of stories about experiences in groups and organizations. Access to these stories, and to the stories about experiences in groups and organizations readers will inevitably then remember from their own lives, will facilitate understanding what forces – and how these forces – bring about or maintain a problematic state of affairs.

This book is designed to help those who, as members or leaders, want to contribute to creating and maintaining work groups do just that. What does a work group look like? In short, members of such a group refrain from selecting a scapegoat to carry what they want to disown, and then isolating, 'treating', attacking, rejecting, or extruding that carrier. Instead, they seek to get in touch with and acknowledge whatever it is they are perceiving, thinking, feeling, or doing; that is, they own it. They endure and share whatever anxiety it arouses in them. They face together and find solutions for conflicts and dilemmas that confront them. They do all this because it enables them to achieve shared goals, to do the work they want to do; the work matters to them. This state of affairs, for however long it lasts, makes any group in which it exists 'a work group'.

Many of the stories in this book are about mental health or educational groups and organizations. If we view organizations and the groups in them as systems that take in raw inanimate things (tin, aluminum, steel …), which answer to our will, and, combining them, convert them into artefacts (automobiles …), or that take in inanimate signs or bits of information and, combining them, convert them into new knowledge, then these mental health or educational groups or organizations have a distinctive property. The 'materials' they take in, process, and change are not inanimate but human, alive. These 'things', these patients or students, wiggle, have wills of their own. They are elusive. They are recalcitrant. They say, 'No.' They bristle. They bite. They surprise us.

A mental health organization transforms patients. A school transforms students. But regarding patients or students as 'materials', as objects to be converted, as 'inputs' and 'outputs', as 'products', suggests falsely that they are as passive in the process of conversion as inanimate materials.

The stories in this book challenge those who participate in such organizations to imagine what must go into a 'process of production' that seeks to change human beings, who are and in fact must be, to one extent or another, *active* participants in their own transformation. They must necessarily have a say about the 'process of production' and the nature of the 'product'. They may facilitate or obstruct the one and influence what we seek in the other.

These human 'materials' may threaten in many ways the members of the organization who work with them. Because they are different from us. The differences that exist among patients or students, and between patients or students and the members of the organization, amplify differences among members and groups in the organization, and the anxieties and pernicious processes to which these differences give rise. The similarities between 'them' and 'us' are also threatening. They involve just what it is that as human beings we share with patients and students but that we do not want to acknowledge, that we want to disown, in ourselves. So we emphasize the differences that divide us and that lead to mutual alienation, rejection, and anxiety.

Because of the characteristically high levels of anxiety in these kinds of organizations, the management of anxiety often takes priority over work. Our ways of managing anxieties are often dysfunctional with respect to work. For example, we may allay anxiety by behaving in a way or adopting a procedure or arrangement that emphasizes our differences. '*We* are the ones that, in every case, know. *You* the ones that, about everything, are ignorant.' 'Yes, you know and we do not.' '*We* possess all the competence available, *you* all the incompetence.' 'Yes, you are capable and we are not.' This polarization, while allaying anxiety in both groups, blocks the bridging of the differences that do exist. But the bridging of these differences must occur if students or patients are to become engaged as active participants in their own transformation.

Even if you work in an organization that is neither in the mental health nor the education sectors (although, even so, you have been or are a student and perhaps have been or are a patient), I hope that the stories in this book will remind you of your own experiences – in families, classrooms, college dormitories, civic and religious organizations, social clubs, professional associations, committees, occupational organizations. And that you will be moved to reflect on these experiences, these stories from your own life, of which you have been reminded. Ideas about groups and organizations will suggest themselves to you, and you, wanting to see whether these ideas are of any use, will try them out in small and large experiments.

This book intends to help you find out how to make use of the constructive possibilities of whatever group or organization you are in – riding the ups and downs, enjoying the company of others for its own sake, harnessing the forces that are unleashed when people deploy their powers in concert to overcome obstacles and bring themselves to a shared destination. It intends to help you be inventive in discovering ways to endure, survive, and even actively manage the pernicious processes that may be found in these same groups and organizations. It intends to make possible your refusing to lend yourself, and to help others refuse to lend themselves, to these processes as either victim or victimizer, neither then perpetuating nor becoming overwhelmed by them.

PART 1

Stories

More and more often there is embarrassment all around when the wish to hear a story is expressed. It is as if something that seemed inalienable to us, the securest among our possessions, were taken away from us: the ability to exchange experiences …

Every morning brings us the news of the globe, and yet we are poor in noteworthy stories. This is because no event any longer comes to us without already being shot through with explanation … Actually, it is half the art of storytelling to keep a story free from explanation as one reproduces it …

The value of information does not survive the moment in which it was new. It lives only at that moment; it has to surrender to it completely and explain itself to it without losing any time. A story is different. It does not expend itself. It preserves and concentrates its strength and is capable of releasing it even after a long time…

Walter Benjamin

CHAPTER I

Arriving at the Idea of Stories

Marshall Edelson

I realized in my sixties that I had come to believe that *knowledge is structured as stories*. Specifically, I realized that the knowledge I used in my clinical work and teaching came to me in narrative form. Stories, not facts, rules, or universal generalizations. Concrete particulars, not concepts, kinds, or types. Talking with patients, I heard their stories and I remembered other stories. I listened for and I drew on memories of specific events, involving identifiable characters and places, and occurring on particular occasions and in a particular sequence.

It may seem strange that, in these first three chapters, I write entirely about the idea of stories, not about group and organizational life. But the idea of stories is central. Any attempt I make to understand group and organizational life depends on it. So in this chapter, I tell the story of how, through various experiences in childhood, college, graduate school, and finally the clinical situation, I came to the idea of stories. In Chapter 2, I describe how I use this idea in my work with patients. In Chapter 3, I describe how I use it in my teaching.[3] It may disorient some readers, perhaps, to discover that these three chapters are introductory, are about stories or 'the narrative approach', and not about group experiences and the use of a narrative approach to understanding them. That subject has its explicit beginning in Chapter 4.

In a sense, however, that group and organizational life appear to be missing from these first three chapters is only an illusion, created by telling *my* story as if it were nothing but an individual story. The discerning reader will see the effects on me of my life in groups and organizations all along the way, as in my career and clinical work, for example, I struggle to integrate personal inclinations with social expectations, and as in the teaching situation I am compelled to pay attention to the impact of authority relations.

The change comes in Chapter 4. I take a step toward our main subject by giving explicit attention to the role of narrative in both psychoanalytic theory (focused on individual systems) and social theory (focused on social systems). I rethink these two kinds of theory. I conclude with the claim that abstract theory in psychoanalysis (its metapsychology), and abstract theory about social systems, about groups and organizations, are scientistic disguises concealing narrative paradigms.

How I came to the idea of story

This book belongs in part to the species 'intellectual *autobiography*'. I begin with stories about my own experiences, rather than, as I have many times in past works, mainly expound theory or construct arguments. I am unwilling to continue to give priority to general abstract statements, although of course they still carry some interest for me. For, I have come increasingly to believe that the knowledge we have and use in the *practice* of anything – clinical, educative, administrative, investigative – exists in our minds, primarily although probably not exclusively, in narrative rather than propositional form. Especially when 'knowing how' rather than 'knowing that' is the kind of knowledge at issue, stories in all their specificity and particularity, not abstract general propositions, seem to be the cognitive schemes to which we refer.[4] So it seems appropriate now, here, in this chapter, to trace the place of stories in my life and, specifically, how they came to take that place.

For many years, and increasingly it seems to me in recent years, a lot of people have been talking, although in quite different ways, about *narrative*. Lester Luborsky has written a manual for teaching psychoanalytic psychotherapy using an explicit narrative paradigm as a basis for the therapist's interventions. He has also reviewed research measures based on such a paradigm, in the context of his own use of such a measure in research on transference.[5] The title of Roy Schafer's most recent book is *Retelling a Life: Narration and Dialogue in Psychoanalysis*.[6] I could cite many other recent works in psychology and the humanities. Maybe something is happening in our culture of which this talk about narratives is an expression.

I don't want to get into a discussion of how my ideas about stories are different from or similar to the ideas of these authors and others. Often, talk about narrative occurs in the context of an interest in hermeneutics, when hermeneutics is contrasted with science. My interest in narrative does not imply a rejection of scientific thought or method.

I could argue, with utmost rigor, of course, that my ideas about stories are different *and* better than those of others. Some years ago, I would probably have done so. Now, however, I am mindful that I often exhort those I teach to permit themselves to be reminded of their own life experience, not theory, as they listen to patients in psychotherapy. I often tell stories to trainees about my own experiences to make a point, rather than lay down rules of technique or give theoretical explanations. It is fitting then that, in seeking here for the sources of my interest in stories, and so for an indication of how I think about them, I turn to my own life, rather than solely to philosophical writings or the technical, theoretical, or research literature of my profession (but including these to the extent and when they have affected me). The particulars of where I'm coming from will differentiate the path I am taking from that of some others who, even though they are also talking about narratives, come from another place, are heading in another direction.

Early movies

To my mother's dismay, when I was seven years old, she had to take me screaming from a showing of the movie *David Copperfield* (1935). The triggering events were scenes involving the cruel treatment of the hero by his wicked stepfather Mr Murdstone (played by Basil Rathbone). At eight I saw The *Prisoner of Shark Island* (1936). The movie was about a physician who was imprisoned, unjustly so in this telling of the story, because he treated the assassin of Abraham Lincoln. He was pardoned because of his valor in coping with a plague on Shark Island. I felt what a fine thing it would be to be a doctor. At nine I saw *London by Night* (1937). The movie was about an Umbrella Man who, having been seen hobbling under an umbrella through the fog, was suspected of a series of murders. The movie featured a montage of close-ups of the terrified faces of London citizens, with an image of the Umbrella Man hobbling through their large heads. As I remember it now, I could not sleep for months, kept awake by images of the terrified faces and the sinister figure superimposed on them. I could not get these images out of my mind. So no one ever had to teach me or convince me that 'merely' imagined stories could have profound effects!

I began to imagine that I might become a writer of stories. When I was nine, I had a little pocket notebook in which I wrote a jungle adventure about an intrepid explorer. By the age of twelve, I was immersed in movies, going to downtown Chicago theaters to sit through as many as three triple features in one day. My life was, and in some important sense still is, in the movies.

When I was fourteen, I went fourteen times to sit through a movie called *Kings Row* (1942). This movie tells a story of two friends, Parris and Drake. Parris, who was a good boy, goes to Vienna at the turn of the century, and becomes the first psychiatrist in America. He returns home because Drake needs him. Drake, who had been a young hellion, had awakened after an accident to find his legs had been amputated. Parris later discovers that a sadistic surgeon had performed an unnecessary amputation to punish Drake for his sexual looseness with women. How would it affect Drake if Parris were to tell him what he had discovered? This movie, which portrayed father-figures as protectors and teachers but also as implacable cruel obstacles to relations with women, rang all sorts of changes on the theme of 'father–son relations' and the related theme of 'becoming a man'.

Such movies provided me with one model for 'the good story': the so-called classic Hollywood melodrama. They also taught me a lot about what you must do to be a *good* audience for such a story, namely, an active, involved, identifying-with-a-protagonist, expectant, questioning, waiting-for-an-answer, inference-making, hypothesis-forming, hypothesis-revising audience. Good training for a psychotherapist-to-be.

College

At sixteen I became a student in the College of the University of Chicago. I participated in Socratic dialogues in small-group seminars, and favored this format when years later I became a teacher. I was exposed to the New Criticism, which imbued me with a sense of the autonomy of the study of cultural objects such as paintings, poetry, novels, and music. The study of such objects need not be dependent on knowledge of history, sociology, or the psychology of the creator. You can ask about such an object: How is it made? How do its parts relate to each other? What choices has the author or artist made? When do conventions, and what conventions, determine these choices? What reading or understanding of the work do the answers to these questions best support?

These are the questions I eventually asked about the stories patients told or enacted. Doing psychotherapy, I found it natural to be attentive to the choices they made. It was not difficult to recognize the stylistic devices, the 'defense mechanisms', the content-transforming operations, and the various other strategies of invention and representation they used in constructing their stories. Or to be alert not just to the content of these stories but to the *ways* patients told or enacted them, their attitudes toward them. Later, as a psychoanalyst-in-training, I read *The Interpretation of Dreams* through the lens of Freud's overarching metaphor of dreamers as artisans, his presentation of how dreamers *make* dreams – by what mental operations, using what materials.[7]

This education in paying close attention to details and to the way in which a work of art was constructed made me suspicious of relativism: that the meaning of a work of art was whatever anyone made of it. How could people claim that one reading was just as good as another, and that the details of a work's construction were irrelevant to deciding among such claims! I. A. Richards' work *Practical Criticism* certainly influenced me. It showed most readers were rather inept or careless, and where they went wrong.[8] My reservations about relativism have re-emerged in my current rather solitary belief that a close examination of the details of clinical materials can support one interpretation of those materials over a commensurate and incompatible rival interpretation.[9] I find it difficult to accept the belief that differences among clinicians are unavoidable and unresolvable.

But my anti-relativism has been shaken from time to time. In the early 1960s, I was co-leader with Art Aronoff of a poetry study group at the Stockbridge

Library. I didn't know what to make of the fact that everyone in the group seemed to understand the same poem differently. Either most of the readers were poor readers or something else had to be added to my thinking about such matters. What was eventually added is well represented by the work of Norman Holland.[10] He studied reading and readers. The same work, though it had observable intrinsic linguistic and organizational properties, which anyone might come to see, might nevertheless evoke a very different unconscious fantasy in each reader, and so a different feeling and interpretation of the work.

It's the same with movies. Different people have very different responses to the same movie. The same person at different times has different responses to the same movie. Whenever we have this kind of situation, we assume that an internal structure mediates the relation between some aspect of reality and a person's response to it. David Rapaport made the point that the observations of 'different responses to the same stimuli, the same response to different stimuli' suggest it is necessary to postulate internal structures mediating relations between stimulus and response.[11] An unconscious fantasy is such an internal structure.

Spellbound

At seventeen I saw Ingrid Bergman and character actor Michael Chekhov in Hitchcock's *Spellbound* (1945). She was a psychoanalyst in love with her amnesic patient (played by Gregory Peck) and determined to rescue him from a murder charge by curing his 'guilt complex'. Chekhov, in the role of her wise former training analyst, tries to help her despite his qualms about the patient. Under the spell of this movie I came to a sudden decision, which from then on I never questioned. I would have a psychoanalysis and then become a psychoanalyst. Later I was convinced – a slight European accent was enough – that my psychoanalyst looked and talked like Ingrid Bergman. Another demonstration of the power of stories in our lives.

The TAT

I first came across the Thematic Apperception Test when I was a nineteen-year-old undergraduate major in psychology at Stanford University. I read about it in a book called *Explorations in Personality* by Henry Murray,[12] which described many methods for studying personality. For my senior project I put a classmate through all of them. It made immediate sense to me that I could learn a lot about people from the stories they made up, so much so that for this project I invented my own TAT, using pictures I cut out of magazines. (I was not impressed that the stimulus had to be ambiguous.)

I mention Murray's work again in what follows. I was not aware of the role his work had played in my own life until I wrote this; I feel I have re-established a relationship that I had lost. His idea that you could use a variety of methods to study one person was a revelation. A person was a domain unto herself or himself and I could make multiple observations in that domain. I set myself to notice repetitions and parallels in the subject's responses across methods. I noticed also when hypotheses to account for responses obtained from one method matched hypotheses to account for responses obtained from another method. These ideas and methods in turn came to influence how I listened, and taught others to listen, in the clinical situation.

Graduate school

At twenty-one I returned to the University of Chicago to do graduate work in psychology. Those were heady days. James Miller was Chairman of the Department and preoccupied with system theory. Hedda Bolgar, a Viennese psychoanalyst, taught me personality theory. I worked with Herb Thelen in his group dynamics laboratory. Carl Rogers, with whom I had little rapport, ran the Counseling Center. I thought, and still do, and now teach, that the psychotherapist should actively process what a patient communicates and do something with it. Rogers thought that, in my work with a young adolescent, which centered around the client's drawings and paintings, I talked too much.

The enthusiasm of William Stephenson, a red-headed Englishman, for his method of obtaining quantitative data within a subjective frame of reference was contagious.[13] I and a fellow graduate student used his method in a single-case study. In addition to a battery of methods for exploring personality mostly picked up from Murray, we arranged for the subject to participate in role-playing dramas we had invented. The situations to be enacted were chosen on the basis of what we had learned about the single subject. Involving the subject in these situations was designed to influence the subject's representations of himself and others in predicted ways. Apparently I already thought that the dramas in which people were involved in everyday life had the causal power to affect internal structures.

Moe Stein was my teacher in psychological testing. I thought his manual, *The Thematic Apperception Test: An Introductory Manual to Its Clinical Use with Adult Males*, splendid in its rigor.[14] What a combination: the richness of stories *and* disciplined thought! That integration became my ideal for myself as a professional, though all too often I was not to achieve it. Stein emphasized standard procedures of administration, reading the subject's responses without knowledge of the case history, and intra-individual comparison of stories. 'Read the first story told by a subject', he taught, 'and formulate hypotheses about that subject on the basis of that limited sample just as you would with any other sample of the subject's behavior. Then, check and revise these hypotheses according to the information in the next story. Iterate this procedure through the twenty stories. Notice parallels. Notice repetitions.'

His conceptual scheme for analysis of the stories was one I already used at the movies. 'Identify the hero.' (His subjects were adult males.) 'What are the characteristics of the setting? Who are the others in that setting? What objects (props) are important? What social pressures and ideologies impinge on the hero? What does the hero need?' (The list of needs came from Murray.) 'How are these needs manifested in the actions the hero initiates toward objects, toward other people, or in the reactions the hero has to actions initiated by others? What attracts or repels the hero? What inner states, what feelings, does the hero experience? What modes – fantasy, planning, motor action – does the hero favor? Is the ending happy, unhappy, indefinite?'

Interpretation of the set of stories depended not only on picking up repeated themes but on careful detailed observation across stories of sequences. 'What conditions precede the appearance of a particular need in different stories? What consequences follow the appearance of a particular need in different stories?'

All these questions continue to guide how I follow and process, and teach others to follow and process, the stories told and enacted in psychotherapy. I would like to attribute whatever confidence I have in teaching psychotherapy to what I have learned over many years, from psychoanalytic training, from doing different kinds of clinical work, and from whatever wisdom age confers. It is a bit disturbing to realize that by age twenty-one the frame for much of what I teach today about psychotherapy was 'in place' in me.

In graduate school, we had a year-long seminar on the philosophy of science and research methodology. (Psychology was self-conscious and defensive about its status as a science.) I am still drawing on that experience. That seminar raised most of the issues in this area about which I have written. Finding that many of the positions I have since taken were explicit or foreshadowed in the papers I wrote for it would not surprise me. Again, it is a little disconcerting to think that by age twenty-one I had most of the ideas I was ever going to have on the philosophy of science and research.

Attempts at integration

My work in psychotherapy and teaching psychotherapy is the better for my having wrestled with such issues as 'the problems in establishing the credibility of an inference'. But for many years following graduate school – through medical school, psychiatric residency, and eventually academic life – I had no particular success in integrating the side of me passionately interested in stories and the side taking great pleasure in the challenge of rigorous conceptualization and argument. The former, I knew, was not likely to impress my teachers and peers; no doubt they would regard it as 'soft'. The latter was likely to command their respect; they would regard it as tough-minded. I became a member of a university faculty. I wanted to be promoted. I did what was required and enjoyed doing it. I gave myself up to the mastery and explication of difficult theories, such as Chomsky's in linguistics, Parsons' in sociology, Bertrand Russell's and other analytic philosophers' in the philosophy of science and formal logic, Fisher's in statistics and experimental design, and Freud's in psychoanalysis (especially his metapsychology). I wielded the weapons of indefatigable scholarship, trenchant criticism, and logical argument. I made implicit assumptions explicit. I examined the consequences for practice of holding one rather than another view. I did careful analyses of relations among theories. But the truth is, in doing all this, I left something important of myself behind, something I needed in doing and teaching psychotherapy.

Now and then, I tried to pull these two sides of myself together. My book *Language and Interpretation in Psychoanalysis* is a peculiar hybrid.[15] The conceptual tools I used in discussing interpretation were Chomskyan syntactic analysis and Roman Jakobson phonemic analysis. But the objects subjected to interpretation included a Bach prelude and a poem by Wallace Stevens.

In my mid-forties, I was much immersed in Stevens' poetry. It had a great deal to say about the effort of imagination to survive the pressure of too much reality. Isn't it strange that psychoanalysis says so little about imagination? The word hardly appears in the psychoanalytic literature. Trainees continue to be uncomfortable when I encourage them to regard imagination as an indispensable aspect of clinical skill. It is as though I were encouraging them to do something disreputable.

Gradually, especially in doing and teaching psychotherapy, I found myself less interested in abstractions and *a priori* rules of technique. Lipton's paper on Freud's technique helped liberate me by taking a stand against dogma. He wrote that no one can know *a priori* that an intervention is correct. You can only assess its validity by maintaining an attitude of inquiry (the indispensable hallmark of the psychoanalyst) and observing its immediate impact and subsequent fate. Not everything the psychoanalyst does or says belongs to the domain of technique, although it is her or his job to discern the effects of everything she or he says or does.[16]

There came a time when I could no longer read metapsychology, and I stopped teaching it. Merton Gill and Roy Schafer seemed to have gone through something similar, judging by their radical swerve from metapsychology after their brilliant studies of it.

An account of psychoanalytic process in terms of telling and enacting stories, which takes narrative as a central concept, regards psychoanalysis as an extension of commonsense or folk psychology. Dramatistic concepts such as desires and beliefs play a central role in its explanations. It attributes causal powers to the contents of mental states: specifically, to what is believed and desired.[17] This characterization of psychoanalysis is not consonant with the aims or language of metapsychology.

Clinical theory in psychoanalysis refers essentially to mental contents. (Mental contents are internal symbolic representations of those states of affairs that a person desires or believes.) Psychoanalysis's explanatory use in its clinical theory of unconscious fantasies, mediating between 'stimuli' and responses to them, exemplifies desire/belief explanation (semantic theory).

Metapsychology, on the other hand, is essentially an attempt to replace commonsense explanation in terms of what is believed and desired with a 'nonsemantic' theory that describes contentless causal mechanisms or processes. A nonsemantic theory involves no reference to and assigns no causal role to mental contents. Metapsychology aspires to be a nonsemantic theory and, in this sense, to be like the learning theory that tries to formulate laws using concepts such as conditioning, reinforcement, and stimulus generalization not requiring any reference to the content of what is learned. Metapsychology so conceived must fail as a psychoanalytic theory, if psychoanalysis is indeed trying to answer just those questions I have previously described it as trying to answer.[18] Stoller makes the same point.[19] My present conviction is that a science of psychology that is a sophisticated extension of folk psychology is an explanatory apparatus that is quite good enough for the psychotherapist.

As my struggle for integration continued, I began to pay more attention to sensuous particulars than to conceptual labels. I think that a psychotherapist is the better for having a taste for nondestructive gossip. I like the highly personal particulars of an individual narrative. I am leery of theories even about narrative or lists of general themes for classifying narratives.

The work of several others supported the direction I seemed to be taking, and the belief that in taking it I did not have to abandon tough-minded empiricism and rigor altogether. There were those few who saw fantasy as core to psychoanalysis: Arlow, of course;[20] Schafer, who argued in a paper on the defense mechanisms that they were not contentless operations but fantasies;[21] Reik (1941) who, in his fine work on masochism, showed beautifully how to lay out the details of the phenomena first before theorizing about dynamics and etiology;[22] and Stoller, who studied sexuality, and so of course fantasies, at a time when psychoanalysis seemed to be losing its interest in sexuality.[23] Theorists may lose their way but any moviegoer knows how important sex is to a story.

Certain philosophers of mind and cognitive scientists were also helpful. Fodor argued persuasively that a science of psychology must be based on commonsense or folk psychology.[24] Hopkins[25] and Wollheim[26] added that psychoanalysis was in fact an extension of folk psychology. They also explicated the important role of fantasy in psychoanalysis. Some cognitive and computer scientists (Schank, Abelson), in the tradition of Piaget's *internal schema*, chose to work with *narrative, script, story*, and *scenario* as key concepts.[27] Lakoff and Johnson focused on the role of imagination and metaphor in studies of reason and category formation.[28] Lakoff, an anthropologist and linguist, wrote a case study of anger. Examining metaphors used in expressing anger, he found that they seemed to 'converge on a certain prototypical model of anger'. Since that model had a temporal dimension and a number of stages, he formulated it as a prototypical *scenario*.[29] Similarly, de Sousa, in his cognitive theory of emotion, referred to how we learn the vocabulary of emotion from paradigm *scenarios* drawn from daily life in childhood and later reinforced by stories that are part of culture.[30]

It is true I did find these formidable books stimulating and exhilarating. But perhaps I list them here mainly to justify my interest in stories to scientific colleagues (one of the reference groups I carry around in my head). Do I continue to be uneasy about owing knowledge and skill to the movies? For, if truth be told, despite this list, I do sound more like a moviegoer than a cognitive scientist when I am doing and teaching psychotherapy.

An important observation

The major shift in my thinking about psychotherapy took place when, a few years ago, the difference between two kinds of sessions struck me. In one, patients mainly told stories (usually but not always) eagerly and expressively. In the other, they repetitively described, catalogued, and offered generalizations about their traits and states. Taking this kind of observation seriously has had apparently felicitous effects on my work as a psychotherapist and teacher. That encourages me to persevere in drawing intuitively on my experiences of movies and in listening to and thinking about stories.

CHAPTER 2

Using Stories in Doing Psychotherapy

Marshall Edelson

Before adopting a narrative approach to understanding group experiences, I used the idea of stories in the clinical work I did as a psychoanalyst and psychotherapist.

A conception of psychopathology

My conception of the *patient's plight* (psychopathology, if you will) influences my work as a psychotherapist and teacher of psychotherapy. I introduce my conception of the plight of at least some patients by telling a story. When I was a child, I listened rapt to a radio program: *The Shadow.* Every episode began with an eerie hollow voice declaiming 'Who knows what evil lurks in the hearts of men? The Shadow knows!' In one episode, a criminal enemy of the Shadow invents a time machine in order to wreak vengeance on him. This enemy captures the Shadow and spends a twenty-four-hour period visiting unspeakable tortures upon him. Then the time machine is set, dooming the Shadow to repeat this twenty-four hours throughout eternity. Unhappily, I can't remember how the Shadow got himself out of this fix!

Now I see patients who are trapped in scenarios of unslaked desire, relentless punishment, and horrifying dangers and their suffering seems terrible to me. Their plight is that they are trapped in such scenarios ('trapped' is the operative word here). Their symptoms may be regarded as signs that they are caught in such a scenario, that they are compelled to participate in the scenario for time without end, and that they struggle to escape from the world of that scenario. This may not be the plight of all patients. So the question of the scope of the particular kind of psychotherapy I am discussing is a live question for me.

I see some patients then as in the grip of a scenario (usually more than one scenario). This scenario is more or less unconscious. (An unconscious fantasy exemplifies 'unconscious scenario'.) I hear the stories they tell or enact as variants of the scenario in which they are trapped. That is, I understand these stories as part of their *active* attempt to shape or interpret their past and present life to conform to the scenario or to match conscious fantasies that derive from the scenario. Sometimes, on the other hand, patients seem, more *passively*, to be simply reminded of the scenario by elements of experience. Then they imagine that they relive it.

The relation between such a scenario and a conscious fantasy derived from it is usually more or less disguised by means of such mental operations as condensation, displacement, iconic symbolization, and translation of verbal elements into imagery. In creating conscious fantasies, as in creating dreams, patients make use of the scenes and dramatic situations of experience as materials. They transform, combine, and embellish these materials.

A conception of psychoanalytic psychotherapy

In recent years, increasingly, I have found myself focally aware of the stories patients tell me, and the stories they enact in which I am one of the characters. (Talking about enacted stories is a way of talking about transference phenomena.) This increasing awareness has led me to a conception of psychotherapy for patients trapped in scenarios, a conception I will also express in the form of a story – the story of Scheherazade.

Scheherazade tells stories nightly to her husband, the sultan, who has gotten into the cynical habit of beheading his queens after one night of love. That she tells these stories, and the way she tells them, are part of a story she does not tell but enacts. She tells these stories to achieve a certain purpose of her own, in the story she enacts with the sultan. She keeps him asking, 'What will happen next? How does the story come out?' Each night she stops her story just at the moment of greatest suspense. Each night she avoids being beheaded at least one more time. She tells him wonderful stories for a thousand-and-one-nights. Then their own story, the enacted story, has a happy ending.

Just so, a patient may tell a psychotherapist stories about her current life outside the therapy hour, about her childhood, and about herself in relation to the psychotherapist. Unlike Scheherazade, she is the hero of most of the stories she tells. And quite unlike the stories that Scheherazade tells, a patient at the same time is both the hero and in a different aspect of herself the real adversary of the hero in most of the stories she tells. Often as adversary, she enters the story disguised as someone else. Such cunning devices of the storyteller convert an intrapersonal drama into an apparently interpersonal drama. I have the impression that psychotherapists often fail to mark this conversion.

Like Scheherazade, the patient tells a story at a particular time for particular reasons, or to achieve particular ends. She may tell the story in a way that helps her to avoid, reject, or disown certain feelings or states. 'They have nothing to do with me.' Or she may tell it to influence the psychotherapist. Just as we can differentiate the story of Scheherazade and the sultan from the stories she tells him, so what a patient hopes to accomplish by telling her story is part of another story, a story involving the patient and psychotherapist, which the patient is enacting rather than telling.

What is a story?

No single simple definition will cover all the instances we might like to include in the category *story*. But a large family of instances have features characteristic of the classic Hollywood movie melodrama.[31]

A protagonist has a wish and a problem in gratifying it. He wants to bring about, maintain, or avoid some state of affairs. By one means or another, he attempts to do so. But, in this attempt, he encounters opposition. An antagonist erects obstacles or imposes constraints that prevent – or threaten to prevent – the protagonist's attaining what he wants. The antagonist may be a person, Nature, or a social system. The protagonist overcomes, makes accommodative adjustments in response to, or fails to overcome the antagonist.

The story, from beginning to end, forms a trajectory from one state of affairs to another. There is a change in the protagonist's situation or in herself. The change may be for the better (happy ending). The change may be for the worse, or, despite the protagonist's efforts, there may be no change (unhappy ending). A change in the protagonist's situation may be a change in her environment, her body, or other persons important to her. A change in the protagonist herself may be a change in her feelings, knowledge, or moral character.

Especially characteristic of the scenarios in which patients are trapped is that the patient himself at the same time is both protagonist and antagonist, both hero and adversary, the one striving to achieve a goal and the other acting as the chief obstacle to achieving that goal. The scenarios are, in this sense, intrapersonal. I have the impression, however, that psychotherapists and patients who favor interpersonal themes tend to neglect intrapersonal scenarios – for example, those that are about the patient's relation to his body and his attitudes toward and feelings about the wishes he has in that relation. Similarly, it is my impression that a patient's *own responses* to his wishes, feelings, and actions play a larger role in character and symptom pathology than we might guess, given the patient's (and sometimes the psychotherapist's) preference for telling stories in which the *responses of other persons* to the patient as well as his responses to them are emphasized.

Psychotherapeutic process

Psychotherapists inquire into the detailed particulars of each story told or enacted, and pay attention to just how a patient tells or enacts the story. They notice relations among the stories told or enacted. They see that some stories, although they have a different setting or occur in a different domain, are quite similar. They discover that some apparently unconnected simple stories are episodes, one perhaps leading to the other, in a more complicated plot.

Psychotherapists pay careful attention to the circumstances that seem to trigger the telling or enactment of a particular story. What particular event, object, or feature of external reality on each occasion evokes the scenario or inspires the creation of some variant of it? How does a patient use the materials external reality provides in order to act in such a way as to bring about an actualization of the scenario, which is more or less disguised? How does a patient exploit aspects of her experience to justify directing feelings belonging in a scenario to objects or persons in external reality?

As the patient comes to recognize the different versions of a 'favorite' story, she increasingly realizes that she has a major hand in writing and directing it, and in assigning herself and others first one and then another part in the play. As she becomes able to identify what evokes her telling or enacting a story on each of many occasions, she increasingly understands its value to herself – the purposes it serves.

Typically, a patient begins by viewing himself as passive victim. He attributes causation to the external situation. Eventually, he comes to see that what he has attributed to external reality stems from what he carries in his own mind, and from what he does, through imagination or action, to make external reality conform to it.

Gradually, the stories told and enacted take center stage in consciousness. The patient sharpens them, and makes them ever more explicit. She fills in details. She tracks the twists and turns in the plot. She comes to recognize a story even as it appears in many revisions and disguises. She observes the parallels among stories involving different characters or settings.

As part of this process, the patient begins to experience more fully what it feels like to have the wishes, beliefs, or emotions that belong to her stories. Of these she previously had only vague or transient hints. She has prevented them from coming into awareness at all or has paid them only peripheral attention. But they have continued to play a part, however disguised or transformed, in the stories she has told and enacted. As these stories are amplified, the patient acquires direct knowledge of what it feels like to have a certain wish, belief, or emotion. She becomes able to appreciate how it has disabled her, led her to form distorted images of herself or others, and caused her to act in ways that previously did not make sense to her. Fenichel, using the technical vocabulary of psychoanalysis, refers to 'the task of reversing displacements, abolishing isolations, or guiding traces of affect to their proper relationships'.[32] ('Unpacking condensations' also belongs in this list.)

A patient may permit himself gradually to recover the more or less unconscious scenario from which his stories are derived, and to free himself from its grip. This does not mean that the scenario disappears from his mind or that he loses all interest in it. It means that the scenario no longer operates secretly and in the darkness to affect his experience of and response to reality. It means that he has become freer to ignore it, to alter its influence upon him, or to play with it.

It is my impression that in psychotherapy this kind of process is repeated over and over. The particular stories a patient tells or enacts may seem to change. But the task remains the same. Each go-around ('working-through'?) is another brick laid. I use that metaphor rather than a metaphor about human development because it does *not* seem to me that as you go further and further in psychotherapy you are doing something qualitatively different from what was done early on. That is why in my teaching, it does not seem to matter what selection a trainee makes from a set of sessions for discussion. The exercise is the same, but the trainee (like the patient) gets better and better at doing it.

It is also my impression that any instance or any number of instances of this kind of process has its effects, even when the unconscious scenario is not recovered. However, the sturdiness and persistence of changes in the patient do seem to increase with each go-around, just as the trainee's skill increases. If enough bricks are laid, the patient becomes capable of doing this kind of work on her own.

The risk, if the unconscious scenario is not recovered, is that the patient may remain in its grip. Perhaps she merely changes who takes what role, for example, but the stories she tells and enacts, even if somewhat altered in detail, continue to be variants – although hopefully less pernicious variants – of the same scenario.

Stories told and enacted in one patient's psychotherapy

Now let me tell a story that begins with a patient arriving late to a psychotherapy session, as she often does. The *content* of the story she tells has to do with the many difficulties that prevent her from completing a work assignment on time, and how her conscientious effort to overcome these difficulties made her late to the session. She describes herself as lazy, unorganized, uncreative, and stupid. She mutters how inflexible and callous her professor is. If she is late with the assignment, he will certainly be upset.

It is important to distinguish the content of a story from the *function* or purpose it serves on a particular occasion or for a particular patient. The same story may serve more than one function. The content of this patient's story focuses mainly on her dialogue with herself in which she blames and criticizes herself. But telling this story serves the function of countering the disapproval she imagines her psychotherapist feels in response to her coming late. She judges herself in the story she tells. But in the different story she enacts, she assigns the role of judge to her psychotherapist.

The *interpersonal* story here enacted with the psychotherapist enables her to escape or evade judgment. (An interpersonal story involves two persons.) She prefers to believe that it is the psychotherapist, rather than to recognize that it is she herself, who judges her. She only has to face the judgments of the psychotherapist during the sessions; between sessions she is free of him. She argues with him implicitly that he cannot fault her for her conscientious efforts as a student to please her demanding professor. But then again, she also heaps criticisms on herself as a way to beat the psychotherapist to the punch. These are some advantages the interpersonal story has over the intrapersonal story.

In the *intrapersonal* story she tells, she blames herself, taking the roles of both judge and judged. (An intrapersonal story involves one person; if more than one voice is heard or there is an interaction between different roles, they are all voices within or roles taken by that one person.) The judge is exceedingly harsh – and she cannot get away from herself. On the other hand, an advantage of the intrapersonal story is that now, identified with the role of judge, she takes on his power to hurt.

One heuristic in interpretation, here as in everyday life, is to infer motive from outcome, to suppose provisionally that the consequence of an action is what the actor intended the action to bring about. The content of the story she tells, then, suggests she may wish to defeat her professor by making him wait for assigned work.

This story reminds the psychotherapist of stories the patient has told in other sessions about how her father dominated and criticized her and her secret strategies for defeating him. The psychotherapist notices thematic affinity among these stories about the past, the stories about what is going on currently in her work life, and the story that the patient seems to be enacting in the psychotherapy situation in which she defeats the psychotherapist by coming late.

The psychotherapist makes an interpretation, connecting the stories from three different domains of her life by noticing their similarity. The patient discusses the interpretation calmly and with great interest, expressing admiration and appreciation of the psychotherapist's ability to bring all these stories together. She adds some details, and remembers some other incidents which fit the narrative pattern the psychotherapist has detected.

In the next session, she tells a story about a fight she has just had with a younger brother. It is clear that even before the fight she had been irritable, belligerent, and provocative. And even now she is beside herself with rage toward her brother, a troublesome adversary who blocks her from achieving what she wants. In a screenplay, the brother would be the villain.

Another heuristic of interpretation: A patient's story may be a response to a recent event. The recent event may have reminded the patient of a story. A story may be her indirect answer to a comment or question by the psychotherapist. It may provide clues to the patient's reaction to an event within or outside of the treatment situation, or to something she herself has felt or said, perhaps a previous story she has told or a fantasy she has had. If you can identify this recent event, you may be able to infer from it the function of the story the patient tells or enacts.

In this instance, 'that the psychotherapist had offered an interpretation' turned out to be what someone writing a screenplay would call the triggering event (like the event in a movie, 'a stranger rode into town'). A triggering event stirs things up, upsets a balance, gets a story going.

'Why', the psychotherapist wonders to himself, 'does the fight story follow my giving an interpretation? Was "giving the interpretation" a triggering event?' It is not immediately clear that, or how, the 'giving-the-interpretation' episode and the 'fight-with-the-brother' episode are linked.

The psychotherapist reminds the patient of similar episodes in which she has been truculent and so provoked a fight. The patient complains bitterly that psychotherapy has done nothing to change her; she still acts as she always has. The psychotherapist notices that momentarily he feels defeated when the patient says this.

However, the patient soon settles down and becomes reflective. 'Why do I get so angry? Why do I make life so difficult for myself by behaving this way with others? I know that there was no reason for acting so provocatively. I just defeat myself. I am my own adversary!' Now she is remorseful and wishes that there was some way to make up to her brother for her treatment of him. She thinks of ways to undo the bad effects of the quarrel.

The psychotherapist remembers the patient's reasonableness in the last session and contrasts it with the fulminations and irrationality with which this session began. That reminds him of a number of stories in which the patient became furious in situations in which, it turned out later, she felt denigrated. He wonders aloud whether she had felt humiliated in the previous session by his superior performance (making an interpretation). She then remembers being peripherally aware of such a feeling. 'But, of course, I couldn't tell you that I envied you, or that I felt resentful because you are always the superior one, and I the inferior. After all, you were helping me. You would become offended. Then you would really send me away.'

In my experience, this kind of response – in which a patient recovers a recent but mislaid conscious thought or feeling – is one of the most dependable indications that an interpretation is on target. That the literature on the validity of interpretations only rarely mentions this kind of response surprises me.

The psychotherapist, if he had been less involved in an attempt to follow and piece together a complicated story, might have relied instead on a theoretical formula. He might have thought, 'The patient has displaced her rage from me to her brother.' As you will see, this shortcut would miss some essential details of what turned out to be a more complex story.

The patient now tells an additional story. The psychotherapist hears it as an episode that connects the episode of the interpretation and the episode of the fight. The additional story: Later in the day following the previous session, the patient had had a conscious sexual fantasy. In it, scenes in which she was forcing someone to do what she commanded alternated with scenes in which she was submitting to another. A fantasy like this was a favorite of the patient's. It seemed always to lie ready in her mind, where she could recruit it for a variety of purposes in responding to many different kinds of triggering events. Circumstances she interpreted as humiliating were especially likely to evoke it. At this point in the psychotherapy, various versions of this favorite fantasy were relatively accessible to consciousness, although, embarrassed, she was always reluctant to tell these stories.

These sexual fantasies are cut off from any contact with her everyday life. As far as she is concerned, they have nothing to do with her ordinary experiences. Why she has such fantasies is a mystery to her. They make no sense. The patient is not aware of any connection between her conscious sexual fantasy and her feelings in the previous session. She is not aware that the fantasy is the fulfillment of a wish stirred up in that session. The contents of the psychotherapist's interventions frequently concern the possibility of such a connection. Providing this kind of connection builds stories out of apparently unconnected episodes.

So the psychotherapist now wonders aloud whether, following the previous session, she had wished to be superior and powerful like the psychotherapist, and able to humiliate someone inferior as she felt he had humiliated her. Her fantasy seemed to gratify this wish, at least in imagination. The connection between the sexual fantasy and an actual event, which had triggered it, now becomes apparent to her. The purpose of the sexual fantasy was to counteract a painful experience.

Further details emerge in this session. She begins to recapture some of the details of the original scene in which she was a torturer, and they horrify her. Why couldn't she stay with this scene? Uncomfortable with an image of herself as a cruel person, first she softens the torture so it seems more like teasing. Then she reverses roles; as the director of this scene, she assigns herself the role of the character who is kind, gentle, and submissive, the one whom the other teases. But this reversal also has consequences, which have to do with how she feels about herself when she is submissive.

She had omitted a piece of the story – how she felt about what she did in her own fantasy and how she got rid of that feeling. Ordinarily, she would not see any act or feeling occurring in her everyday life or psychotherapy session as a result of what she more or less obscurely felt and thought as she observed herself playing a particular role in a sexual fantasy. (It is just this piece of the story the psychotherapist would have lost, had the story of the fight reminded him of a theoretical formula about 'displacement'.)

The psychotherapist wonders aloud: Had the patient been worried that the submissiveness she experienced in her fantasy might emerge in a real relationship? Seeing that she is submissive, someone might despise or take advantage of her. The patient then remembers that just before the fight she interpreted something that had happened as indicating that she had unwittingly invited her brother to treat her as an inferior. This was especially galling, because her brother is younger than she. It was her desire to cancel this invitation that she now believes compelled her, as it had on so many other occasions, to be obnoxious and domineering. Clearly, what is important here is her own response to herself as she is in her fantasy, and not what she imagines someone else's response would be.

Further details of this story about the fight between herself and her brother suggest its links to the sexual fantasy. I think it inaccurate, therefore, to regard this fight-with-the-brother story as *only* or even primarily a disguised expression of 'the transference'.

Finally, telling the story about her brother is part of an enactment in the psychotherapy of a story of vindictive attack and reparation. For telling this story makes it possible for her to take the psychotherapist down a peg or two by showing him that the psychotherapy is not working; she still behaves as she has always behaved. At the same time, by cooperating with him in doing the work of psychotherapy, she repairs the damage she fears she has done him, both by the acts of cruelty in her fantasy and by what she feels are ungrateful cruel reproaches about the inefficacy of the psychotherapy that she hurls at him because of her envy and resentment.

CHAPTER 3

Using Stories in Teaching Psychotherapy

Marshall Edelson

Since the late 1980s, I have been increasingly primarily involved in teaching individual and group psychotherapy to trainees. Before adopting a narrative approach to understanding group experiences, including the experiences I had as a teacher in my seminars on psychotherapy, I used the idea of stories in talking with my students about problems they encountered doing psychotherapy.

Problems I encounter teaching psychotherapy

The problems I encounter all seem to have some connection to the trainees' relation to authority. For example, they attach themselves to theory (usually their teacher's theory). They fear taking risks, making mistakes, being criticized. They avoid committing themselves, going out on a limb. They are reluctant to make specific statements to patients, especially statements involving inferences that, no matter how 'close to the surface', 'commonsensical', or 'self-evident', they can't be sure are correct. They are vague, noncommittal, inexpressive, so that they both conform to some image they have of the 'neutrality' they imagine authority figures prescribe, and at the same time avoid saying anything so definite or specific that it might offer an opportunity for someone to criticize what they said or how they said it. It seems to me then that a teacher of psychotherapy must address the matter of authority relations.

Authority

Out of anxiety, trainees turn to authority, theory, a supervisor, presumably to give themselves something to hold onto while they are learning largely from their own experience how to do their work. But before long that solution gives birth to a new anxiety. 'What will be the response of the authority figure to my work?' 'How can I please or placate this powerful authority figure?' 'Am I doing this right – following the rules of technique, using the theory, this author has laid down?' Ironically, the authority figure has this terrible power in part because trainees, overwhelmed by the gap between their knowledge and skill and the daunting demands of their work, have endowed her or him with it.

I have developed ways of teaching that seem to be effective. But as I look at these ways of teaching, I am struck now with how much they have to do with enabling trainees to free themselves from an anxious submission and attachment to sources and figures of authority – first of all, myself, their teacher, and then others in the social system with whom, in treating and caring for their patients, they have to deal, and whom they may have to challenge, question, and stand up to. But at the same time, I see that until recently I have been innocent about what as a teacher I was up to, just as in my efforts to create a therapeutic community described in Chapters 25 and 27 I was not aware that I sought to empower patients in their relations to authority figures in a residential treatment center.

Preference for generalities

I find many psychotherapists-in-training have already been 'well taught'. As anxious beginners, they cling to the theories and rules or precepts to which they have been exposed. Early, I was struck by the fact that what seemed to pop into their heads when a patient said something was a theoretical idea about the patient, a generalization of some kind, a characterization of the patient, a diagnosis. What popped into my head was some other episode or story the patient had told; a story I knew from my own reading; a scene, event, or character from a movie; a scene involving the patient that the patient had somehow conveyed but not described; or an image such as 'mother holding infant'.

A patient denigrates a psychotherapist who is about to go on vacation. A beginner is inclined to say, 'You sound very angry.' Perhaps, but less often, he may utter a generalization such as, 'You devalue what you cannot have.' However, I might ask the patient, 'Have you ever heard the story of the fox and the sour grapes?' If she says, 'Yes,' that may be enough. If she says, 'No,' I might continue, 'Let me tell you the story. A fox saw some luscious-looking grapes. They were hanging too high for him to reach, so after a few futile jumps, he went off muttering, "Who wants those grapes anyway! They're sour."'

A patient comes into a session furious at his psychotherapist. He had been vividly imagining on his way to the session a scene in which the psychotherapist criticized him unreasonably for something he had done. A beginner is inclined to say, 'You sound very angry.' Perhaps, but less often, she may make what she considers to be a 'transference interpretation', which again is in the form of a generalization: 'You expect me to treat you like your father did.' I might ask, 'Have you ever heard the wrench story?' The patient will usually say, 'No.' I continue:

'Let me tell you the story. A man's car broke down on a lonely stretch of highway in Nebraska. He needed a wrench to fix the car, and he didn't have one. So he set out on foot toward the one farmhouse in the distance he could see. As he walked, he thought to himself, "I'll get to the farmhouse, and then the farmer will refuse to lend me a wrench." He got madder and madder as he approached the house. When he got there, he knocked. When the farmer opened the door, he immediately shouted at him, "Keep your god damned wrench!"'

Letting the patient do all the interpretive work

A typical view psychotherapists-in-training seem to have about interpretation is that it is a generalization about the patient that explains a lot. Their interpretations rarely contain any indices of time or place or any reference to specific occasions; they are general timeless truths. Most feel that patients should come to these truths themselves, so that they are hesitant to offer them explanations.

When they say anything to the patient at all, they usually ask a question, either about a fact or about why the patient has done something. It often seems to me that the request for a fact is not followed by any indication from the psychotherapist-in-training about what she or he intended to do with this information. The preference for asking questions seemed to have its origin in a disinclination to take the risk of making a mistake.

The why-question seems to me mostly to leave patients at a loss, because their motives are in fact a mystery to them. But patients feel they should know the answer to a question, for otherwise the psychotherapist would not have asked for it. The result: a drop in self-esteem, which is an undesirable outcome of what is intended to be a helpful intervention. Or patients may make up an answer, which leads both patient and psychotherapist down a path paved with rationalizations and surrounded by thickets of intellectualization.

In my teaching, I began to express some doubts about the notion that the patient should come to these truths by himself, and that the psychotherapist should stand by waiting for the patient to shout 'Eureka!' Why pass the entire task of making sense of their experiences over to patients, with the psychotherapist mainly providing empathy and acceptance? What might the contribution of the psychotherapist be? Psychotherapists are after all supposed to know something about how minds work.

Naming feelings rather than narrating the scenarios they belong to

Another intervention preferred by psychotherapists-in-training is to comment about how a patient is feeling. Empathy is 'in', and a good thing for a psychotherapist to have. Since some inference seems to be involved, however arrived at, the intervention is counted as an interpretation.

However, I do not think that naming a feeling is the same as understanding how the patient feels. Understanding a feeling seems to me to require knowing the contents of the feeling, knowing what was going on and who was involved when the feeling arose. What specifically did the patient imagine or remember that led him to feel as he did? The frequent comment, 'you feel very angry', rarely includes a statement of what it was, on a specific occasion, to which the patient responded with anger. I began to suggest that it might be useful when talking about feelings to mention in some detail particulars belonging to a time and place.

Preference for colorless, abstract or vague, impersonal language

The various kinds of things psychotherapists-in-training imagine saying to a patient often tend to be colorless, as indeed a number of texts recommend. They avoid colloquial language, so much so that I can usually guess almost without mistake which patients have had previous psychotherapy and learned to talk 'psychotherapese'.

It is difficult to realize that some words are 'theoretical' in tone, even if they refer to a feeling. For example, people rarely use the word 'angry' in everyday exchanges, talking instead about being mad, irritated, annoyed, pissed off. Furthermore, when a psychotherapist uses the word 'angry', it almost always for most patients connotes a faintly negative evaluation. No matter what the justification, anger seems not to be a good thing to have, even where getting mad is okay.

But most prominently, the talk trainees use with patients is vague and general. It rarely evokes an image, describes a particular scene, or narrates a series of specific events. An intervention having the following form hardly ever occurs: 'Such-and-such happened on that particular occasion, and you reacted in this particular way, because it reminded you of the time that ... , and you probably figured that the best way to prevent what happened then from happening again was to do such-and-such.'

The talk of beginning psychotherapists is almost never vivid or dramatic. They rarely tell patients stories, retell a patient's story by re-ordering or adding events to it, or suggest what links exist between a series of particular events, involving a specific cast of characters, and occurring at a particular time and place. They use pronouns, often ambiguous or of uncertain reference, instead of definite descriptions or names. They use conceptual labels (usually in the form of noun phrases like 'your sense of loss', 'your terrible loneliness', 'your dependency') to refer to feelings, motives, apparently contentless defenses, and enduring traits as abstract entities.

What especially disturbs me is that the things said to a patient do not sound *personal*. I can imagine them being said to any number of patients and being accepted by all of them as true. I think, on the contrary, that what a psychotherapist says to a patient should contain the particulars of that patient's experiences, so that it would be exceedingly unlikely that anyone would ever say exactly that to any other patient; it wouldn't make sense to anyone who had not had just those concrete experiences.

I have observed that if a psychotherapist made a timeless generalization, was somewhat vague, or dealt in abstractions, a patient's response was frequently in kind, or simply ignored what the psychotherapist had said and made no use of it. If a psychotherapist, making use of particulars imparted to him by a patient, told a good story, the patient was likely to feel listened to and to take in and use what the psychotherapist had said. Similarly, if a patient made a vague general statement about herself or himself, it made a difference whether the psychotherapist got all interested in these timeless truths, or asked instead, 'For example?'

Among other things, I tried language reform, repeatedly questioning a trainee's use of 'it' and 'that' wherever they occurred, for example. Since the user of a pronoun usually knew what its referent was, and was sure the patient knew, too, trainees experienced me as nitpicking, inducing self-consciousness, and not especially helpful. The use of 'anger' and 'angry' appeared to be ineradicable; I notice myself slipping into using such unnatural language to this day. These observations will come as no surprise to anyone familiar with the work of Roy Schafer.[33]

Three objectives

Helped by members of my seminar groups and the trainees I worked with individually, I began to develop a teaching strategy with three main objectives.

The first objective

My first objective was *to loosen the stranglehold of theory*. I had previously given lengthy demanding reading assignments. I have now stopped assigning readings in my beginning and intermediate courses on psychotherapy.

Beginners, having the notion that they are doing a very difficult job about which they know nothing, understandably cling to theory. Of course, beginners have to have something to draw upon when they listen to patients. I now tried to convince them that they knew a lot more than they thought they did, and that they could draw upon their own deeply entrenched knowledge and a well-honed body of skills. It was just that it had never occurred to them that this knowledge and those skills were relevant. The knowledge and skill I thought they probably had were about stories. They knew how to listen to, respond to, and tell a story.

I might say, 'When you are doing psychotherapy and want to get your bearings, call to mind childhood experiences of wanting someone to tell you a story, how you got your mother to tell you a story, memories of how you listened and responded to stories, what you liked and didn't like, what you wanted and especially enjoyed, what made you restless or turned you off, and what went on between you and the storyteller.

'Call to mind sitting with a friend at lunch, talking about what's been happening in your life, and your friend's life, asking and answering, "What have you been doing? How has the week gone?" What kinds of things would each of you say and ask as the other told about various happenings? What did each of you do to arouse the interest of the other? How did each of you know when the other was not interested? How did that affect what each of you told the other?

'Call to mind watching a movie. Reflect on how a movie went about affecting you. What made you feel that it was a great, a good, a lousy movie?'

In attempting to free those I teach from the iron hand of theory, I might say, 'Pay special attention to what comes into your mind as the patient talks and include that in your account of the session.' Then, when a trainee felt comfortable about including what came to her mind in what she told me, the difference between what was going on in her mind and what she said to the patient often left me dumbfounded. The former sounded so natural and on the mark, the latter so stilted and stereotyped. 'Why didn't you say that!?' I would cry out. 'Do you really think I could have? I wasn't sure that would be right. I thought it might be too much for the patient', she would reply.

'Don't make an effort to figure things out', I might suggest. 'Instead perk up when an image of any kind, a daydream, or some story you know pops into your head. Notice when the story the patient tells you, or something about the patient, how he looks or sounds, reminds you of a movie. Notice when you suddenly find yourself remembering some story the patient has told you – maybe even months before, so that you remember it surprises you. These images, stories, and memories are comments about what the patient is saying, and may often lead you to something you might say to him in turn. Indeed, you may find that you use just what pops into your head in what you say to him.'

The second objective

A second and related objective was to get trainees *to eschew the vague and general, and instead to pursue the particular.*[34] 'Out with conceptual labels summarizing or classifying experiences! Out with vagueness! Use pronouns sparingly. Repeat the particulars of the patient's story.

'Ask yourself as you listen to the patient: Can you see a scene in your mind, a particular time and place, particular characters? Can you see what they are doing? Hear what they are saying?

'If the patient speaks allusively, generally, although perhaps expressively, you provide the scene. Say things like "What you convey to me, the image that comes to my mind, is a mother and child, and the child cries, and the mother knows instantly what the child feels and wants."

'Where the patient has dropped a narrative line, ask, "What happened next?" In telling about a fight with his mother, a patient said in passing, "she tried to get my father on her side", and then went on to describe his mother's various demands and threats. The psychotherapist, as if he were watching this scene in a movie and there was a fade, found himself wanting to know whether the mother had succeeded in getting the father on her side. So when there was a pause in the descriptions of the mother's demands and threats, he asked, "How did your father respond to your mother's attempts to get him on her side?"'

The third objective

A third objective was to focus the trainee's attention on *the immediacy of the therapeutic moment*.[35] I do not mean by this emphasis on the here-and-now an emphasis on what is going on here-and-now between patient and psychotherapist. I mean an emphasis on microdynamics, the ebb and flow, the perturbations, the implied connections, the similarities, in the patient's speech flow, whatever the content of speech, whether it is about the past or present. I mean an emphasis on the minute-by-minute emergence in what the patient says of wishes, impulses, and feelings; and the reactions to their emergence (anxiety, stirrings of conscience, regret, remorse, self-criticisms, changes in levels of self-esteem, reality-testing).[36]

I direct the trainee's attention to the moment-by-moment dynamics in a single session, the blips and perturbations, the minute changes of affect and emphasis. 'Let's focus on the details of microprocess. Be a mole with your nose on the ground following the twists and turns in a barely discernible trail, not an eagle surveying a vast landscape, the valleys and peaks. Give your attention to the microprocess of this single session, not just to the macroprocess occurring over months and perhaps years of sessions.' (I do not say that this is the only way to *do* psychotherapy, but rather that it is one way to *learn* how to do psychotherapy.)

I might say, 'Try imagining that what the patient says is in some way a response to what you have just said, even though it does not seem to have anything to do with what you said.' An example: Toward the end of psychotherapy, a patient told a psychotherapist how much she had gotten out of psychotherapy. She felt she now had a handle on many problems. The psychotherapist, ignoring her grateful comment about psychotherapy (and indirectly about him), asked for a further explication of these problems. The patient became vague, and muttered some fragmentary phrases about 'shame'. The psychotherapist realized that he had been unable to accept her thanks and that she responded to the absence of an appropriate response by becoming ashamed of feeling grateful.

Another patient told a psychotherapist how much she meant to him, how important it was to him to have someone like her in his life. The psychotherapist wondered why, in that case, he made so little effort to make friends. Out of the blue, he began a furious argument about another matter. The psychotherapist said, 'Did you feel pushed away from me when I talked about making friends?' He said, 'I was just thinking that. It reminded me of my mother, when I so much wanted to be with her, telling me to go out and play.'

I might say, 'In a stream of communications by the patient, hear what the patient says at one moment as a reaction to, an assessment or correction of, what she herself has said at a previous moment. She may be saying, however indirectly, "I don't like that I said that," "I didn't mean that, I want to take it back," "I'm ashamed of what I just said," or "I regret I made that hurtful comment."'

Interpretation

I suggest thinking of interpretation as storytelling. 'The patient reports a series of events. You make a story out of these events. Show how they might be causally connected to each other. Where there appears to be a gap, where you cannot provide one of the causal links from what the patient has reported, ask about the event that is missing.

'Tell the patient a story that answers the question, "Why is the patient telling this story now? In response to what event? To accomplish what purpose, to deal with what feeling, to arouse what feeling in me?"'

It is striking to me that a psychotherapist will often give an interpretation when it is not clear either to her or the patient just what puzzling concrete particular, what question about a particular happening, that interpretation is intended to clarify or explain. I might say, 'Often the stories the patient tells belong to the genre "mysteries". Something has happened that puzzles or does not make sense to him. That moment when the patient is aware of a question is the ideal context in which to tell your story to the patient. Like the *Just So Stories* that answer questions like "How did the elephant get his trunk?", your story is one that answers a question the patient himself has raised. Because the patient is just at that moment curious and interested in the answer, he is most likely to listen to and take in your story.'

Clearly the interpretations to which I refer stay close to the surface. They make use of the stories the patient is telling or has told. They draw the patient's attention not to what she has repressed (which is inaccessible as experience) but to what she has temporarily mislaid or recently forgotten, or from which she has withdrawn her attention. When the focus is on the dynamic relations among events 'at the surface', these relations change, enabling new (that is, previously inaccessible) contents in their turn to rise to the surface.

I occasionally cast my interpretation in the form of reminding the patient of a particular movie, saying a bit about the story of the movie, and asking – if the patient hasn't mentioned it – if he has seen it. It is very rare in my experience that the patient has not seen the movie. Often it turns out that the movie was important to him and aroused strong feelings in him.

A patient once reported a dream in which she was wearing a red dress. She said she would never wear such a dress out in the open. Trees rustled in the dream. This dream report reminded me of the scene involving Mammy's rustling red petticoat in *Gone with the Wind*. My asking about the possibility that this scene was in the patient's mind led to the following revelations. The patient was deeply identified with Scarlet O'Hara, but disturbed by this identification. The particular scene was one she often remembered and had thought of recently. As I guessed and eventually asked about, she was menstruating. This discussion led to many more stories, including one in which, remembering how Scarlet tore down the green drapes to make a dress out of them, she imagined the pleasure she might have making bold colorful hats. This image, quite unlike how she thought of herself, came as a surprise but it led to some gratifying developments in her life.

We underestimate the extent to which people in this culture are obsessed and affected by movies and movie-going. Patients rarely mention movies in their 'associations' to dreams, for example, because they assume that the psychotherapist is probably not interested or that these are too trivial to bring up in such a serious setting. Often, a psychotherapist will not pick up an allusion to a movie the patient does not specifically mention, nor does the patient think of it spontaneously – unless it has become clear to him that the psychotherapist is in fact interested in such experiences. Movies that in my own work have been important to patients and provided them with narrative threads running through the stories they told and enacted in psychotherapy include *Alien, Great Expectations*, and *Nicholas Nickleby*.

The troublesome possibility remains that the psychotherapist may introduce subject matter that has special meaning for him and no special meaning for the patient. Can we depend on the patient to ignore the intrusion of material that is 'off target'? From my experience, my answer is a tentative 'yes'.[37]

Stories, lyrics, and criticism in the psychotherapy session

As I think about close listening and about strategies of interpretation in the psychotherapeutic session, I drift ever more back to the humanities. In the frame I currently use in listening and interpreting, the patient in psychotherapy is at one and the same time a narrator or a storyteller; an actor who enacts a story; a director who draws others in, assigns roles, decides on cuts and where to focus attention; a lyricist who conveys a state of mind; and a critic of his own stories, enactments, lyrics. At any one moment in a session, which patient does the psychotherapist address? To which patient, does she listen? To which, respond? At that moment, does she speak as an observer or an interpreter? These are the possibilities.

TELLING STORIES

The patient talks about events. These events have a *then* and a *there*. They are in a particular time and place. They involve specific settings, characters, props. In these events, the patient interacts with others. The patient has wishes, objectives, or goals, which meet obstacles, including the patient's fears. The collision between wish and obstacle has an outcome.

The psychotherapist encourages the patient to tell the story, notices omissions and reluctances, observes especially the order of events. The psychotherapist wants to get the story straight, in all its particularity. If the psychotherapist asks questions, they are likely to be of the kind 'What happened next? What happened before that led up to this event?', not the 'Why?' 'What did all this mean?' kind. The psychotherapist's objective is to help the patient tell the story wholly, completely.

The psychotherapist becomes an appreciative interpreter. I use the term 'appreciative' to distinguish two kinds of literary critic: the one who arouses in the reader appreciation of an illumined work; and the one who, often showing off his own knowledge or cleverness, leaves the reader with a sense that a work has been reduced or belittled, however subtly.

The patient may or may not make the nature of the *links* between events or patterns of events (similarity, causality) explicit. The patient may or may not make the 'moral' of the story, what the story demonstrates, what the patient concludes from the story, explicit. If not, the psychotherapist may infer, point out, provide or make explicit links between events or patterns of events, or suggest what 'moral' the patient has drawn from a story.

Events or patterns of events may be related or associated by virtue of some *similarity* between them. The psychotherapist may suggest what particular feature or property of an event reminded the patient of another similar event. Particular features or properties of events may include the kind of event it is, the type of character(s) it involves, the nature of the relations between its characters, its setting, a prop. Features or properties of a group of events may include the sequence in which they occur or the 'moral' that together they imply.

The nature of the links between events or patterns of events may be *causal*. The patient's own feelings and other motives, including those stirred up by previous events, are 'privileged' causes of events – privileged, in that they are of special interest to the psychotherapist and patient.

ENACTING STORIES

The patient is an actor and/or a director, in a story of his own making, which is enacted with the psychotherapist in the here-and-now. The psychotherapist's objective is to participate in the story being enacted in the here-and-now just enough to catch on to what role the patient is assigning her. ('Participate', in the sense, 'be in touch with'.) The patient evokes or elicits feelings and impulses in the psychotherapist, or acts toward the psychotherapist as if the psychotherapist had the motives the patient perceives or attributes. The participation of the psychotherapist is primarily, but not always completely, internal; it is limited or contained. The psychotherapist observes what feelings and impulses to action are aroused within her, and then – noticing what images, what scenes, what memories, what fantasies, come to mind – guesses at the nature of the story the patient is inviting or inciting her to enact or reenact. The psychotherapist says things like: 'What is it you want me to feel, to do?' 'At this moment, I feel you want me to feel or to act in this way.' 'Do you remember the story you told me or mentioned? I am reminded of it. What is going on between us right now is the same kind of story.'

The psychotherapist, in an act of self-transformation, becomes a storyteller, who interprets the patient's enacted story by *telling* in full the story the patient prefers to enact, rather than as actor joining the patient in enacting it.

COMPOSING LYRICS

The patient tries to convey a state of mind. The patient speaks as 'the self when it is alone with itself'. Its social identities (gender, race, ethnicity, socioeconomic class, age, occupation, sexuality) are suspended, are felt to be absent, to be in abeyance. It is abstracted from the specificities of time and place. This self may be incarnate or embodied, or it may be abstracted even from the body.[38]

The psychotherapist tries to grasp this state of mind, to become acquainted with this timeless incarnate or bodiless self. The psychotherapist listens to the patient's voice, and observes the tone in which things are said – the words and phrases chosen. The words and phrases, the rhythms and tonalities, in their properties *parallel* or are an *analog* of the properties of the state of mind presented or the self speaking.

The patient may provide images and figures of speech. If the patient does not, the psychotherapist may ask for an image, a scene, which might serve as an *objective correlative* of – a *metaphor* for – the patient's state of mind or self. 'What is that like?' 'What scene or image does that call to mind?' 'What you say or how you sound reminds me of a scene or image.'

In contrasting or clashing words and phrases, in different rhythms and tonalities, the psychotherapist hears multiple voices. 'Who is that speaking now?' 'Whose voice is that?' 'I hear this kind of voice.' 'Are you speaking in your mother's voice? Your father's? Mine?' 'Are you speaking in the voice of the tempter? The teaser? The savage critic? The internal saboteur? Is this the voice of reason?' The psychotherapist distinguishes the voices of the patient's many-selved self. She observes what is distinctive of each voice – observes its tone, its diction, when it speaks, and what other voice it responds to or addresses. She brings to the patient's attention the differences in the various voices she hears

– which the patient is likely to experience as one undifferentiated voice – and how these voices relate and react to each other.

The psychotherapist tries to understand what has brought about this state of mind, what it is in response to. Who is this self? What is it experiencing? The psychotherapist may provide an image or scene, if the patient does not, which is offered to the patient as an objective correlative of – a metaphor for – the states of mind presented. The psychotherapist may take what the patient has said and recast the one voice the patient hears as a conversation, a quarrel, a collision between, or a harmonious intermingling of, the multiple voices of the many-selved self overheard by the psychotherapist in the session.

CRITICISM

The patient responds to, adopts an attitude toward, and criticizes (rarely appreciates but is rather ashamed of or feels guilty about) his own tale, own voice or voices. Often the patient experiences his responses as caused by the attitudes of another, or attributes them to or perceives them as coming from another – or, more often, the activity of self-criticism goes unnoticed by him. The psychotherapist observes this activity, and calls it to the patient's attention.[39]

The patient may be mistaken either in experiencing this self-reflexive, self-monitoring, self-critical activity as emanating from the self or in experiencing it as emanating from another. In either case, the psychotherapist locates its proper source and helps the patient return it to whom it belongs.

Assessing the accuracy of interpretations

In view of the inevitable degree of indeterminateness and ambiguity in clinical material, I encourage those I teach to generate more than one interpretation of the same material. It is a good idea to get out of the habit of thinking, 'Obviously this patient is ... , This patient's story is certainly ... ', and into the habit of thinking, 'What is going on with this patient today, given what I have observed, could be this, *or* this ... The story the patient is telling or enacting today could be this, *or* this ... Given the stories the patient is telling or enacting, he may be in the world of this scenario, *or* in the world of that scenario ...'

I remember the report of four psychoanalytic sessions by M. Silverman.[40] A structural theorist, two developmentalists, a self psychologist, a Kleinian, an interpersonalist, an eclectic, and an object relations theorist responded to the report. They intended their commentaries to clarify the way in which theory shapes technique.

In these sessions the patient alluded to three stories: the film *Now Voyager*, the novel *Don Quixote*, and the story of Helen Keller and her teacher Anne Sullivan. What do these stories have in common? They are stories in which someone rescues someone else from a bad situation or hurtful person. Does the patient wish the psychotherapist to rescue her? Is she enacting a story of *a rescue*? But the three stories also depict wondrous transformations. In each story, a person (not simply the situation she is in) changes. Does the patient wish the psychotherapist to transform her? Is she enacting a story of *a transformation*?

Stories of rescue and stories of transformation are not incompatible. Both may be of interest to the patient. But surely one is closer to consciousness, or has a greater charge of feeling or sense of urgency attached to it. That is the one that is more appropriate as a basis for interpretation, on this particular day, in this particular session, here and now. The patient reports a fantasy in which a mad scientist does something to give her bigger breasts. This fantasy provides some evidential support, however weak, for the inference from the other three stories (which are not reported as fantasies) that a story of transformation, rather than a story of a rescue, is most saliently on the patient's mind.[41]

It is important that you cannot guess psychotherapists' theoretical preferences from their descriptions of observations in terms of stories of rescue and transformation. In other words, observations so couched, while influenced by knowledge of narratives or stories, and of course then not *non*theoretical, are nevertheless and importantly uncontaminated by the very rival psychoanalytic theories or hypotheses about the clinical material that are in question. They can be used therefore to favor one of these rivals over another. If trainees learn to observe at this level, they are unlikely to force what patients say onto Procrustean theoretical beds, or to hear only what they expect to hear. Then they are more likely to be in touch with what their patients are experiencing here-and-now.

In the eight theory-driven commentaries on these four sessions, only two mention *Now Voyager* – although the psychoanalyst writes in an aside, 'She repeatedly brings up *Now Voyager*. Is that the script for the analysis?' None considers the story of *Now Voyager* in any detail. One commentary mentions the allusion to Helen Keller. No commentary mentions the allusion to *Don Quixote*. Infatuation with theory, and with explicating theory, leads to ignoring details in the clinical material solely on the ground, as far as I can see, that they don't lend themselves to promoting a general theory. The mischievous witch, Theory, banishes what otherwise might be fascinating particulars clear out of the picture.[42]

Most of all, I give priority to a patient's actual subjective experience in assessing the credibility of an interpretative intervention a psychotherapist has communicated. An interpretative intervention is not about just any story that might in fact be somewhere in the patient's mind. It is about a story the psychotherapist believes is engaging the patient here and now.

Therefore, these are the kinds of responses that are important in concluding that a psychotherapist who has made an interpretation is on the right track: 'Now, I remember an episode just like that which I forgot to tell you. On the way here today, I thought, or wondered, or imagined … Just yesterday, this morning, right after the last session, I … That reminds me of something that happened with my mother …'

These new events are of a time or place. They complicate, enrich, or complete the story, add a missing piece to it, provide a clarifying flashback to an earlier event, give some necessary background. The patient's response may include other stories that are similar to – or be an attempt to counteract – the story she or he has told or enacted about which the psychotherapist has commented. The patient may deepen a mood evident in the story commented on, or may give more details about its setting. The patient may burst through to an emotional state that is clearly appropriate to the unfolding story and therefore, no matter how embarrassing or painful, makes sense.

I am inclined to think I am on the right track if the patient's response to my communication tells me more than I knew before, surprises me, adds a new twist to a story, carries the story further, or involves an intense expression of feeling – as I may begin to laugh or cry, sometimes quite unexpectedly, when something about a movie, I am not always sure what it is, touches me. I am inclined to think I am on the wrong track if the patient convincingly challenges what I say by pointing out particulars that are inconsistent with it or not encompassed by it, if the patient ignores what I say, or if what I say has no impact on him or the story he is telling or enacting.

Mere assent or dissent is evidentially irrelevant. So are timeless generalizations or generalities, no matter how eagerly or enthusiastically the patient offers them.

A ready-made set of stories?

Wouldn't it be useful in teaching psychotherapy to a beginner just to give her a set of stories often told or enacted by patients so that she would recognize what story she is hearing or caught up with the patient in enacting? Psychotherapy research might come up then with a set of stories from its empirical studies that a psychotherapist should have ready at hand when listening to patients. Maybe psychotherapy research can even show that patients with different personality or character disorders, for example, are partial to particular kinds of stories. Indeed, we might regard psychoanalytic theory itself as an effort to provide a set of common or typical scenarios.

A set of stories ready at hand? I don't think so, for a variety of reasons. I am, as you can tell from what I have said so far, leery of anything that promotes reliance on formulas, even if these are archetypal narratives rather than abstract or general concepts. I would recoil from the prospect of stretching the patient's material on still another Procrustean theoretical bed instead of focusing on the particulars in what the patient tells.

But mainly, I don't think that there is a finite list of stories any more than I think there is a finite list of sentences in a natural language. Narrative competence can generate an infinite set of stories, including completely new never-before-created stories, just as linguistic competence can generate an infinite set of sentences, including completely novel sentences, from a finite set of components. For example, see the computer program 'for the writer of novels, short stories, plays, screenplays and television episodes' called *Plots Unlimited* – 'a creative source for generating a virtually limitless number and variety of story plots and outlines'.[43]

CHAPTER 4

Psychological and Social Theories as Narrative Paradigms

Marshall Edelson

I have a problem with my colleagues. They hear what I am saying about stories as a sign that I am abandoning science. The intellectual climate of my workplace, my social world, respects theory and cannot take stories seriously. That makes it difficult for me to stick with stories. It draws me against my will into making a theoretical argument. It impels me to take up the cudgel against the champions of theory. But what I want to argue is that the theories we use to understand individuals, groups, and organizations are storylike, are scenarios, scripts, narrative paradigms.

In practicing as a clinician, teacher, and consultant, I have become ever more convinced that remembered stories help me know what to do or say. When a problem, on a specific occasion, in a specific situation, with all its particularities, faces me, I experience myself as a protagonist in a scenario. I represent the experience to myself as a narrative. And it then reminds me of some other story, which turns out to be relevant. Remembering this story, I now seem to have some notion of what is going on here-and-now and what to do. For better or worse, on the way *from* participation in a scenario that reminds me of a relevant story *to* understanding and action, I do not necessarily pass through the terrain of general theory.

But I cannot shut out the world in which I live and work, which respects theoretical knowledge and thinks stories are for children or recreation. So, despite my inclination to avoid abstract theorizing and argument, I am not telling stories here. Instead I am arguing for taking an interest in stories.

I am not arguing for junking theories in favor of constructing stories. I am arguing, first, that we should make a strenuous effort really to hear the stories others tell us in all their particularity. These stories are privileged, windows into the world we are trying to see and understand. I am arguing, second, and most importantly here, that the theory we do use and that we should be using to understand the meaning of those stories is a *narrative* theory, both a theory about narratives and a theory whose schemas, templates, or paradigms are narrative in form – are structured like a story. (I include, as part of 'understanding the meaning of a story', answers to the questions, 'What evoked the story? How is the story being used to do something about whatever it was that evoked it?')

Listening to the story

Patients tell psychotherapists stories. Psychotherapists in turn tell their consultants or teachers stories. The teacher/consultant, just like the psychotherapist, participates in this storytelling in some skillful, that is, appropriate way. Above all, we to whom the story is told should be interested in it. We listen as children do, wanting to know what happened next, curious about how this situation came about, who did or said what, how it all ended. We make the gestures and noises that elicit the story, that encourage the patient or those who consult us to go on with it, to tell us more, to bring up the events that do not come out immediately but that we know are there.

Clinicians and teachers/consultants sometimes say, identifying what they regard as a problem, 'There are many perspectives on any story, many ways of hearing it.' But for me what is salient, what comes first, is just the story the patient tells, before all the perspectives on it. Do we actually hear the story on the patient's mind? Are we primarily interested in it, in listening to it, in eliciting untold aspects of it? Or are we instead rushing to fit some fragment of it into a favorite perspective or theoretical scheme of our own, using this incomplete piece to justify our confidence in that perspective or scheme? If we do not hear and pay close attention to the details of the particular story that here-and-now is on the patient's mind, then whatever we say is likely to be somewhat vague, general, or formulaic, or to belong to the world of some other scenario – and it will not touch that patient.

The problem is that, apparently inevitably, we fit any story we hear to the frame we bring to it. Guided by a theory, our own life experiences, our own preoccupations, both personal and occupational, we pay attention to certain details and ignore others. I have the experience over and over watching movies with friends that each of us seems to see a different movie. One of us sees the television miniseries *Brideshead Revisited* as a story about the self-destructiveness of an alcoholic, whose alcoholism is fueled by an unconscious conflict over homosexuality. Another sees the same movie as a story about an empty loveless man who falls in love twice and both times is failed by his lovers, or about a woman who keeps choosing the wrong men. Still a third responds to a story about a family belonging to a minority (Roman Catholic) in a Protestant England, and about the fate of its various members in that society. Another responds to a story about the role of religious faith in society, and about the clash between skepticism and faith, the reluctance of the believer to bear the burden of belief, and the attempts of the skeptic to escape the emptiness and despair that are the consequence of disbelief.

One might agree that all these stories are indeed there in the movie and told, and that it remains for the viewer to become aware of the frame that prevents him from receiving more than one. However, the viewer may also choose to scan a number of possible frames – this is where group discussion of experiences watching movies can be helpful and fun – and decide consciously that one of these encompasses more of the detailed particularities of the story than any other, or matches better the intentions of the storyteller, if these intentions can be inferred from the context of the story, from how it is told, or from its outcome.

Where does theory come in?

Of course, those who regard a theoretical framework as indispensable in such listening are going to be suspicious of my apparent dismissal of general theory, certain that I smuggle it in somewhere.

I have asked myself, 'What is the role of ideas in my life, in my work? Do ideas come first, before experience? Do I impose these *a priori* ideas on my experience? Do I organize and interpret experience in the light of my ideas, as documents are placed in preexisting labeled files?

'Or does experience come first, before ideas? Do I extract my ideas from my experience, as I squeeze juice from fruit?'

In my clinical work, I have examples of both these possibilities. At times, patients, whose ideas are often in the form of stories, expediently use, adapt, and select from the material of experience, fitting it to some favored preexisting story they choose to remember and to tell themselves and others. Similarly, as a clinician, infatuated with a theory, I have had to resist the temptation to use, adapt, and select from what a patient says or does to 'confirm' that theory.

At other times, one story reminds a patient, who, for example, is constructing a dream, of another story, simply because the two stories have something in common or are in some way alike. The patient may then use elements of one story in the dream to allude to the other story. Similarly, as a clinician, infatuated with a theory, when one story a patient tells me (for example, about current experience) reminds me of another story the patient has told me (for example, about childhood), I have had to resist the temptation to leap from observation of a similarity to a statement of causal connection.[44]

Of course I agree that, in any practical enterprise, ideas are important tools. Of course I agree that we use some theoretical framework in listening to any story. The crucial questions are, 'What theoretical framework? What is its function in our practice?'

I put my answers to these two crucial questions in this way: Theory may guide us about how best to elicit a story, or how best to enable another to tell it to us, because a theory may help us to understand what difficulties the teller may have in telling the story. Theory may suggest to us how to help the storyteller bring to light scenes, episodes, characters she may have wittingly or unwittingly omitted, because a theory may help us to recognize clues to the existence of these omissions. A theory may show us how to let the storyteller know that he is in fact unwittingly enacting or telling a story and indeed what story, because a theory may help us to identify and reconstruct the links connecting apparently unrelated events, and making these events then part of that story.

But I think the theories that help us in this way are capable of doing so just because they are not sets of more or less general propositions, logically (that is, deductively) related to one another, and made up of more or less abstract concepts (variables), which are functions of each other. The theories that help us are elaborations or complications of a theory we already possess and that we learned when, as children, we were told stories, sometimes the same story over and over, or shown movies of increasing complexity.

This theory that we possess and use is, first, a theory about stories: how they are constructed, what conventions they use, how the significance of various (repeated) elements is recognized, in what way stories are related to reality (have referential meaning), and in what way they have more or less explicit meanings (as in the moral drawn at the end of a fable or the point made in propaganda) as well as implicit or symptomatic (nonreferential) meanings.[45] Our theory is, second, also a set of narrative paradigms, scripts, scenarios, which have been constructed from experience as well as taught to us, and which we use in perceiving and understanding what is happening in the world in which we live.

When I write that the knowledge required as a base for clinical skill is represented and stored in the form of stories, I am making a strong *theoretical* claim. I do not dismiss theory, but rather make the point that the theories we use, that we find valuable, are themselves narrative paradigms or schemata. Only an overlay of misguided scientistic abstractions disguises the nature of these theories from us.

Psychoanalytic theory

Psychoanalytic theory emphasizes *fantasy*, the *dreamwork* we use in constructing works of imagination; *conflict, castration* and other dangers; the *oedipus complex*; the *primal scene*, the *phallic woman*; the *family romance*; and internalized 'objects', and the dramas of love and hate, of loss and seduction, of anxiety and desire, of prohibition and sabotage that these figures enact on the stage of our minds. Isn't psychoanalysis then a theory about remembering (and forgetting) stories, constructing or inventing stories, enacting stories, the impact of stories on our lives, and the process of storytelling itself, as well as a set of narrative paradigms evoked by, and used by us in interpreting, the stories we are told? (Freud noted with some discomfort that his case studies read like works of fiction.[46]) Why not frankly acknowledge the kind of theory we have in psychoanalysis, rather than engage in sterile linguistic exercises meant to show that psychoanalytic theory (in particular, its metapsychology) is as 'scientific' as a theory in physics!

Social theory

The same is true of the theories about groups, organizations, and social systems to which we are drawn and which we use.[47] These theories are redolent of the stories that underlie their sometimes portentous abstractness and give them whatever meaning they have. Movies that tell group stories – *The Women* (1939), *Executive Suite* (1954), *Patterns* (1956), *Twelve Angry Men* (1957), *The Group* (1966), *Bloodbrothers* (1978), *Diner* (1982), *The Decline of the American Empire* (1986), *Dead Poets Society* (1989), *Glengarry Glen Ross* (1992), *The Age of Innocence* (1993) – are better answers to the questions 'What is a group?' 'What are its distinctive properties?' 'What influences what happens in the life of a group?' than any theoretical statement.

The journey

What is a group? It is the values, task, purpose, or goal members of a collectivity *share* that make it a social system (a group, an organization, a society). We form a group or organization to achieve one or more than one task and to reach the subgoals that lie along the path to that task-achievement. This definition immediately draws us into a narrative paradigm (one of the most common): *the journey*.

Resources and obstacles

What resources does a group need for its journey? What obstacles does a group meet on its way?

A collectivity must have access to resources needed to achieve its task. Access to resources depends upon the collectivity's relation to its external situation. Here the intergroup story of an organization's relation to other organizations, for example, becomes important. In general, we want to know the story of the relations between a collectivity and its situation, about relations across the boundary that divides a collectivity and its situation.

I tell stories about boundaries that groups or organizations use fearfully to keep dangerous others and dangerous things out, boundaries that groups or organizations make more or less permeable, welcoming what may come from 'out there', and boundaries that are so leaky that the group or organization is no longer able to tell what is distinctive about it or who belongs or doesn't belong to it. These stories are about opening or closing borders, about unhindered passage or perilous secret smuggling across borders, about whether 'we' allow strangers in and whether 'we' regard what they bring with them with friendly interest or suspicion.

A theoretical interpretation of some problem the collectivity is having may point to the impact of its current relative lack of access to resources such as knowledge, facilities, money, personnel, opportunities. These resources come from the outside. This explanation or interpretation, although we may dress it up in such language as 'the collectivity's adaptation to its external situation', comes down to depicting an episode in the story of the group's or organization's journey.

To tell a group or organization story is to tell about what supplies the group or organization needs for its journey, and how it goes about acquiring them. It is to tell about the obstacles encountered in preparing for the journey ('the hard-hearted merchant', 'the keeper of secrets') and on the journey ('the dragon guarding the gold' or 'the plea addressed to a reluctant helper').

Can I depend on others? Can they depend on me?

The group or organization also needs internal resources to reach its destination. We may speak in theoretical language of the level of capacities and skills available. We may ask about the motivations people bring to their participation in the collectivity, and the degree of commitment various members have to a set of high-level values. We may worry about problems of morale.

I hear stories of inspiration, enthusiasm, and readiness to make sacrifices for a higher good or an ideal. I hear stories of disappointment and cynicism, of those who have lost their way or given themselves over to evil. Although our language may be arcane, we are in Camelot, in the realm of ideals that people seek to realize together, or in the name of which people fight bloody and interminable wars.

The questions every character in the group story is asking about every other are, 'Can I depend on him?' 'Is what is important to me important to her?' 'When it comes to a choice – this group or that one, this path or that one, this action or that one – can I depend on him to make the choice that follows from the values we share as members of this group and our shared commitment to realize those values in reaching our common destination?'

Strains develop when there are differences, as there inevitably are, in the extent to which members of a collectivity share these values and this commitment. These strains may be of such intensity that we are justified in speaking of an episode as a crisis of confidence, which indeed may have as its consequence the dissolution of the group. But more ordinarily a group or organizational story may follow the vicissitudes of such strains: how the group or organization confronts or avoids these strains, how it negotiates them and what – usually uneasy – balance results from such negotiation, or how instead they result in disappointment, anomie or alienation ('we have lost our way'), emigration ('here is where I leave this wagon train'), 'scapegoating', 'blaming' the group within ('the saboteurs', 'the troublemakers'), or conflict with 'foreign' groups ('the enemy', 'the bloodthirsty Indians').

Who gets to play what part?

We *organize* a group or organization. The way we organize it ideally has to do with what will help get the job done. Types of organization are structures. I suppose someone might claim that a structure is not a narrative idea, because it does not denote a process or implicate time in any essential way. But a 'type of organization' might be considered a description of the parts in a play or the team positions in a game, and what action we assign to each one, and how these parts or positions and their actions relate to one another. I think then of a structure such as a *table of organization* or an *analysis of a task* as the product of a process. As such, it is essentially a *plan* and so inextricably part of a process of human action. But, like a map on a journey, it continues to influence what happens next, because the human players choose to consult it and to let it guide them.

Each member of a collectivity (individual and group or subgroup) has one or more than one role, that is, plays a 'part' or 'parts' in attempts to achieve the collectivity's goals. Roles reflect the way in which we have organized a task. Who may or must do or say, or does do or say, what to whom? How are decisions legitimized? What decisions are, and which are not, regarded as legitimate? Do people see themselves functioning as exquisitely intermeshed team members, each one doing exactly what is needed to make it possible for another to make her or his contribution, or do they feel that they are always stumbling over each other, getting in each other's way, interfering with and obstructing each other?

Ordinarily, we relate roles to one another hierarchically. That is, we invest each role with *authority* to carry out a *responsibility* or more than one responsibility. Ideally, we define roles by the tasks those who occupy them bear responsibility for achieving. Role-relations result from an analysis of the relation of tasks to each other. Which task is supraordinate, and which subordinate? ('Supraordinate' and 'subordinate', in the sense that a supraordinate task, if we are to achieve it, requires the achievement of a variety of subtasks, perhaps simultaneously, perhaps in a certain sequence.) A supraordinate role bears responsibility for coordinating the performances of subordinate roles each of which in turn bears responsibility for the achievement of some subgoal. We vest the supraordinate role with the authority those who occupy it need to adjudicate conflict or competition for resources that may arise in the interaction of these subordinate roles. So the relation of roles to one another, again speaking of an ideal, is not arbitrary, capricious, or an expression of individual desire or predilection, but legitimized by our understanding of task-requirements.

Problems may occur when a member's power, the ability of that member to influence others, is unrelated to the authority and responsibility attached to the role the member occupies. (I hear a story about a 'kibitzer' or a 'loose cannon'.) Other problems occur when authority and responsibility do not match. Typically a low-status person – guard, nurse, trainee – has a lot of responsibility but little authority. (I hear a story about 'burnout'.)

Different stories go with 'role' and 'wish', although both may be properties of the same concrete individual. To regard an individual's behavior in the light of the role that individual occupies and its relation to other roles is to tell a group story, in contrast to the individual story we tell when the focus is on this same individual's behavior as an expression of non-role-related wishes or fears.

How do we deal with the deviant?

Norms are rules, situation-specific prescriptions and proscriptions designed to see that roles fit together in order to achieve goals. We extrapolate norms from high-level values. Values are essentially preferences for making one kind of choice rather than another when faced with alternatives. This language is abstract but the reality to which it refers is dramatic, for it refers to situations in which group members face choices. The group sanctions one alternative over another, and so a group member is always faced with the possibility of making a *wrong* choice.

Given the uncertainties involved in such extrapolations, people often have trouble making the connection between specific norms and more general values and over-arching goals. They simply automatically rebel against or conform to 'the rules'. They have no sense of the relation between the rules and any general values they may or may not have consciously committed themselves to realize in a wide variety of situations. How much do people care about and how much are they actually governed by norms that specify who shall do or say what to whom in interactions with others? (Am I going to hear a story about the person who goes through the red light whenever no policeman is watching?)

I hear stories of deviance and the control of deviance, of reward and punishment, of moral imperatives and their violation. Others may be interested in telling individual stories about a bad person, a criminal. In response, I may tell a group story about an individual whom other group members *scapegoat*, whom they choose to see as the cause or source of some difficulty so that they may avoid dealing with a problem and recognizing their own contribution to it, which make most if not all of them anxious.

Leaders

The theoretical statement is: Leaders function at and control boundary exchanges. How does a leader go about identifying what obstacles interfere with access to external resources? How accurately does she or he anticipate and identify these obstacles? How does a leader plan to overcome such obstacles, and how does she or he as part of that plan interact with representatives of other groups or organizations?

Confidence in a leader, and therefore the motivational commitments of members, will depend on how clearly and with what integrity a leader represents in her or his own actions the values and task faced by a group or organization. Can we trust her? Is the way in which he has organized, or proposes to organize, the individual or group constituents of an organization an effective and rational means for achieving collective goals? Or does it seem that other personal motives or considerations do determine, or have determined, a leader's moves and designs? Is a leader of a collectivity interested in, and good at, evoking the value-commitments necessary for maintaining the collectivity members' task-related or goal-relevant motivations?

A leader may be dysfunctional in a variety of ways. A person may occupy a position of leadership for nontask or antitask reasons. She may have little or no interest in the job, but accepts it because it offers some personal opportunity or advantage. Or someone gives him the job, because of a level of incompetence that ensures that he will cause no trouble for his superiors. So then we may have a leader who doesn't seem to care, or who is unavailable. I hear stories of demoralization and chaos.

A leader may be a martinet, preoccupied with rules, making demands, with very little interest in the concerns or feelings of his subordinates. Such leaders appear frequently in movies: Gregory Peck in *Twelve O'Clock High* (1949), Charles Laughton as Captain Bligh in *Mutiny on the Bounty* (1935), John Mills as the tormented new leader in *Tunes of Glory* (1960). The same indifference to subordinates may occur in corrupt leaders, whom personal advantage or ambition, ill-concealed by hypocritical postures, preoccupy: George Macready and Adolphe Menjou in *Paths of Glory* (1957) or Broderick Crawford as Willie Stark, the bullheaded and brutal demagogue in *All the King's Men* (1949).

A leader may be so overidentified with her subordinates, or so concerned with popularity, that he is unable to make task-required decisions that might upset or hurt them: Gary Merrill in *Twelve O'Clock High* and Alec Guinness in *Tunes of Glory*.

A leader may be so driven and single-minded about reaching a particular destination by a particular route that he is not able to make use of new information, or respond to changing conditions (John Wayne as Tom Dunson in 1948's *Red River*) or take into account a larger context or supraordinate goals (Alec Guinness in 1957's *Bridge on the River Kwai*).

A leader may mesmerize followers by personal example and fantastic feats, becoming the hero of myth or legend (Kirk Douglas in 1960's *Spartacus*), but fail entirely to master the mundane or technical details necessary if a spectacular tactical victory is to result in lasting gain (Peter O'Toole as T. E. Lawrence in

1962's *Lawrence of Arabia*). Robert Redford in *Brubaker* (1980) is unable to maintain the prison reforms he has achieved through acts of personal heroism, because he is inept in dealing with crucial groups in his situation, for example, the legislature.

A leader, his eye on the task but also identified with his subordinates, may make an agonizing decision: to ask for sacrifices from a few now to save the many later, to ensure the continuity of the collectivity in the long run. Johnny Weissmuller as Tarzan in a movie the title of which I cannot remember eats what scarce food is available rather than sharing it with the women and children he is shepherding across a mountain, because if he does not survive to lead them they will not survive the ordeal of such a journey. Tyrone Power in *Abandon Ship!* (1957) has to decide who in an overcrowded lifeboat will go overboard. Clark Gable in *Command Decision* (1948) also makes such a decision, sending airmen against targets to their deaths in order to minimize casualties in a coming battle. His superiors, in their relation to other groups with which they must deal, judge that he has asked for an unacceptable level of sacrifice, and they take his job away from him.

I do not grasp what the theoretical language offers in the way of an understanding of these phenomena that the movies do not. To put it another way: Is the theoretical language merely a scientistic translation of the knowledge that is already more vividly and usefully contained in story form?

In each case, questions arise about a leader and followers, about the group and collectivity that chooses or suffers a dysfunctional leader, about the situation of that group or organization and the conditions in which it strives to maintain itself and achieve its goals. What brought about our coming to have this particular kind of leader? What function does it serve – who benefits from – our having just this kind of leader? What is the 'real' problem? To what extent can we say that it does not depend on leader-characteristics alone? In an effort to understand how it happens that we choose or suffer such a leader, do we tell an individual, interpersonal, group, organizational, or intergroup or interorganizational story?

The hold our reference or identity groups have over us

Each member of a collectivity has internalized reference or identity groups, and often asks herself, 'How will those important others respond to what I am doing or saying as a member of *this* group?' Depending on the answer to that question, a member may occupy her role with greater or lesser degrees of ease.

No matter how task-effective a way of doing things is, if it conflicts with what a reference group values or prescribes, it will arouse discomfort and people will tend to avoid it. Requiring behavior from people that does not match their professional identity as they and important others see it, however appropriate to a particular task or to the values of a particular institution, will create problems that leaders need to recognize and explicitly address. This is especially difficult to do, when sacred beliefs and values (for example, equality, democracy) are involved.

Group members classify themselves and others in the group classify them according to achievement, or according to given attributes (for example, gender, age, race, ethnicity, socioeconomic class, professional discipline) that define identity groups. When are such classifications relevant or irrelevant to – how do they facilitate or interfere with – task-achievement? There are many stories, often painful and usually complex, about gender, race, class, ethnicity, age in group life. In the movie *Diner*, for example, a group of men coming of age band together to protect themselves from relationships with women: It's easy to talk to each other, but what do you talk to a woman about?!

MEMBERS OF A GROUP IN AN ORGANIZATION KEEP LEAVING

Here are some stories from my own experience illustrating the way in which reference to an identity group can influence behavior in a work setting. In the 1960s I was asked to consult at a community mental health center. This was at the height of the therapeutic community movement, which espoused egalitarian relations among the various mental health disciplines. The administrators of the center found that at the end of each year they were losing the psychiatrists they had hired the year before. This, no matter the level of skill, personality, goals, or espoused ideals of the psychiatrist.

One finding had to do with the team's determination to keep the doctor from taking over and giving the orders. So all decisions had to be by vote. Furthermore, the team was suspicious of any contacts or meetings a doctor had with other doctors that took her or him away from the team.

Each psychiatrist gave a different reason for leaving. None expressed any discomfort with the 'team approach'. In fact, all were enthusiastic about it. One of the factors in psychiatrists leaving the mental health center, despite their enthusiasm for the team approach, was that this system defined the role of psychiatrists differently from the way in which their major reference group defined it. Their education as physicians had trained them to be leaders, to make decisions, to accept authority and responsibility, as a necessary part, and a realization of the values, of the practice of medicine.

MEMBERS OF A GROUP IN AN ORGANIZATION BALK WHEN ASKED
TO PERFORM 'INAPPROPRIATE' TASKS

Similarly, when in the 1960s I was trying to establish a therapeutic community on an inpatient unit, I suggested that the appropriate task for nurses, given their continued presence on the unit, was to work with the entire group of patients rather than nursing or doing psychotherapy with individual patients. I saw nurses and patients as two interacting groups both having a stake in the quality of life on the unit. The nurses' goal might then be to deal with disruptions in group life:

antagonisms, conflicts, competitions for spaces or resources, among groups of patients and between nurses and patients. Such disruptions, of course, interfere with adherence to norms designed to maximize the therapeutic enterprise.

In response to my vision, the nurses for the most part became demoralized. They could not accept such an assignment. However appropriate it was from the point of view of the task as I conceived it, the role was too foreign to their conception of their profession and too distant from their actual training.

In the same setting, when as Chief of Service I asked the residents to play baseball with patients in the interest of achieving socialization and rehabilitation goals, they would only do so because I did so myself. Even then they never could see any connection between what they were doing and what they imagined their professional role suggested they should be doing.

Anxiety, the hidden saboteur along the way

Role demands and dilemmas evoke anxieties (frequently shared). A poor fit may exist between personality or capacities, on the one hand, and role-requirements, on the other. (How did we get into that fix?) Conflicting requirements may beset a person who at one and the same time occupies two roles. (How and why did we get into that fix?) Authority-relations up and down a hierarchy arouse anxieties. Do people imagine disagreeing with a leader? What do they imagine the consequence will be? What happens when someone actually does disagree with a leader – in private, in public?

Being classified in a certain way by other members of a group, given your own way of classifying yourself, and the connotations of particular classifications, arouses anxieties. The imagined responses of members of other groups to which you belong to your participation in *this* group arouse anxieties. What would *they* say if they knew you were agreeing to do this or that? Would they throw you out as a traitor, a betrayer, as disloyal, or an incompetent?

The sheer difficulty of the task, and the frequent ambiguity about whether or not I, you, we have failed or succeeded, arouse anxieties and demoralize. This is especially so when the task involves processing and transforming 'human materials'.

When I notice odd, dysfunctional, nontask, or antitask ways of going about doing things, I guess that these weird arrangements and procedures serve as collective or shared solutions to which group members turn to rid themselves of anxieties. I try to discover in each case what kind of anxiety these apparently peculiar arrangements and procedures mitigate. It is critical for a collectivity how it deals with anxieties, for the way in which it deals with them affects task-achievement for better or worse.

David Berg has put it on occasion in these words: 'What's bugging the members of the group, and what are they doing about it?' Clinicians (for example, group psychotherapists), teachers of group psychotherapy, and organizational consultants give answers to that question in interpretive interventions. Ezriel and Sutherland and, also, Whitaker and Lieberman, in their writings on group psychotherapy, emphasize listening for: (1) those wishes that are not idiosyncratic but that group members share, albeit often unconsciously or unavowedly; (2) as well as the shared fears associated with these wishes; and (3) the ways that group members collaborate, wittingly or not, to promote particular resolutions of such wish–fear conflicts. Some of these solutions are enabling. They are on the side of both wish and fear; they provide both gratification and security. Some are restrictive. They favor the fear and ignore the wish.[48]

The kind of story I have tended to tell

Here is the kind of story that I have been likely to tell about a group or organization. My interest has tended primarily, although of course not exclusively, to be in what brings people together, where they are going together, what ideals and values and goals they share.

There is an agreed-upon explicit task. People and groups are interdependent with respect to achieving this task.

There are imagined and real difficulties in accomplishing the task (obstacles and dangers on the road to a destination). Shared anxiety about the imagined or real dangers associated with what might happen during the journey, or even upon reaching the destination, fracture shared commitment to reaching that destination.

It is true that the source of the anxiety may be different for different group members or different groups in the organization. These differences often arise from role differences: the different parts people or groups have been assigned, what they are expected to do, how they are to contribute to achieving the task.

Interdependence among members holds the group together and makes its achievements possible. The failure of interdependence is identified as *the* problem, leading to feelings of disappointment and blame: I/we can no longer do my/our job. (Because) I/we can't depend on you/them. NOT: Because, for this or that reason, this is a tough job to do. However, I regard this 'being a tough job' as very often *the* problem. It is a very important part of the story, which may be covered over by preoccupation with disagreement and quarrels, differences, tensions, and conflicts, among members of a group or among groups in an organization.

Often, members, more or less unwittingly, in order to mitigate anxiety, join together to abandon the task, to make antitask arrangements, to develop antitask procedures, to accomplish other goals that have little or nothing to do with reaching the agreed-upon destination. Harmony is restored. At a price.

There are a number of important possible interventions open to any leader in the group. A leader may encourage and make possible sharing and reality-testing the imagined dangers. What are the facts? A leader may help a group or organization anticipate and plan for possible obstacles. Why don't we change the route to the destination!? A leader may invoke commitments. Let's remember what we have actually joined to do, the importance to all of us that we succeed, and what we all stand to gain if we do succeed. The collective processes initiated by such interventions are what make it possible to resume the journey.

A narrative approach to understanding experiences in groups and organizations

We use many abstract concepts (we call them 'themes' or 'motifs') in making or describing a novel, play, or movie. They are the stuff of dramas of deception, betrayal, sabotage, corruption, revolt, sacrifice, survival, rescue, pursuit, escape, help, missions, quests, bold enterprises, fights, the newcomer who upsets the way things are, the tragedy that results from a miscommunication or a chance mishap or a lost opportunity, the loneliness and dilemmas of leadership. Is there any doubt that our concepts about collectivities – no matter how impressively abstract we make them – help us to tell and elicit stories, precisely because they belong to a narrative framework for organizing experience?

CHAPTER 5

Essential Plot Ingredients
Diversity, Conflict, and Dissent
David Berg

Marshall's definition of a social system – 'the values, task, purpose, or goal that members of a collectivity *share* make it a social system (a group, an organization, a society)' – is too limited to fit how he and I actually think and work in groups. We need to qualify it to take into account two kinds of observations both of us make.

The *pattern* of actions and statements we observe, from which we infer what group members share, makes clear two things. One, whatever group members share (commitment to a task, purpose, or goal, or a belief, assumption, feeling, or value), different members share to varying degrees. Two, the attitudes members have toward what they share, including what to do about it, differ (sometimes markedly) from member to member. ('I don't like it, I'm uncomfortable with it.' 'I'm all for it.' 'It's obviously true.' 'I don't admit it.' 'Let's get rid of it.' 'Let's go with it.' 'I have no hesitation in expressing it.') Observing such differences and the pattern they make provides much of the content or at least the starting point of our clinical and consultative interpretations.

In making such observations, I think of them as pieces of a picture-puzzle, rather than as episodes in a story. The image I carry in my mind when I am trying to understand a group or organization is putting together a jigsaw puzzle. Each thing said or done by anyone is a piece of the puzzle, and I will not understand what is going on in this group or organization until I have all the pieces of the puzzle and can put them together in relation to each other, so that I can see the pattern they form. The pattern for me is likely to be an image of interrelatedness, rather than a narrative form.

Conflict

Rather than emphasize what group members *share*, or deplore the problems caused when they do not share it equally and there are strains rather than harmony, I emphasize instead that *conflict* is inevitable, and one of the sources of creativity, in groups. A leader who relies on her ability to motivate others by invoking shared values, and who is less concerned about how she responds to and manages conflict, may rush to bring about a premature consensus, coming together, or integration, rather than take the time to encourage the expression of differences and the acknowledgment of conflicts.

The story I like to tell starts with the *differences* among members of a group or organization, and in particular those differences that have to do with their memberships in other groups: organizational groups (with different functions or hierarchical positions); as well as identity groups (gender, race, ethnicity, age, socioeconomic class, professional discipline). In one such story the influence of memberships in identity groups on the distribution of power, authority, and responsibility is unacknowledged. One of the dysfunctional effects of this distribution is that people occupy the wrong positions; they are doing the wrong jobs. Their actual skills and potential contributions may be sacrificed. So, perceiving waste and unfairness, they withdraw commitment, perform incompetently, rebel ineffectually, and are disabled by impotent rage.

Protest or dissent often results in scapegoating, when peers withdraw or dissociate themselves from the one who is different or from the one who dissents – out of fear of authority. Those in authority regard differences of perception, thought, and feeling as disruptive and dangerous to the togetherness they think is necessary for task-achievement. They may try to suppress differences. That suppression interferes with the group's efforts at problem-solving; it disables the group. One way I define dysfunctional leadership is leadership that carries out activities designed to suppress within-group differences (in the service of harmony).

Those in authority instead may encourage and make possible the sharing and acknowledgment of differences, including different life experiences, different values, and commitment to different goals, and the conflicts, as well as the different approaches to problems, arising out of these. This kind of collective process gives birth to new and creative solutions to problems, even including perhaps the alteration of an existing authority structure, or the abandonment of a previous destination in favor of a new one.

What is the source of a leader's concern about the existence of differences and similarities among group members, about which predominates, about which should be emphasized or encouraged? A leader may prefer a predominance of the latter over the former in all cases. Or, in composing a group, for example, may wrestle with such questions, as 'In what kind of group do you emphasize difference (a clinical team?) and in what kind of group do you emphasize similarity (a psychotherapy group?)? And similarity and difference with respect to what?'(Marshall expresses this concern and raises these questions in Chapter 14.)

Anyway, whatever the leader's answers to these questions, and whatever reasons seem to him to support the answers as appropriate, my guess is that the underlying anxiety is about the possibility that if differences are emphasized or diversity dictates or characterizes the composition of a group, the group may build in, create, or maximize what the leader worries will turn out to be dysfunctional conflict, that is, conflict that will interfere with the degree of solidarity necessary for success.

Of course, the reasonable position is that the members of any effective group need both a sense of the ways in which they are similar (that, for example, they share certain goals and values) *and* an appreciation for their differences. But let me set aside this reasonable position, because the concern of the leader who raises such questions is often about the risks of creating conflict or encouraging the expression of conflict in any kind of group at all. Anxiety about conflict in groups is well-nigh universal among those who participate in them, and is one reason that some people, who have searched in vain for a transcendent or complete harmony, solidarity, and togetherness, 'don't like groups' and flee from them or try to avoid them.

My response to this anxiety is that competition and differentiation, even conflict, are inevitable in groups. You can work as hard as you want and you will not be able to keep these out of group life. This is true for at least two reasons.

The first reason is that groups come together, and have the capacity to create something (insight, health, ideas, decisions, strategies) precisely because the individual members are different. Put another way, these differences are the source of creativity in a group. The similarities (or common purpose, objective, feeling) are what hold the group together as they explore and struggle with their differences. A group's creativity arises out of its disagreements and conflicts. So, if you are going to convene a group, you are going to have some conflict if the group is to reach its capacity for creativity. I do not think you can structure such conflict out of the group. No matter how homogeneous *you* (or I) think the group is, its members will find the dimensions of difference (because these differences are the source of its potential) and struggle with them.

The second reason groups will always have conflict, whatever their composition, is because of the nature of collective life. As Ken Smith and I have written, group life is, for most of us, an ambivalent affair, fraught with likes and dislikes, hopes and fears.[49] Group members tend to organize their participation around these ambivalent reactions, for groups provide a vehicle for expressing both sides of complex emotional states by distributing these as either one or the other among the group members. In so doing, groups simplify for the individual the often distressing experience of holding within her or his inner world contradictory or opposing feelings.[50]

Scapegoating in groups, the process by which group members isolate and get rid of an unwanted or unacceptable thought or feeling and then react harshly to the person they now imagine has it, is a uniquely collective (as opposed to individual) phenomenon. Especially if the scapegoat can be kept around, the group members have the benefit of both sides of an issue being expressed. The scapegoat is on one side, everyone else is on the other. Most group members have thereby also reduced whatever stress they would have experienced trying to hold both sides within themselves at once.[51]

Familiar and recurring subgroupings also serve this function. Each of two subgroups in a larger group expresses one of the opposing 'sides', while members experience the group as tensely trying to hold both subgroups together.

If conflict is not only inevitable but an important source of creativity, which I believe it is, then the question becomes, 'How does leadership manage conflict in a way that *enables* rather than disables the group?' This is a challenge and one that does not get a facile answer from me.

I have become convinced of a few things. It never pays to run away from conflict, although running away is also inevitable. (Fighting and fleeing are complementary aspects of the same process.[52]) Running away can take the form of using one's authority to ignore conflict, or to suppress it, or to seek only and compulsively after immediate compromise in the interest of an illusory perpetual harmony.

It is usually necessary, if something useful is going to emerge from conflict, to provide legitimacy for both sides. A group learns from conflict if both sides survive the emotions and build on each other's ideas. For this to happen, both sides need to be present in the conflict. If one side is obliterated, if the desirable outcome is the domination of one idea rather than the search for that which connects the two polar opposites, the process of collaboration (creative connection across differences) will not be possible, and the group may not survive as a group.

Dissent

It is not an accident that disputation, conflict, argumentation, and legalistic debate (as well as legal debate) are part of contemporary Jewish life (and contemporary Jewish stereotypes). We are and always have been (if one reads the Bible as history) a disputational people. Abraham, the first Jew, argues with God over the fate of Sodom and Gomorrah. Such impudence. Such courage. Such compassion. And this is not an isolated case. Jacob, Jonah, and Moses also struggle with God, opposing the will of the All Mighty. And although obedience too is a part of the story of the Jewish people, opposition, and especially opposition to authority, is present in full measure.

The Talmud asks whether God prays, and after much disputation the answer is that God does. Then comes the question, 'What does God pray about?' The Talmud says that God prays that His harsh, punishing, severe side will not overwhelm the compassionate, merciful, loving side of Her being. If God is made in our image, then we have created a God to represent perfectly the opposition in ourselves. In return, God's prayer suggests that both sides, and indeed the struggle itself, are divine.

The Talmud, of course, is a legal code, the very structure of which is disputational. It often has two parties – the House of Shammai and the House of Hillel, for example – who debate the points of law raised by a particular pragmatic question or dilemma; after much dispute, in which the arguments on both sides are allowed to develop fully, the law is said to follow one or the other of the Houses.

Since it is written that the law usually follows the House of Hillel, and if this is divinely revealed law, why is the other side, the side that is *not* law, present? Why is it included in the Talmud at all? Perhaps this inclusion is meant to suggest that the 'other side' is also inside the law and inside us. The presence of both sides allows us to examine more fully, to understand the complexity of, an issue, without reducing it to a simple rule. The fullness of our understanding, an understanding that carries with it the other side, enables us to empathize with, make a relationship with, and listen to the other side within us and within our social lives.

Perhaps the presence of the other house in the Talmud is telling me to be careful not to disown the other sides of my internal struggles, especially the sides I dislike even as they are a part of me. Our most intense anger is often directed at others or other groups who embody a characteristic of ourselves that we have succeeded in disowning.

Consider the story of King David, as told to me by Leroy Wells.[53] After David sends Bathsheeba's husband Uriah to die in battle so that he, David, could marry her, the prophet Nathan confronts the king. Nathan tells him a story about a rich man and a poor man. The rich man steals the poor man's only lamb to feed a guest rather than slaughter one of his many sheep. David is enraged and asks Nathan who the rich man is, so that he, the king, can punish him and restore the poor man's lamb to him. Nathan replies that King David is the rich man. Listening to the story, David did not recognize an image of himself. For he had succeeded in disowning his dark side, a side that was always with him, and which, disowned, he could only see and respond to in another. The rage we feel at others for their transgressions, the self-righteous rejection of them, may stem in part from our inability to accept within ourselves the desire to transgress.

In a profound way, the presence of both sides, in opposition, is an acknowledgment that dissent, difference, and opposition are necessary parts of any law, because their presence inspires and supports responsible opposition, responsible reinterpretation. The opinions of the House of Shammai constantly reinvigorate the opposite point of view, and in so doing make room for, invite, other points of view possibly not yet considered. It is as if by carrying along the loyal opposition, the Talmud acknowledges the potential contributions (to law, to knowledge, to understanding, to insight) of all responsible oppositional stands.

This legitimation of opposition also serves as an antidote to dogma, intolerance, and bigotry, since the respectful way in which both sides are presented and explored makes it difficult to come away from any dispute with a belief that there is only one way to think or to act. It is the other side of an argument, the dissent that is part of the law, that informs our lives by symbolizing respect for principled disobedience, responsible dissent, and the voice of the minority.

The Supreme Court of the United States usually issues a dissenting opinion when handing down major decisions. This dissent has important implications at two different stages at least. First, in preparing the majority opinion, an image of the anticipated dissent helps shape the argument of the majority opinion and hence the law itself. Take away the formal requirement for dissent and you take away an important influence on the development of the law. Second, when applying the law in subsequent situations, the dissenting opinion functions to temper the majority, to permit and even invite interpretation of the majority opinion. The dissent provides a space in which the debate can continue; there is more to be learned, understood, or debated as the law is passed down through a changing society.

It seems to me that the disputational format of the Talmud serves similar functions. 'How else could it be', I ask myself, 'that learned rabbis, steeped in study of the law, *disagree?*' The message is that disagreement is a fundamental part of law and by implication the social life law seeks to order. Perhaps more fundamental than the issues themselves, disagreement is a way of uncovering the issues that matter. This kind of disagreement needs to be nourished, especially by those who have the power to suppress it.

I think of four examples of the importance of opposition and dissent in group life. It is interesting that in some sense they are all about pairs; except for a look at what goes into a two-person collaboration in the last two chapters of this book, we haven't chosen to explore the dynamics or to tell stories of couples: the romantic couple, parent and child, siblings, psychotherapist and patient, marriage, friendship. What do we have to tell about pairs, which have at least some dynamics different from personalities, groups, intergroups, organizations? Movies do an especially good job when it comes to telling stories about pairs; they are a veritable treasure mine of such stories. According to one authority Marshall has quoted, in maybe 85 percent of movies the major plot is a romance, and in maybe 10 percent more it is at least an important subplot.[54]

First among my four examples is the example of a two-person collaborative relationship (co-authors, co-teachers, co-therapists). Inevitable differences simultaneously enable and endanger any such collaboration. There are times collaborators feel in 'sync' *and* times they fall out of step, areas in which they come to share a perspective *and* areas in which they retain different perspectives. In a 'rush to harmony', it may become difficult to hold on to a 'realistic' picture of the collaboration, or to tell a story of it that is true to the actual experience those who collaborate have of it. This can impair work together, not the least because the 'pretty picture or story' discounts the value difference and dissent may have for the work.

Many years ago, the Ford Motor Company found that its aggressive hiring campaign to recruit assembly-line workers was having unintended, disastrous consequences. By trumpeting the high salary and significant benefits of work on the line (in an effort to entice people into the work), and giving no information about the long repetitive hours and the often boring tasks, the company was doing a great job of hiring but a lousy (and expensive) job of retaining new hires. The more they emphasized the positive, the greater the retention problem became. So the company produced a 'realistic job preview' to use in the recruiting process, a short film about the assembly-line titled 'Don't Paint It Like Disneyland'. The film showed what it was *really* like on the line. People who applied for these jobs after hearing about the benefits *and* seeing the film were much more likely to stay on the job than those who had only been given the rosy picture. Collaborative relationships are not like assembly-lines, but they are not like fairy tale romances either.

The second example is marriage. The union of two individuals includes the struggles of each partner to develop her or his own individuality while simultaneously developing the partnership that is a marriage. Conflict in marriage is often considered a necessary but unwanted part of this process. Yet conflict is often a window into the issues that matter most to the people involved. It is not just a problem to be overcome, coped with or solved, but a sign that important issues are being engaged. If we can hold or carry along and respect the conflict, it may teach us a great deal about ourselves, the people we love, and the relationships we have with them.

The third example involves boss–subordinate relationships. Remember the archetypal encounter between the gruff, opinionated, powerful company president and the bright, ambitious, usually loyal subordinate? The subordinate respects the boss but disagrees with several important decisions. The subordinate decides to confront the boss, fully expecting to lose her or his job. When the list of opposing views is complete and the subordinate expects to be fired, the boss says, 'I like your spunk. You've taught me something. You deserve a promotion.' (No doubt Marshall could come up with a list of the movies that contain this scene.) The story rarely unfolds this way in real life, but the moral of the story as I see it is that both the boss and the subordinate must fully play their roles, including their willingness to take a position and defend it. If both are willing to do this, *and* if both can learn from their encounters, then insight, growth, and understanding are possible even in hierarchical relationships.

My final example is about children (and their parents). As my children grow, there are inevitably conflicts about a variety of daily decisions. Since my children are small, the conflicts are, largely, small ones. There are times when the law is the law (as I see it) and for good reasons that I can explain and that satisfy me. When one of my daughters rebels, defies me, or opposes my decisions, I hold my ground. But inside I rejoice at the independence, the rebellion, the dissent, even the conflict, painful as it may feel to both of us. My child senses this joy, I am sure, and we both learn something because we can allow this conflict to happen without rancor and with respect.

CHAPTER 6

Stories and Theories

David Berg

I am not ready to give up on non-narrative theories of language. I believe they may provide an occasionally powerful means of communicating experience. Are we kidding ourselves if we believe that we will be able to forswear such theory altogether? Is it too much in our blood, our way of thinking and being in the world, no matter how much we acknowledge the limited value of theoretical discussions (or presentations) in the teaching of the 'learned' professions? Is our inclination to conceptualize an experience, when it occurs, and the way we choose to conceptualize it, rather than something to be prescribed or proscribed, also a piece of a story to which we want to attend?

I have found that theory may guide our choice of 'method', how we listen to a story, who we talk to, and what we do with our temptations to 'believe' one or another version of a story we have heard more than once. But it is also true that, when we want to defend ourselves against the anxieties that may attend really listening to individual *or* collective stories, we often use the generalizations and abstractions of theory to do so.

When I was in graduate school in organizational psychology, for example, it was acknowledged with deep irony that you could get a doctorate in this field without ever spending any time inside an organization other than the university! *Conceptualization*, although of course important in any learning process, became a defense against the anxieties of *experience*, and *reflecting* on experience, which are also important ingredients in a learning process. Going out into the field meant giving up some control or at least holding in abeyance the meaning or moral of the story and any course of action that might follow.

When I reflect on the stories I enjoy telling, and those I enjoy hearing, I realize that they are about an experience and at the same time give meaning to that experience. People tell the 'same' story in different ways. This suggests both that various 'tellings' can emerge from the same series of events and that different meanings can belong to the same story.

When my daughter tells me a story about her day, I listen to the ups and downs, the unfolding of the 'plot', the funny, sad, angry, and touching parts. I also listen for the reason she is telling me the story, which is another meaning of it. I am curious about the events and actions, and their unfoldings, but also about the meaning these events and actions have had for her, how she has experienced them. Both tell me something about her life.

Theory, too, is an attempt to capture the experience of events and acts and to attach meaning to that experience. Classical science would have us believe that events and acts themselves, 'objectively' observed and described, offer up their own intrinsic meaning. Few of us are prepared to concede this claim, since it is often clear that the scientist, like the storyteller, is describing what he or she experiences through various lenses. Some of these lenses are an *a priori* theory, a prescribed method, politics, culture, and identity. All of these combine to draw a certain meaning from events and actions.

Replication studies, where a scientist strives to duplicate precisely the results that others have obtained, are not a popular form of research – unless they fail and so cast doubt on the work of others. Although they are crucially important in the scientific process, they do not allow the 'replicator' to tell his or her own 'story'. That this is so is not merely a matter of denying the replicator the opportunity to achieve fame, promotion, and prestige. Creative research enlists the researcher in a process of discovery, of extracting meanings from experience (or 'data'); replication research does not call for that kind of creativity and stands in its way.

Both stories and theory are attempts to capture something about experience, not merely describe it. Both intend to convey meaning as well as information. Both evoke a wide range of responses from those who listen, depending on their vantage points and life experience. Stories, I think, engage a broader audience. They invite the listener to have his or her own unique relationship to characters, plot, obstacles, struggles, and resolution. Theories, too, can be engaging, but often they discourage us from getting involved in the same way, because abstraction is the language and objective of theory.

Is there any benefit from the use of theoretical language as opposed to narrative language? Perhaps theoretical language can serve the same function *in a narrative world* that narrative language serves in *a predominantly theoretical world*. It heightens aspects of experience that we have come to take for granted, by raising questions about them. Theory can inform us about what to look for, what motifs to expect, what roles to anticipate. It may help us listen to what's missing in a story, and therefore lead us to ask about it. Perhaps abstraction and stories have complementary parts to play in enabling us to listen and understand – even when abstraction is not essentially narrative in nature.

What kinds of stories do we tell? Theory influences my answer to this question.

We are most familiar with *individual stories*, accounts of an individual's struggle to make her way in the world. How much of the struggle is with internal forces and how much with external ones varies, as does the role played by other individuals and social systems in the 'main character's' story. But in these stories we focus our attention on the individual, and the rest of the characters, the environmental forces, the impact of time are all organized around this person's journey.

Interpersonal stories focus our attention on the relationship between two people, their tensions, compatibility, attraction, rivalry, intertwined destinies, or the evolution of their connection over time. These stories are plentiful in literature and film since, just as with the individual story, it is easy to recognize and identify with the interpersonal story.

There are also *group stories* in which the focus of attention is a collective. These stories are rarer in literature and film (though I would contend not in life) and depict the struggle of a group to manage its own internal dynamics as well as its relationship to a wider social or organizational world. The film *12 Angry Men* (1957) dramatizes the struggle of a jury to come to a verdict and, while individual personalities play an important role in the film, the story is about a group's evolution and development.

Intergroup stories are about the relationship between two or more groups or between two or more group representatives. In these stories, the central theme involves the current or historical circumstance of two or more groups. 'The immigrant experience' is a phrase which describes millions of individual experiences, but it is a story about the relationship between a host culture and an immigrant culture at one or more points in time.

One can, of course, follow the threads of all these stories in most life accounts. The movie *Hester Street* (1975) is about life on the Lower East Side of New York City around the turn of the century. It tells simultaneously: (1) the story of an individual immigrant and his struggles to find a life in a new world, (2) the story of a relationship between two people (a man and a woman) who meet in this shared circumstance, (3) the story of a group of immigrants as it struggles to manage the competing pressures to maintain traditions rooted in their cultural history and to assimilate the values and practices of their new society, and (4) the story of tension, discrimination and acceptance in the relationship between two groups, those whose immigrant status is generations in the past and those who are themselves new immigrants.

Finally there are *organizational stories*. Variations on the intergroup story, the organizational story tells of the internal and external life of an organization. You know you are in the presence of an organizational story when someone tells it in answer to the question 'What happened to the Psychiatry Department?' or 'What happened to IBM?' These stories often involve individuals, interpersonal relations, group dynamics, and intergroup relations, but the focus is, the driving curiosity is about, the organization.

CHAPTER 7

Intergroup Stories Everywhere!

David Berg

What do I mean when I use the phrase 'intergroup story'? Intergroup stories refer to those events in organizations that involve the relationship between two or more groups (or their representatives). These can be either organizational or task groups (shared task or level of responsibility) or identity groups (shared biological, cultural, or historical background). In its simplest form, I mean by intergroup relations what happens between these groups.

If, for example, we put patients and hospital staff in a room together (say, at a community meeting), what goes on in that room would be an intergroup event. That is, each group's awareness of the other group and the history of their relationship with each other would influence the dynamics in the room. Conflicts between patients over whether to confront the staff about allowing pets (described in Chapter 27) seemed to be in part a response to the presence of staff in the community meeting. The presence of the staff and the authority they represented may have made it difficult for some patients to 'rebel' because of fear of retribution or the intense dependency in the relationship between staff and patients.

It is relatively uncommon (except in sporting events, Congress, or group relations conferences) for two or more groups to be in the same place. Most often, we see intergroup dynamics enacted by representatives when they meet together to talk, decide, socialize, or work. In these settings, too, the history and current relationship between two or more groups significantly influence the behavior of individuals who are functioning as representatives or whom others see as being representatives.

I should note that this is not always a conscious process. I may be unaware that I do represent the views and values of a particular group or that others are treating me as if I were. In addition, this lack of awareness can be a result of my never having attended to my group memberships, or of my desire to protect myself from the consequences of group membership, both of which are characteristic of many white people's relationship to their racial identity.

As soon as we are willing to consider the possibility that individuals are also representatives of the groups to which they belong, our way of understanding interpersonal relationships and group dynamics changes dramatically.[55] Now when we see a 45-year-old male physician talking to a 30-year-old female nurse, we have more than just personality to consider in our attempt to understand the attitudes and behavior each exhibits toward the other.

Or imagine you are walking across the floor of a manufacturing plant and see two men arguing about a machine. You might come to the conclusion that these two people don't like each other. Suppose I tell you that one man is a supervisor and the other a union employee. Now you might think that the enmity between their two groups (historically) might be contributing to their personal animosity. (See how dramatically the frame changed with just one piece of intergroup information!) Then suppose I tell you that negotiations between the union and management were at an impasse, and that a strike is likely within the week. It would be extremely difficult now to convince you that this argument is simply between two individuals who do not like each other.

My experience is that intergroup forces often exert an influence on a group that goes unnoticed. Hierarchical concerns may influence a group (as in the story of the community meeting told in Chapter 27) because its task or interest involves dealing with those in authority, without members of the group becoming focally aware how much these concerns are influencing what people are saying and what positions they are taking. On the other hand, a group that is explicitly concerned with problems in how one or more groups having different tasks, functions, or roles, are collaborating may be especially attentive to the professional identities of its members.

The context or setting in which a group is embedded also plays a role in defining which issues, and particularly which group memberships, are salient for those involved.[56] I predict that a community hospital located in a predominantly minority setting will be more attuned to the racial and ethnic identities of its patients and staff, and to the state of racial and ethnic relations in the wider social environment, than its counterpart in a primarily white suburb.

I see intergroup dynamics everywhere I look. There is an element of representativeness in almost every interaction between individuals in an organization. The conversation or disagreement between two *individuals* may also be an interaction between *representatives* of two parts of the authority structure. I know I experience it that way when I 'speak for' other graduate students or junior faculty, or when I receive a 'complaint' from a student or subordinate that seems 'typical'.

In a hospital, clinical teams are often composed of individuals who belong to different groups. Nurses, physicians, social workers, psychologists are also men and women; black, white, Hispanic, and Asian; middle class and working class; senior staff and junior staff. These various group memberships comprise the identities of the team members. A nurse, I would venture to say, is always aware of the source of a suggestion or proposal, as is the physician, the social worker, and the psychologist. The relationship among the various groups has an impact on each person's assessment, for example, of the risks and benefits of public disagreement, the likelihood of having significant influence, and the 'real' factors governing an individual's stance on an issue.

The naive observer of team meetings (and by naive I mean uninformed by an awareness of the groups to which team members belong) might notice certain dysfunctional group dynamics: people are not listening to each other; certain people dominate the discussion; there are lots of interruptions; there is an absence of leadership. By changing the frame and attending to the intergroup aspects of the situation, we might develop other explanations for the group processes we observe. The people dominating the discussion are physicians in this medical institution. Alternatively, the issue is a trivial one to the physicians and one or more of the other groups dominate the conversation. The interruptions have a pattern to them; people only interrupt down the hierarchy, never up. That a psychologist is the team leader may account for an apparent absence of leadership, if psychologists have little authority in a hospital that has male physicians in the vast majority of senior administrative positions.

I would argue that it is only our (understandable) wish to transform the difficult complexities of intergroup relations into the relative simplicity of interpersonal ones that explains why we don't see the influence of organizational and identity groups more clearly in our everyday institutional life. As the example of the supervisor and the union member illustrates, a knowledge of the group memberships people carry with them, especially those known to others in the situation, shapes our understanding of what we observe. Perhaps even more important, it can shape the actions we take. We would follow different paths depending upon our 'diagnosis' of the problems we see in the team meeting. If we believe that the members of the team need group-process skills (in listening, agenda setting, leadership, conflict management), we try to provide help in these areas. If, on the other hand, we suspect that the physicians are not open to any input from nurses, or that the assignment of a psychologist to the role of team leader reflects the institution's unwillingness to commit physician resources to this implicitly downgraded task or its inability to persuade physicians to take on this responsibility, we find our efforts pointed in very different directions. No amount of 'listening training' (to take the simplest example) will affect the professional relationship between physicians and nurses or between physicians and psychologists.

Individual, interpersonal, group, and intergroup dynamics influence all team meetings, department meetings, psychotherapy sessions, and classroom discussions. How do we know *which* factors are at work in any given situation? *All* factors are always at play. Often, one or more of these factors are especially important in shaping the life of the group. An enduring conflict between two strong personalities may overwhelm the impact of the group identities of team members. On the other hand, it may be the presence of representatives of two or more levels in an organizational hierarchy that is making open communication extremely difficult.

However, I pay special attention to *intergroup* factors for two primary reasons. First, when the group dynamics of a team or the institutional dynamics of an organization remain the same in the face of personnel changes and group reorganizations, something is going on that is not attributable to individual and group dynamics. This is a variation on the 'characters change and the plot remains the same' theme.[57]

Second, intergroup issues are so difficult to address, so hard to change and so emotionally powerful, that we shy away from this 'diagnosis'. I look for the intergroup forces because, frankly, I am afraid no one else will. Few of us want to examine the role of hierarchy or identity in organizational life. It arouses too much feeling, carries too much baggage, and feels too hopeless (at times), leaving us with a sense of our smallness rather than the stature to which many of us aspire. To acknowledge that we all represent a variety of groups – our membership in them influences us when we talk and act, and others inevitably perceive what we say or do in light of their knowledge of the groups to which we belong – is to acknowledge that we do not transcend them and cannot escape our membership in them, and this, by implication, is an acknowledgment of our limits as individuals. I am willing to take the risk that I am distorting my understanding of a given organizational event by seeing group representatives where there are none, and by interpreting the actions of individuals in light of their group memberships when they are *just* being themselves, because all too often the powerful effects of intergroup relations are ignored, overlooked, or denied.

A student once said to me after learning, first, small-group dynamics and, then, intergroup dynamics that we can reframe almost all within-group dynamics as intergroup dynamics. Individuals, she said, are always also group representatives, or at the least carry with them their group memberships. Subgroups inevitably develop stereotypes and images of each other, and go on to relate as if to an 'other', filtering what they see and hear through the history and status of their relationship. (I think of the story about the 'committed' and 'uncommitted' students in my organizational diagnosis class, which I will tell later in the chapter 'Individual Frames, Intergroup Scripts, and Scapegoating'.) And, of course, authority relations are not simply 'member-leader'. They, too, are transformed into interactions between representatives of different levels in the hierarchy. (The resident is *always* a representative of the medical hierarchy in the eyes of the patients, no matter how much she or he may feel differently.)

I believe that what this student said to me is right. It is not that all group happenings are intergroup events and only intergroup events, or that all groups are deliberately composed of representatives of different task or identity groups, but rather that intergroup *dynamics* affect all groups, and that we ignore this influence at some risk to our objectives and our effectiveness.

CHAPTER 8

What Stories Does a Group Psychotherapist Hear?

David Berg

We tell our stories, listen to the stories of others, and work together to uncover what they might mean. Our understanding will deepen if we attend to the many kinds of stories that may be contained in one. This is especially important because each of us will be drawn to one or two particular types of stories, and may need to rely on someone else to draw attention to the other stories embedded in the story being told. Especially if we reflect on a story as part of an attempt to develop a course of *action*, we must be able to hear and respond to the multiple stories embedded in it. But it is easy to fall short of this ideal.

Clinicians are trained to conceive themselves as working primarily in two-person systems (e.g., doctor/patient). Marshall and I, as teachers of group psychotherapy, have noticed that, when clinicians become group psycho-therapists, they tend to continue to favor individual and interpersonal stories. Stories that reveal the dynamics of social systems strike them as of little use. Such stories more easily attract the interest of a teacher in a classroom or an admin-istrator in an organization, although even teachers and administrators often give most attention to individual stories.

Group psychotherapists, preoccupied with responsibility for the care of individual patients, are not likely to see the point of paying attention to the stories about groups and organizations that are embedded in the individual and inter-personal stories of which they are most aware. Especially in an era when medication plays an increasing role in many psychotherapies, the impact of social systems on therapeutic process comes to seem a trivial consideration.

Yet the group psychotherapists we teach do live and work in an organization. This organization is involved in supervising their work in groups, as well as in the intake, assessment, and monitoring of the treatment and ultimate disposition of patients. Performing these functions well enhances services to patients. But imagine a group psychotherapist who must walk into a session when he or she is filled with frustration or anger at some 'system' malfunction: a therapy room door is locked at the time of the session, some other group is in the room, two clinical supervisors give conflicting advice which is inadequate as well, a disposition takes months to complete. Despite inner turmoil, that psychotherapist must go ahead and strive to fully engage his or her work with a group of patients.

Similarly, trainees repeatedly are made to experience the limits of their authority. But at the same time they are expected to take a great deal of responsibility for the treatment of six or eight group-psychotherapy patients and the management of extraordinarily complex situations that arise in the course of that treatment.

In order to do the work of group psychotherapy, the psychotherapist must understand and manage both the dynamics of the psychotherapy group and the dynamics of the system in which the psychotherapist and the group are embedded. He must face 'upward' toward the system and his relation to its authority as well as 'downward' toward the psychotherapy sessions with patients. I have observed that psychotherapists often do not see the job of system management as part of the work they must do in order to do group psychotherapy well. But the stories told in this book make clear the ways in which being embedded in an institution can affect psychotherapeutic work in groups.

Group psychotherapy is, at its core, about collective processes. It is difficult for me to imagine working with patients in a group without some appreciation of the social processes that recur in these settings. It is crucial that group psychotherapists be able to recognize the role group forces (for example, conformity, leadership, conflict) play in the behavior of individuals. Since a psychotherapy group is a small social system, complete with hierarchy, authority, roles, historical identities, and competing tasks, the psychotherapist should have some understanding of social systems to augment his or her understanding of the biological and psychological systems of the individual, at the least so as not to 'misdiagnose' events in the clinical setting. Such misdiagnosis can, and often does, result, for example, in scapegoating an individual member of a psychotherapy group as *the* problem, a process that is likely to exacerbate the psychopathology of that member.

There is another reason clinicians ought to know something about group and organizational life.[58] Any clinician ought to draw on her own experiences in groups and organizations in doing clinical work – at least, let these experiences come to mind. Without doing so, how can she understand what a patient is talking about when he tells about life in a family, classroom, school, job, club? These kinds of settings evoke responses within the patient, and have particular meanings for her or him, some of which are idiosyncratic, but some of which reflect common themes of collective life.

Finally, among the reasons group psychotherapists need to know something about groups and organizations, one has to do with the answer to the question: 'What is the curative impact of doing psychotherapy in a *group*?' Or to put it another way, 'What is it about the dynamics of a group that has the potential for improving individual mental health?' In our work together as co-teachers of a group of group psychotherapists, Marshall and I have come up with the following answer.[59]

Group psychotherapy is achieving its goals when members become ever more able to express fully what is on their minds, their thoughts, feelings, hopes, expectations, and imaginings. When this happens, group members come to possess aspects of themselves they have rejected, hidden, neglected, or suppressed, and which often they have put into others, whom they then attack, blame, or try to get rid of. As group members take these lost pieces back into themselves, they increasingly come to be themselves, to accept who and what they are and feel and think. At the same time they come to see others more as they are, and to connect with them. They are then able to offer the many newly accessible aspects of themselves freely to the group in which they participate. Group members experience a shared process of this kind as creative, and this enhances the sense of competence, worth, and self-esteem of all who participate in it. Many of us have had such experiences in groups, when we have a heightened sense of who we are and how much we are able to contribute just by being who we are.

This process is never completed. As groups face new tasks, their members confront new information about themselves and the others around them. Over and over individual members struggle with disclosure in the context of their hopes and fears about the group's reactions to them, the group of which each is a part. The more feelings and thoughts that are expressed, the greater the opportunity for discovery, acceptance, and connection, but also the greater the risk of conflict, rejection, and isolation. The old saw about progress being two steps forward and one (or two!) back is not just a refrain of some frustrated committee member. It is a realistic depiction of the inevitable emotional ebb and flow of group life.

Have I made a general theoretical statement about the mechanisms of therapeutic action of group psychotherapy? Perhaps instead I have told a kind of story about what we expect to happen in a psychotherapy group when things have gone well.

PART 2

The Problem of Interpretation

Which Story Are You Receiving?

Since behavior is multidetermined, organizational processes can be examined and understood in terms of any or all of these levels [intrapersonal, interpersonal, group-as-a-whole, intergroup, or interorganizational processes]. Organizational processes are analogous to a radio broadcasting band. If one tunes into 107.5 FM, this does not mean that 96.0 is not broadcasting, but rather that one has just amplified a particular station ...

[At the group-as-a-whole level,] the unit of analysis is the group as a system ... Group members are considered interdependent subsystems co-acting and interacting together ... Group-level analysis assumes that when a co-actor acts, he or she is acting not only on his or her own behalf, but on behalf of the group or part of the group. Co-actor behavior from a group-level perspective cannot be simply examined by assuming that the motivation and genesis of the co-actor is merely a function of his or her own idiosyncrasies. It must be viewed as a synthesis of and interaction with the group's life and mentality. Simply stated, the co-actor is seen as a vehicle through which the group expresses its life ...

In essence, each member is called upon to assume role(s) ... that provide a service to the group. These differentiated roles divide and distribute expressive, cognitive, instrumental, mythical, and reparative elements within the group. Fundamentally, roles in groups, in part, serve to manage anxiety, defend against deindividuation or estrangement, structure the group's élan vital, and get work done.

Hence, each group member performs important functions on behalf of the group. In this regard all services and functions (that is, roles) performed in groups are interdependent. This individual role behavior must always be analyzed in the context of the constellation of roles distributed in the group. In short, individual role behavior is embedded in the field of other roles.

Leroy Wells, Jr.

CHAPTER 9

Tuning in on the Group-as-a-Whole

Marshall Edelson

In group and organizational life, we see others locate *the* problem in an individual, believing that doing something about that individual will solve a group, intergroup, or organizational problem. But it is necessary for us to go beyond individual psychology in thinking about what we see and hear, in trying to understand the problems that face us, in choosing the target of our analyses and the interventions we make that we intend to be helpful. It is important for us to turn to a social-systemic or group-as-a-whole level of analysis, even when the plausibility of an individual story makes it irresistible. Otherwise, we too are likely to participate in instigating or contributing to a process of blaming or scapegoating.

There are those who may challenge this conclusion. Group psychotherapists, for example, are likely to be anxious that choosing a social-systemic or group-as-a-whole level of analysis puts them at risk of neglecting, failing to respond to the dire needs of, or not doing anything to help individual patients for whose treatment and welfare they feel responsible. Teachers are equally convinced that an individual's learning difficulties or behavior problems disrupt the class and must be dealt with as such, if the teacher is to be fair to others in the class and the problem student. In the same way, it is obvious to administrators that some individuals just don't have what it takes to do their jobs competently or to get along with other people, and that failing to address that as *the* problem, for example, by counseling or discharging that individual, endangers the enterprise for which they are responsible.

These seem to me to be reasonable concerns. I share them. In responding to them, I would like to address the following questions. Under what circumstances is it advisable to avoid giving priority to individual stories and to tell group, intergroup, and organizational stories instead? In other words, what are the indications for choosing a social-systemic or group-as-a-whole level of analysis (or 'frame') in preference to an individual level of analysis (or 'frame')? Indeed, when should we feel compelled to make such a choice? If such a choice is indicated, why is it so difficult to make?

Why not tell individual stories?

We have seen that different kinds of stories are present even in a single movie. They are present in every experience as well. Ideally, it would seem that if I tell you a story about an experience in a group or organization, I should tell you the individual stories as well as the group, intergroup, and organizational stories that can be told about that experience.

Why then do I emphasize group, intergroup, and organizational stories over individual stories? David Berg has suggested that it is as a participant in the former kinds of stories that we are most likely to find our understanding of what's going on faltering. Perplexity exacerbates our distress. Second, he has noticed, and so likewise I have come to notice, that it is just those stories that others neglect, as they try to get a handle on problems they confront as administrators in organizations, teachers in classrooms, or psychotherapists in psychotherapy groups.

But of course I am not entirely at ease with my emphasis. There is something woefully inadequate if not wrongheaded about it. Why should I make it social system *or* psychological system? Why not *both/and* rather than *either/or*? After all, if I function as a complete human being, in doing any complicated job or trying to understand any complicated experience, I draw on all the kinds of knowledge or stories I know or can remember.

But it does not seem to me to be reasonable, in every attempt to understand what's going on in some particular group, intergroup relation, or organization, that we should be expected to describe all the knowledge (tell all the stories) that we, that any clinical practitioner, teacher, or administrator might remember and use, knowledge of personality systems, of psychological processes, of lives, of pathologies, of biological and social processes. It is impractical to compose an encyclopedia of all the knowledge or stories that are relevant in grappling with even a single puzzling experience.

Yet, ideally, every time I run into a phenomenon, problematic or not, in a group or organization, I should consider the personalities and invoke the psychological processes of each individual who is involved in order to arrive at an adequate explanation of it. So, when I tell a story about an experience in a group or organization, why not include an account of the personalities and psychological processes of the individuals who play a part in the story? At the least, I should point out the propensities individuals have to provoke groups into assigning them certain roles, wittingly or unwittingly. That is, in any complete story, I should refer to each group member's attraction to or *valence* for a particular role in a group or organization. I should identify the propensities individuals have to provoke others to regard or treat them in certain ways, for example, to fix upon certain classifications of them (gender, age, race, ethnicity) over other possible classifications, along with the particular connotations these classifications have. I should also include stories of the way in which idiosyncratic (not shared or collective) individual wishes, fears, and ways of thinking conflict with, undermine, or support either explicit or covert shared purposes or tasks. Why don't I?

Sometimes, of course, because I have no appropriate way of obtaining the private personal information I would need to tell each individual story. I don't have that information. But even if I did have a way of obtaining such information, or wanted to include in my story guesses about what I would find out if I could, there are still other reasons for focusing on group, intergroup, and organizational stories rather than individual stories.

The third, and not the least of my reasons for favoring group, intergroup, and organizational stories, is the extent to which I find, in one experience after another, that telling individual stories serves a malignant collective process. That process is the scapegoating of individuals as part of a shared strategy for avoiding or denying collective responsibility for certain problematic phenomena: 'She or he causes this problem, because she or he is this or that,' rather than 'We create this problem, because, whatever the consequences for the particular task we are trying to achieve or goal we are trying to reach, this problem in fact arises out of, or serves, other purposes of ours that we prefer not to acknowledge.'

My students, faced with a problem in a psychotherapy group, or in their lives in an organization, tend automatically to identify the problem as a person. They go on to describe the behavior, personality or incapacities of that person as clearly responsible for getting in the way of achieving desired goals. My colleagues, when we talk about a program in trouble, teaching, or something happening in the organization in which we work, tend to make the same kind of judgments.

In general, when a clinician, teacher, or administrator trying to accomplish a task meets an obstacle, she or he locates the problem in some individual. A trainee is incapable of learning, can't get along with others, refuses to learn, is overreactive or underreactive, complains too much, or can't get her or his act together. A teacher doesn't prepare, can't tolerate challenge, plays favorites, is boring, dogmatic, or inaccessible. A patient in group psychotherapy is sicker than other group members, monopolizes group time, intimidates others in the group, or doesn't show up. A staff member or administrator is incompetent, is untrustworthy, doesn't care, is hard to get long with, or is someone no one else wants to work or be on a committee with. A leader, in allocating resources (persons, facilities, money), favors one part of the organization at the expense of another, never consults with others, is secretive, power-hungry, indifferent to the plight of others, or weak.

To counteract this tendency, I emphasize going beyond individual psychology, that is, changing the *conceptual frame*. I remind myself of, I call my student's or colleague's attention to, properties of a social system, to conditions, to group or organizational processes. I ask, for example, 'Is it possible that we may profitably regard the behavior of some particular member of a group as a clue to collective processes?' For that individual behavior may represent an attitude, wish, belief, or feeling that others share but cannot acknowledge or express. It may divert the group from a consideration of a problem about which everyone is anxious. It may make a contribution to the group's achieving some covert nontask or antitask objective. It may be an inevitable consequence of the way a task, a role, an organization is structured.

Often, however, the individual story comes so easily, even I, trying not to take it at face value, forget all else. Or, when I tell a group story, I encounter incredulity or blank incomprehension in others. This is frustrating, because I have learned over and over that such a change in a frame can be helpful in understanding a particularly thorny clinical or administrative problem. It is worse than frustrating when I see that locating the problem in an individual leads to interventions that turn that individual into a casualty and make things worse for the clinical or teaching enterprise.

Difficulties in changing the frame

Why is it difficult to 'change the frame' – to tell a group story rather than an individual story, to adopt a social-systemic conceptual frame rather than an individual-psychological conceptual frame for explaining behavior or solving problems in groups and organizations? After all, if you go through medical school, you know without thinking about it, that, depending on the problem in which you are interested and the question you ask, you pay attention to and describe the properties of a cell (or cellular processes), of a tissue, of an organ, of a system of organs, or even – at least sometimes – of a motivational system (the overall behavior of a patient). Ordinarily, you don't get mixed up about which set of concepts or language is the one to use.

Perhaps here we are dealing with what John Dewey called an occupational psychosis: a disability that arises from overattachment to the narrow language of a profession. Putting the problem in an individual may be a linguistic-conceptual habit in those who specialize in the treatment or education of individuals.

Or perhaps, in trying to understand a difficulty in changing the frame, paradoxically enough, we should pay attention to the characteristics of the particular social system to which we belong. For example, in the system to which I belong, group psychotherapists are not held responsible simply for how the group goes. They are held medically responsible for each patient in the group, and are expected to prescribe and monitor each patient's medications and respond to each patient's symptoms and crises, in the group if possible but also outside the group if necessary. Given that responsibility, it seems obvious that group psychotherapists would hold onto what seems to them the appropriate 'focusing on the individual' frame, however much that may prove a distraction from attending and responding to group processes in order to do *group* as opposed to individual psychotherapy.

Making the diagnosis that a change in frame is indicated

The ubiquitous inclination to focus on the properties of an individual when trying to understand some event in a collectivity suggests an important scenario that a leader in any kind of group (committee in an organization, class, psychotherapy group) must be prepared to recognize. In it, group members (perhaps and indeed often including the leader) may be enacting a story of scapegoating. Because the outcome of such a story is often destructive to individual and group, the possibility that it is being enacted makes considering the diagnosis that a change in frame is indicated necessary and sometimes urgent.

I use the phrase *making a diagnosis*, because I do believe that a focus on an individual or a psychological explanation is sometimes relevant, useful, or constructive in group or organizational life. But, how do busy clinicians, teachers, or administrators, struggling with all sorts of problems, make the diagnosis that a change of frame from psychological to social system is warranted? What will lead them to think, 'In this particular case, in trying to solve this particular problem, I had better find and focus on causal properties of the group or organization to which I belong rather than locate the problem in my patient, my boss or subordinate, or my student or trainee. In this case, using a social-systemic or group-as-a- whole level of analysis, I can most fruitfully understand what is going on, and can most effectively direct my intervention at a collective process rather than an individual'? How do we know when to try to formulate a social-systemic explanation instead of simply locating a problem in an individual? How do we know when an individual explanation *by itself* is likely to prove useless? How do we know that social-systemic properties or processes are playing a significant role in bringing about, exacerbating, and/or maintaining behavior that is an obstacle to achieving the goals of a group or organization? What are the consequences of failing to make a social-systemic diagnosis, not only for the person who is mistakenly identified and scapegoated as *the* cause of a problem, but also for the clinical, administrative, or teaching task that continues to bear the burden of having the real obstacle go undetected and unmitigated?

I have found three ways to arrive at the diagnosis that some property of a social system may be causally involved in bringing about disturbing, troublesome, or negatively valued behavior.

One way of arriving at this diagnosis

I become aware that a number of group members, despite having different motives, pathology, or personalities, are behaving the same way at the same time. So, for example, when early in my career I was chief of an inpatient unit, a number of patients made suicide attempts in the same period, or left the hospital against advice, or ran away. For me, it seemed implausible that there was a different cause for each instance of such behavior. It made more sense, on the usual probabilistic grounds, that a common cause was responsible for this rash of similar behaviors. The obvious candidate for such a common cause in these cases was some property of, or process occurring on, the inpatient unit where these people lived together.

Later, working as a psychiatrist in a residential treatment center, I presented a graph at a community meeting. The graph showed that, over a period of time, the total amount of medications (whether given when and if requested by patient or given on a prescribed schedule) that were consumed in the community increased or decreased in relation to major events in the community. Both patients and psychotherapists found it difficult to give up their belief that each psychotherapist prescribed medication for each particular patient in response to symptomatology exacerbated by a unique process of psychotherapy with that patient. 'Nothing to do with anyone else but us' was the idea.

A second way of arriving at this diagnosis

I observe a discrepancy between a way of doing things in a group and the ostensible task of that group. Sometimes, someone with the authority to do so suddenly and inexplicably changes a way of doing things that has proved itself efficacious in carrying out an ostensible task. More usually, reluctance, indignation, outright rebellion follow any attempt to change procedures or rules hallowed by tradition, despite their obviously having little to do with the ostensible task of the group or interfering with carrying out that task. In fact, whenever I have attempted to bring about such a change, even merely raised a question about such procedures or rules, others have always made me feel that I had unwittingly and clumsily trampled on sacred ground.

A resident came out of a room and told a nurse that the patient she has been seeing seems on the verge of becoming violent. She suggested taking an appropriate step. The nurse told her that as a resident she had no authority to give that order. The rule was that the chief resident had to give such an order, and at that moment he was off the floor.

The nurse represented the permanent staff, who are anxious to protect patients from inexperienced residents. So a procedure had been instituted toward that end that apparently had to be followed no matter what the particular circumstances were. In this instance, the resident had in fact had considerable clinical experience prior to the residency, and had been correct in making such assessments on previous occasions in this setting. But the rule did not admit taking into consideration this particular resident's competence.

The resident was frustrated by the rule, but that was difficult to express. For she was only assigned to this clinical unit temporarily. As a resident she was expected to get along with other mental health professionals and not to act like a doctor who wants to be boss. The upshot was that she was left wondering anxiously if she was just being, or if the nurse saw her as, overfearful or overreactive. The patient in fact shortly after did become violent.

Dysfunctional procedures or arrangements may represent an attempt to cope with or accommodate to, or be an expression of, the effects of an organization having multiple missions. The commitment to multiple missions may result in a state of continuous perplexity or anxiety about priorities. It may also result in leaders, each of whom represents a different important mission, engaging in relatively unconstrained competition with one another for resources and opportunities.

Such procedures or arrangements may represent an attempt to cope with or accommodate to, or be an expression of, the effects of scarcity, a shortage of money or personnel, or difficulty in holding onto a subgroup of professionals who are needed but difficult to recruit. Funny kinds of arrangements may help to raise or maintain morale when members doubt that the collective mission of a group or organization is achievable or even any longer valued. Above all, practices or policies that seem to have very little to do with getting a job done may help members cope with shared anxieties: for example, about their safety in the face of patient violence, whether they can count on holding onto their jobs, or their lack of skill or fit given what is expected of them.

However, in all these cases, people's need to defend, sometimes with considerably sophistry, a questionable arrangement or procedure as helping the group carry out its ostensible task exacerbates the system's difficulties. In each case, we must ask, 'What stands in the way of acknowledging openly that some other goal has taken precedence?'

A third way of arriving at this diagnosis

I notice that the behavior of a member of a psychotherapy group, a seminar, or a committee leads to indictment of, or obsessive solicitude for, that member by other members. If that member leaves or ceases the behavior, someone else begins to behave in the same way and elicits the same response. It is very difficult for clinicians, teachers, or administrators to believe that, in this behavior, the member is representing something for, or acting as the representative of, other group members, despite the existence of evidence favoring such a belief.

A paranoid patient becomes disruptively argumentative. A depressed patient makes everyone uneasy by talking of suicide. It is easy to see these behaviors as manifestations of a patient's pathology. A student comes late, is too busy to do a reading assignment, prefers to remain silent in seminar discussion, or interrupts the seminar's work by insistently arguing with a teacher. It is easy to make judgments: irresponsible student, poor student, disruptive student. The patient becomes sicker. The student drops out of the seminar. The indictment seems justified, until someone else begins to behave in the same way.

Then I notice the way other group members participate in making sure that someone in the group is behaving this way. They may remain silent, for example, rather than coming in with an attempt to move the work of the group forward. They may accept without rebuttal a person's version of events or attribution of attitudes to other group members. They may incite a person to this behavior, for example, by facial expressions, questions, and remarks.

I remember one paranoid patient who found herself a leader in a community meeting whenever everyone wanted to fight with the staff. But others treated her as sick, or criticized or ignored her, when they were no longer in a fight mode. These swings in others' reactions to her unchanging interventions were confusing and far from helpful to her.

A typical story in an organization involves the repeated failure of different individuals in a leadership role in a particular program, apparently in each instance through some fault of their own. They are eventually seen as incompetent or as having defective personality characteristics, having in every instance sooner or later behaved in ways that made others angry or uneasy. Whatever type of personalities these individuals have, and the type differs from one individual to another occupying this role over time, there is always eventually some such objectionable behavior or egregious incompetence. This despite the fact that these individuals are often chosen because they have demonstrated the required competence in other administrative roles.[60]

In situations like these, we gain little by blaming an individual person or particular group for ineptitude, stubbornness, thoughtlessness, or stupidity. Often, either the program is so situated in the organization or the role of director so structured that the outcome is inevitable almost no matter who occupies the role, or some goal other than achieving the ostensible shared task has priority for the group members and so we need a diagnosis of what that covert or latent shared goal is.

Making an interpretation

Telling the appropriate *explanatory* story (that is, making an appropriate interpretation) requires clarity about the nature of the system, the protagonist, whose story we will tell. We identify a system by picking out the particular elements whose interrelationships constitute that system.

A psychological system

A *psychological system* is a structured set of relations between different *dispositions*, such as wishes, beliefs, and values (and different groupings of these). It includes a higher-order executive function, which perceives, responds to, and controls and manages these dispositions. It includes operations that bring about transformations of these wishes, beliefs, and values, in their content or interrelations.

So, if I am trying to understand such a system, I might tell the following story (make the following interpretation). What I observe is the result of an individual's own attitudes and reactions to his own particular wishes, thoughts, and values, and of what the individual does about these (for example, rejects them, suppresses them, exports them outward by imagining them to exist in others, gives one priority over another).

I listen for stories that are versions of scenarios in which an individual is trapped. Aspects of experience are forever reminding her of them. She is forever making an active effort to relive them by bringing about their actualization in experiences.

Sometimes these scenarios are in the form of fantasies. These fantasies may involve images of what the individual who does the fantasying desires. They may also involve strategies for projecting or introjecting whatever (including desires) that individual feels to be unacceptable or dangerous. That is, individuals may imagine that some bad or dangerous wish, belief, or value, or response to it (a feeling is such a response) is in some Other, rather than within themselves, because then they can get rid of or avoid that Other (along with the thought or feeling). Or they imagine that something bad or dangerous, rather than in some uncontrollable Other, is within themselves where they can suppress or contain it.

In these stories an individual is protagonist. The explanation of the protagonist's actions and states (including feelings) shows that these actions and states arise from the nature of particular constituents of the individual system (particular wishes, beliefs, and values), their content and interrelations, and particular operations transforming their content and interrelations.

Interpersonal system

The prototypical *interpersonal system* is a structured set of *interactions* between two different psychological systems. What is primary here are *not* the reactions each has to her or his own wishes, beliefs, and values. What is primary instead are the reciprocal or complementary interactions between the two, the ways in which each tries to influence, control, or manage the states or actions of the other, the actions each takes toward, away from, against, or with the other. Perceptions each has of the other, beliefs each have about the other, and the feelings each arouses in the other influence these interactions. Dyadic interactions and not individual dispositions are the constituents of this system.

This system includes a higher-order executive function, which is an image of the couple (its history, its interests, its purposes, the experiences associated with it) that each member of it has internalized. To the extent each of them has – and gives priority to – this image, it governs or influences their interactions. It includes those operations that are available to the couple for jointly effecting transformations or changes in their interactions, in how each perceives the other and how each believes the other perceives her or him in turn, how each acts toward the other, and what adjustments to make where and when the wishes, values, and beliefs of the two psychological systems are in opposition. The use of human language in communication is high on the list of such operations.

Interpretation tells a story in which a couple is the protagonist. The story explains the states or properties of the couple and what as a collective entity it does. The story is about the couple and not primarily about either member of the couple. As an explanation it relies on showing that the states or properties of the couple, the way *it* is and what *it* as a collective entity does, is the outcome of the interactions between the members of the couple. These interactions reflect how each perceives the other and how each believes the other perceives her or him in turn, how each acts toward the other, and where and when the wishes and beliefs of the two systems are reciprocal or nonreciprocal, similar or contradictory.

Small group system: group-as-a-whole

The constituents of a *small group social system* are *roles* occupied by persons who share some values(s) and goal(s). The roles are patterned so that each makes some distinctive contribution to the realization of the shared values or achievement of the shared goals; no single member can realize or achieve or realize them alone. The contribution that a role makes to the achievement of shared, overt (recognized or acknowledged) or covert (unrecognized or disavowed) goals defines that role.

A group's executive function resides in a leadership or management role. A group evokes and maintains motivational commitments to group goals. It controls deviance with respect to the group norms that enter into the definition of any role and that integrate roles with each other. It relates to its external situation in order to acquire needed resources and prevent intrusions that could disrupt its own functioning or alter its own identity. It makes collective decisions and takes collective action.

The personality systems of the group members enter the group story only as far as they influence what roles members choose or what roles somehow gravitate to them, and the ways in which they inhabit, and how they perform in, their roles. We may also implicate personality systems when someone recruits others to join her or him in satisfying idiosyncratic desires that have nothing to do with the group's task or interfere with its accomplishment. (I do not mean to deny here that there are needs for personal satisfaction that a group must meet to some extent, if it is to maintain motivational commitments to the achievement of its tasks.)

In a group story, the group members have not been selected with an eye to their membership in other groups; they have not been selected to represent these other groups. If, on the other hand, we are telling a story about a small group of representatives, any group story we tell is likely to be significantly embedded in and overshadowed by a story about intergroup relations.

An interpretation of group phenomena tells a story in which a group is the protagonist. The story is about the group and not about a single group member or about the leader of the group alone. It explains the states or properties of the group, what it is and what as a collective entity it does. Among its properties are the patterns of relations among the roles of group members, what goals it pursues at any given time, how it goes about pursuing them, and its degree of success or failure in reaching them.

The explanation may point to roles, goals, or values that conflict or compete and how the group resolves such conflicts or competitions. For example, different roles may give priority to different values, norms, or goals as well as compete for resources. A collective resolution to the anxiety aroused by such conflicts may be to give priority to ways of avoiding anxiety, no matter what the cost to accomplishing the group's task.

There may be different degrees of motivational commitment to a value or a goal. Group members may flout agreed-upon norms for role behavior, so that they experience each others' behavior as unreliable, unpredictable, or unexpected. External obstacles, such as scarcity of resources, facilities, or opportunities, may hinder or prevent a group from reaching its goals.

Relations between the members and anyone who is officially the leader of the group, or anyone whom members see and follow however transiently as a leader, may govern the way group members relate to each other. (Redl has a particularly evocative discussion of these leader–follower dynamics as observed in the classroom.[61])

The organization as system

Groups are the constituent elements of an organization. Each group is differentiated by the subtasks for which it is responsible. Each group meets a different goal, which is necessary to accomplishing the mission(s) of the organization.

Interpretation tells a story in which the organization is the protagonist. It explains the collective actions of the organization, the vicissitudes it undergoes, its properties, its successes and failures. The explanation refers to the vicissitudes of relations among an organization's constituent groups, and how these intergroup relations may affect or be affected by the organization's relations to other organizations that make up a significant part of its external situation. A common story tells how within-organization strains and malintegration between groups result in difficulties in the relation between an organization and its external situation, or how problems in the relation between an organization and its external situation result in strains in the relations among within-organization groups.

Intergroup system

Happenings in an organization are quintessentially intergroup events, involving concrete groups in an organization or their representatives in actual relation to each other. We may compose a group in an organization (for example, a clinical team or a committee) so that the relations among representatives of different task or identity groups in the organization are what is most relevant and salient.

Other kinds of intergroup events or intergroup processes, more broadly conceived, occur both in and out of organizations, in small groups, for example, or in clinical teams, wherever the membership of persons in identity groups as well as task groups influences what is going on in the setting observed.

In the past I have thought of systems as intergroup systems only if (1) they were groups or organizations in relation to one another, or (2) they were groups the members of which are there to represent *other* groups. But I have become more cognizant, as a result of conversations with David Berg, that in a broader sense intergroup processes can occur in *any* group. Even if members of a group are not there for the purpose of representing other groups, they may still perceive each other as representing other groups, especially identity groups (gender, race, ethnicity, socioeconomic class, age), and they may still respond to each other as representatives of these groups.

In this view, an individual story may also be told so that explanatory interpretations refer to intergroup events or processes. If the protagonist of a story is an individual, interactions will occur between internalized figures. The individual imagines these figures as actors on an inner stage or instead experiences them as 'different aspects of myself'. Usually, the internalized interacting figures, even when they are different selves, are representations of members of past groups (such as the family of childhood) to which the individual has belonged, or of present groups to which the individual does belong (so-called reference or identity groups). The individual imagines and responds to what other members of these groups 'would say about *this*' – or in imagination reenacts old interactions with them.

However, the difference in these ways of looking at intergroup phenomena is important to me because it has implications for making interpretations in a group situation. What kind of story will we tell?

We can tell individual, interpersonal, group, intergroup, and organizational stories about any sequence of events. That means we can use any kind of story to divert attention from another kind of story, when one arouses more anxiety than the other. Although I agree with David that group members are most likely to ignore intergroup phenomena, I have encountered instances in which an insistence on telling an intergroup story has served to suppress another kind of story, more relevant to the avowed task of the group but associated with more anxiety. More important in my experience, we should expect a different response to an intergroup story told to a group of representatives of other groups from the response we get when we tell such a story to a group whose members do not perceive themselves as representatives of other groups.

For practical reasons, then, I want to maintain the difference between *intergroup systems,* which are explicitly structured around intergroup relations, and *intergroup processes* in groups, which are often covert and unacknowledged. Such a differentiation helps me to think about how to intervene, interpret, or participate, in a particular context.

In an intergroup system, interest in intergroup relations is manifest and no one questions that the task requires attention to these relations. Everyone acknowledges that these relations have to work for the system to accomplish its goals. Suppose, for example, we consider the situation in which different tasks belong to the different groups that make up an organization. Each group contributes in some way to the particular output that is the organization's reason for being. Management is responsible for coordinating the work of these groups so that they make their contributions in a timely and efficient manner, and for mediating conflicts among them over priorities and competition for limited resources. A group of representatives come together to deal with a problem of interest to all the groups they represent (these groups have a common cause), or to negotiate a solution to a conflict among them. In either case, the differences among these groups, in their interests, in the consequences different ways of proceeding or different solutions have for each of them, are front and center, and an interpretive comment about them is likely to touch those to whom it is addressed.

But this is not the expected outcome of telling an intergroup story in a psychotherapy group, for example. In general, members of a psychotherapy group are *not* there for the purpose of representing other groups, but nevertheless they often unwittingly perceive each other as representing other groups, especially identity groups (gender, race, ethnicity, socioeconomic class, age). They treat each other as representatives, and endow each other with the attributes imagined to be characteristic of the members, of these other groups. This, then, is an example of an intergroup process. Since an intergroup process occurring in such as a small group, one that is not explicitly structured around intergroup relations, is usually covert or goes unnoticed, its members may regard calling attention to it as odd and as having no obvious relation to the task that is this group's reason for being.

Stories about work

An individual, interpersonal, group, intergroup, organizational, or inter-organizational story presents a pattern of causally linked events. The events are usually reciprocal actions or interactions between social agents (between different voices within an individual, between members of a dyad, between group members, between groups, or between organizations). Reciprocal actions between an agent and another are determined by each one's expectations of what the other's actions or reactions will be in return. Reciprocal actions are also the responses of an actor to the actual actions or reactions of another – as the actor perceives or understands them.

Another kind of story, instead of presenting a pattern of causally linked events, depicts an enduring property, the character, or the structure of an individual, group, or organization (its protagonist). The property, character, or structure is manifested throughout the protagonist's history. It may also be illustrated by or revealed in the actions the protagonist takes and has taken in different circumstances. These actions do not so much lead from one to the other as arise in every case out of the character of the protagonist. Properties of individuals include character traits or persistent dispositions.

But an interest in group and organizations may also focus on *work* itself rather than the interactions or characters of *social agents*, on the nature of work, its structure, and the demands it makes and how a social agent responds to these. Often a focus on work takes the form of a desire to explain, to detect what influences, the behavior of an individual *as an effective member of a task group*, that is, purely in that abstracted aspect of the self we call *the worker*, the one who works. What is it about the work itself and the worker's relation to it that influences how a teacher in a classroom teaches? What a student in a seminar does with this teaching? How an administrator leads a clinical enterprise? How a therapist goes about treating a patient? How a psychotherapist does psychotherapy?

Here we want to know what influences people's/group members'/workers' behavior – not only in their interactions with each other, but in their relation to the work they do. How do they do their work? What does a particular kind of work call out from them? Remind them of? What metaphors for the work are at play in them? What do they imagine – at different levels of the imagination, with different degrees of awareness – that they are doing? Some nonwork activity – perhaps some bodily activity? Is this a source of unconflicted or conflicted pleasure? What is their attitude toward, their feelings and beliefs about, different phases or aspects of a work process? What motivations do they bring to the work? How do they inhabit or perform in task-related roles? What influences how and what they contribute to the production of a product or a sought outcome? How do they relate to, what are their beliefs regarding, their work functions and roles? What kind of match exists between their capacities and work-requirements? What anxieties are aroused by the activities they perform and by the prospect of success or failure?

The relation here is not an interaction. It is one way. It is the relation of a worker not to an actor, not to some purposeful entity, but rather to an *activity* – a work process, or some phase or aspect of it.

But to the extent we are also interested in a social psychology of work, we attend to the ways in which the task group to which a worker belongs modifies, regulates, channels, constrains, and exploits the meanings work has for that worker. In addition, we notice and want to explain differences and variations in the way task groups work. How does the kind of work to be done affect the way a task group works? How does a leader go about focusing a task group on a mission or goal, and how effective is that way? What is the relation between means and ends, between a method or procedure and what we use it to achieve? How appropriate is the choice of a method or procedure to what it is intended to achieve? How felicitous is the relation between means and end? What are the effects of unsatisfactory conditions or unexpected opportunities? How do task groups respond? How effective are these ways of responding? What are the ways task groups recruit motivations, values, and attitudes needed for accomplishing particular tasks? What are the ways a task group compensates for their absence when in particular instances it cannot recruit them. How effective are these ways? How successful is a task group? What is the outcome of its work? How does it assess outcomes? Is it able to acknowledge unfavorable outcomes? To what extent? Does it assess outcomes directly or must it rely on indirect and therefore not always valid indicators of success?

At the *phenomenal level* then there is great variety. We may notice patterns of linked interactional events. Or we may concentrate on observations of a social agent's properties. We may focus on a worker's relation to the work process itself. Perhaps we see as well that it is not only the nature of the work and the conditions of work that affect the relation between worker and work, but that also the task group to which the worker belongs may modify, regulate, channel, constrain, or enhance that relation. Then again, we may take a special interest in the differences and variations in the functioning of a task group qua task group, or the functioning of different task groups compared to each other. Any of these phenomena may provide the material for a story.

Techno-structural dynamics

An organization's task is to take in material or various materials and to convert or transform the material[s] to bring about a desired *output*. Call the material[s] the organization's *input*. Call the process of conversion or transformation a *process of production*. Call the output the organization's *product*. The product has value to those in the situation of the organization (consumers, customers) that the material[s] did not have before being converted or transformed.

An organization is made up of task groups. Some of these task groups are on the boundary between the organization and its situation. Such groups are responsible for obtaining materials at one end of the process of production, or for marketing or distributing or otherwise shipping out the product at the other end of the process of production. Other task groups are responsible for various steps or phases in the process of conversion or transformation.

These task groups are mini-systems. Each one that is not on the boundary between the organization and its situation has an input from some other task group in the organization, has its own particular process of conversion or transformation (its contribution to the entire process of production), and has an output to some other task group in the organization.

I will arbitrarily designate the relations among these task groups as a *techno-structural dynamic*. One kind of theoretical explanation tells a story about a techno-structural dynamic, that is, describes relations among task groups, in particular, conflicts and competitions among them. This story emphasizes the characteristics of the work-process, the material conditions in which work is done, and the way work is structured. It identifies different task groups. It describes the different values (preferences), norms (prescriptions), and standards each such group holds and promulgates. These values, norms, and standards define an *acceptable* or *appropriate* input; a *good* process of production (how people in a group responsible for a particular phase of a conversion *should* relate to one another and how various such groups *should* relate to one another); a *desirable* product or outcome; and when a worker *should* accede to the group's norms, standards, conventions, or rules, or deviate from them (be creative, do it differently). It also takes note of what resources each task group needs and its access to them. Different values, norms, and standards, and differences in access to resources, are the basis for conflict and strains among task groups.

This story may focus on *the product* and conflicts between different product standards. By what standard should a product be evaluated? What standard should be given priority? Even if a standard is accorded primacy, whether a product satisfies it or not may be more or less difficult to decide.

The story may focus on different *production practices* and conflicts that arise over which one to choose. Needs for cooperation and standardization come into conflict to one degree or another with needs for individuality and creativity. Individuality and creativity to varying degrees are necessary to awaken or re-awaken consumer interest or demand, and so will be valued and promoted – but, given that norms of production are also valued, within what limits? A changing external situation – aggressive competition, new technology, fluctuating demand, changing government policies – will stimulate the need for individuality and creativity. External change creates strains within an organization, as needs to maintain valued norms and standards come into conflict with needs to anticipate and recognize change and to experiment in order to be able to respond adaptively to change. Different task groups will represent these different priorities, and so see each other as 'the problem', as the one to fight. A change in one area, to one degree or another, affects everything else. How are such unanticipated consequences perceived and dealt with?

The story may focus on *resources* and their acquisition and allocation. Themes will include scarcity, competition, and justice. What is possible? What is fair? Norms for evaluating a product come into conflict with *practical constraints* (limits to the availability of resources). In other words, conditions of production (accessibility of resources, costs) come into conflict with product standards. Task groups compete for limited or scarce resources. How does the competition play out? How is it adjudicated?

So stories that function as techno-structural explanations tell about conflicts between roles; between different task-related values, norms, or standards; between a norm and some standard, on the one hand, and practical constraints, on the other; or between task groups, competing for scarce resources. What do we need to know to tell such stories?[62]

We need to know who has the power to make decisions, how decisions are made, when decisions are made. We need to know the norms for the product and those for production processes, and to recognize strains between product conventions and production conventions – and how these strains affect work. We need to know what materials production processes are supposed to use, and what interactions among workers in a task group and between different task groups an organization permits. We need to know what the norms are that give rise to formulas and what norms regulate innovation. We need to know what procedures are used in evaluating whether a product or process of production satisfies a standard. We need to know how deviance – failure to meet a standard or violation of a norm – is perceived and dealt with, and how this affects people.

Human-process dynamics

To the extent the members of any concrete group are committed to, and do, act together and relate to each other in order to achieve a defined task or arrive at a defined goal, they belong to a *task sentient group*. The task sentient group is an abstract entity, an abstracted aspect of a concrete group.

But wherever there is a task group, there are nontask groups and antitask groups. Stories about human-process dynamics are not concerned primarily with relations between task groups. They are about relations among task groups, nontask groups, and antitask groups.

The members of a task group also bring to the group values, wishes, fears, or beliefs that do not arise out of their relatedness to the task, but are instead idiosyncratically personal, arise from membership in other groups, or are based upon some particular group identity (gender, age, profession, ethnicity, race, religion, socioeconomic class). To the extent that these values, wishes, fears, or beliefs influence members of any concrete group in their group-bound or group-related actions, and in their relations to and feelings about each other, these members belong to a *nontask sentient group*, which may or may not interfere with the work of the task group.

Similarly, values, wishes, fears, or beliefs that inevitably and by their nature oppose the aims and therefore the work of the task group may influence these same members in their group-bound or group-related actions, and in their relations to and feelings about each other. To the extent that this is so, these members belong to an *antitask sentient group*, which does interfere with the work of the task group. Because of these values, wishes, fears, or beliefs, these members act in concert, although not necessarily everyone in the same way or taking the same part, to sabotage the work of the task group. Each one plays a part, more or less wholeheartedly, more or less wittingly, to bring about that end.

At any one time, task, nontask, and antitask sentient groups are more or less apparent, more or less active, more or less salient in considering what is going on in a group. Every member who is a member, to one extent or another, belongs to a task sentient group, nontask sentient groups, and antitask sentient groups. One of the functions of leadership in a task group is to take responsibility for managing the relation among these sentient groups, most especially to harness the energies of nontask sentient groups in the service of the task group and to thwart the aims or mitigate the effects of antitask sentient groups.

I will arbitrarily designate the relations among these sentient groups as a *human-process dynamic*. A second kind of theoretical explanation tells a story about a human-process dynamic. It describes relations among the various sentient groups. It answers these kinds of questions. In what phenomena do we detect the actions of a sentient group? To what is it responding? What is its composition? How is its influence manifested? What strategies does it use? On balance, which sentient group's strategy, at any one time or in any one process, seems to be winning or losing?

In these stories, then, we are interested in identifying wishes, fears, beliefs, finding out where they come from, recognizing the strains and conflicts among them, describing a group's here-and-now strategy for resolving these, and evaluating the outcome of that strategy. Has the group's strategy favored the expression or gratification of a wish over the mitigation of a fear? Of one wish over another? Of the mitigation of a fear over the expression or gratification of a wish? Or has the group found a way to balance, make room for, or achieve the expression or gratification of apparently competing wishes? Has it found a way both to express or gratify a wish and mitigate a fear associated with that wish?

Two kinds of stories

A human-process dynamic story is likely to explain phenomena as the result of an attempt to avoid, get rid of, or manage irrational anxiety. Such anxiety arises primarily from the mere fact of membership in a nontask or antitask sentient group; a work process or task group demands do not cause it. It is usually largely unconscious and therefore apparently inexplicable. A techno-structural dynamic story, which is about how *work* itself is organized or structured, is likely to explain phenomena as the result of an attempt to avoid, get rid of, or manage anxiety that is work-related – a response to conflicting task group demands and norms, or to disparities between what is required and practical constraints. It is usually largely conscious and therefore apparently explicable.

In the first case, anxieties arise from collectivity, from the social, from groupness itself, and how individuals experience it. What we must know are individuals' subjective experiences in collectives qua collectives. We usually don't need to specify the nature of a task or work process, the technical details and the specific norms or standards involved, and the objective conditions prevailing as attempts are made to do the work and to meet these standards, in order to understand these anxieties, for they arise from the experiences of individuals in groups as groups. In the second case, we do need to specify them.

For full understanding, neither kind of explanation is sufficient and both are necessary. However, my own criterion for deciding that I am in the presence of a concrete group that is functioning primarily as a task group is that its members are especially invested in, talking about, and struggling directly with techno-structural issues.

Stories about a *human-process dynamic* and stories about a *techno-structural dynamic* both, it turns out, tell *intergroup stories*. I have already described how an individual story can also be told as an intergroup story. So here then we ask an even broader question than the one posed by the difference between intergroup systems and processes, discussed above. Is it possible that social-theoretical explanations are most usefully, in general, *intergroup* stories? Influenced by David Berg's thinking and our work together, and from what I have written above, I have increasingly come to think that this may be so.

CHAPTER 10

The Characters Change, the Plot Remains the Same

David Berg

My realization at a particular time of my life of the importance of membership in groups was an unsettling one.[63] It raised the possibility that I, as an *individual* agent, was no longer the sole or even a primary determinant of what happened to me in my life.

From that moment on, I have fought the individual vs. system battle many times. I have found that no matter how compelling the evidence, it is difficult to accept how powerful the impact of social systems can be on the behavior of their members (individuals and groups), precisely because I feel so powerless to affect these social systems. So, periodically, I have found myself asserting the importance of individual explanations for organizational events, because the assertion points me in the direction of some action I can take and so reaffirms my sense of personal efficacy.

As any clinical administrator, team member, or classroom teacher can acknowledge, however, such a sense of personal efficacy does not always translate into organizational effectiveness. It has often been the case that individual explanations for organizational events have simply not equipped me adequately to solve a whole raft of problems.

What's going on in this outpatient clinic?

As a graduate student, I studied an outpatient psychiatric facility for my dissertation research. I was interested in relationships among staff groups: psychiatrists, psychologists, social workers, nurses, residents, and lay analysts. As part of this research (which involved interviews, observations of team meetings, and reviews of memos and minutes), I developed a questionnaire to further explore some of my nascent hypotheses. One question asked: 'When work difficulties arise in the outpatient department they usually result from…' The organization members were asked to respond by choosing 1 for 'Personal Problems', 7 for 'Organizational Problems', or any number in between to express some mix of the two. All the mental health professionals in this outpatient facility were at the 'Personal Problems' end of the scale. And the psychiatrists were *two standard deviations* closer to the Personal Problems end of the scale than the others. Since then, I have discovered that others besides mental health professionals tend to choose 'personal problems' over 'organizational problems' as responsible for work difficulties.

How do I address the concerns of the conscientious clinician who asks, 'How does one know, if an individual is singled out in a group, when to focus attention on the group and when to intervene at an interpersonal or individual level?' It seems to me that we do no harm in exploring group-level issues before acting on an individual-level hypothesis. The problem usually is that we do not know how to explore group-level issues competently or effectively. At the same time, we have to cope with the pressure to act on the individual level that is coming from the group, our training, and in some cases a supervisor. It is often possible to follow group-level interventions with individual-level ones. It is much more difficult to go the other way.

What's going on in this classroom?

How do I answer the diagnostic question about indications for changing the frame? I walked into my daughter's first-grade classroom on parents' visitation day to observe a piece of her day. I soon noticed that one boy, Billy, was obviously the class troublemaker. (It will come as no surprise that I sort of liked him.) I had heard about Billy from my daughter; his reputation preceded him. What I saw fitted what I expected.

However, the longer I watched, the more my attention was drawn to the elements in the classroom that made it difficult for this active kid to behave well. For example, the teacher had placed five colored cubes on the children's desks – and then told the kids not to touch them! Eight or ten kids routinely violated this injunction. Billy got more than his share of scolding. The math lesson that went with the colored cubes had some obvious conclusions to be drawn: $2 + 2 = 4$; $3 + 1 = 4$; $4 + 0 = 4$. The teacher asked, 'Can anyone think of any more ways?' When Billy suggested the off-quadrant answer, '$1 + 1 + 1 + 1 = 4$', the teacher politely acknowledged that this was correct, but 'not what we are working on today'. Giggles from the class – and a smile from Billy.

My twenty-minute diagnosis was representative of increasing attention to social systems as agents affecting individual behavior. Billy, clearly a rambunctious kid, was in danger of being placed in a role: troublemaker. He was likely to remain in this mischief-maker role because others expected it of him, it produced a form of social acceptance, and it expressed the mischief other kids would have liked to express but would not for fear of the consequences.

The role of troublemaker was also likely to shape how others responded to Billy. For example, his intelligence and creativity were ignored in favor of labeling his behavior 'disruptive'. He was frequently sent to the principal's office, which had costly consequences for him. His role was extremely difficult to get out of since *everyone* (teachers and classmates) had a reason to keep him in it, so he gradually resigned himself to it.

Billy's trips to the principal did nothing to address the underlying issues in the classroom: How do you encourage creativity when certain facts must be taught to twenty-four children in a set period of time? How do you handle the energy, physical and social, of twenty-four first graders in a confined space? (The fact that these issues have given rise to alternative approaches to space, teaching techniques, and schedules testify to the possibility of attending to social-systemic elements in classrooms as well as individual students.)

What ultimately convinced me that Billy was not 'the problem' was my observing that when Billy left the classroom or was absent, someone else replaced his behavior in class, and the *function* that behavior served continued to be served. It was especially startling when it was Bryan who was 'disruptive', for he was 'the good boy' in the class, who usually misbehaved only when he was under Billy's direct influence. The teacher and my daughter both expressed surprise when Bryan became disruptive in Billy's *absence* (since they had expected such misbehavior instead from one of four or five other boys who routinely 'filled in' for Billy when he was out).

The moral of this story is: *The characters change. The plot remains the same.*

What's going on in this meeting?

When I first attended a full faculty meeting at the management school where I taught, I was amazed at how unproductive it was. In particular, one or two senior faculty members were terribly disruptive, consistently sidetracking the conversation and rendering any collective action impossible. After a few such meetings, I became disheartened and joined my junior colleagues in the various hallway laments that were a regular post-meeting ritual. They convinced me that if these two faculty members would leave, we could have productive discussions. The rest of the faculty seemed reasonable.

As luck would have it, one of these two faculty members left and the other drastically reduced his attendance at faculty meetings. A naturalistic experiment presented itself to me. My expectation was that things would now be different. When other 'reasonable' faculty suddenly began to act irresponsibly in meetings and the overall quality of the discussion did not improve or change much at all, I was shocked. The offending individuals had been removed. Why hadn't the dynamics of the group changed?

When the characters change and the plot remains the same – that's when I make the diagnosis that a social-systemic level of analysis is required. Nevertheless, I found it extremely difficult to consider alternative explanations for the robustness of this group's apparent dysfunction. I was convinced that the disruptiveness lay in a few individual members. But the experiment forced me to think again. It was only then that I began to notice features of the larger system that gave me a different picture.

First, I had to acknowledge that no one had stopped these faculty members from behaving as they had. No one had confronted them about their disruptive behavior and no one (except a few naive junior faculty members) had suggested that we do things differently. This led me to the conclusion that there was something useful about the role these faculty members were playing for the whole group and especially the senior faculty. This conclusion was reinforced when other faculty members came forward to take up these roles when the offending parties left.

Second, I began to realize that faculty meetings, if they were used to raise important issues and decide significant questions, would undermine the influence of the senior faculty on matters ranging from curriculum to research support to teaching obligations. The arrangements that faculty members make with the dean they traditionally make in private and reflect the status, reputation and negotiating skill of the parties involved. For senior faculty members in particular, collective decision-making runs the serious risk of diluting their individual influence and autonomy. I was forced to articulate an 'organizational' hypothesis to rival the individual one for explaining dysfunctional faculty meetings: the less effective the faculty group, the more powerful the individual members. So, there were 'good' reasons for the majority of people at faculty meetings to contribute, actively or passively, to these meetings never accomplishing anything.

Whereas the individual-level hypothesis led to some clear action implications (for example, a wish for the departure of the offending individuals), the organizational hypothesis pointed to some much bigger issues, most of which seemed outside my control. When we feel powerless to affect the larger system of which an individual or group is a part, we may prefer to locate the problem in an individual. That diagnosis suggests an action that is possible to carry out, which is to change or get rid of the individual. Knowing there is an action – and what action – we can take, we feel effective, instead of powerless.

Our flight from our helplessness in the face of social-systemic problems leads us to favor individual explanations precisely because we feel less helpless when armed with this kind of diagnosis. But, unfortunately, the explanation that makes us feel most efficacious (or least helpless) may not be and often is not the one that leads to effective intervention.

It is clear that not just persons but any part of an organization – a particular group, a committee, a meeting – may be scapegoated, seen as *the* problem. People may dread attending a group's meetings (the meetings are boring or silly), or may be reluctant to refer business to a group (nothing will happen). They have little inclination to consider in what way something about the larger system of which that group is a part may in fact favor the group's functioning in just the apparently terrible way it does.

The value of changing the frame

Here is an illustration of how a 'change in frame' can lead to an understanding that poses difficult dilemmas about action or intervention. Two 'preceptors' (teachers) were meeting with six group psychotherapists about the special problems involved in doing group psychotherapy. The teachers and other group members examined together process notes from the psychotherapists' group-psychotherapy sessions as well as reflected occasionally on parallel processes occurring in this 'preceptorial' group itself, that is, processes that were similar to those occurring in some of the psychotherapy groups.

In one particular meeting, the discussion centered around the difficulty psychotherapists were having getting patients for their psychotherapy groups, when attempting either to form new psychotherapy groups or to add members to existing psychotherapy groups. The difficulty was paradoxical, given the pervasive view in the institution that resources were tight, and that therefore, although patients were clamoring for treatment, their treatment needs could not be met.

One of the psychotherapists recounted her attempts to call patients whose names her team leader had given to her as appropriate candidates for her newly formed group. In spite of her willingness to consider adjusting the meeting time of the group and her individual face-to-face contact with over half of the eight individuals on her list, only one patient of those she contacted arrived for the first session. Two others attended the second session. Her consultation with colleagues and her team leader resulted in terminating 'the group that never was a group'.

In examining this familiar experience, the preceptorial group was tempted (as were the teachers) to find the psychotherapist's actions wanting. Should she have been flexible or firm about the meeting time? Should she have met with everyone or should telephone contact have sufficed? Was she sensitive enough to the harrowing transitions (from individual psychotherapy, from another disbanded group, from an extended evaluation process) these patients were being required to manage?

Slowly, the conversation turned to the reasons such a situation had developed. Why was the psychotherapist given a list of names and asked to call them? Ordinarily, the first step in a patient's entering treatment, after a referral is made to a group psychotherapist, is the act of calling the psychotherapist and expressing a desire to get psychotherapy. Did not the trainee's calling and trying to induce patients to enter her psychotherapy group itself put things on an odd footing, and teach the psychotherapist to behave in a way that in a private practice setting might be considered inappropriate, even unethical? How did it come to be that a trainee with little experience in forming a psychotherapy group was given this very difficult sensitive task, which required that she 'pursue' the patients? Answers to these questions required looking at the social system itself, and what about it made it likely that it would be difficult for anyone, no matter what their individual characteristics, to find patients for a new group or to add patients to an existing group.

First, what about the authority structure and organization of the group psychotherapy program? Was there anyone in the organization who both knew enough about group psychotherapy, and was willing, to be responsible for all the work involved in screening patients for group psychotherapy, and making a clinically competently managed referral to a group psychotherapist trainee? What kind of advice and guidance did the psychotherapist receive concerning forming a group, the anxieties that are likely to influence this task, and what might be done to address them?

One of the psychotherapists said that someone ought to have known that the people on the lists given to trainees were not really interested in group psycho-therapy. The trainees discussed their experiences chasing down uninterested and unresponsive patients. That discussion reminded one of the teachers of the real estate salesmen in the movie *Glengarry Glen Ross* (1992) talking about the lists of prospects their boss had given them. 'In that movie', he told the preceptorial group, 'the boss instructed the salesman "to make a sale or get fired". He favored some salesmen with "good leads", in this way enabling them to succeed, and eliminated or tested other salesmen by giving them "bad leads". The latter recognized bitterly that the lists he had given them were dead prospects.'

Second, what attitudes about groups, group psychotherapy, and patients were part of the culture of the social system? What part was played by the pervasive focus on patients' disabilities, and the lack of confidence that these patients were capable of contacting someone to whom they had been referred? What about the skepticism or at the least lack of enthusiasm of clinicians in the organization about the efficacy of group psychotherapy? Who in the organization did have the conviction that group psychotherapy was efficacious? What attempt had been made to follow and evaluate the outcomes of group psychotherapy and to communicate this evidence to others as the grounds for such a conviction? Were people worried that no such evidence existed?

Another social-systemic question had to do with clinical teams, who were always on guard lest they be flooded beyond their capacity to work effectively. So the boundaries of teams were difficult to permeate. A team did not readily accept patients referred from another team to a psychotherapy group that came under its aegis, because these patients would then be added to the list of patients for whom the team was responsible.

More questions, then, about the authority structure and organization of the group psychotherapy program. What was the basis for forming particular psychotherapy groups? Who had the authority to assess what groups were needed, to form them, and to see that each patient was assigned appropriately to just the kind of psychotherapy group that might help that patient with the specific problems she or he had, no matter to what team she or he belonged?

The preceptorial group began to discuss the ways in which referrals were made, the absence of supervision on a regular timely basis, the trainees' experience that they were often, as one put it, 'hung out to dry' when facing a variety of obstacles to their getting training in which they are interested. But the real rub came when the two teachers looked at each other and realized that to take these social-systemic explanations seriously, to shift some of the responsibility for the difficulties in getting patients for psychotherapy groups from the psychotherapist to the organization, they had to confront their own participation in these events.

The two teachers might well ask, 'How so? We weren't involved in the team evaluations and referrals. We weren't involved in the day-by-day supervision. We have no clinical-administrative authority to tell the group psychotherapists what to do and what not to do. We did not conduct the seminar on group psychotherapy for trainees; we had nothing to do with the administrative decision postponing the beginning of that seminar to a date long after the group psychotherapists began to meet their groups. We are not responsible for interteam relations, nor for deciding upon the kind of groups that are needed, forming them, and seeing that patients were assigned appropriately to them.'

But, then, who failed these trainees? Were they themselves unable to identify the help they needed and to seek it aggressively from the administration of the institution? Or did their supervisors and preceptors, including the two teachers in this group, for many good and complicated reasons, contribute to their 'failure' through, first, lack of attention to the requirements of the job the trainees were asked to do, and, second, through lack of attention to, and acknowledgment of, the way characteristics of the system in which they worked affected what they could accomplish.

I am all too aware as I write of the potentiality, in moving from an individual frame to a social-systemic frame, of shifting blame from an individual to some leader or group, and so simply shifting who gets scapegoated. What seems to be crucial is the extent to which we deal with problems and anxieties by *blaming* some individual or group, rather than attempting to understand what often seem to be overwhelmingly complex networks of factors and processes. In the latter case, each time we are tempted to say, '*That's it! That's* the cause' we go on with the inquiry and ask once more, 'And what brings that about? What maintains *that*? In whose interest is it for *that* to be that way? What purpose does *that* serve?'

In this example, 'fixing' the trainee (her approach to forming a group, her technique, her knowledge about the referral process) is *relatively* easy, compared to 'fixing' the organization (overlapping unclear authority relations, resource scarcity, intergroup competition, professional status, the role of group psychotherapy in the treatment of a large patient population). So we often tend to overemphasize the individual explanation as we (in this case *we*, the co-authors of this book, who were the two teachers) quail before the daunting task of even beginning to *consider* how to change – much less how to *participate* in bringing about change in – the organization.

PART 3

Individual vs. Group

I never in all my walks came across a man engaged in so simple and natural an occupation as building his house. We belong to the community. It is not this tailor alone who is the ninth part of a man; it is as much the preacher, and the merchant, and the farmer. Where is this division of labor to end? and what object does it finally serve? No doubt another may also think for me; but it is not therefore desirable that he should do so to the exclusion of my thinking for myself...

Above all, as I have implied, the man who goes alone can start today; but he who travels with another must wait until that other is ready, and it may be a long time before they get off...

The value of a man is not in his skin, that we should touch him...

Do not seek so anxiously to be developed, to subject yourself to many influences to be played on; it is all dissipation...

What are men celebrating? They are all on a committee of arrangements, and hourly expect a speech from somebody...

I never found the companion that was so companionable as solitude.

Henry D. Thoreau

For every infraction of the rules of silence and attention the whole group has to suffer together with the culprit – although the suffering is likely to consist only in an interruption of some pleasant exercise...

In his instruction, to be sure, he [Alcott] addressed individuals as much as possible, but all matters of discipline and many matters of taste and judgment were referred to the entire group for final decision. This was a detail of teaching about which Miss Peabody was most doubtful when she began her work with Alcott. To her the education of children meant the sedulous 'drawing out' of the individual as such, but to him it was primarily the development of social beings. Her own method had been to deal with 'stuff of the conscience' in private interviews, and she was somewhat shocked, at first, to see Alcott bring it boldly forward for public discussion. In no other respect, however, was she more completely converted to Alcott's opinion as the months went by. She came to agree with him that ... the conscience of a whole school of boys would be more sensitive than that of the average individual, and she also came to understand the high moral value of making each erring individual see his misdeed as by no means a private matter but as one in which the entire group was concerned...

This little controversy, although it was argued out in terms of the moral problems of children, had larger implications. Miss Peabody's original contention in favor of an appeal to the isolated and private conscience was in keeping with the whole tendency of New England Puritanism and its long struggle of souls alone with God. Alcott's disciplinary method, stressing the general truth that no man liveth unto himself alone, was in accord with his own social nature.

Odell Sheppard

To recapture the naive response of the film-fan is the first step towards intelligent appreciation of most pictures.

V.F. Perkins

CHAPTER II

On Being a Group Member I

Marshall Edelson

When I was a young boy, the stories of Louisa May Alcott influenced me. Her father, Amos Bronson Alcott, founded Fruitlands, that ill-fated community where, of course, no orchards grew. Unlike other utopians, he believed that social order must start from within the individual, not in an imposed order. Unlike some other transcendentalists, however, he stressed that the moral life is lived not in solitude but with others.

His Temple School, described by Elizabeth Peabody in *Record of a School*, was established upon principles that obviously also influenced the regime at Plumfield in *Little Men*, an account by his daughter, Louisa May, of the successful treatment of delinquency and character problems in a 'therapeutic community'.

At the heart of both the real and fictional school was a great teacher. He sought never to lie. He appealed to the affection of his students. He joined them in moments of delight and avoided dull routine. He ruled kindly but firmly so that impulses might be disciplined and directed. He used 'the conversation' as a pedagogical method, as did Socrates, Jesus, and the Talmudic rabbis. He asked questions of group members in the belief that truth is within, that the task of the teacher is to help the student find and face it there, and that the students in their replies could teach him as well as themselves. Moral, spiritual, and philosophical lessons were drawn from words and experiences of everyday life. (At one time approximately one-quarter of the children participating in these 'conversations' at the Temple School were between ten and twelve, one-half between seven and ten, and one-quarter six years old or less!)

Alcott's unique emphasis was on the social milieu and the idea of social responsibility. When physical punishment seemed necessary, it was his custom to have a child who was fond of him strike him rather than his striking the child. This custom – dramatically recalled in *Little Men* – exemplified his belief that all wrongdoing has social effects and reverberations.

These days, of course, we would be very jumpy, justifiably so in my opinion, about the possible adverse consequences of using guilt as an instrument of education. An enduring problem for me as clinician and teacher is how to make an observation, tell a story about, or discuss, the effects and reverberations of particular actions or ways of thinking, without evoking in those to whom I speak an image of Jehovah's wrath.

Nevertheless, I think that, although clinicians are not supposed to be judgmental, I do bring a strong moral sense to group and organizational life. I don't think that's necessarily bad. I seem to remember a comment by Erik Erikson that clinicians (or teachers?) lacking a capacity for moral indignation would be handicapped in their work. But 'moral' is not 'moralistic'. How do we mark the difference?

The doubts expressed by Elizabeth Peabody about Bronson Alcott's methods returns us to the dilemma just examined in Chapter 9. When, in what particular endeavor, do we appropriately give primacy to a focus on the private individual, whose actions and experience are determined from within by intrinsic capacities and dispositions? When do we appropriately give primacy instead to a focus on the individual as social being, whose actions and experience are determined from without by the nature of the external situation and specifically by the groups or organizations of which that individual is a member?

Thoreau in *Walden* speaks for the side of myself, valuing individualism and privacy, which is always getting in the way when I participate in group life – creating doubts, making me wonder, 'What am I doing here?' How do I mediate between these two in me, Thoreau and Alcott, who seem such poles apart in their quarrel? What would I say to them? Is there any way I can make them friends?

The problem of accomplishing an inner integration of these divisions is one that all of us face. For me, Thoreau and Alcott are still as different in temperament and outlook as ever, still as quarrelsome, still as intolerant of each other, still moving in different directions. Is this antagonism between me-as-individual and me-as-group-member irreconcilable? I don't like to think so.

Problematic aspects of group membership

I have always approached groups eagerly, wanting to belong, to be part of some collective achievement, and at the same time ambitious to make a personal contribution that others would value. I imagine, 'This will be my family. Blessed order will reign. We will read aloud to each other, and discuss what we read. We will not fight. We will not treat each other with indifference. We will give up things for each other. We will need each other to do what we want to do. Each of us will have a recognized legitimate place in this small society, and the part each of us plays in enabling all of us to reach our common goals will determine that place, justly and rationally.'

Bewitched by this ideal image, of course I eventually become disillusioned. Other members of a group rarely seem to share my vision of it. I fret impatiently over their lack of serious purpose. They espouse beliefs and values, but they do not seem to me to live up to them. I reject such hypocrisy; my own sickens me as well. (Is anyone ever truly honest in a group?) Moreover, prizing competence, I wince whenever I find myself as a member of a group thereby associating myself with the incompetence of others. And it is in groups that carelessness or malice, my own and others', most keenly wounds.

Throughout my life in groups and organizations, I seemed to see so clearly, so vividly, in *others*, what group life threatened to arouse or did arouse in me – with which I wanted nothing to do. I often reacted by not wanting anything to do with *them*. Often, eventually, I would 'quit', resign, or wander away, becoming preoccupied with my own inner life or with enterprises I believed I could do better on my own. In this book, I want to write something about these troubling experiences, hoping that, in doing so, I and others, reflecting on my stories, will learn something about groups and organizations, and that in the telling of these stories I will also learn something about myself, about the relationship between what is individual and what is social in me.

Child

When I was a child, I did not fit in. Others respected me as a 'brain' or teased me. I did not play with them. It seemed too risky; I was afraid I would be hurt. Classes in school were safe while the teacher was there. But, in a group from a multiracial multiclass neighborhood, a lot went on when the teacher was not there. And I was the teacher's pet. I shrank, holding my breath, not wanting others to notice me. Sometimes the teacher would leave me in charge. Terrified, I saw only bad boys – a group out of control. The question for me was how to placate the bully and satisfy the teacher. I did not think about the impact of identity – ethnic or racial, socioeconomic class – on what went on in classrooms; I had no idea of it.

Adolescent

In my adolescence, I belonged to a Zionist group. I spoke with others about the beauty and dignity of labor, but one day's bending over in the fields pulling onions was enough for me. Since I spoke well, knew Jewish history, and read the Zionist literature, I was chosen to be a leader. I disapproved of those charismatic leaders who exhorted others to emigrate to Israel but then did not do so themselves. I was uncomfortable when I thought of myself encouraging people to emigrate. I must have known in my heart that I had no intention myself of doing so. Nevertheless, wanting to belong, I did and said all the right things. I went to meetings. I sang the songs. I danced the dances. At times, I ceased being the observer and experienced the exhilaration of togetherness. Even so, it was not really my group. In my late teens I left the group and turned to a personal psycho-analysis for what I needed. I did not go easily beyond individual psychology.

The group punished me. It stole my brother. Following my example, he also joined this Zionist organization, but unlike me he did emigrate to Israel. Since then, nothing appeases my loneliness, because in losing him I lost what I could not acknowledge was part of myself: not only a Jew proud of the history and trad-itions of his people but a gentle, sweet-natured, loving, artistically creative human being.

Of course I know this to be a not completely accurate portrait of my brother. I notice that, on occasion, he can also be dour, impatient, and sharp-tongued. But since when have the mental processes to which I now refer – the splitting off of some part of oneself ('nothing to do with me') and imagining it in another – ever bothered with 'objective' reality! These mental processes, of course, are among those that are rife in group life, making it both messy and difficult to understand, which is why I tell the following intrapersonal and interpersonal story here, although it is not obviously in itself about an experience in a group.

My brother was the person I wanted to be but felt through my early and mid-life I could not allow myself to be. I would not give up the person I felt I must be – someone masculine, aggressive, logical, ambitious. Bent on wresting from others the respect I imagined went with success, I was determined to get ahead. I remained unaware of subtleties and nuances of feelings I had about my own ethnic and gender identity. I gave away a part of myself. I became somewhat estranged from and occasionally uncomfortable with what I experienced as a softer more feminine me. To some extent I gave it over to my brother (in my inner comparisons of us) and when he went it seemed to me, I was half-afraid, that perhaps that part of me might have gone with him.

Young adult

Groups continued to fascinate me. And I did not altogether abandon what I felt to be more expressive, artistic, dramatic, more feminine, in myself. In my twenties and thirties, I gave parties. I gave a Scheherazade birthday party for a friend and a Bach party for my wife. I organized, for a group of East Coast exiles in Oklahoma City, mostly theater people, a party of tableaux about New York City. Its highlight was a woman in a fringed sequin gown, draped across a piano, singing, 'Ten Cents a Dance'. What I most remember of all these parties occurred at the Bach party. I was rehearsing a group learning to dance a minuet. I saw a woman coming out of the kitchen and grimacing with distaste as she watched her husband, who was a member of the group, dance the minuet. Her expression passed a judgment. 'Not very masculine, that.' I believe some years later they were divorced. This may have been my first conscious awakening to the impact of gender stereotypes in group life.

I remember the reluctance of my friends to perform. It did not occur to me to connect it to the powerful impact of gender stereotypes on behavior I had glimpsed. I reacted to their reluctance by wondering guiltily if I were some kind of monster. Was I simply bent on enforcing my will on my shy friends? Did I merely use them as material to create a self-gratifying and self-aggrandizing spectacle?

I have always dreamed of a brilliant salon, with witty people gathered regularly for dazzling conversation, good food, and entertainments. However, most of my friends throughout the years have been mental health professionals, not performers, not intellectuals for whom the play of the mind is everything. So I settled for the quiet enjoyments of subdued conversation with intimates who, having worked together, know each other well, and do not feel they 'have to' perform or impress each other. I sought more emotional, open, deeper exchanges in one-to-one relationships. But an unhappily unrealized ideal for me continues to be the intense group life and the achievement of a string quartet.

Group conference staff member

As a graduate student, I had studied group dynamics. In my late thirties, I became active in an organization that sponsored group conferences. This organization designed conferences to confront their members with the nature of authority. Eventually, as a member of the staff, I found myself wanting to dissociate myself from what I saw as the incompetence of other staff. I felt, uneasily, that some of my colleagues exploited the conference to pursue what I regarded as impure ideological and political goals. These goals were far removed from the disinterested study of group phenomena to which I felt committed and which I understood to be our common task. In addition, there were rivalries and conflicts among the leaders of the conferences; I came to feel that some of them shamefully treated others about whom I especially cared, and I recoiled.

Psychoanalyst and educator

In psychoanalytic training, I once told a teacher that attendance at a group conference might result in my missing one of his seminars. I was enraged and baffled when, in response, he questioned my commitment to psychoanalysis. I did not apply ideas about overlapping group memberships and intergroup relations. Instead, I sought to simplify my group life, eventually, by resigning from the board and staff of the group conferences. Later, I became a psychoanalyst and a professor responsible for educational programs – and sighed with relief. No longer would competing group memberships pull me apart.

But there was to be no escape from groups and organizations. In my forties, during the 1970s (you remember what the 1970s were like), medical students challenged my syllabus for a first-year course in behavioral sciences. They said that it was too demanding, and that the readings did not seem relevant to what they would be doing as physicians. I knew nothing of negotiation. I was the authority who knew best. I had my own vision. I would not compromise it. Naively, I expected the Dean and the Medical School Curriculum Committee to support me in my dealings with students. To my surprise, they went along with the students. Indeed, they responded to my stubbornness by taking time away from behavioral sciences teaching.

For me this experience was a version of a familiar scenario: I make trouble for my father and my father turns away from me. I realized too late that those in authority may want people in 'middle management', above all else, to do their jobs in a way that not only does not cause trouble for those above them but in fact protects them from it.

This was one of my more spectacular failures. I resigned as leader of the course. I wonder what the outcome would have been had I known more, or thought more about what I did know, about authority and leadership.

A slow learner, I came to repeat this experience with candidates in a psycho-analytic institute. They wanted to meet with me to discuss their objections to the syllabus I had distributed in advance of the course. I said I would be glad to discuss it with them at our first meeting, but not before. Stalemate. I expected the Education Committee of the Institute to back me up as a member of the teaching group. I was shocked that, fed up with the ruckus and annoyed with me for not dealing more skillfully with it, the Committee instead responded to the stalemate by canceling the course.

So, there was something stiffnecked about me, some need to stand on my dignity, some edginess about whether others respected me, some reluctance to do anything that others could interpret as weakness – which are important in understanding these events. But there was also something about the way people in authority treat, and what they expect from, those who work for them, that we need to take into account, if our understanding is to be complete. At the least, the messages I was getting in various social settings seemed bewilderingly complex. Be masculine. Be strong. Be tough. But not too much so. Be a leader. Take a stand. Don't be a wimp. But know when to negotiate, compromise, yield. My failure to think more about the impact gender stereotypes had on me in particular, and on leaders and followers in group and organizational life in general, was a real handicap in participating in that life effectively, in avoiding unnecessary hurt to myself and problems for others.

I did not last long either as a member of a psychoanalytic society in my community. Although in my forties, I was completely oblivious of the varied agendas that brought people to the meetings of the society. I assumed I was participating in scientific sessions, and that direct rigorous discussions of presentations were appropriate. Once, a member of the society rebuked me for being 'brutally' critical of the speaker, who was after all a guest of the society.

'How can we have any kind of pleasant after-the-meeting socializing if our guest's feelings are hurt?'

Two groups, clinicians in private practice and full-time academics, met together in these society meetings. The members of each gave primacy to different values. There were differences in perceived status and income. The dynamics of the relation between these two groups no doubt played a part in the events I have recounted. But no one (including myself) formulated the problem in an intergroup relations frame. Instead, the frame was individual. The focus was on the kind of person I was.

On another occasion, one member of the society, worried I would criticize, asked me not to comment on his presentation. I did not agree to his request. Somewhat self-righteously, I thought of myself as indignantly refusing to be silenced. When I did comment, he and others looked at me angrily and reproachfully; I had betrayed him. I must have looked stunned as I saw their expressions. 'Well, what did you expect?' someone asked me. Was this group scapegoating me as the brutal critic in its effort to manage unacknowledged anxieties and purposes? If so, I lent myself to it, with what I regard, when I see someone else doing it, as tragic innocence. But then again we might more fruitfully regard the incident of the young man who asked me to be quiet, who asked for my protection, as an example of a miscarriage in a cross-generational relationship.

In my thirties, when I first attended an annual meeting of the American Psychoanalytic Association, I witnessed a senior psychoanalyst shaming a younger colleague by saying to him before a large audience, 'What right do you have to present such views! You are not even Bar Mitzvah yet.' To me it was horrible to see an elder treating a younger man in that way.

The age difference aside, I do not enjoy caustic putdowns – like those that occur regularly in the literature of academic philosophy, for example. Humiliating someone has never been any part of my idea of direct rigorous discussion. So I was especially distressed when members reacted to what I said in my own Society as if that had been my intention.

I went to fewer and fewer meetings. Instead of turning my attention to the dynamics of cross-generational relations when such relations were especially difficult, or to the dynamics of the intergroup relations in these meetings, I fled. I do not know that in my forties I could have done differently.

I experienced similar dissatisfaction, being the odd-man-out, in a continuing seminar of psychoanalysts and faculty from the humanities. I wanted to take seriously the problems involved in relating the humanities and psychoanalysis. Others told me early in a planning session: 'No program of study. No assignments. We work hard enough during the week, committees, classes. We just want to get together, hear a presentation, talk, have a good time.' This attitude to me was not serious. But, oh well, a good time is a good time.

But was it a good time? Neither group was willing to listen to or learn from the other. The psychoanalysts enjoyed showing off their ability to play with works in the humanities. They did not seem to me to want to achieve any deep knowledge of its methods. Those from the humanities seemed to me remarkably and irresponsibly uninterested in how psychoanalysts do their work and think about psychoanalysis. I eventually withdrew from these meetings also. Again I couldn't find any way to think about these meetings as an intergroup relations event, or any way to use my knowledge of intergroup relations to help these two groups relate more effectively to each other. Not the least of my difficulties was that in the meeting I could never persuade other members that any problem in intergroup relations existed, although in the hall or on the way home I heard that some at least were having a similar experience. That the two groups united to keep this unsatisfactory state of affairs from changing must have been paying off in some way. It was not immediately obvious to me what it would be that would be worth giving up any idea of a more productive relationship.

Similarly, the members of a psychoanalytic study group refused to choose anyone to serve as a designated leader. I saw this refusal as an expression of un-acknowledged feelings of competitiveness and a determination to prevent any serious leadership from emerging. Often the members allowed someone to dom-inate the discussion, to talk on and on, to everyone's obvious distress and irritation. (No one was to act like a leader. So no one interrupted, despite lots of *sotto voce* grumbling.) Talk but no study. Short meetings and long luncheon breaks. 'Edelson, lay off, stop your nagging. This is a social occasion for us. We work hard all year, committees, clinical work, meetings, meetings, meetings. We want to have some fun.'

How did I, over and over, get into the role of 'group conscience'? Am I not interested in fun, just like everyone else? But is a bad group meeting, an aimless cliché-ridden discussion, fun? Why did I lend myself repeatedly to others' attempts to manage their anxieties by boxing me in with a stereotype? Why did I let myself be caught between 'work needs' and 'feeling needs'? Why did I polarize these needs, put them at odds? I knew it was legitimate for members of groups to want to satisfy social needs in them. I had such needs too. Often, I have felt convinced I could do the job just as well and more efficiently on my own, but still joined a group just because it gave me a chance to be with and to relate to people I liked. But nevertheless sooner or later the demands of the work would begin to weigh heavily on me. If I felt it was not being done, I could not relax and enjoy the togetherness. The socializing seemed to me to lack genuineness. It didn't seem based on anything solid – a shared achievement, for example.

Anxieties associated with being a group member

The anxieties that have made me unhappy as a member of a group are, I believe, inevitably part of the experience of being a member of a group. Three anxieties especially: loss of individuality; shame; and difference.

First, I have feared groups' encroaching on, restricting, refusing to recognize, rejecting, and so denying me, what I feel is uniquely individual about myself. I haven't liked being caught in the boxes others stuffed me in, from which there seemed no escape. In fact, everything I would say in my struggle to get out of the box others in the group perceived as confirming that I belonged in it, that they were right about me.

Second, I have feared the power of a group to sweep me up in some collective turbulence. I seemed to lose control of what I said or did. I would blurt something out. Hostile comments, embarrassing self-disclosures, would erupt. I felt I was shaming myself in front of others.

Third, I have feared my image of the group would differ from that of other members, and that I, being seen as different, would be isolated, alone, an outcast. Difference raised frightful specters of conflict, of struggle, of winners and losers, of being hurt or even destroyed.

In and out: a lover's quarrel with groups

Sometimes I seem to see groups as impinging on my individuality through constraint. Other members seem to suggest that if they were to respect me, I had to be rigorous, scientific, tough-minded, manly, restrained. I cannot let go and be as flamboyant, emotional, and artistic as I want to be. Others draw back, are uncomfortable, are overwhelmed by what they experience as excess.

On the other hand, groups also interfere with my individuality by adopting standards more lax than my own and expecting me to accommodate to them. I strive to achieve, to work with others in a disciplined way to reach an end. I expect each member, myself and others, to give his all in a strictly coordinated effort. But others see me as a puritanical pest, a rate-buster, a control freak who is demanding, does not let others have any fun. I feel rejected and in turn judge those who cannot or will not make the effort to keep up, and who are envious of those who can and do. Adopting a stance of moral superiority, I see myself as struggling against others' determination that everyone in the group shall finally sink together to the lowest level of performance. No one will be allowed to stand out, to do better, to work harder. No one will have to feel bad because they lag behind or cannot or do not do as well.

My ideal group continues to be that group that not only lets me be fully me but enjoys me, and knows how and wants to use me. But I anticipate that groups will prevent me from being everything I can and want to be. To belong to them, it seems to me, I run the risk of having to be less than what I might be.

I find holding an image of a group and what the group exists to do that other members do not share is somehow intolerable. It's disorienting and demoralizing. Like knowing what scenario you're in, but having your fellow actors acting as if they are in a different one. Apparently I feel I'm a member of a group to the extent that I feel that others and I inhabit the same world, enact the same scenario. I feel that someone else is not a member of my group if the lines they speak seem all wrong, as if these lines were part of some other script.

I try 'heroically', foolishly?, usually futilely, to change the groups to which I belong, so that they can then be the kind of groups to which I feel I belong. But sometimes I seem to do so without any deep realization of what it takes – the kind of attention to relationships, for example, that it takes – to foster the development of a working group.

I like warmth, friendship, people being together and taking pleasure in each other's company. I also like people working in a disciplined way together to bring something about. Finding groups interesting, exciting, dramatic, gemütlich, and sometimes productive, I seek them out. But also finding them messy, restrictive, undisciplined, at times overwhelming, at times frustrating and boring, I recoil from them.

Now, in my sixties, I seem to be changing. I am fond of the people in my study group (we have been meeting together for many years), the students in my seminars. I look forward to seeing and being with them. They seem to have similar feelings toward me. At this time in my life, human relatedness is becoming more important to me. Even the most difficult group has good moments. I know that in the experiences I have been describing I have not taken a balanced look at – I have not been fair to – myself or the groups I describe. I have not gone out of my way to give a thoughtful analysis, either psychological or social-systemic, of the various meanings of these experiences. I have not considered at any depth my own motives. I have not elucidated group dynamics. I have not drawn attention to the conditions which impinged on these groups and affected how they functioned.

As all of us do, struggling with the anxieties that go with being a group member, I need a perspective on the individual and the group. To the extent I have one, as is the case with all of us, my hold on it when I am a group member has seemed periodically tenuous and precarious. Returning to a theme mentioned at the beginning of this chapter, I realize that the perspective I want includes the realization that to be a moral (not a 'moralistic') *person*, which is important to me, is to be a member of a group, and that the idea of *morality* is meaningless in the absence of the reality of group membership. Such a perspective also includes the realization that neither the properties of a person nor a social system alone are totally responsible for failure. But how do I know what weight in particular circumstances to give to each of these: the person, the social system?

I don't want to duck the problem of understanding what I contribute to my own unhappiness. (This, for me, is part of being a moral person.) But I also want to understand how the groups in which I participate manage to have an uncannily accurate sense of my dispositions, and how they go about exacerbating and exploiting these dispositions.

I remember the Smith and Berg book on paradoxes in group life has a description of a particular paradox: 'the more you are in, the more you want to be out, and the more you are out, the more you want to be in'.[64] Most of us, as individuals who are also group members, live and relive forms of that paradox. If we can't get altogether free of it, at least we can come to understand it better.

CHAPTER 12

On Being a Group Member II

David Berg

My awareness of the role groups play in my life began early. Growing up as a Jew had a significant impact on my awareness that people belonged to groups, and that group memberships influenced the way people experienced the world and the way in which the world responded to them. It is only now, as I get older and can meaningfully use phrases like 'thirty-five years ago when I was a kid', that I realize how much World War II and the Holocaust affected my early family life. As I watched the images on television and heard my mother's sobs, I began to realize, although I could not have used these words, that people are not just individuals. They belong to groups. What happens to us, how we think and feel, what we notice, how others respond to us, are a function of our personalities and talents, but also of our group memberships and the relationships that our groups have with others now and in the past.

This is not a uniquely Jewish story. I suspect that many of us are aware of how our group memberships may be shaping our experience of the world. For me, ethnicity was one of the first group memberships I understood in these terms. Race, gender, social class and sexual orientation came later. I was also aware, at an early age, that my place in a hierarchy was not merely an individual condition, but a *social* status, a characteristic of organizational identity. This social status connected me to others and explained the convergence of our sentiments about things such as school, teachers, and rules. For me, then, knowledge about groups and intergroup relations became central to understanding human behavior and myself in the world in which I live.

Social relations in elementary school

I watch the wonder and pleasure in my daughters' eyes. I listen to the full-bodied laughter preceding or following a fit of the giggles. I observe the deep satisfaction that accompanies a small but meaningful accomplishment. I think that children see, feel, and enact the world in ways much clearer and more straightforward than those of adults. Sometimes, however, this 'clarity' of thought or feeling, especially when group members share it, can be upsetting, as in the cases when children visit cruelty upon one another.

A few years ago I thought back on the social relations in my elementary school. My reflections focused on the role 'identity' factors (like race and gender) played in the life of my classmates and me. Who was 'in'? Who was 'out'? Who did we pick on and why?

As I thought about these questions, I realized that the three kids we picked on – one girl and two boys – all had 'special' characteristics. The girl was the only child I knew whom a single parent was raising. In the mid-1950s, there was no such concept as 'single parent'. I remember we all knew there was something strange about her home life. There was only a mother in her apartment. One of the boys was the only black kid in the class. The other boy occasionally had an epileptic seizure in class.

What brought all this back to me was remembering that when my parents divorced after fifth grade, I hid my changed status from my classmates. I refused my mother's attempts to encourage me to have parties at my house, and I never spoke of my parents' divorce.

In hindsight, it seems that I was not only ashamed of my difference. I feared that my classmates would seize upon this difference in cruel ways, just as I had. Finding someone who was different, and joining together in identifying those who were different, gave the rest of us a sense of being 'in' when we worried about being 'out'. It was as if our feeling of belonging depended on someone else's feeling rejected. Without the layers of social veneer that most of us acquired in subsequent years, we were free to enact these feelings, to define our group or club in terms of those who could not join.

Zionist youth movement in adolescence

It is an interesting coincidence that involvement in a Zionist youth movement in late adolescence left a legacy that I also remember vividly. Judaism, and especially Labor Zionism with its emphasis on collectivism and responsibility, proved to be fertile ground for confrontation between burgeoning adolescent individuality and peer group conformity.

After years of participation and leadership in a Zionist youth movement, I found myself representing my high school age peers at a meeting of college age alumni of the movement. These 'graduates' were planning to emigrate, as a group, to Israel in the late 1960s, and I was privy to their conversations and concerns. I had been invited to attend this small conference to serve as a liaison with the high school age group, but I was not invited to join this pioneering group of emigrés.

I remember feeling two things simultaneously. I was aware that I did not want to emigrate to Israel at the age of eighteen, although those in the movement, adults and teenagers alike, would have applauded such a commitment by someone in my leadership position. I felt too young to make a decision of that magnitude. I was about to enter college and I was scared to even think about leaving home. (Golda Meir came to speak to this group of fifty, and she said, as if speaking to me personally, 'Don't think, just come!')

At the same time, I was angry and disappointed that the group of emigrés would not let me join them as they made plans. These were people I respected and admired. This was a group I wanted to be part of. I was hurt and angry when they did not allow me to be a member – even when I did not share their collective commitments.

Already then I realized that my state of mind was bizarre. How could both feelings coexist within me? I desperately wanted to be part of this group and equally intensely wanted nothing to do with the shared goal of its members.

College

In my early adult years, I found that my interest in groups and organizations centered on the tension between what people in organizations espoused and how they behaved. Living according to what we espouse is always difficult. It is tough enough for me to live up to whatever expectations I have for my individual behavior, the way I treat my spouse or children, the way I conduct myself in the face of racist jokes and ethnic slurs, the ways I act on what I value. It is significantly more difficult to compel the groups and organizations to which I belong to behave in ways that are consistent with the values they espouse.

When I was in college in the late 1960s, one spring semester brought with it a strike by the maintenance workers of the university. Student supporters championed not only improved economic conditions for the employees, but improved working conditions as well, including humane treatment and respect on the job. As a result of the strike, supervisory personnel staffed the university dining hall. One evening, entering the dining hall, I watched a fellow student, who was shouting support for the union's demands, walk up to a supervisor – struggling in vain to keep up with the work – and dump a full tray of food at his feet. A small band of students cheered this 'protest' and my stomach turned over.

I understood then, as I think I do now, the politics of organizations. But I could not help wondering how people who espoused humane treatment for all employees could use a tactic that was so pointedly humiliating to another human being. On the other hand, I can imagine the response that would have greeted a student who dared to voice a criticism of the strategy used in the dining hall because such a strategy violated those values that presumably united students and employees. I hear an indignant voice, 'What self-righteous, holier-than-thou individual would say such a thing in the midst of such an important struggle?!' I think in response, 'But don't we live most of our lives in the midst of important struggles? Isn't that what makes it so hard to live what we espouse?'

Groups and organizations are complex creations

Perhaps these gaps, and the disappointments in self and others to which they give rise, occur because groups and organizations are complicated creations. We stitch them together to satisfy a whole range of human needs, for accomplishment and achievement, as well as for inclusion and community. Some of these needs we identify and explain easily. Others we find more difficult to acknowledge and understand. Some we share with others in our groups. Others are unique to single persons. Some needs serve to bind us to a group. Others, when frustrated in a group, drive us away from it. Most often we feel needs that bind us and needs that drive us away at the same time. So our experiences in groups evoke strong and conflicting feelings in us.

As I think about my own experiences in groups, I find myself noticing that the landscape has *both* hills and valleys, success *and* failure. I feel deeply satisfied when a group meeting produces something new, something original, something none of its members on their own before coming to the meeting could have imagined.

Groups are important to me, both personally and professionally. Because they are important, I fear them as much as I am drawn to them. The intimate connection I feel to some groups gives them the power to arouse intense emotions, both positive and negative. I often find myself cast as 'complainer' or 'the dissatisfied one'. I often volunteer for this role as a way of balancing my hopes and fears about group membership. When I feel the derision that in that role comes my way, I feel angry and alone precisely because I want to feel included and accepted. And I feel betrayed because I know others are dissatisfied too but unwilling or unable to join me in saying so.

It can be useful to focus on the problematic, frustrating, and alienating aspects of group life. To highlight what troubles us about our experiences in groups encourages us to better understand ourselves in groups as well as the dynamics of groups themselves. For example, focusing somberly on the problematic nature of living and working with others, I am reminded that, in spite of myself, every time I join a group or meet with an existing one, I expect or hope the experience will be ideal. Coming with such expectations and hopes, however implicit or unconscious they are, any group member is likely to experience as failure what is natural and inevitable: The ebb and flow of group life. The necessary conflicts. The strong but mixed feelings. The frustrations that lead sometimes to participation and other times to withdrawal.

Idealization of groups contributes to a potentially disabling sense of failure. This sense of failure contributes to our impulse to leave the group, to take it over, or to sabotage its work. These impulses, acted upon, debilitate the groups to which we belong, as well as organizations and the individuals who depend on them.

The following questions are shared by those of us who wouldn't want to live without, but have trouble living with, groups and organizations. From where does authority in groups come? By what right is it exercised? What does membership in a group or community require? What can a group expect of its members and what can the individual member expect of the group? How do our memberships in some groups (e.g., race, gender, ethnicity, class, age, family, profession, culture) shape our experiences in others? These are some of the questions that the stories we tell raise – and attempt, however partially, to answer.

CHAPTER 13

The Movie Group

Marshall Edelson

I am going to tell a story about the vicissitudes of a movie group. In it psychotherapists-in-training and I tried to discuss with each other our experiences as we watched a movie together. This story illustrates what it's like to be a member of a group, any group – and especially the tensions between the individual and the social that are always associated with group membership. The illustration of these tensions is vivid, I think, just because the story involves movies and responses to movies. Movies themselves and the responses of audiences to them, I shall argue, are implicated in the most extreme expressions of individuality and sociality.

There are other reasons that I choose to give such a detailed account of this group – of the obstacles that stood in the way of its achieving what might seem to be a simple goal, of its quarrels, of its failures and successes. Certainly, a group of psychotherapists-in-training responding to movies and to each other as they discussed their responses is an ideal context in which to pursue our interests both in *narrative* and in *understanding experiences in groups*. In addition, some of the responses members of the movie group had to the movies we saw together paralleled just those responses they had to their patients in psychotherapy that adversely affect a psychotherapeutic process. Becoming aware of these across-context similarities helped us to understand experiences in groups and also, a bonus, contributed to the development of attitudes and skills needed in doing psychotherapy.

Movies and audience response: extreme expressions of individuality and sociality

Movies are associated with an enigma. Why do responses to a movie differ so much from individual to individual, and in the same individual from occasion to occasion? What meaning can we give to the notion *a collective response*, the response of an audience, which is not merely the sum or aggregate of the individual responses of the members of that audience?

We do write as if audiences were homogeneous collectives. Some writing about movies is concerned with how movies shape the ideological and value preferences of *the* audience. Some writing about movies is concerned with how the ideological and value preferences of *the* audience determine what finds its way into movies. But I observe that members of audiences differ. Different viewers have very different experiences as they watch the same movie, and evaluate the movie very differently.

Even if I focus on those who presumably have specialized knowledge about and wide experience with movies, I find unexpected disparities. The emphasis and rating of one reviewer or critic and those of another may diverge radically. Creating a movie is a collective process – and more of a bricolage (that is, an object put together from what just happens to be available) than it is considered to be by those who think of it as the deliberate design of a single 'auteur'. Any individual review of the movie or evaluation of it may be partial, a response to only one or two of the individual pieces that went into making the movie.

In addition, I know from my own experience that even the same individual at different times in her life will respond differently to the same movie. (I might say the same about responses to other art objects as well, including music, novels, plays, and so on, but I do not strive for an ambitious generalization here.) All of us have had the experience watching later in life a movie that meant a lot to us in childhood, only to find that what was magic and compelling about it has disappeared. This has something to do with the difference in the way a child watches a movie from the way an adult watches a movie, not simply with changes in movie conventions over the years.

Is this variability individually or socially determined? Does it follow from differences among personalities, from differences in intrapsychic dynamics, or from differences in the extent to which individual viewers have the common ground of knowledge taken-for-granted by the moviemaker? Does it follow rather from the different identity groups to which viewers belong and from differences in the values, ideologies, and interests associated with these memberships?

In the past I have accounted for this variability along the lines of Holland's ideas about readers.[65] It depends on which unconscious fantasy (or fantasies) is (or are) evoked in an individual by a movie and an individual's particular response to the fantasy. Is the fantasy accepted or rejected? Does it make for pleasure or arouse anxiety? How does the individual defend against that anxiety? In other words, I have told individual stories to solve the enigma of response variability.

But when I read a review, as I often have, in which the reviewer comments that a particular movie will be of interest only to a minority or special group, and this comment is associated with a lower rating (number of stars) than I would have given the movie, then I think group memberships must have a lot to do with the variability I notice. When I catch a reviewer making this comment repeatedly about movies that tell a story about members of the same particular minority or special group, it lends weight to this impression.

I have the same thought when I notice in the groups in which I participate that members of different generations respond differently to a movie. These differences in response are often associated with differences in the conventions with which each generation is most familiar. Responses are different, for example, to how much talking characters in the story do ('it's too talky'), to voice-over narration ('it's too slow'), to black and white in contrast to color ('it's not as much fun' or 'it's not as real or involving' or 'I'm not used to it'), to 'old movies' in contrast to 'new movies'.

Perhaps the decisive divide is between *mis-en-scene* and *montage*.[66] Older movies invite the viewer to contemplate *the scene* – what is in it, how objects and people are arranged – and to become involved in it. Scenes are prolonged, leisurely, dense with information, filled with objects and figures. These co-exist in many planes; they are in sharp focus from foreground to background. People in the scene *talk*, and the talk has weight, is expressive, expands. Continuity between shots is seamless; the shots flow invisibly one into the other.

Newer movies invite the viewer to react to montage, to the juxtaposition of shots or scenes. Often it is the juxtapositions themselves that convey information and suggest meanings. Information and meaning tend to be subliminally absorbed, for there is little time for reflection. Scenes and events shift rapidly from one to another. A viewer must meet the challenge to find her way continuously and quickly, to keep re-orienting. It is the movement from one event to another that matters, and the nature of the connection between them that intrigues. Cuts occur frequently, abruptly, calling attention to themselves. The movement is so swift that events and lines seem almost 'thrown away'. Talk is minimal. It is brief, to the point, fast, overlapping, mumbled, or obscured by sound effects or musical background. Scenes do not call for contemplation or effortful attention. Each scene is shallow. It has little information, and that in one plane, the foreground. Information, a detail, an object, a facial expression, is highlighted in close-up so that no viewer can miss it.

The difference is not a difference in genre. It is not simply that current movies are action movies and older ones 'weepies' or women's pictures. A comparison of two versions of *Little Women* (1933 and 1994) shows the same contrast.

I find this gap between generations especially poignant. In the movie group, it was one among many obstacles that stood between me and other members of the group, who were of another generation.

I do want to know something about an audience. But not about an audience en masse, not about a generalized audience, and not just about one member or a few members of it. I want to know about the particular experiences of *all* its members.

For it is only from these particulars that I can construct a story about the group-as-a-whole.

I wanted to know why, for example, in any attempt by members of the movie group to share with each other their experiences of a movie, conflicts arose over which experiences of a movie, and which mode of experiencing movies, are legitimate. How did group members express these conflicts? How did collective perceptions of the significance of these conflicts emerge? How did group members forge out of different proposals collective resolutions of these conflicts? Perhaps to know these kinds of things about an audience's response to a movie is not only to know about a group, a social entity, but also to know something about how the movie, a cultural artefact, is constructed and how that structure works.

Movies seem to me to be the most extreme expression of *individuality* and at the same time the most extreme expression of the *social*. In experiencing movies, I experience again the tension between the individual and the social. I often feel that every graceful thought, every impulse, every nuance of feeling, every curiosity I have ever had was born – and every wish and curiosity satisfied – at the movies. In the dark, watching, and then discussing movies with others, my individuality, the desires of my mind and body, which strive for expression and satisfaction, mingle and collide with my sociality, my curiosity about others, about the society in which I live, about how others live and what they believe and value. Movies themselves, results of a collective effort, represent life in society, which puzzles, intrigues, and sometimes torments me.

Like many others, I experience a movie as if it were a dream I was dreaming. So movies seem to me to be the most extreme expression of individuality, for I – and no one else – dream my dream. In watching movies, as in dreaming, I am in touch with bodies, with faces, limbs, and genitals, with my own body, and with the desires of my body. The characters in a movie appear to me as figures on the stage of my mind. Since I dream them, they are all aspects of myself. They perform in an internal drama. I write it, stage it, direct it, and act in it – all the roles are mine. I am also its audience. So it is with me and my dream.

A mental process, according primacy to pleasure as an end in itself, creates my dreams. It assimilates or uses contents from external reality to that end. It does not seek to fit, to accommodate or adapt to, external reality. So, many of my body's physiological processes have a rude autonomy from external reality. They are triggered by *internal* events. They have their own rhythms. The rhythms of my body's desires are in many ways independent of external reality. My dreams, my body, and my body's desires form the core of my *individual* identity. Their relative autonomy from the causal pressures of my external situation guarantees the integrity of my individuality. [67]

When I relate to others in actual social situations, feel connected to them, and join them in enterprises that matter to us, my dreams and my body's desires stand between me and group pressures and seductions. They mitigate my receptivity to thoughts and feelings others don't want and, not wanting, pass over to me, pour into me. They protect me from the shame I feel when I succumb to this contagion, when I am swept up by and act upon others' thoughts and feelings as if they were my own. Remembering and remaining in touch with my dreams and bodily desires, which experiencing movies helps me to do, I am able to resist my own temptations to disown who and what I am. I am able to say to others what I feel and believe with a voice that is my own.

Yet, as a form of popular culture, movies also seem to me to be the most extreme expression of collectivity. Investigation of the psychology of the screenwriter, the director, or a character in the work will not lead us to the movie. Neither will investigation of the psychology of a single member of the audience (a single 'reader'), which tends to leave out the movie as an object, to lead away from it rather than toward it, to result in something partial if not idiosyncratic. If a movie were the product of an individual mind, an examination of it might tell us something about the way the mind works, and understanding something about the way individual minds work might tell us something about the movie. But since a movie is the product of a collective process, perhaps it is in understanding another kind of collective process, evoked by the movie, that we also learn something about the movie itself.

I make a jump to consider what parallel might exist between cinematic and collective processes; I wonder if there might be correspondences between cinematic and collective process. I play with the conjecture that the content and form of a particular movie, its story and the way that story is presented, coincide somehow with the collective process it evokes and to which it appeals. Perhaps since we deal here with mass or popular culture, it is not only individual psychology that is relevant in considering the impact of a movie, but group psychology. What if we do not look to understand how the motives of some putative creator of the work as an object 'out there' influenced what it became, and we do not look to understand how some abstract generalized collective 'mind' receives a movie? What if we seek instead correspondences between cinematic process and a group narrative or a pattern of responses in an audience?

We want to see if there are parallels between cinematic and group processes that will help us understand what goes on between members of an audience as they are affected by a movie and what goes on in the movie itself. A method comes to mind. We might learn something about a movie from the dynamics of a group's discussion of its members' experiences of it? *Group process* might reflect, parallel, or correspond to *cinematic process.*

That there might be a correspondence between cinematic process and group process seems plausible. When a group as an audience responds to a movie, and then *if the group members are able to engage each other fully* over their differences in ex-periencing the movie, it is possible that the different responses and the dynamics of their engagement will parallel the dynamics of the cinematic process – the movie's content and structure, and the operations, devices, and techniques used by it in achieving its effects.

Even if we were to regard the movie as the product of an individual mind, the director's, the screenwriter's, the actor's, it is still the product of an individual mind that has struggled in the making of the movie with collective processes.

> [For example,] the director conducts all the elements comprising the cinematic orchestra. He or she must have the artistic integrity and toughness of mind required for making the final decisions on the screenplay as an equal partner with the writer and producer; playing a decisive role in the selection of cast and staff; directing the acting, cinematography, lighting, and other aspects of production; supervising the visual effects; and exercising the right of the first cut in editing. The director must cope with unions and a staff of cinematographers, gaffers, stagehands, and electricians; set designers, scene painters, costume designers, and makeup experts; major and minor performers. The director must charismatically inspire them all to do their very best. Finally, the director must complete all this within the limitations of the budget and the uproar of an ongoing production.[68]

Everyone has a finger in the pot: the producer, the screenwriter, the novelist of whose work the movie is an adaptation, the set designer, the director, the actors, the cinematographer, the editor, the sound designer, the visual special effects person, all relate to each other, all influence what becomes the final product. It is not unusual to have many screenwriters, or to have more than one director, among these some that go uncredited. Even the audience has a say. In response to comments from previews, the movie is changed to delete what audience members didn't like and to give them what they wanted. Many motives, many different kinds of considerations, compete in the process of construction: ideological, commercial, aesthetic, logistical, what resources are available. There are also unexpected accidents, which may turn out to be opportunities or obstacles. Negotiation and compromise, people mutually influencing each other (whether this influence be acknowledged or unacknowledged), and the interaction of many factors or circumstances (anticipated or unanticipated) are hallmarks of the collective processes that produce a movie.

But it is this diversity – not necessarily 'individual genius' – that is likely to produce 'the sleeper', something new or unexpected, a magical unpredictable combination of elements no one person, motive, or circumstance alone could have brought about. The making of that quintessential movie *Casablanca*, for example, comes to mind.

Paradoxically, this social diversity, these various contributions to a final product, also makes it possible for me to use a movie, as many others do, to construct my own individual dreamlike experience. For at least one progenitor of the movie is likely to provide me with the hook to which I can attach – the material which I can use to create – my own experience of pleasure, of wish fulfillment. Perhaps I take off from a mere moment or fragment, which had found its way into the movie during the messy collective process that made it. Perhaps its many progenitors provide me with all the materials I need to construct a dreamlike experience in which I condense many different kinds of pleasure or wish fulfillments.

Responses to movies and parallel responses to patients in psychotherapy

I saw parallels in the movie group between the way members experienced movies and responded to the stories they told, and the way these same group members experienced patients in psychotherapy or psychoanalysis and responded to their stories. Each illuminated the other. I was able to observe these parallels, because these same trainees were or had been students in other seminars of mine on psychotherapy or psychoanalysis, or were presenting or had presented their clinical work to me in individual preceptorials.

Psychotherapists in general respond more or less frequently in three unwanted ways to stories patients tell or enact. All three ways of responding have their origin in our need to disown or disclaim something in ourselves. We split it off, see it not in ourselves but in our patients, and we reject it in them.

1. We find ourselves experiencing patients as different from ourselves. What they are like in their stories, what they do, has to do with their badness, their sickness, which has no correspondence to anything we accept in ourselves. They have pathological traits and commit odd or bad acts. 'It has *nothing to do with me*', is what we feel. It is just in this sickness, this incapacity, this defect or deficit, that we feel we are different from our patients, and we congratulate ourselves that it is just because of this difference that we are able to help them.

   So, we are led to objectify and distance patients. They are *out there*. We cannot understand their acting like *that*. They *resist* our efforts. Thus, as we describe them, we use a language that, if used in describing ourselves, would make us unrecognizable to ourselves. Faced with what we experience as alien and inexplicable in another, we pull away. We become discouraged. A note of belittlement or criticism sounds in what we say.

2. We find ourselves experiencing impulses to make moral judgments. 'She is cruel, mean, selfish, exploitative, manipulative, sociopathic.' 'I do not like him. I do not like what he does to others.' Sometimes, in the middle of a psychotherapeutic process, we suddenly begin worrying, ruminating, playing with ideas about our patients' diagnoses. Diagnoses have pejorative connotations, and can serve as respectable masks for more primitive irritations.

3. As we listen to a patient's story, or feel ourselves pulled by a patient into a scenario as one of its characters, we turn to authority. We want to understand the story, to know what to say, or to justify something we have said. We draw on theory. We make use of technical language in formulating our thoughts. We remember what a preceptor, supervisor, teacher, or expert said or wrote. We refer to a rule of technique or good practice. Distrusting the spontaneous response that might betray us, we shrink from it as 'countertransference', and rely instead on formulas. We prefer to listen to the introjected voice of authority, rather than notice and pay attention to what goes on in our minds, which we dismiss fearfully as too 'personal', irrelevantly 'idiosyncratic', merely 'imagistic', or excessively 'emotional'.

But the relief the voice of authority affords us comes at a price. It is an obstacle to our finding a voice that is our own. Because we cannot admit that our own everyday life experience is relevant to what we prefer to believe is *strange*, we cannot draw on our experience. So we are shut off from the everyday competence we all have before our formal training in psychotherapy – our competence in listening to stories, telling stories, and using stories to understand our own or others' experience. That leaves us depending on theory, teachers, the voices of others, so that we may know how to respond to our patients' stories in a way that keeps them Other and at the same time constrains our impulse to criticize and condemn that Other.

The beginnings of the movie group

It all started when, several years ago, I participated in a movie group run by psychiatry residents.

The residents' movie group

Three residents had organized the group out of their interest in movies. The group ran into a number of difficulties. Different goals clashed with each other.

One goal was for residents to get to know faculty members. So each meeting a faculty member was invited to choose a movie and come to the group to lead a discussion of it. The other goal was to find some way to enjoy and discuss movies together. But often the faculty member was not especially into movies and would choose a movie without regard to its value as a movie but simply because it provided an opportunity to discuss something about a psychiatric phenomenon or practice. The faculty member might not be invested much in movies but was often very invested in the topic having to do with psychiatry and was happy to have the opportunity to discuss it with a group of residents. The result was that especially those who had organized the group out of their interest in movies were left unhappy about the movie they had had to sit through and with the discussion that had little to do with the movie as a movie.

The three residents who had organized the group acted as hosts, taking responsibility each time for inviting a faculty member, getting the film, setting things up, providing refreshments, and preparing an announcement for the department bulletin. They did not try to get a commitment from any group of residents but left attending up to anyone interested. The result was a heterogeneous group, made up of residents, spouses, friends, and members of other disciplines. Moreover the group membership, who attended and how many attended, changed each time. So the group never came together as a group.

The group leaders felt increasingly a sense of resentment about being left with all the chores and with the lack of commitment from the members who came or not as they pleased. Moreover, it became apparent that no one else in the next generation of residents had become involved enough in the group to want to take over the reins. So the three group leaders (one of whom was leaving the residency), after asking if anyone in the group wanted to take over and getting no volunteers, disbanded the group.

The birth of the movie group

Following that event, I offered an elective seminar on movies and the problem of interpretation, which – despite a yearly, sometimes partial, sometimes total turnover in membership – became in its different versions known as 'the movie group'. The remaining two leaders of the residents' movie group elected to join the movie group each year over the next three years.

The seminar met in my home. It was elected by members of a university department of psychiatry, including residents in psychiatry, psychology fellows, social work and nursing staff, and rarely a faculty member, and in one of its versions by candidates in a psychoanalytic institute. The members of the movie group for the most part were, or had been, students in seminars of mine on psychotherapy or psychoanalysis.

I chose some movies from the 1920s and 1930s, the largest number from the 1940s, and a few from the 1950s and 1960s, almost all in black and white. They were classic Hollywood movies – not 'great cinema' or 'film art'. I assumed that many movie group members might not have seen these movies, some of which were 50 to 75 years old, and wondered if the movies would seem strange to them. But I wanted to share movies with them that had some meaning to me, and that were movies I thought would result in a fresh first-time experience that would bring them together as a group.

The task: a rigorous exercise

I wanted to use the movie group to mitigate those tendencies (related to the three unwanted ways psychotherapists respond to stories their patients tell or enact) that interfere with trainees learning to do psychotherapy. The trainees tended to respond diagnostically to what a patient said or did, to objectify and characterize the patient by describing his states, traits, symptoms, or dysfunctional behavior. They made inner statements *about* the patient that began 'She...' or 'He...' or made statements to the patient that began 'You...' I wanted them instead to begin noticing their own internal events, images, memories, fantasies, reveries, voices, and to make inner statements that began 'I...' For, reflecting on these internal events, they might then come to realize that frequently the patient evokes them and ask, 'In what way has my patient evoked this in me? What motivates her to bring about these events in me, and just now? What drama does she imagine on the stage of her own mind and strive to realize in what happens between us? What role, what figure from her inner life, what aspect of herself, am I assigned? Am I comfortable or uncomfortable in this role? Do I bear it and sit with it and explore what it is like to be in this role, and in so doing possibly learn something about her – and inevitably also then something about myself? Or do I find the role intolerable? Do I reject and refuse and return it?'

I also wanted trainees to have the opportunity to find their own voices, and to come to speak to the patient in that voice. That meant enabling them to give priority to images, memories, fantasies, reveries, and the dramas that took place on the stage of their own minds over the hectoring, warning, critical, constraining voices of external authority – whether these voices took the form of august theory, indisputable rules of technique, or the pronouncements of admired and intimidating teachers or supervisors. It is true that theory, rules of technique, and a teacher's suggestions can be useful, especially if trainees give themselves permission to consider them, try them out, and accept or reject them in the light of experience. But they are not useful when they come between psychotherapists and their patients, interfering with spontaneity and innovation, and substituting what is general and formulaic for the unique, specific, and personal.

I set then the following task for the movie group. I asked members to pay attention to and to report their experiences watching the evening's movie to the group. Together we would try to thwart our tendency to focus on the movie as an object 'out there', to describe its characteristics, and to evaluate its characters or itself as a work. Instead, we would tell just what we felt, thought, remembered, or imagined at various points in the movie. When did we cry, laugh, wander, get restless, want out? When did we remember an experience (and which experience?) from our own life, or an episode from another movie?

I also suggested that in our discussions we avoid using technical jargon or professional language, and use instead the language of everyday life or conversation. The focus was to be on the subjective experiences evoked in us during a viewing of the movie: feelings, images, memories, fantasies. Talk was to be about ourselves and our own here-and-now experiences, not about the film as an object 'out there' or about its properties. No film theory. No learned discourses on philosophy, mythology, Marxism, psychoanalysis, semiotics, psychology, or sociology. No call to rank the movie or to evaluate it in any way. No talk of the techniques or skills of the director, actors, writers, photographers, set designers, or camera positions, at least not right off. No analyses or interpretations of the movie, at least not until we could ground them in, and they had something to do with, detailed accounts of a variety of members' experiences.

We did try, with varying degrees of success, to reflect on our own experiences. 'What did I feel or think? What image or fantasy did I have? At just what point in the movie? When did I laugh or cry? When did my mind wander? When did I get bored, restless, want out? When did I remember an episode from another movie or a novel, or an experience from my own life? Which episode? What experience?' We did try, but often failed, to refrain from expressing global evaluations or ratings and to talk instead about details and the internal events to which they gave rise. We did manage, more successfully than most such groups do, to exercise tact and reticence with regard to offering analyses or interpretations of the movie – at least until such interpretations could be grounded in and had something to do with detailed accounts of a variety of members' experiences. But, although we wanted to talk about ourselves and our own here-and-now experiences, often we talked instead about the properties of the movie as an object 'out there'.

Obstacles to accomplishing the task

Two kinds of obstacles stood in the way of the movie group's accomplishing its task. First, certain factors made it difficult for members of the group to stick to talk about their own experiences. Second, at least two very different modes of viewing movies emerged. These modes were so different they seemed at times incommensurate. Members of the group had great difficulty connecting with each others' experiences. Quarrels and then a sense of futility resulted. It seemed impossible to accord legitimacy to those who experienced movies in a mode different from one's own. What was the point of even trying to share experiences that were fated for rejection?

Sticking to talk about one's own experiences

The first kind of obstacle was that, for various reasons, it was not easy for group members to stay with their own inner experiences. They had some difficulty focusing on these experiences, much less articulating, elaborating, and sharing them. There seemed to be a number of easily discernible reasons for people's reluctance to discuss their experiences of movies in a group, making that reluctance both understandable and apparently unavoidable. Some of these had to do with member differences. Some had to do with the impact of membership in other groups in the system in which we all worked.

PERCEPTUAL PROJECTION

As humans, our customary projection of the experience of perception onto objects in the external world leads us almost automatically to formulate responses to a movie in sentences that are assertions about the movie rather than in sentences about ourselves. The group discussion usually started with 'The movie…' and almost never with 'I…' The recurrent slide into discussing the object rather than the experience seemed irresistible. Of course, if someone makes assertions about the movie as object, other group members are hesitant to describe experiences that now seem to them 'mistaken', 'invalid', or 'ignorant'. They apparently accept that the 'objective' characterization of the object they have just heard was 'correct'.

THE AUTHORITY STRUCTURE

Trainees elected to take the movie group as a seminar. It had an authority structure. I was the teacher. More familiar with movies than most of the members, and especially with movies of the 1930s, 1940s, 1950s, and 1960s, I chose the movies that we were to watch. I led the discussion. Some group members continued to appreciate my introducing them to movies they would otherwise have been unlikely to see. But others came increasingly to attribute their discontents and difficulties in the group to my usurping the prerogative to choose the movies. They sought to respond to the movies as they thought I wanted them to. When I seemed to respond to a movie differently from the way they responded, they felt that was a criticism of their response.

Carl, feeling criticized, and representing other group members who felt as he did, defended himself by saying, 'You have set it up for us to fail to give you what you want by choosing movies that are especially important to you but with which we cannot connect, because of their age or because they have no special meaning for us.' This said by someone who had been so taken by *Double Indemnity* and *Sunset Boulevard* that he had gone out to find and see as many Billy Wilder movies as he could!

It is not usual in an academic seminar for members to reveal personal responses. Ordinarily, the teacher expects that students will suppress these in favor of intellectual objective discourse, and sets the example for such discourse. I regularly made personal comments about my experiences watching the movies we saw together. But it was clear from what members said that they couldn't quite believe that that was what I wanted and all I wanted from them, that they also were permitted to make such personal comments.

That the movie group *was* different in many ways from the usual seminar did help with all this. It met in the evening and at the teacher's home. Certainly it was more informal; in some years, for example, the meeting began with members sharing pizza provided in turn by each of them.

PROFESSIONAL IDENTITY

The group members had been educated to think of themselves as tough-minded scientists. They were to be objective, to stick to the facts, to eschew personal bias. To pay attention to and express personal feelings and opinions was to be flighty, nonprofessional.

GENDER

The usual gender stereotypes were in full operation. Men tended to be reluctant to confess experiences they did not consider manly. During the movie group's early history, few women joined. Those who did attended sporadically or left the group after a half dozen meetings. The majority of members were men. A man led the group. Men occupied most of the higher-status positions in the hierarchy of the department of psychiatry. Perhaps some women did not want to spend their evening off re-experiencing what they frequently felt during their workdays, that they were more or less shut out from or on the periphery of a man's world.

FEELINGS AND OPINIONS ARE DANGEROUS

Almost every member was more or less anxious that his feelings or even opinions might harm another. This anxiety tended to inhibit discussion. It was only in discussions with individual members outside the group that I heard things like, 'I didn't want to spoil someone else's experience by saying something bad about the movie.' 'I felt such-and-such about this-or-that in the movie, but I didn't want to say so, because I thought I would upset Lou or Rosa if I did.'

I could not tell if this apparently ubiquitous belief in the harmful effects of expressing feelings and opinions was due to an overestimation of one's power to affect others. (Even some experienced psychotherapists fall prey to this omnipotent fantasy.) Was it due to an underestimation of others' strengths, resiliency, and ability to take care of themselves, to stick to their guns and to reply with feelings and opinions of their own? (Even some experienced psycho-therapists fall prey to a tendency to see everyone as a patient, and patients as fragile, helpless, or victims.) Was it related to a wish to avoid conflict, difference, and dissent? Could it be an appropriate response to something intrinsic in experiencing movies? Is that experience particularly fragile?

PROFESSIONALS' QUEST FOR RESPECT

As is usual, people were reluctant to express apparently unconventional feelings, ideas, and so on, lest others think them odd or ridicule them. Maybe a reluctance to seem odd is greater than usual in a group of people who want others to respect them as 'mature' and 'reliable' professionals.

One member confessed to me that he had particularly liked the movies we had watched (for example, *Gilda*) that he hadn't seen before and that had something sexually perverse or kinky about them that wasn't obvious but that became clear to him in group discussion. Of course, he had never said anything even remotely like that during the group discussions.

This vignette suggests one goal that members of any group (including a psychotherapy group) might have in sharing their experiences – in this group, the feelings, thoughts, images, and memories a movie had evoked in them. In giving these experiences as gifts to, and receiving them as gifts from, one another, they enrich, and are enriched by, one another. They become aware of *possibilities of thought, perception, feeling, and imagination* that prior to group discussion had gone unnoticed or were altogether inaccessible. This expanded awareness beyond the boundaries of what one can attain in a life lived alone is in and of itself a value of life in a group – in addition to the advantages it confers on those who have occasion to take collective action in dealing with a task or problem.

Two different ways moviegoers experience movies

I did gain something valuable from the differences among us that emerged in the movie group, differences that resulted occasionally and painfully in quite bitter quarrels. I became increasingly aware of peoples' different modes of experiencing movies, and the reluctance of people to accord legitimacy to experiences in a mode different from their own. These different modes of experiencing movies constituted a second kind of obstacle to our accomplishing our task.

ENTERING A NARRATIVE WORLD

Probably for many reasons, viewers are transported to different degrees when they watch a movie. That is, they more or less actively enter into a narrative world.

We know that a movie may seem very different to any one of us on a second viewing, and different again on still another viewing. We know that each one of us may tell a somewhat different story about a movie we have watched together. But in each of these cases the movie as an object has remained the same from one viewing or viewer to another. It follows that viewers are not simply the passive recipients of a narrative world. They actively participate in constructing it. Something in them makes a difference, takes part. They collude with the movie in creating it. They raise questions and then find answers – from one shot or scene to the next. They form hypotheses (for example, about what is going to happen or what has happened) and seek pertinent evidence for or against these hypotheses. They make inferences (for example, about the motives of a character) and check to see if these turn out to have been correct or incorrect. They notice mere hints and respond to them with necessary internal detailed elaborations. Not everything they think of themselves as 'seeing' is actually visible on the screen; they fill in what is missing but implied. They make use of knowledge to which they but not some character in the story are privy. They interpret signs of all kinds: conventions, symbols, conjunctions of images that are metaphors. Bordwell's work, among others, and my own experience have encouraged me to say that *the viewer and movie create the movie's narrative world together*.[69]

When viewing is in this sense *active*, viewers collaborate with the movie to create a narrative world for themselves to inhabit. If 'inhabiting a narrative world' is what we mean by 'experiencing a movie', then it is possible for a viewer to watch a movie without experiencing it. V. F. Perkins' comment is pertinent. 'Of course it is possible to cultivate... aloofness, rather as Victorian ladies were said to distract themselves from their husbands' nocturnal attentions by thinking over problems of household management. But one cannot analyze, or understand, an experience which one has refused...'[70]

The distinction between merely watching a movie and experiencing it comes to mind when I become aware of differences in how viewers feel not only about particular movies, but about the act of watching a movie. There are viewers who watch a movie without inhabiting the narrative world it creates. They say about going to the movies, 'I can take it or leave it.' There are other viewers – clearly, I am one – that are turned on simply by the act of watching a movie, any movie, almost no matter what narrative world the movie creates or how skillfully it creates it. It is the dark, the screen, the movement on the screen in the light in the dark, the staring at the light in the dark and at the movement in the light. Like addicts, these viewers become restless if too much time passes without seeing a movie. They are, to others' incredulity, indiscriminate in their choices and the pleasures they take in their choices. They say, 'There is always *something* to enjoy in any movie.' Often, these 'addicts' are ashamed of their greed, their omnivorous appetite for movies, their lack of discrimination. In a group that contains such addicts and a lot of 'I-can-take-it-or-leave-it' moviegoers, the latter are bemused by the former and the former tone down their enthusiasms. This member difference, like others, interferes with people talking openly with each other.

Nevertheless, I have never heard these addicts – no matter how ashamed they might be to confess their addiction and the lack of taste or discrimination that goes with it, or how reluctant to have it marked and ridiculed by others – express any desire to be cured of it. Quentin Crisp writes in his 1989 book *How to Go to the Movies*, 'Life is a disease for which the movies are a cure...'[71]

There are parallels here to clinical work. These differences and their consequences have implications for what we espouse as the ideal way for a psychotherapist or psychoanalyst to listen. Watching a movie, one may say, 'I was not involved. I felt distant. I was not transported.' Listening to a patient, one may say, 'I was bored. I couldn't get into the story he told.' If I am the viewer or psychotherapist, I notice with regret that my refusing to inhabit a narrative world has left me withdrawn or passive and unable to manifest that activity of the mind I need if am to be transported, involved, if I am to enter into the world of the narrator. I am inclined to wonder whether I have refused the experience because it might have touched on something in myself, involved me in something that I did not want to own.

TWO MODES OF EXPERIENCING MOVIES

Once viewers are transported, they tend to choose one of two modes of experiencing movies. Having entered and inhabited a narrative world, they seem to have primarily one of two different kinds of interest in it. Furthermore, their grounds for evaluating a movie as good or bad seem to depend on which of these two kinds of experience or interest they have had.

In the movie group, these two modes of experiencing movies often conflicted. There were struggles over which one was legitimate, which one was right, which one was to dominate. Such struggles had all the passion of ideological warfare, with one side rejecting and belittling the perceptions, cognitions, and feelings of the other.

I tend to feel that arguing leads to polarization, the *blues* and the *reds* squaring off against each other. I want group members to stop fighting each other long enough to reflect, hoping then that they may realize each of them to some extent within themselves is both blue and red. That means the task is not to reconcile blue-member and red-member combatants, or for blue members to defeat red members. The task for all group members is to help each other find a way to acknowledge and integrate the blueness and redness within themselves. (But, even as I write this, I wonder about its adequacy as a generalization about group and organizational life. What about the *real*, irreconcilable value-differences and conflicts of interest that certainly must sometimes exist within and between groups. What is the risk of approaching such conflicts with the idea that they can be resolved somehow at an intrapsychic level? What place does the brutal struggle between armed forces, the naked use of power to win, have in everyday group and organizational life? When is the task for the blues and reds to mobilize for war, each using whatever resources and power they have to ensure that they eject the opposition and make the group or organization theirs?)

THE REALISTIC/MORAL MODE

The first mode of experiencing a narrative world is 'realistic' and 'moral'. A viewer comes to the movie with the desire to learn from the narrative world what the actual world is like and how to behave in it. 'How to behave in it' also includes what values to hold, and how to sustain, strengthen, and realize values in a world that may not be especially friendly to them. The movie is expected to represent the world as it is, and as it ought to be, which is assumed to be the function of 'true art'. I notice that if a movie disappoints these expectations, those who view it in this mode seem to criticize it with an especially intense moral indignation, bitterness, or cruelty, denigrating it as a 'Hollywood' product, and making insulting comments about actors' physical appearance, or about the audience's or other reviewers' mental deficiencies.[72]

In the realistic/moral mode, it is the proximity of the narrative world and the actual world that is a source of satisfaction. Any similarity between them, but especially similarities in what is *possible* in these worlds, enhances a viewer's experience of a movie. If a viewer in this mode were dissatisfied with a movie, that viewer's recommendation for improving the experience would be to make the movie in some way more relevant, more applicable, to problems and challenges in the actual world, or to make it contribute by its example to the way the actual world could and ought to be. 'I don't want these false dreams, this sentimentality. People suffer when they believe in illusions. They look for life to be like that, and invariably are disappointed and misled.'

What makes a movie, viewed in the realistic/moral mode, good? It is good if it is informative, if it adds something truthful or useful to the viewer's knowledge. It heightens the viewer's awareness of the human condition, of the complexities of human nature. Perhaps it provides the viewer with a 'script' that – remembered – will turn out to be helpful in navigating through an unfamiliar situation, or creates for the viewer a vivid sense of place not yet, but possibly some day, visited.

We should not suppose that a movie viewed in this way transmits its information, its message, intellectually, dryly, or baldly and directly. It arouses, inspires, elevates. The knowledge it offers is grounded in feeling, in tears or laughter. A novel thought, a fresh perception, an insight, as an object of passion, can make a viewer's heart beat faster. An experience of a narrative world that is as the actual world is, but ought not be, can make a viewer's blood boil with indignation and perhaps with determination to bring about change.

The ideas a movie conveys make possible a new way of looking at and understanding oneself and the world. It is transformative. It brings about some significant and lasting change in viewers, just because it is subversive. As it adds new ways of looking at the world, new knowledge about the world, new ideas, it subverts existing beliefs, views, knowledge, ideas.

Since the ideas (including values) a movie presents may contradict social norms, it may choose to represent these ideas indirectly. It may disguise what it wants to say by presenting its opposite with deliberate irony. The subversive message may be delivered ambivalently. It may be merely suggested by, or an unwitting side effect of, plot exigencies. Along these lines, Basinger in her 1993 book *A Woman's View: How Hollywood Spoke to Women 1930–1960*, writes of the woman's film,

> A woman's film is one that places at the center of its universe a female who is trying to deal with the emotional, social, and psychological problems that are specifically connected to the fact that she is a woman. These problems are made concrete by various plot developments, and since they are often contradictory, they are represented in the story as a form of choice the woman must make

between options that are mutually exclusive... The presentation of the woman's world allows for both an overt indication that women should lead conventional lives and a covert form of liberation in which they are shown doing something else or expressing anger about this need for conformity...

To convince women that marriage and motherhood were the right path, movies had to show women making the mistake of doing something else. By making the Other live on the screen, movies made it real. By making it real, they made it desirable. By making it desirable, they made it possible. They gave the Other substance, and thus gave it credibility. In asking the question, What should a woman do with her life? they created the possibility of an answer different from the one they intended to provide at the end of the movie.[73]

In this mode, a bad movie is one that misleads a viewer. It provides no clues, it does not indicate in any way, that its picture of the world is a lie. It implants false beliefs in viewers about groups of people who are 'different' or 'other', supporting bigotry and injustice. It may lead to 'romantic' illusions about love, friendship, or family life, therefore to expectations that are inevitably disappointed, and so to troubled interpersonal relationships and personal unhappiness. It may model amoral or immoral behavior, which might be imitated by the viewer, to the world's sorrow.

THE HEDONIC/ESCAPIST MODE

The second mode is hedonic and escapist. (*Hedonic* is from the Greek word for *pleasurable*.) A viewer's desire is to be transported into a narrative world that contrasts in crucial respects to the actual world and is an alternative to it. This viewer comes to the movie with a wish for a pleasure that, for various reasons, is very probably (and sometimes certainly) inaccessible in the actual world.

V. F. Perkins cautions us not to be snide about escapism, writing, 'Too strong an emphasis on what the movies allow us to escape *from* (the rain, overcrowded houses, financial problems or whatever) distracts us from the more positive function of escapism, ignores the importance of what we escape *into*.'[74]

In the hedonic/escapist mode, while some similarities between the narrative world and the actual world are necessary if a viewer is to be able to enter the narrative world at all, *similarities* between what is *possible* in these two worlds is *not* what enhances a viewer's experience of a movie. Rather, it is what is possible in the narrative world that is *impossible*, or at least that is very *improbable*, in the actual world – or that perhaps the viewer would not want, hope, or expect to be possible or to become an actuality in the everyday world – that enhances a viewer's experience of a movie.

A movie is enjoyable, not because it presents recognizable aspects of the actual world, but because it draws the viewer into a fabulous, a mythical, a fictive realm of imagination. To the extent it reminds the viewer of any other world at all, it is because it contains allusions to other fictive worlds. It evokes memories of other movies, stories told and read, pictures seen and music heard. The viewer selects a movie of a certain genre, values what is remembered and familiar, enjoyable just because it is familiar – familiar genre conventions and fragments, personas, voices and gestures, props. But a good movie does something with these, gives a twist that is a bit of a surprise.

What makes a movie, viewed in the hedonic/escapist mode, good? It is good, if it more or less covertly subverts, not beliefs in this case, but social rules, codes, proscriptions having especially to do with pleasure. To some degree, it opens a door to pleasures in the imagination that society may regard as perverse or kinky. Quentin Crisp is frank, and speaks for many others when he writes, 'What I always want from any movie is a saga of human depravity...'[75]

Literally intoxicating, using cunning strategies, a good movie skillfully overcomes, sneaks by, or soothes away those of the viewer's anxieties or moral imperatives that are obstacles to various kinds of pleasure in the actual world, and so makes them realizable in imagination. It takes a viewer who is willing to drink and then makes that viewer drunk with words, stars, close-ups, gestures and movements, song, dance, spectacle. To some degree, it transcends the ordinary, freeing the viewer from the actual world. It heightens experience. It expresses the inexpressible. It releases what is pent up and imprisoned. It soars. Exhilaration, elation, and piercing delight are its effects. Its gifts to the viewer are great moments, great scenes or set pieces, memorable faces, over-the-top performances. While a viewer in the realistic/moral mode tends to like performances that are understated, laid back, minimal, detached, which, by convention, are experienced as more realistic, ordinary, everyday – and disdains or is uncomfortable watching performances that are over-the-top – a viewer in the hedonic/escapist mode tends to value performances that are extravagant, operatic, pull out all stops, and to experience the understated performance as flat. Needless to say, neither style of performance is more realistic nor less realistic in any absolute sense; depending, for example, on culture or occasion, we can – easily or with difficulty – find either style in everyday life.

A good movie experienced in the hedonic/escapist mode is magical, flaunts its use of magic unashamedly, evokes wonder. Spells are cast. Passions are storms or consuming fires. Impossible events occur. The movie takes the viewer to distant times and exotic places she or he has never before visited and is never likely after to visit.

Whatever else, a movie viewed in the hedonic/escapist mode gives pleasure. It is interested in the body and in the pleasures of the body. A good movie viewed in the hedonic/escapist mode is – and for some viewers this is the ultimate accolade – entertaining.

Like other dreamers, quasi-reclusives, and those stuck-at-homes who are confined by the external circumstances of their lives, I am grateful to movies for such experiences as these. They widen my actual life beyond the walls that contain it. Through them, many places, events, objects, people, feelings, and pleasures become part of my experience that would otherwise remain foreign or unknown.

Crisp's advice to us about how to go to the movies declares its allegiance to this mode of experiencing movies.

> The way to go to the movies is incessantly. The more often we visit the cinema, the more exciting the experience becomes, not the more boring, as one might have expected. Films teach us how to see them; they are written in a language that we must learn... The way to go to the movies is reverently. We must be prepared to believe in the most improbable hypothesis, provided that it is presented to us with sufficient conviction, enough passion. We must surrender our whole beings to whatever reaction the story demands – gasping, laughing, weeping, wincing, sighing with utter abandonment... If we go to the movies often enough and in a sufficiently reverent spirit, they will become more absorbing than the outer world, and the problems of reality will cease to burden us.[76]

In the hedonic/escapist mode, a movie may be judged to be bad by a viewer when it has not been skillful enough to overcome, sneak by, or placate that particular viewer's anxieties or moral imperatives. These, operative in the viewer's everyday life, remain obstacles to the dangerous or forbidden pleasures the movie offers. Viewers are uncomfortable, turned off, hate the narrative world they have entered.

A movie may be judged bad because it is neither daring nor creative. It fails to transcend the prosaic and ordinary. There are few if any moments and few if any things in it that are memorable. It is tedious. It imitates without variation elements of other narrative worlds, other movies. It does not find a felicitous mixture of the new and old. It does not surprise.

If viewers in the hedonic/escapist mode were dissatisfied with a movie, their recommendation for improving the experience would be to make the movie more airborne, more fantastical, more gratifying. They would try to join with the movie in creating a narrative world that is different in crucial ways from the actual world and that may substitute for it for a while. These viewers make their insistent demand that a movie have a 'happy ending' – no matter how inconsistent that ending is with what they do know, and know they know, about the actual world.

WORRIES ABOUT MOVIES AND BEHAVIOR IN THE ACTUAL WORLD

Those who view movies in a realistic/moral mode are especially likely to be concerned that people may be moved to terrible deeds, recklessness, or imprudence as they imitate what they see in the movies. I cannot find evidence for anything like that in me. I feel that, seeing movies, I become a better person. Even when scenes violate my own norms, it is as if they drain pools of tabooed potentiality out of me. Whatever impulse in me corresponds to these scenes, it finds relative satisfaction in the viewing of them.

I have rather the difficulty sometimes, escaping into a movie's pleasures, of later becoming more impatient with my life, with others. A movie will remind me of, and leave me with, unslaked desire. If it does, since I have chosen to view it in the hedonic/escapist mode, I consider it to have failed as a movie.

Violence in the actual world is unpleasantly frightening. The prospect of violence in the actual world arouses anxiety. Sexual acts under certain circumstances or of a certain kind may in the actual world be morally repugnant or regarded as disgusting. But a viewer in the hedonic/escapist mode regards a narrative world as an alternative world, as a substitute for rather than as a guide to the actual world, and in that sense regards the movie *as having nothing to do with the actual world*. For that kind of viewer, the movie's narrative world does not serve as an occasion of temptation that is likely to lead to action in the actual world.

Similarly, a dreamer permits transgressive desire and action in dreams, because at the moment of this experience sleep makes action impossible. It is unlikely that the dreamer will repeat actions from dream scenarios in waking life. It may be the same with a viewer of a movie. The possibility of acting to obtain again in the actual world what the movie's narrative world has offered is remote, when there is a reliable boundary between the two worlds. That boundary helps to render quiescent the anxieties and moral scruples aroused by what is transgressive in the movie. The viewer accepts the movie's pleasures.

It may be quite otherwise for a viewer who regards a movie as a guide to the actual world and, therefore, *as having everything to do with that actual world*. Of course, that approach to movies may have useful consequences, because – like any stories – the tales movies tell may have a moral, may instruct, may provide information that can serve as a guide to action, may influence beliefs, may impart or invoke values, and may even call for and inspire actions. But there is a worrisome danger in this approach. There are movies most of us – and then we say society itself – would prefer not serve as models for action in the everyday world.

A THIRD MODE?

It might prove useful to distinguish a third mode of experiencing a movie, an aesthetic mode. But I am inclined to see viewing a movie in this mode as a specialized instance of viewing a movie in an escapist/hedonic mode. Here, as in the escapist/hedonic mode, the emphasis is on pleasure. But the pleasure comes especially and additionally from an appreciation of craft. The viewer focuses on and responds to skill, to the director's cunning, the actor's exciting vivid performance, the screenwriter's inventiveness, and the techniques the art designer, cinematographer, composer, and sound editor use to achieve their effects. This pleasure is apparently independent of any response to the narrative's content. 'Who cares what the movie was about! It was so brilliantly done.'

My guess is that many viewers who experience movies primarily in this 'aesthetic mode' are more likely than others to possess specialized knowledge or who are more than usually conversant with technical matters. However, it is also probable that many viewers respond unwittingly to the 'formal properties' of movies and derive pleasure from them. For example, such viewers may be drawn to and relish a Hitchcock movie without necessarily being able to articulate just what it is that Hitchcock is doing, just exactly *how* he makes a movie or tells a story, that gives them pleasure.

QUARRELING OVER MODES OF EXPERIENCING MOVIES

I do not think that I consistently favor one of the two major modes over the other. I have experienced movies in both ways. At various times in my life, I have gone to movies to learn about the world. It would be a mistake to underestimate the urgency of this quest just because it is directed to a movie. When I was a child, trying to understand my family, and the members of my family, I went to movies to find out what people are all about. When I was an adolescent, I wanted to figure out sex. At a still later time in my life, I wanted to learn how to face illness, aging, death. Furthermore, I have a strong personal disposition to adopt a moral stance in my everyday life, to maintain standards, to condemn laxity, to struggle to tell the truth, to tell the story of things as they are, and to despise prevarication and hypocrisy in myself and others.

But movies for me can also provide and increasingly have provided a blessed relief from the rigors and repressiveness of this stance. Movies are my preserve, where fantasy flourishes and pleasure wanders free. I go to movies to escape *from* and to escape *to*, to be delighted and entertained. It is not that at this point in my life I do so more than before, but that I am more willing now to say that that is what I seek.

Just formulating such a dichotomy tempts one to use these two modes to polarize people, to set one person or group against another, to take one stance and in taking it to dismiss another. But these modes may alternate in the same viewer, appearing – now one, now the other – in different responses to the same movie, on a particular occasion, or on different occasions or at different times in a viewer's life. Or the same viewer may bring one set of attitudes, responses, and standards to one movie and the other set to another movie. Furthermore, though two viewers may be in the same mode, a movie may not work for one, and be judged to one degree or another bad by that viewer, and still work for the other and be judged to one degree or another good by that other, because – this is just one possibility – they differ in the extent to which they are active, the extent to which they inhabit the narrative world of the movie.

In addition, a movie's success or failure, viewed in a realistic/moral mode, depends in part on viewers' background knowledge, because that will determine in turn whether they come with a lack – a desire to learn what the movie can teach – and whether they have the prior knowledge that is necessary to learn the something new the movie can teach them. Its success or failure for viewers in the hedonic/escapist mode depends in part on the extent of their willingness to go along with its strategies for evading their objections to the kind of pleasure it offers. No strategies for overcoming, evading, or placating a viewer's anxieties or moral scruples are foolproof. Movies that call upon background knowledge many different groups of people already have, or that have strategies of seduction that go over well with many different groups of people, are 'popular'.

All this I have said in an effort to avoid using these modes to dichotomize, compartmentalize, and stigmatize viewers. But, given what I have experienced in the movie group, I am still stuck with a problem. How incompatible are these two modes of viewing? How much does adopting one interfere with gaining access to the other? Are some movies, at least, able to sustain a viewing in both a realistic/moral and a hedonic/escapist mode?

Let us take *Pretty Woman* (1990) as an example, since it has aroused polar-opposite responses and evaluations. It is a fairy tale. A wealthy businessman hires a prostitute as a companion. The viewer is reminded of other stories or movies (for example, *My Fair Lady*, 1964) by the questions this story asks. Can this prostitute be educated to fit into the businessman's world? Of course she can. Will she pass the test? Of course she will. She falls in love with him. He struggles against his love for her. Is he the Prince she has been waiting for? Yes, he is. Will he rescue Cinderella from a life of squalor and carry her off to his castle? Yes, he will.

Pretty Woman evokes fantasies of transformation and rescue. It gives sensuous pleasure. We see, and we see the effects of, beautiful bodies, elegant clothes, jewelry, cosmetics, bubble baths, and simple lessons in table manners. We are in the narrative world of Cinderella, where there is much that is entertaining. In a hedonic/escapist mode, we enjoy all this, and evaluate the movie as 'good'.

On the other hand, in a realistic/moral mode, we may reject the prettification of the prostitute's life, the equation of personal desirability with access to and possession of material goods, the presentation of consumerism as the means to personal change, and the suggestion that a woman is dependent on men to change her life, that she must wait for a man to come to rescue her. We evaluate the movie as 'bad'.

But, in these evaluations, we have taken the story as the woman's story. Suppose we take the story as the man's story. Then we may experience the movie in a realistic/moral mode as having a piece of valid knowledge to transmit. We are in a position to learn something serious, that if you are going to have a relationship, you have to take some chances with your feelings, even if you have been hurt or betrayed before. So that now, although still experiencing the movie in a realistic/moral mode, we may evaluate it as good.[77]

Perhaps the popularity of this movie has to do with many viewers' ability to experience it in a way that gives them both pleasure and knowledge. The narrative world in which the woman is protagonist gives pleasure, when that world is experienced in a hedonic/escapist mode. The narrative world in which the man is protagonist imparts knowledge, when that world is experienced in a realistic/moral mode.

Movies give more leeway than is commonly appreciated to a viewer in choosing whose story the movie tells. A movie does not absolutely determine whom a viewer will choose to regard as the protagonist of its narrative world. Nor can the movie prevent the viewer from experiencing an apparently single story doubly, as two stories each with a different protagonist.

Similarly, as Basinger has explained about the woman's film, a lot of what a viewer might experience or say about such a film depends on whether the focus is on how it all ends – or on the various subplots or alternatives or obstacles encountered along the way to that ending. The so-called 'feminist' film *Alien 3* (1992) is an example of a film apparently quite different from those 1940s movies Basinger describes. It has a strong independent heroine, who faces danger, who is a leader, who needs no man, who is not interested in home or marriage – but who is boiled in oil at the end. What do we enjoy in this movie? What image of women, of the fate of independent women, does it leave with us?

If, on any occasion, we are each one of us capable of both viewing modes, and each mode has its value, and in that sense each is legitimate, why in group discussions should someone who favors one mode feel it necessary to reject the other mode? Why should another's response to the kind of experience a viewer has had in a movie's narrative world have such an impact on that viewer?

In the movie group, I have heard viewers who favor one mode, even if it be only on one occasion or in relating to one particular movie, dismiss the experience of those who favor the other mode. 'Love isn't like that at all', they say severely. 'That was totally sentimental. How could you let yourself be taken in by it? Do you mean that you were actually crying during that scene?!' At the same time they brace themselves against being similarly dismissed by someone saying, 'It's only a movie. It's fun. Whether it's "true" or not is beside the point. The very criterion of truth is inapplicable. It's not a documentary. Lighten up!'

Dismissive comments in a group discussion of a movie disinvite conversation. Making attributions of the movie as an object, as the text, rather than focusing on the inner experience that leads a viewer to want to make such an attribution, may shut people up or make them feel isolated, wrong, wanting to defend themselves. Discussions in the movie group provide many examples of one of the potentially pernicious processes discussed in Part 5: splitting, projection, and scapegoating.[78]

Suppose a group member, in a realistic/moral mode, is eager to talk about the ideas she gets from a movie, and another group member, who is in a hedonic/escapist mode, says with dampening effect, 'You're taking it too seriously! It's just a movie!' Perhaps this critic wishes to emphasize fun or pleasure, because he is especially reluctant to confront the implications the movie may suggest for the actual world. He disowns his own responses in a realistic/moral mode, and seeing what he rejects in her, deflates her and dismisses her ideas. Ashamed that she might yield to a movie's pleasant seduction, she, on the other hand, may have embraced ideas to abort feelings she otherwise might have permitted the movie to arouse in her. So, seeing in her critic what she wants to disown in herself, she rejects him as a lightweight, a romantic. Both have split feeling and thought. In each case, the experience rejected is discovered in the other and derided there.

I do know first-hand that someone *can* spoil an experience for me by putting down my values, taste, emotionality, or knowledge. 'How can you enjoy *Gone With the Wind* (1939) when it portrays African-Americans in the way it does?!' 'How can you enjoy *Pretty Woman* (1990) when its picture of a prostitute's life is so false?!' Or: 'Didn't it bother you that they got all the facts wrong?'

I feel different from others in that movies do not seem to mean as much to others in groups to which I belong as they do to me. I imagine the scorn of serious colleagues that I should take movies so seriously when the world is in such trouble and there are so many responsibilities serious professionals must accept to make it better. It is as if I stand condemned of frivolity in the face of others' suffering. But somewhere I myself must feel I should be taking care of someone, instead of fooling around. It is this rejection of the frivolous in myself that makes me especially vulnerable to those who wish to deal with their ambivalence by attacking one side of themselves in me.

Entering a narrative world depends on a willing yielding to illusion, a shutting out of illusion-shattering distractions. To experience a movie, to inhabit it, may hang on a precarious juggling of scruples and fears in a quest for fantasied wish-fulfillments, or a precarious juggling of a desire for new knowledge and anxiety about its implications. A viewer wants to avoid being thrown off balance. In that sense, experiences of movies are fragile, easy for others to destroy.

So easy, that if I learn something offputting about a star, I may find my pleasure in her or his performance spoiled. The old practice of keeping the true lives and personalities of stars secret, and of building a star persona the facts of whose life and personality were largely concocted or implied by a series of roles, had some sense to it. It was that persona and not the 'real person' who inhabited each different role.

Having done all that I can to escape splitting, projection, and rejection of another, I still cannot escape the impression that the two modes are crucially different and do seem to be incompatible, at least in some respects. Succinctly, the point of reference or context for experiencing or interpreting a narrative world in a realistic/moral mode is what is existent and actual, while the point of reference or context for experiencing or interpreting a narrative world in a hedonistic/ escapist mode is psychic reality, what gives pleasure in imagination. It is clear to me that, for the psychotherapist at least, exclusive adherence to the realistic/moral mode will not do.[79]

Tuning in on the group-as-a-whole

In discussions of group processes or dynamics in the movie group, I encouraged members to view events, various interactions, for example, as episodes in a group-as-a-whole story. I also encouraged them at the same time to reflect on their individual responses to particular movies, and also on the way they worked as psychotherapists. From time to time, we would become aware that stories, themes, and motifs in all three contexts were similar. Reactions to each other, to movies, and to patients, and what ensued from these reactions, were similar. Becoming aware of these parallels seemed to hold out the promise of helping us struggle with our problematic responses to narrative worlds, which recurred over and over in all these different contexts.

But there was more than just promise. Out of the sometimes exhilarating and sometimes difficult experiences I had in the movie group, I came to some understanding of my own feelings about, and relation to, group life. Here, as I and others struggled with the problems that arose when we attempted to share experiences with each other, I did find some little piece of the integration of the individual and social aspects of myself I had set out to discover.

Three ways of listening

In telling about the events that occurred in the movie group, I use three ways of tuning in on a group-as-a-whole.[80] I emphasize thematic or formal affinities, or similarities, among the various things group members say, and so infer from these affinities or similarities a wish, fear, or solution they *share*. I listen as I would as an individual psychotherapist or psychoanalyst, treating the flow of speech in the group as if it came from a single person. In both cases it is probably an oversimplification to think that only one thing is being expressed or represented, but one may want legitimately to focus on what is dominant, primary, or most 'highly charged'.

Influenced especially by my work with David Berg, I listen a second way. I observe a *pattern* of contributions, each one representing a different aspect of a group dynamic, each one quite different, but fitting together like pieces of a jigsaw puzzle. One person's role may be to represent a disturbing wish, feeling, or impulse to express such a wish or feeling. (Such disturbing wishes or feelings in group life may be reactions to some feature of or change in the group's situation – an opportunity, the availability of a facility, an inducement, a threat. In this particular group they were often evoked by the movie seen.) Another person's role may be to represent a reaction to that disturbing wish – for example, a fear aroused by it. The roles of others may be to represent possible resolutions, each giving a different weight to the gratification of the disturbing wish relative to the weight given to the fear-motivated rejection of that wish.

Whitaker and Lieberman's *Psychotherapy through the Group Process*[81] may be read (oversimply, perhaps) as proposing that one of these, the wish, the fear, or the resolution, were primarily at a particular moment being expressed in some form by most group members. In the same way Bion in *Experiences in Groups*[82] seems to suggest that at a particular time all group members join in one basic assumption about what the group meets to do. But it is also possible to listen as if what we have in what group members say are parts, each person giving an incomplete piece of the whole, each person specializing in some part of the dynamic process. If I listen then to the group-as-a-whole as if I were piecing together a jigsaw puzzle, what I come up with is a picture of a dramatic situation, with all its elements in tense relation to each other.

However, if I listen to the group-as-a-whole in a third way, as if I were watching a drama enacted, then the pieces are linked the way a story links episodes or a scenario links scenes. I am not now interested in a picture, an at-this-moment dramatic situation. I am interested in a process of action, in sequences of events, in a succession of states and states of affairs. What's going on? How did it get started? What is the problem, desire, obstacle, conflict? How is it expressed? How does it eventually come to be perceived by the group members? Toward what end does this series of linked events seem to be heading? Does it get there?

In listening to a discussion of a particular movie, if we put the pieces of the discussion together and see what pattern they form, rather than choose any piece as dominant or primary, and especially if we link the pieces as episodes or scenes in a story, then we may get back to the movie itself. We may ask, 'What is it about the movie that makes it capable of evoking these different responses? What is it about the movie, the story it tells and the way it tells that story, that produces this parallel process, this story the group is enacting?' (This last question is a difficult one. I discussed it early in this chapter. It is hardly addressed, and certainly not adequately addressed, in my story of the movie group. But it is raised by the method used, the discussions held, in that group.)

Movies often do tell a story about wishes, the fears associated with them, and the way conflicts between wishes and fears are resolved. But it may be the way the movie tells its story, not just the content of the story told, that represents, suggests, or evokes the different and often conflicting wishes, fears, and resolutions in the members of the group watching it.

The psychoanalytic candidates

In one movie group made up of psychoanalytic candidates, we watched *Kings Row* (1942), *The Magnificent Ambersons* (1942), *The Picture of Dorian Gray* (1945), *Black Narcissus* (1946), *Jezebel* (1938), and *The Big Sleep* (1946).

The movie *Black Narcissus* (1946, color, British) is about a group of nuns who start a mission in a remote outpost in the Himalayas. The movie begins when a young nun is made the sister superior of the new mission. There are questions about whether she has the wisdom and experience to take on such leadership. She is told by her superior: 'The superior is servant to all.' She struggles throughout the movie with her pride in being elevated over others, exhorting herself 'to learn not to be superior to others'. This theme evoked no responses by group members – who were psychoanalytic candidates – that involved their experiences encountering or exercising authority.

One of the nuns, Sister Ruth, is jealous of the young sister superior, feels belittled by her, and resents her relationship with a male British government agent in the outpost. She decides to leave the order. Suddenly she appears in a red dress and makeup, and makes her way through the jungle to the house of the agent, where she declares her feelings for him.

There were gender differences in the group members' responses to this episode. The two women in the group felt more involved in the movie than the men in the group seemed to be. Furthermore, they were pleased and excited by the transformation of Sister Ruth. They did not see her as the men in the group did, as crazy or demented, but rather as breaking free from the restrictions of the order. But they felt sad and disappointed that her leaving the convent hadn't led to anything but her subsequent attack on the sister superior and her falling to her death. The men in the group, on the other hand, were not exhilarated as the women were, but instead felt uneasy, anxious, and frightened during the scene where Sister Ruth appears in a red dress. The men saw her as looking like a character in a horror story. One of the men saw her as physically exciting in this scene. I had remembered the dress as a vivid scarlet although on this viewing I saw it was actually burgundy. (Another contrast in the responses of men and women in the group appeared in a later discussion of *The Big Sleep*. The women thought that the wit and repartee in the movie were erotic; the men didn't think of it as having to do with anything sexual, in a physical sense.)

Many men in the group felt disconnected from the film. 'Nuns are weird.' One man told about seeing nuns play sports when he was a child and thinking with astonishment, 'They are people!'

Black Narcissus depicted the nuns as overcome by the erotic atmosphere of the mission. Disturbingly sensual paintings are everywhere on the walls of the mission, which had once housed a harem. Erotic statues loom up in the jungle. A young prince runs off with a seductive native girl. The camera focuses on the agent's naked thigh. But a number of men in the group commented that the heterosexual elements seemed pallid and unexciting to them. The sister superior's memories about the time before entering the order when she was in love seemed to them to lack vividness. For them the man she loved had no reality. We then noticed that the most intense relationship in the movie is between two women. The disturbing paintings show naked harem women sporting with each other.

Men are portrayed as intruders, outsiders, nuisances; they are dissolute, unable to love, callow, or macho.

There was a strong moral tone to the discussion about the end of the movie. These candidates seemed to be very disappointed that the women continued in the religious order. The group members had hoped for some dramatic change. 'There was no real change in these people. Nothing happened in the end.' By implication, it seemed to me, deciding to continue a religious life, homosexual choices, and renunciation of desires were for the group members not 'good outcomes', although they presumably had been exposed in their training to the idea that psychoanalysts ordinarily do not have a stake in what particular life choices analysands make as a result of a psychoanalysis.

Presumably, they also were attentive in their work as psychoanalysts to small apparently unimportant details, especially as signs of inner change. Yet the momentous hand touching between the sister superior and the dissolute agent at the end as they take leave of each other (she does not pull her hand away but lets it linger in his) was experienced by the group members as 'nothing'. To me, however, this scene clearly signified that he who had been unable to love now loves, and that she loves him in return even while accepting that this love will find no expression in action.

Representations of women

In the first version of the movie group whose members included psychiatry residents, psychology fellows, social work and nursing staff, and rarely a faculty member, all from the Department of Psychiatry, we watched movies linked by the theme 'the way movies have represented women': *Pandora's Box* (1928, silent, Louise Brooks), *Morocco* (1930, Marlene Dietrich), *Now Voyager* (1942, Bette Davis), *Gilda* (1946, Rita Hayworth), *Double Indemnity* (1944, Barbara Stanwyck), and *Sunset Boulevard* (1950, Gloria Swanson).

The group had approximately three women and six men. The women participated less than the men in the discussion. Instead of being struck by the strength of the women film stars, the men responded to the physical attributes of the women these stars portrayed. Perhaps put off by the way the men clubbily discussed the representations of women, or by the representations themselves, the women in the group did not return to the following year's version of the movie group.

Representations of monsters and others who are different

In a second year's go-around of the movie group, with the essentially all-male composition of the group in mind, I chose three movies that told stories about 'a man who is a monster or in some way beastlike, savage, grotesque, or defective': *King Kong* (1933), *Wuthering Heights* (1939), *Laura* (1944). Then, as what was going on in the group influenced my choice of movies, I expanded the theme to include stories about 'a man who is different or deviant': *Maurice* (1987, color, British), *Women in Love* (1969, color, British), *The Barefoot Contessa* (1954, color), and *12 Angry Men* (1957).

The group did include one woman, who at first said she would be unable to attend, then said she would try to come, but each time canceled. She did come for the last few sessions, after having asked me repeatedly if she was welcome in the group. In the final meeting that year of the group, she upbraided a male resident who referred to women as 'girls'. Perhaps having expressed how she felt enabled her to join the group during the following year.

In this 'men's' group, comments about the absence of women were made in every meeting. The men had mixed feelings about their inability to draw women into the group. They felt it would be a better discussion if their women colleagues were present. There was something anxiety-arousing about talking intimately with other men. On the other hand, they also felt there was something relaxing and fun about being an 'all-men's group'.

LAURA

The group members ran into difficulty in the discussion of *Laura*. They could not mention, much less talk about in any matter-of-fact way, the various perverse trends depicted in the movie: for example, the epicene aesthete, who was jealous of the heroine's relationships with men with 'strong bodies', relationships he did everything he could to destroy with his viperous wit; the detective with a metal leg who fell in love with a dead woman, as he voyeuristically gazed upon her portrait and read her intimate letters.

MAURICE

The ability to talk about sexuality and various kinds of sexuality in a matter-of-fact nonjudgmental way is indispensable to the psychotherapist. I chose *Maurice* for our next movie. Homosexual desire and relationships were depicted with relative frankness in this movie, based on the posthumously published novel of E. M. Forster.

The movie begins by picturing two relationships. One is between two friends, Maurice and Clive, who meet at school. Clive thinks that anything physical will spoil the purity of the love between them. The text they study together is Plato, where the relationship is between an older and a younger man.

The second relationship is between a superior, a young lord, and an inferior, a soldier he is accused of degrading, for which he is imprisoned. His fate serves as a terrible example to Clive. He entirely rejects Maurice's love, and enters into what promises to be an unhappy marriage. Throughout the movie the shadow of social rejection and punishment lies over the lives of the characters, just as the group members became preoccupied with being rejected by others because of thoughts and feelings they had watching the movie.

The movie raises a question about Maurice and Alec, an under gamekeeper whose muddy boots the camera emphasizes. They are of different classes. Maurice at first treats Alec with contempt, and Alec Maurice with angry suspicion, but they come to love each other. Can there be a relationship between these two men – superior and inferior in terms of class, and therefore distrustful of one another – that is loving and lasting?

Viewers evaluating the movie in terms of knowledge of the actual world could not accept its attempt to portray the apparent realization of a loving, lasting relationship between members of different classes. They rejected a 'happy ending' that is clearly a wish-fulfillment: What after a while would the two men find to talk about?!

Early in the discussion, one group member, Ralph, criticized the aestheticizing of homosexuality in the movie, and made it clear that he was criticizing it as a person who was gay. Although this was as frank as anyone had been in the group, his criticism of the movie as an object left us in the dark about his actual experience watching the movie, which had led him to make such an evaluation of it. What was he thinking of that he felt had been left out? What was he thinking of that was not as 'pretty' as the movie presented it?

Joseph spoke next. He made no acknowledgment of what had just been said. 'I was interested until there was actual physical contact between the men. That was disgusting.' Others, as I learned later, were worried how Ralph felt when Joseph said that. So they did not confess to reservations similar to Joseph's, although they too had them. Instead, they argued with Joseph. As they condemned and disowned what he was saying, he became more and more extreme in his statements. 'It is like you are asking me to accept as all right someone's murdering their mother. You all discuss the movie as if something ordinary is going on in it.'

Bernie said, 'I am hesitant to confess that I was drawn into the movie. What does that say about me? How will others respond to such a confession? I cannot go into any detail about my experience watching the movie for fear of offending Ralph.'

Ralph said in turn that he had been unable to be honest in the previous discussion of Laura, in which everyone had ignored the gay subtext, for fear of offending the straight group members. Joseph immediately broke in to talk about spirituality in a love relationship. I found myself thinking about the importance of male bonding in social life. If I had been able to say something about this, I might have made a connection with Joseph, who was becoming increasingly isolated. But I felt that any comment about 'sublimation' would be heard as condescending or rejecting by Ralph.

So what we had was a number of men who didn't want to express the feelings aroused in them by depictions of homosexual relationships in the movie just after someone in the group had revealed he was gay, out of consideration for that person. But their refusal to acknowledge their own feelings resulted in isolating, dissociating themselves from, and rejecting someone else in the group, who was in some sense chosen and willing to be chosen to express the most unacceptable of those feelings for everyone else. Other members were horrified at how thoughtless, inconsiderate, and dense he was.

Joseph, who was left 'holding the bag' rather than regarded as a spokesman for others, and provoked into making more and more extreme statements, was ethnically different from other group members. That difference made it easy for them to project onto him attitudes they felt ashamed of, and to disown them and him.

Ralph told me later that he was struggling with whether or not he was being a wimp by not challenging Joseph who, apparently ignoring him, was condemning homosexuality. He also felt the protection of him by others was a kind of condescension implying that he was not capable of managing such attacks.

A lot of these processes got worked on in individual discussions with me, rather than more ideally in the group itself. I talked with Joseph about his complicity in his being scapegoated. Outside of the group, he understood what had happened. With me, and in subsequent meetings of the group, he was much less extreme and provocative, expressed his ideas quite differently, and so became much less a target.

WOMEN IN LOVE

There were two contrasting responses to Ken Russell's *Women in Love*, the next movie we watched. 'It was phony, pretentious; I hated it.' 'It was operatic, camp, fun.' The movie was about two sisters, Gudrun and Ursula. Despite Ursula's demanding from her lover his love, entire and exclusive of others, a number of members liked 'the blonde chick' (Ursula), because she 'looked normal' and 'it's normal to want to be loved'. I heard the use of such an expression as 'the blonde chick' and the concern with normality as a protection against the development of more intimate relationships among the men in the group. The pull to normality was also a recurring reaction against the inevitable polymorphous perversity in the narrative world of movies.

The group members did not like the aggressive women in the movie (Gudrun and Hermione), who made them uneasy. I commented that no one condemning these women seemed to remember that Hermione had in fact become especially controlling after she made a sexual overture to Rupert and was rejected by him; cruelly, he winced and pulled away. Some members again brought up the absence of women in their group and the need to have women as members.

Male–female couples

However, when in an effort to make the group more welcoming to women, I asked a woman resident to help me lead the next year's version of the movie group, a number of men in the group were outraged that I would raise one of their peers above them, even though they understood what problem I was trying to solve. I had invited this particular resident to work with me because she had asked to speak to me, and told me something about her difficulties in the group when she was a member of it. She expressed a wish to help me with the problem of bringing men and women together in a group where they could talk together, since in the residency they had to work together.

We recognized that our acting as the group's co-leaders might backfire, because it again presented women with a version of their everyday world: a woman working with (in the shadow of?) a senior male professor. But we felt comfortable enough with each other and with how we intended to work together to accept the risk.

The major problem I had was to deal with my impulse to respond to the men's hurt feelings by downplaying the importance of my co-leader's position. I avoided doing this, and indeed made it clear to her and to others by my behavior that I took our collaboration seriously. The men more or less threatened not to rejoin the group the following year, but we were able to work through their feelings in a number of one-on-one discussions. They did rejoin the group, which on its next third go-around had something like twenty applicants (the previous enrollment had been seven), half of whom were women. Interestingly enough, for the first time, enrollment in the other seminars I offered turned out also to be roughly half women and half men rather than mostly women or mostly men. During this third year's version of the movie group, we saw movies that told stories 'about male–female couples'.

FLESH AND THE DEVIL

The first was *Flesh and the Devil* (1927, silent, Greta Garbo). There were two reactions, both about the character played by Garbo. Neither was exclusively a reaction of just men or just women. One was moral, treating the character played by Garbo as a real person, and condemning her as a bad woman. She had come between two friends and, in the absence of one with whom she was supposedly in love, she married the other, apparently for his money. But Charlotte, a resident and the co-leader of this version of the movie group, said after quite a while into the discussion that she had had a pleasurable fantasy in which she was a beautiful seductress and had great power over men. Her comment was ignored by others in the group. The second reaction was hedonic and focused on Garbo the actress rather than on the character she played and on the sensual pleasure of looking at her body and watching her gestures and movements as if watching a dance. This was not an instance of the 'male gaze', 'objectifying and fetishizing the woman', for in fact one of the two who were able to confess responding in this way was a woman, interestingly enough a woman from another culture. (I was the other.)

PRIDE AND PREJUDICE

After watching the next movie *Pride and Prejudice* (1940), the group members, again taking an objective moral stance, praised the character Elizabeth played by Greer Garson for her spirit and intelligence, expressed reservations about the character Darcy played by Laurence Olivier, and rejected the character Lady Catherine played by Edna Mae Oliver as arrogant and overbearing. I, on the other hand, expressed being stirred by the moments of leavetaking in the movie. I was especially moved to tears by Olivier's voice at such moments. My comments led nowhere. I also introduced some recollections evoked by the movie of what it was like, after going off and becoming educated, to feel ashamed of one's uneducated family – likewise, no one picked up on these. What did engage group members was a 'sociological' discussion of what it was like to be a woman at that time and to have to consider the economic consequences of not marrying or not marrying well.

I was impressed by the largely 'realistic', moral, judgmental, and evaluative tone of the discussions to date, which had also been full of silences, heaviness, a palpable reluctance to speak. All this invited a consideration by the group of its own process or dynamics. We discussed what kept us from achieving our goal, which was, viewing a movie, to be able to pay attention to our own experiences and speak openly and freely to each other about them. Certainly that at sixteen members we were not quite a face-to-face group. Certainly that we only met once a month and so did not have the time or continuity that would be necessary for us to come together as a group. But most certainly that we were a group whose members were divided by their differences.

Although both movies had centered on relationships between men and women, watching them had not so far stirred up any apparent interest in sharing observations or experiences of the relationships between men and women in the group. But the gender division in the group, the history of the relationships between the sexes, was not the only division leading to distrust and the inhibitions of expression that were apparent. What was the contribution of the divisions between old and new group members, between those who met together with me in some other seminar each week and those who had no other contact with me, between psychiatrists, psychologists, and nurses, between members of different ethnic or racial backgrounds, between members of different generations, between those who had dinner together before the movie and those who did not join the group for dinner?

THE SEVENTH VEIL

In our third meeting, we watched *The Seventh Veil* (1945, British). Ann Todd plays Francesca, a concert pianist who is unable to play the piano after her hands are mildly burned in an automobile accident. Though her physical injuries are minimal, she tries to kill herself.

In an attempt to 'cure' her, a psychiatrist elicits her story while she is under narcosis. As a young girl she had been left as ward to her second cousin Nicholas, played by James Mason. He is a misogynist recluse who in many scenes sits beneath a portrait of his mother. His mother had abandoned him to run away with a man. No one is ever to mention her. He had vowed that no women shall ever enter the house. When Francesca first comes into her new home, she tries to embrace him. He pushes her away violently and limps off, leaning on his cane. The house is a house of men; it is silent and lonely.

Discovering Francesca's musical talent, Nicholas lures her into playing for him, devotes himself to making her into a fine concert pianist, controls every detail of her life. She desperately wants his approval. Her first concert is a nightmare; throughout it, she is remembering when she had been caned on the hands while a young girl in school, resulting in her losing a musical scholarship. She is in terror that she will lose the use of her hands during the concerto.

Nicholas prevents her from marrying when she falls in love with a young bandleader. Later, she tells Nicholas defiantly she is determined to go off with the painter whom he had hired to paint her portrait, even if this means giving up her career as a pianist. Enraged, Nicholas tries to hit her on the hands with his cane while she is playing the piano. Terrified, she runs off with the painter, and they wind up in the automobile accident in which her hands are burned.

Now, the question posed by the movie is: 'After her psychiatric treatment, when she recovers her ability to play the piano, to whom will she choose to go – Nicholas – the bandleader – the painter? Whom does she love and who does she feel is the one that loves her and cares for her?' She comes down a long staircase and goes past the psychiatrist, the bandleader, the painter, who wait in the great hall, to Nicholas who has limped off to his lonely den.

Ruth said she was deeply affected by the movie. She is a pianist and it stirred up memories of her own life experiences. Dick said he always identified with the oppressed. He felt Francesca was oppressed by Nicholas and he didn't like Nicholas. Carl said she had chosen the wrong man at the end; he didn't like Nicholas either. Maureen said she hated Nicholas. There were other voices expressing disapproval of Nicholas, categorizing him along with other sexual abusers of women.

I, on the other hand, spoke of my reaction to the wordless scene in which Nicholas sensitively lures the shy young girl Francesca, who has refused to play for him, to the piano by playing the piano himself until, rapt, she joins him. I also said jokingly in a deadpan voice that Nicholas was a vampire. I meant to convey that he was a creature of the imagination, the dark man, who could be appreciated only as a reappearance of the silent limping Byronic hero who inhabited the world of literature. However, people seemed puzzled by my comment if they noticed it at all; no one responded to it.

The chorus of moral condemnations of Nicholas and discussions of sexual abuse continued. I was too inhibited by the force of these denunciations to point out that those seeing Francesca as a helpless victim ignored her own self-characterization when, in narrating her story, she had said about herself that her childhood girl friend Susan was always getting her into trouble and that she always went along with Susan even knowing that she, Francesca, was the one who always got punished. I imagined with what disapproval such an observation would be received. But I felt the disapproval coming at me from others, rather than recognized that something in me was not happy with what I myself must have experienced as my own apparent callous complacency in the face of Nicholas's cruelty.

Indeed, I was caught up in judging, in being cruel. For I found myself asking myself, 'How can these people be psychotherapists, when they are so self-righteously rejecting of what they regard as "bad" in people?' In this, I am Nicholas, impatient with the one he is teaching, her betrayal of her own calling. The process in the group is parallel to the one in the movie, and I no more than any one in the group can escape participating in it.

I remembered how, as a teacher, I struggled with what to say when a trainee was comfortable enough with me to burst out with, 'I hate this patient! He uses and abuses women!' I was baffled. Could she actually feel that there was nothing in her that corresponded to what she found so reprehensible and distasteful in him? The tragedy was that it was just that that stopped her from seeing he hated himself for what he did. That was why he had come to psychotherapy. She saw only the defensive bluster, the smooth arrogant self-satisfaction, which excited her loathing. I didn't know how to say to her, 'But if you cast him out, how do you help him to change?' without betraying her trust in me, without her hearing my question as the deepest criticism of her, as stigmatizing how she feels ('yours is not an appropriate attitude for a psychotherapist to have'), as my casting her out.

I shrugged off, I fled, from these complexities. I argued the position I had taken. I told the group that after I had seen the movie for the first time, it had lived on in my imagination. Some years after seeing it I was working at an army post as a psychiatrist. I was called in as consultant. A young private had been brought into the hospital, unable to speak. Every time he tried to speak, his jaw went into spasm. The doctor was about to perform an invasive diagnostic procedure.

I tried to interview the patient with no success. Dimly remembering *The Seventh Veil*, I decided to try sodium pentothal. The nurse brought in the tray just as in the movie, but I found the patient asleep. I thought to myself, 'Why wake him up just to put him to sleep again. Why use the sodium pentothal at all? What if I just wake him gently and while he is still half asleep interview him?' That's what I did. It worked. Without hesitation or difficulty, he told me his story.

His commanding officer had sent him to sick call. The doctor, a captain, said there was nothing wrong with him and sent him back to duty. His commanding officer observed him and sent him back to sick call. The captain told him angrily that he was malingering, and that if he appeared at sick call again he would have him court-martialed. Whereupon the young private fell to the floor, silent, his jaw in uncontrollable spasm. This was a highly adaptive symptom, since if in his frustration and fury he had attacked the captain even verbally he would have been in serious trouble. As soon as he had told me his story, the symptom disappeared. He turned out to have double pneumonia and remained in the hospital for treatment.

As the hero of this story, I saw myself practicing creatively, and furthermore as rescuing someone who was a member of a system in which authority may be and in this case was abused. I was taken by surprise then when Bernie made a jibing, mocking comment that he guessed he would learn how to be a psychiatrist from the movie *Silence of the Lambs* (referring to the murderous, cannibalistic Dr Lecter in that story). I said with some feeling that his was a very cutting comment. I felt but did not say that the cruelty in his comment paralleled the cruelty depicted in the movie. I experienced Bernie's voice and the judging voices as other incarnations of Nicholas.

I went on to say that I felt oppressed by the judgmental tone of the discussion, the righteous attitudes expressed. Bernie was joined by Carl (both members of the group previous years) in complaining that they didn't know what I wanted from them. I seemed to want people to be more personal, but when they said they hated Nicholas they were speaking out of strong feelings and so felt they *were* being personal. What would satisfy me?!

Those group members who had been studying their own group process in another seminar and in particular talking about authority and how they depended in unnecessary ways on me alluded knowingly to those discussions, which Bernie and Carl had not been part of. Boris said heatedly to Bernie and Carl that they were 'old members', that it wasn't their group anymore, that there were new group members who were going to make this group the kind of group they wanted it to be. Bernie and Carl wanted to know why I got to choose the movies; Ron said that he liked that I chose the movies because then he saw movies that he would not otherwise ever see.

I tried to clarify that the question for me was not being 'personal' or autobiographical, but rather of talking about one's own inner experience watching the movie rather than about the movie or the characters in the movie as objects 'out there'. This continued to be puzzling to group members, who thought when they talked about Nicholas they were talking about their own inner experience.

However, the tone of the discussion began to change somewhat. In particular, both Ruth and Maureen became less vague and spoke movingly and in more detail of the actual experiences they had had in their lives involving conflicts between the demands of career and relationships.

Boris raised a question about whether the 'old members' of the group resented that one of them, a woman, had been chosen by me to be the co-leader of the group. I thought that Carl confirmed this impression by then attacking Charlotte while seeming to defend her, saying in effect that she was a sham co-leader because she didn't participate in choosing the movies. So I said, 'In this group right now, not just in the movie, a woman is being abused!' I thought to myself that these same people, when they presented their own clinical material for group discussion in psychotherapy seminars, were nervous about their colleagues' criticisms. What kind of experience would Charlotte have had if she had chosen a movie, only to have it criticized and rejected by group members?

Charlotte asked others how they experienced her as a co-leader. Many said in effect that they didn't experience her as a co-leader. She replied that she had thought that many times she had spoken and contributed something to the discussion as a co-leader but that she found that, unlike what happened when I made a comment, group members largely ignored her comments. She was not concerned about choosing the movies because she thought there were other ways she could function as a leader and she was willing to treat the whole experience as an experiment, to go with the flow, and to see how things went. It seemed to me that group members silently treated what she had said as if it was merely a self-deluded rationalization by a woman who could not see that she was being 'abused'.

In the end, I interpreted what was going on. I saw an effort by group members to ignore their own role in creating or unmaking a leader, and in particular their competitiveness with each other and their refusal to permit any one of them to emerge as a leader. They disowned the fights going on among themselves. They sought instead to focus on fostering a quarrel between the co-leaders and watching that fight 'out there' that for each one of them then had 'nothing to do with me'.

Many group members remained silent. Boris said that he would not talk about his own experiences in this group, not because he was afraid of the leader, but because he felt in danger from other group members. The meeting ended with a strong shared sense that this had not been much fun and that the evening had been a difficult and rather unpleasant one.

After the meeting, Charlotte told me that she felt that women in the group desperately wanted my approval and thought that they could not get it. This was the story of Francesca and Nicholas relived in a group whose members were unable to talk about it!

I learned during the week following that Bernie and Carl had felt the jibe about *Silence of the Lambs* was justified by their concern that psychiatry as a discipline not be made ridiculous by associating it, as I did, with movies. Bernie felt that perhaps he and Carl didn't belong in the group any more and should leave it. Boris felt that Bernie and Carl were seething with resentment over the choice of Charlotte as co-leader and were so preoccupied with that they could not join or permit any discussion of the movie. Amy told me she was worried about just what sort of person I was; I experienced again the chill of belonging to a group in which everyone, including myself, sat as a judge over everyone else.

THE WAY WE WERE

Charlotte and I met again. She had said repeatedly that perhaps it would be best to let people discuss the movie any way they wanted. I now agreed with that. I felt both I and the group members had to be freed from the yoke of my image of what a good discussion would be like. They would only hear any further explanation by me of the group's goals or reasons for discussing movies in a certain way as evidence of my continued dissatisfaction with them. So we decided to lighten up, and at the next meeting simply to acknowledge, without a heavy discussion, the difficulties we had been having, and just see how the meeting went. I would as much as possible let people know how I experienced a movie, but not in the spirit of 'do it like me' but rather curious about differences in the way we had experienced it. Having been made aware in the meantime of how much many group members hated talking about the group, at the last minute, before the meeting began, we decided together not even to say anything about the previous meeting.

I showed the movie *The Way We Were* (1973) in our next meeting. In this movie a couple struggles with and is ripped asunder by differences in their images of the ideal life, just as the group members and I seemed unable to agree on an image of the group and its goals. In particular, he finds her idealization and expectations of him dispiriting and ultimately intolerable, just as the group members felt burdened by my expectations.

I had not been able to think of a way of talking directly about what happened in the previous group's meeting without its being heard as an argument, a criticism, an expression of dissatisfaction with the group members or with the way the group was going. I thought that perhaps by picking a movie that was quasi-contemporary and in color, the kind of movies some of them said they would like better, I might communicate, 'I have been listening; I have heard you.' By responding to the plight of the couple in this movie, I could convey, 'I know how it feels for people when someone about whom they care imposes an ideal and expectations.' Increasingly, but especially when I am caught in a situation where I find that the very act of interpretation exacerbates the problem I intend my interpretation to illuminate and mitigate, I have preferred in my clinical work to see if I can begin the process of confessing to a mistake and exploring its consequences or the process of making an interpretation by telling a story.

The Way We Were meeting turned out to be quite enjoyable. People were involved with the movie; one member had seen it many times and cried throughout the viewing. Men as well as women talked about the star presence, the intense magnetism and attractiveness, the ability to light up the screen, of Robert Redford. There was a good deal of talk about the nature of the problem the couple had. He can write; she cannot. He is attractive; she feels ugly. She is passionate and full of conviction; he jokes, is detached, and full of doubts. She is Jewish; he is gentile. Group members were even able to mention in passing experiences and fantasies involving relationships between Jews and gentiles.

Group members alluded to similar difficulties they had had in relationships in which opposites attract. Why are such attractions so intense? Why is it so difficult to get out of such a relationship? You are dissatisfied with yourself. Something is missing. Something is unacceptable. You see in someone else what is missing, what you would like to be or have. You grab onto any hint that this someone else has what you would like to have. You idealize that person. She or he struggles against expectations that cannot be fulfilled, but at the same time is attracted to you for the same reason you are attracted to him or her. You have something that she or he feels is lacking. Each member of the couple is intensely attached to the other who is carrying a valued piece of herself or himself. Though neither can stop trying to control the other or struggling against being controlled by the other, they cannot separate either. They cannot abandon what each feels is a missing valued piece of themselves.

The reemergence of 'moralistic' judgments occurred in response to the scene in which Barbra Streisand seduces a drunken sleeping Robert Redford by getting in bed with him. How could she permit or enjoy his having sex with her when he was drunk and asleep and could not even remember what had happened the next morning?! No one in the group seemed able to imagine simultaneously what this experience was like for each of them, identifying with both of them, and imagining the experience from inside their skins in a way that would make what was exciting or pleasurable about it self-evident.

GREAT EXPECTATIONS

For the next meeting, I chose the movie *Great Expectations* (1946, John Mills and Valerie Hobson). I commented to the group before the viewing that, in response to their curiosity, I had been thinking about what led me to choose the movies I chose. I thought, in addition to being meaningful to me, a movie had a good chance of being chosen if it reminded me of some other movie we had seen or of something going on in the group. This was an example of the same attention to similarities that I found useful in my psychotherapeutic work.

The discussion that followed was lively. Ron began it by saying he wanted to guess what other movie *Great Expectations* had reminded me of and why. He thought I had been reminded by Pip's embarrassment when his brother-in-law comes to visit him in London of the shame Elizabeth had felt about her family in *Pride and Prejudice*. A number of people talked directly and movingly about the experience of rising socioeconomically or leaving their country of birth. These changes to a new world had led to feelings of distance from their families. With the differences in level of education or style of life, it felt like there was nothing any more that was shared, nothing any more about which they could talk together. (For one person, on the contrary, it had led to a greater appreciation of the family's qualities and values.)

I talked about the importance to me in my relationship to them of trying to bridge the gap between generations, so as not to repeat the experience of separation and loss in my relationship to my origins. Myra said, 'Perhaps that is why it is important to you to show us movies in black and white, from an earlier time, important to you in your life. Perhaps you want to know that we will not reject you as old-fashioned or be unable to talk together about something that is not part of our lives.' I expressed appreciation for this insight.

No one brought up the way in which the many instances of cruelty in Dickens' world might have reminded me of *The Seventh Veil*. I told the group that such was the case. In the discussion that followed, the members' attitude toward a man's cruelty (Nicholas's) seemed quite different from their attitude toward a woman's cruelty. The woman (for example, Miss Havisham in *Great Expectations*) was perceived as sad, as having suffered; it was difficult to remember that the same might have been said of Nicholas. We talked some about the universality of cruelty, its origins in experiences of being hurt, and the terrible remorse that follows one's realization that one has been cruel. The judgmental tone that had previously so disturbed me seemed to have disappeared from this discussion.

The last two movies we watched were *The Postman Always Rings Twice* (1946, Lana Turner and John Garfield), and *Notorious* (1946, Ingrid Bergman and Cary Grant).

The moral of the story of the movie group

Was the enterprise of the movie group, the task I had set it, not merely difficult but impossible? Somewhat discouraged, I wondered if the gap between me and the group members was inevitable. Often, it felt to me as wide as the Grand Canyon, and quite possibly, given where they were in their lives and careers, unbridgeable. (I see now how splitting or polarizing aspects of oneself, disowning one of these, and rejecting it in others and so rejecting others led to discouragement in the movie group just as in clinical settings.)

The way I put it to myself was that the gap between us was not merely a difference in our modes of experiencing movies, but – what amounted to the same thing – a difference in our stance toward psychic reality. For them, or so it seemed to me, a movie had something to say about the actual world. It illuminated 'real life'. For me, a movie illuminated, if anything, a possible world, the world of imagination. It was not a documentary. I experienced a movie as a work of imagination, the imaginations of those who created it, and in my viewing it a work of my own imagination. A movie and its characters were not for me things 'out there' with objective properties of their own, but were instead an expression of my own subjectivity. A movie for me was, while I was watching it, my own dream, daydream, fantasy. I realized that to watch a movie as a realization of one's own fantasy is the criterial attribute of a mode of experiencing a movie that I was beginning to identify and call hedonic or escapist.

The characters in a movie were figures on the stage of my own mind, imagined by me, part of me. Watching *The Seventh Veil*, I was Nicholas, I was Francesca, I was the bandleader, the painter, the psychiatrist. Each one was an incarnation of some aspect of myself. What one of them was capable of, I was capable of. Under circumstances in which one of them felt remorse, I too would feel remorse. No one of them was disowned by me, put out there to be judged by me. No one of them was 'the other', and 'nothing to do with me'. They were all me, and I regarded my creations, these selves of myself, as no more to be judged, as no more providing evidence of my moral irresponsibility, than the actions of figures in my dreams.

When Nicholas, 'mon frère, mon semblable', was attacked in the group, I also was attacked. No wonder I experienced such distress during the group's discussion! It was as if I had reported a fantasy or dream to a psychoanalyst, and she had responded, 'What a bad, cruel person you are!'

It is my enduring quarrel with group life that it is so often dominated by scapegoating processes. Members join together in disowning rejected aspects of themselves, attributing what is disowned to a chosen Other, and then attacking or in some way getting rid of the Other. Groups judge. Groups arouse guilt. Groups shame. Groups extrude. But I have wanted instead – and this was true even before I participated in psychoanalysis – to live by what for many is merely a cliché: Nothing human is alien to me. That I brought such a wish with me to psycho-analysis may have been what made psychoanalysis such a 'right' experience for me when I came to it.

To the extent I can avoid participating in the pernicious group processes of splitting off what is rejected from what is accepted, projecting what is rejected and unwanted, and attacking what is now 'out there', there is nothing human that is unimaginable to me, that I cannot find somewhere in myself, that I would regard as 'nothing to do with me'. But, of course, I cannot always avoid these pernicious processes. I am enmeshed in them when I become impatient or discouraged with other group members, when I oppose – as I just have – 'them' and 'me'.

I do not wish to condemn but rather to observe, to wonder at, to be curious about, what I or others *imagine*. Further, even when I cannot take pleasure in *what* I imagine, I take pleasure in the act of imagining. For me, this attitude has everything to do with whatever abilities I have as a psychotherapist and psychoanalyst. But, my moral self now hastens to add, a commitment to 'nothing human is alien to me' does not mean that I do not hold myself responsible for what I actually *do*, or actual others responsible for what they *do*. It may be that a psychotherapist cannot function without a capacity for moral indignation. But it's also true that a psychotherapist cannot work with a patient he rejects as alien. He needs some link to the patient, some feeling, even when the patient behaves badly, that 'there, but for the grace of God, go I. I don't like what he does, I think it's wrong, but I can imagine myself capable of it.'

I said to myself then after *The Seventh Veil* meeting that, if this is me, then my uneasiness in this group and in other groups as well, and my enduring lover's quarrel with group life, are honorable. I decided then and there that I would no longer deplore my uneasiness as if it were simply a matter of social awkwardness or being a difficult person. I would no longer regret the pain this being at odds with others brought. I knew once and for all about myself – here I imagined myself taking a heroic stance – that I would not give up this necessary quarrel.

In retrospect, that heroic state of mind, even if it has some truth in it, strikes a false note, because it does not do justice to the mind's complexity. Now I would emphasize that this quarrel is essentially within myself, between the severities of my own morality and the seductions of my own imagination. Now I wish that I had found some way to say to the group, 'We all experience impulses to judge, criticize, and condemn. Just as you reject characters in the movies we watch, so I criticize you for doing so. But what we want to work on together is how to understand these attitudes, and what to do with them when they are unwanted, other than to ignore or deny them. Can we in some way use our awareness of them to understand whatever process it is in which we are engaged when they surge forth?'

What is the moral of this long story? Here it is, in a memorable excerpt from a poem by Suniti Namjoshi, quoted by Marina Warner in her 1995 book *Six Myths of Our Time*.[83]

> *And all the little monsters said in a chorus:*
> *You must kiss us.*
> What! You who are evil,
> Ugly and uncivil.
> You who are cruel,
> Afraid and needy,
> Uncouth and seedy.
> *Yes, moody and greedy.*
> *Yes, you must bless us.*
> But the evil you do,
> The endless ado.
> Why bless you?
> You are composed of such shameful stuff.
> *Because, said the monsters, beginning to laugh,*
> *Because, they said, cheering up.*
> *You might as well. You are part of us.*

CHAPTER 14

Diversity and Group Formation

Marshall Edelson

I find that occasionally, and especially after strife-ridden meetings, or slow sticky beginnings, I feel, 'This group will never get off the ground! Its members will never draw together, will never connect!' Remembering the quarrels and the periods of apathy and withdrawal from participation that I had encountered – for example, in the movie group – I am tempted to think, 'Suppose the leader of a group – a community meeting in a residential treatment center or inpatient unit, a psychotherapy group in an outpatient clinic, an executive group in an institution, a committee, a seminar – had the power, as it was being formed, to decide on its composition, to choose who its members would be. Wouldn't it be great, really help get the job done, if he chose members for the group who were homogeneous!'

I am especially likely at such a moment to remember trying to treat both patients with schizophrenia and patients with asocial or antisocial predispositions in the same group on an inpatient unit. The two subgroups responded very differently to the same intervention by the therapist, a comment concerning, perhaps, the way in which some members in the group had treated other members of the group as they lived together on the unit. A blunt confrontation, cutting through evasions, lies, justifications, would, sometimes at least, get the attention of some members of the asocial/antisocial group, even result in their being at least transiently thoughtful about the consequences of what they had done, while at the same time members of the schizophrenic group would spiral into a despond of guilt. It seemed a bad idea even to have such different kinds of patients living on the same unit, for those who were asocial/antisocial exploited and victimized in various ways the more vulnerable schizophrenics, making the setting far from a 'therapeutic' community for either.

But then, of course, reservations kick in. There are many dimensions on which people can be alike or different, age, gender, socioeconomic status, race, ethnicity, interests. I ask, 'Homogeneity on which dimension?' I answer, 'Well, it would be nice if the members were homogeneous on just that dimension where difference is likely to generate obstacles to the group achieving its goals. How pleasant it would be to watch and discuss the experience of seeing a movie with people whose mode of viewing was like my own! No quarrels. No hurt feelings. No spoiled experiences. No stretches of silence and heavy-going. Instead, like-minded people glad to be together, feeling safe with each other, wanting to share their responses to the movie, their thoughts and feelings, their fantasies, with each other.'

But, of course, this is no answer at all. I had seen often enough, even where there is likeness on one dimension, other differences interfere with achieving a valued goal. I certainly don't mind the differences in capacities, skills, knowledge, role, and life experience that contribute, often each different contribution indispensable to achieving the goal. I just wish – futilely of course – that we could do without the differences that divide members of the group from each other and them from me, that keep us from coming together, from feeling safe with each other, from enjoying and being together. But what if you can't have the differences that make a contribution without the differences that seem to make trouble?

A work group's identity, its boundaries, depend on its task(s). To figure out who needs to be in the group, what its ideal composition would be, I have to have analyzed that task, so I know what steps must occur or parts exist, and how these are to be coordinated, and who will do what, if the group is to accomplish its task(s).

But each person I select is at the same time an individual personality and a member of one or more than one identity group, and in an organization also a member of one, and sometimes more than one, subtask group, which is responsible for a particular step or steps that must be taken, or a particular part or parts that must be in place, if the group's goal is to be reached. Inevitably, given differences in the subtask groups and the particular values associated with, and skills and knowledge needed for, each of their particular task(s), and the differences in the identity groups, how they are perceived, and their different histories, including the histories of their experiences with each other, no matter how much solidarity or shared commitment there are, there will also be conflict, competition for resources, and ways of experiencing the same events that clash with each other. And I realize that these inescapable differences will exist, and will have helpful, problematic, or indifferent consequences, before I have even taken in the inescapable presence of various idiosyncratic motivations, traits, histories associated with different personality systems, which will have in turn their helpful, problematic, or indifferent consequences.

In deciding how to select the members of this task group I am forming, I struggle with dilemmas – questions each of which seems to have equally good but contradictory answers. But underlying all the questions is a question about the value of heterogeneity or difference compared with the value of homogeneity or similarity in a task group.

In forming the group, should I give priority to division of labor, which means differentiation of roles, or to an egalitarian diffusion of responsibility for the task? If the first, each group member is responsible for a specific step, aspect, or subtask needed to achieve the group's objective. On a clinical team, then, every relevant discipline is represented, and each member of a different discipline is responsible for a distinctive specific subtask.

But emphasizing differentiation will usually result in hierarchy and differences in status. It usually leads to members competing for resources. It may lead to splitting and polarizing group members along fault lines having to do with the different competing and sometimes conflicting values, norms, or priorities that are associated with different steps, aspects, or subtasks. It also may lead to the envy and resentment that go with the perception that someone has a subtask – for example, psychotherapy or pharmacotherapy – that current ideology favors, or that is less unpleasant or more gratifying than one's own. In other words, in making the choice to maximize differentiation for the sake of efficiency in use of resources to achieve tasks, I run the risk of unwittingly encouraging conflict, the strains that go with conflict, and the possible stalemates that may result from conflict.

Then, for the sake of harmony, solidarity, and morale, should I diffuse responsibility for each step or subtask among all group members? No one is held to only one role. Anyone may substitute for anyone else in representing or carrying out a step or subtask. On any matter, the opinions of all carry equal weight. Everyone on a clinical team, for example, is an expert on everything. Everyone does everything.

But then what happens to accountability? How do we locate where responsibility lies? If everyone has it, no one has it. If no one has responsibility, some things that need to be done fall between the cracks. What about the costs of having those less competent carrying out subtasks that other members of the team are more competent to carry out? What about the demoralization of those who are unable to exercise the special skills and competencies they have?

Should a psychotherapy group be composed with an eye to maximum diversity (along what dimensions?) or with an eye to maximum homogeneity (along what dimensions?)? The first choice (diversity) again maximizes the probability of conflict, of polarization (men against women, ethnic or racial minorities against the majority, the young against the old), of scapegoating and even extrusion of someone felt to be alien or different (he is different; it's his problem, not ours). The second choice (homogeneity) may result in the absence of experiences, points of view, knowledge, skills that might be helpful in trying to solve a shared problem.

When selecting members for a group, and charging the group with specific responsibilities, should I make sure that every other group that the work of this group I am forming is likely to affect has an explicit representative? Should I convey the expectation that each of these other groups so represented will organize itself, so that its representative, before participating in this group, will have consulted with its members, who will have adequately informed her about their views, wishes, fears?

I believe in clear assignment of responsibility, knowing and explicit representation, and the allocation of skills and resources with more regard for what will get the job done than for the prestige-and-status-seeking needs of the people involved. Yet I also value experiences of harmony and solidarity (although my tendency to embrace the role of gadfly and questioner often deprives me of this that I value). I shrink from polarized arguments and combat. I know that people's commitment to getting the job done will diminish if they feel demeaned, slighted, frustrated, or threatened by differences in authority.

I am strongly tempted to simplify by creating a polarity. One can be a feisty battler for what's right, someone who likes to organize powerless groups so that they can take on authority, who loves a good fight, who doesn't mind calling to people's attention the unbridgeable gulfs that divide them. Or one can be a peaceable person, wanting groups to organize themselves so that they can carry on rational conversations with each other, resulting in the solution of problems they are willing to acknowledge sharing. Either/or not both.

It is preposterous – this wish we humans have to rid ourselves of the complex dilemmas we ought to have the strength to contain and integrate within ourselves! To disown either I have to forget much of what I know about myself.

What I have tended to do (this is only one kind of solution of some of these dilemmas) – for example, in organizing a clinical team or community meeting in a residential treatment center – is to emphasize differentiation of roles and explicitness of representation, and try to deal with conflict by creating adequate opportunities for consultation. Each group has the chance to share with all other groups what its particular goals or responsibilities are, and so what associated values, interests, and resource-needs it has. Each group shares with all other groups its fantasies about how any proposed step or changes will affect it. Others take these fantasies seriously, testing their reality in discussion, and developing joint plans for dealing with and mitigating possible adverse consequences for any particular group.[84]

In composing a psychotherapy group, on the other hand, I go for homogeneity at the level of a shared goal or problem. Every group member struggles to reach this goal or wants to solve this problem. I go for heterogeneity or diversity within that homogeneous group. Collective attempts to reach a shared goal or deal with or solve a shared problem then can draw on a variety of cultural, economic, generational, gender, class, and occupational experiences, points of view, knowledge, capacities and skills in the group.

Homogeneity at the level of goal. Heterogeneity at the level of means. Solidarity here – as in the clinical team with highly differentiated roles and explicit representation – comes from the sense that 'we're all in the same boat making for the same destination' as well as from the sense that 'we all have something distinctive and valuable to contribute to getting us at last to port'.

I do try to avoid one situation: having only one member of a particular identity group assigned to a psychotherapy group (or, if I can possibly avoid it, on a clinical team or any work group as well). In such a situation, all of the group members are like each other but different from that one member with respect to identity (one woman/man in a group of men/women; one nonwhite/white in a group of whites/nonwhites; one old/young person in a group of younger/older persons; one psychotic patient in a group of nonpsychotic patients with character disorders). The other group members tend to perceive everything the person who is different says or does, without regard to its relevance to the shared problem, as expressive of his or her idiosyncratic identity. That person may end up feeling undervalued or overvalued, but in any event is likely to be isolated as 'different from us', and therefore to become the repository of everything we would like to disclaim or disown in ourselves: 'nothing to do with me'.

There are very few Prosperos in group life, willing to acknowledge that what they regard as dark, ugly, bad, weak, or deplorable is in themselves and not just in the other, and to say then of themselves, as Shakespeare's Prospero did of Caliban, 'This thing of darkness I acknowledge mine.'

CHAPTER 15

Morality

David Berg

I would like to use the two Houses of the Talmud, which I described in Chapter 5, to comment on the struggle that any clinician or teacher and indeed any group member participating in group and organizational life needs to wage to retain a sensitivity to moral distinctions. And, under certain circumstances, to take stands founded on these distinctions without becoming moralistic, that is, without succumbing to what we might call 'moralism' (as opposed to 'morality').

Moralism is the presentation of one view, one House of the Talmud, without any acknowledgment of the other side and its role in creating that view. Moralism prefers a single outcome, certainty. It brooks no dissent. It sets itself against a process in which dissent is honored. Moralism satisfies our desires for order, clarity, and certainty with respect to questions of right and wrong, sometimes at the expense of our acceptance that actual situations are in fact chaotic, complex, and all too often much more ambiguous than we would like them to be, and therefore equivocal with respect to questions of right and wrong.

As I comment on the moral, I am aware of venturing into very treacherous (I use the word knowingly) waters. But I do think that morality is the system of values and beliefs that emerges from a commitment to follow a certain process, and for me that process always involves at least two sides or points of view and room for dissent.

Similarly, the dilemma that the works of Alcott and Thoreau pose is like the never-ending dilemma posed by the two Houses of the Talmud. Even though neither of us chooses to live in isolation nor to become fully enmeshed in a utopian community, we feel the need to bring both kinds of longings, however opposed they seem to be, along with us as we confront organizational life. Alcott's views help us reclaim our idealism and hopes for collective life – that things can be better – when our frustration with others, and with intractable obstacles (apparently unalterable conditions), threatens cynicism and despair. Thoreau gives us each a place to go when we are in danger of being oppressed, suffocated, overwhelmed by the demands (psychological and physical) pressing upon us in our communal involvement.

PART 4

Using and Abusing Authority

There was an Eastern king who heard about Moses. He heard that Moses was a leader of men, a good man, a wise man, and he wished to meet him. But Moses, busy wandering forty years in the desert, couldn't come. So the king sent his painters to Moses and they brought back a picture of him. The king called his phrenologists and astrologists and asked them, 'What kind of man is this?' They went into a huddle and came out with a report which read: This is a cruel, greedy, self-seeking man. The king was puzzled. He said, 'Either my painters do not know how to paint or there is no such science as astrology or phrenology.' To decide this dilemma, he went to see Moses, and after seeing him he cried out, 'There is no such science as astrology or phrenology.' When Moses heard this he was surprised and asked the king what he meant. The king explained, but Moses only shook his head and said, 'No. Your phrenologists and astrologists are right. That's what I was made of! I fought against it and that's how I became what I am.'

Old Jewish Story, as told by
David Rapaport

CHAPTER 16

Leaders and Followers

Marshall Edelson

A leader knows he needs information if he is to be able to cope effectively with malintegration within a group (or organization) and with its relations to other groups (or organizations) in its external situation. An effective follower provides such information, about both happy and unhappy developments. An effective follower does not come to a leader mainly with requests for help in doing a job, nor repeatedly with burdensome requests for additional resources. He reports problems, usually with a proposal for dealing with them or at the least a set of options for the leader to consider. An effective follower sees his role as one requiring him to mediate between those above him and those below him; he interprets, so to speak, the values, goals, situation, and problems of each to each.

However, there are leaders who want to avoid experiencing themselves as uncertain, ignorant, or incompetent, so they split off such feelings, disown and project them. There are followers who want to avoid experiencing their own sometimes cruel wishes to attack the authority on whom they depend, so they split off such wishes, disown and project them. The result of these and similar processes is that followers perceive leaders, and leaders perceive themselves, as containing whatever competence, memory for past experiences, or wisdom exist, and as exclusively able and inclined to evaluate and criticize others. And leaders perceive followers, and followers perceive themselves, as containing whatever incompetence, failures of memory, and silliness exist, and as exclusively deserving – and the injured objects of – evaluation and criticism.

When there is a collusion between leaders and followers to maintain this state of affairs, both act as if they are in agreement that leaders are never incompetent, forgetful, or ignorant, and never deserve or need to be evaluated or criticized, and that followers are never competent, never remember or know, and are always in need of being found out and corrected. So, it may seem, in the intergroup relations between healers and patients, for example, that healers contain all wellness and maturity, and patients all illness and immaturity. Similarly, in the intergroup relations between teachers and students, it may seem that teachers contain all knowledge and students all ignorance.

In such a world, leaders do not act as if they need information from followers. They do not seek to know what followers know, believe, feel, or think, or what experiences followers have. They do not want to be troubled; they insulate themselves. If followers try to communicate these matters, recognizing that to do so is to act responsibly as a follower, leaders disparage both what is communicated and the communicator. 'You are probably responsible for this state of affairs about which you are telling me. The problem about which you complain is your own fault, the result of some mistake or failure or defect of yours.' 'You've got it all wrong.' 'You're distorting.' 'You have limited access to what's really going on.' 'Your personal problems are getting in the way of your seeing things clearly.' 'That's interesting, but I don't think it's really as important as…' 'Why are you bothering me with this. That's just what I expect you to take care of. I've got all these other things to do.'

Both leader and follower collude to keep from exposing any mistake the leader may have made, or difficulty the leader is having, for any 'weakness' in the leader threatens both leader and follower. The follower communicates such criticisms clumsily, if at all. The leader learns to deflect such criticisms with explanations, assertions of good intentions, or counter-criticisms. 'This is what I was trying to do.' 'I did it for your good, the good of all, for the sake of the task.' 'I wouldn't have done it, if you had only…'

Other followers observe the unhappy fate, the putdown, of someone who questions or challenges a leader. So they learn to convey their criticisms of a leader indirectly, by attacking a follower, or the position of a follower, who is identified with, obeys, or agrees with the stand of, that leader. A pseudo-harmony between leader and followers is bought at the cost of strains among followers.

Such considerations lead us to ask, 'How do such processes affect the ability of the leader to lead? The ability of group members to carry out their tasks?' 'How does the nature of the relation between leaders and followers determine what kind of relations exist among followers?'[85]

My own experiences

I have been struggling with questions and feelings about authority all my professional life. As a psychoanalyst, I am of course familiar with the irrationality that swirls around relations to authority, and some of the reasons for it. However, it is one thing to understand those irrational currents when I am working in my office under controlled conditions that permit me access to the irrationality and at the same time permit me to reflect upon it. Keeping my head above water when I am participating in collective processes in everyday life poses problems of quite another order of difficulty. I have not noticed that psychoanalysts outside their offices are much smarter, more rational, or better behaved in their group and organizational lives than other people.

I am going to tell you some of my own experiences as a medical student, graduate student, resident, and junior faculty. I want to draw a moral from these stories. The moral has to do with contrasting my experience, for example, as a resident – what I felt and how I acted toward people who had authority – with how I treated residents when I became a chief of service, a person who had authority.

I would say in general that as a graduate student or trainee, I was a pain in the *tochus* to my teachers and my supervisors and administrators. At the same time, I feel that it was just this that helped me to gain confidence and to find my own voice in my practice as a psychotherapist. Without your own voice, there can be no spontaneity, and without spontaneity, what can the result of psychotherapy be? So, *pace* my teachers and administrators, I think in retrospect that it was useful that I was not easy for them.

Now the problem is that I believed – and all the trainees to whom I talk these days apparently also believe this about themselves – because I had certain experiences when I was in training as a fellow or resident, when I got to be in a position where I was working with residents, fellows, or medical students I would never treat them as people had treated me. I made that a promise to myself. Unhappily systems are so powerful, and the anxieties that go with authority roles are so strong, that the very people who say, 'When I grow up, when I get to the top, and am a teacher or a supervisor, I promise I will never act the way people acted toward me,' turn out to do just that. Generation after generation, each new generation treats the people under them in just about the same way they were treated.

Medical student

As a medical student, I spent six weeks on psychiatry. I was told to go in, interview a patient, and get a history. By God, I was going to do a good job! So I went and saw this middle-aged woman who was depressed. I did an extremely thorough examination. Among other things, I asked about her sexual history: I was going to do this; I wasn't going to be nervous about it. I was somewhat startled when the patient told me quite a bit about what was traumatic in her life in this area.

Then the Chairman of the Psychiatry Department met with all us medical students. I had written up and handed in the report of my interview. In front of all my fellow students, he accused me of damaging this woman. He said, 'We had worked very hard to get her to cover over. She is recovering. How could you do this!? How could you go in there and stir up all these traumatic experiences!? What the hell is the matter with you?' I cried (afterwards).

That was a very upsetting humiliating experience. No one had told me anything about the treatment plans. I suppose no one expected a medical student would do an interview like this. It was expected that I would be hesitant, lack confidence, and not pursue potentially embarrassing matters, in the usual way of a beginner. So that was my first experience being taught how to do interviewing.

This professor thought he would teach me a lesson, or protect my next patient from me. The next patient he assigned to me was mute. 'You can do no harm,' he seemed to be saying, 'because this patient can tell you nothing.' But I would not be punished; I was determined that he would not defeat me. I wrote a very long report for him of what I said as I mused out loud before the patient, and my detailed observations of the patient's nonverbal responses to what I said.

Graduate student

When I was a graduate student in psychology, I was in a seminar. The teacher of the seminar assigned the writing of a series of one-page papers. I wrote papers that were invariably two to three pages long. The teacher began to write notes on my papers: 'Grade: A. Please turn in one page!' Finally, he called me in for a conference. He said, 'I assigned one page. I want one page. Why aren't you giving me one page? I'm going to give you an F if you continue to do this.' I said, 'Well, it doesn't make sense to me that I should stop writing a paper arbitrarily at the end of a page when I still have things to say. I usually stop writing when I've said what I want to say. However, I understand that you have a right to ask for one-page papers.' (Here I indicate my recognition of and respect for his authority.) 'What I'm saying to you is that I'm going to continue to do what I've been doing. I'm going to write until I've said what I want to say. You can give me an F. I won't fight with you to get a better grade. I won't argue with you. But I'm going to do what I'm going to do.' And he said he was going to give me an F. He never did actually. I kept handing in two-to-three-page papers. He kept giving me As.

I felt good about this outcome. I hadn't questioned the legitimacy of his authority. I also understood that he didn't want to go blind or spend all his time reading papers. At the same time he heard me out. He didn't put me down. And apparently what I said did influence him.

We tend to forget that the self depends for its existence on social nutriment. Without some experiences like this, an individual's ability to stand up to authority shrinks and eventually dies. If rebellion is always treated as bad, if the outcome is always humiliation, suppression, failure, you give up. If no one values the self that is creative, challenging, and feisty, it dies. But if, for example, someone in authority gives you a job even though you come with a reputation of 'being difficult', as someone later on in my life did, in fact gives you the job just because of what makes you difficult, in other words, does value this very self that might make life less easy for him, then that self survives.

Resident

When it came time to take a residency, I looked for a residency where I could pretty well learn on my own. I wanted to learn from my experiences with patients. I didn't want to sit in classrooms. I did not enjoy meeting and presenting my work to supervisors, because I always felt overcriticized and paralyzed. If the supervisor said something to me, I felt I had to go do what the supervisor said.

I hated continuous case conferences because I would present work and everybody in the room knew better than I did what I should be saying to my patient, what was going on with the patient. I would go into a room with the patient, and all these voices now in my head would be saying, 'Say this. No, say that. No, better to say that.'

The person I liked best during my residency was the Psychiatrist-in-Chief who was in charge of teaching. He had no administrative responsibilities. His sole responsibility was teaching. Fortunately for me, he never wanted to say anything to me about my process notes or about my experiences with patients; he always wanted to tell me instead about his experiences in Budapest with Ferenczi and what had happened in his own life. So he and I got along splendidly. Everybody else complained about him, because they would go to him and say, 'I want to know what to do with this patient!' And he would launch into one of his stories about Budapest. All of the residents would get together and say, 'He's an awful supervisor. He never tells us what to do.'

Actually, he had written a paper called, 'Being rather than doing in psychotherapy'.[86] He said, 'Once you start getting preoccupied with the question "What should I do with this patient?", it means you don't understand something. So the answer is not to be told what to do. The answer is to figure out what you don't understand that's leading to the question "What to do?"'

I read omnivorously. I liked to read books. I would get very infatuated with a book and try out ways of thinking about what patients told me. Then I would get another book and it would tell just the opposite story and I would get infatuated with that story. I would try out ways of thinking, stretch them, and then finding them lacking in one particular or another, throw some things out, and retain others.

I also wanted to learn by trying things out that were not necessarily 'by the book'. 'This is the right, this the wrong, thing to do.' I was curious to see what happened when I was on my own. Of course, now I have no difficulty imagining people who are responsible for and have authority in the area of clinical care, their hair standing on end as they envision residents wandering about trying things out with patients just so that they can learn.

But there is a way of a trainee doing this responsibly. It involves knowing a lot about yourself (I had twice been in extended psychoanalyses before my residency), listening carefully to the details of the patient's stories and ways of telling them and relating to you, paying a lot of attention to your own inner experiences and to the patient's responses to your interventions, and while not being constrained by ideologies and theories not being ignorant of them either. (You cannot intelligently challenge or test a rule, attitude, prescription, or scenario unless you have absorbed it, know it inside out.)

Also, if you know how to listen, you will hear in what the patient says a message about some mistake you have made. (In Patrick Casement's book about psychotherapy *Learning from the Patient*, he discusses how the ability to listen to what patients try to tell you, most often indirectly, about some mistake you have made or are making, enriches your work as a psychotherapist.[87] When I was a teacher, a resident brought this book to my attention, and I ended up using it in my teaching.)

But I understand why those who have responsibility and authority are anxious about what residents might do as they learn, and it raises the question for me, 'How do we create a system where trying things out can be done responsibly, while still protecting the welfare of patients?' Is one answer to this question to work closely with a trainee, in a form of apprenticeship, but one in which the trainee is not kept down by criticism and constraints?

The first day I came onto the residency, I went to see a patient. Everybody else had just been assigned patients. They were all reading the charts. I said to myself, 'I'm not going to look at her chart. I'm just going to go in and see her. I'm not going to know anything about her. I want to see what's going to happen if we just meet as two people without my having information that might affect what might otherwise spontaneously occur between us. It is possible that I will learn from her what is in the chart but in a form that will be useful to our work together because it will be her own perceptions, her own way of putting things, that I will be getting.'

I found a very dour-looking woman in a rocking chair, rocking back and forth, her arms folded across her chest, glaring at me, not saying a word. So I said to her, 'Have you lost a baby recently?' because she looked sad and she was rocking with empty arms. She leaped to her feet and said, 'I'm not even married!' She was furious. But we were engaged. This very silent withdrawn suspicious person, who wouldn't talk to anybody, talked with me after that. (But I don't recommend, now that I know better, starting work in this way with an angry suspicious person who wants to maintain distance.)

I worked with another patient who had what I thought was a delusional system. Needless to say, he didn't regard it that way. He had written a 500-page manuscript arguing for his system. He got better as we worked together. About a year passed. He had given me the manuscript to read and study, because I was interested. Close to the time he was going to be discharged, he asked for the manuscript back. I said in essence, 'I've thought a great deal about it. I feel your illness is encapsulated in this manuscript. I would rather not give it back to you. I don't think your holding on to it would be helpful to you.' I received an urgent call from the medical director's office. 'Dr. Edelson, the medical director wants to see you.' I went to see the medical director. 'What are you doing!? I'm getting complaints this patient and his family are going to sue the hospital. You have to give this manuscript back. You cannot keep it.' I said, 'It's not good for the patient.' He said, 'Give it back.' I gave it back. (I would not now take the position I did then, in part because it would not simply convey my concern or caring; it smacks too much that I know better than the patient what is good for him.)

I had another experience in which I was treating a catatonic patient and I suddenly got an idea – I don't know where or how I got this idea – that maybe liquid rather than solid food would help this patient, who was not eating at all, to eat. Maybe if she would use a straw to draw liquid up, that might get some nourishment into her. So I tried to find straws.

I had left a message asking an aide on the unit to bring me in some straws while I was sitting with the patient. I wanted to be there with her while she was eating. The aide came in and said to me, 'I can't find any straws.' And I said in my most Sergeant Edelson voice, 'Get me some straws!' So he disappeared out of the room. I found out later that he went immediately to the Clinical Director and complained about being treated in this belittling way.

The Clinical Director was already annoyed with me because I never talked with him, consulted him, brought him my problems or thinking. Probably he interpreted my ignoring him as contempt for him and his position. He took away three or four of my patients and gave them to other residents. I felt humiliated in front of my colleagues, having my patients taken away and given to other people to work with them, with the to-me-especially-horrifying implication that instead of helping I was hurting these patients. I went to the Psychiatrist-in-Chief, the one with whom I liked working. I cried for an hour. The Psychiatrist-in-Chief didn't say much about my experience, but he let me cry and then suggested I have a glass of wine with my wife and go off together for the weekend to New York to see some plays. The Clinical Director never talked to me about the complaint of the aide. Another aspect of this situation I only found out later, although I must have had some sense of it at the time. The Clinical Director and Psychiatrist-in-Chief didn't like each other or work well together. Apparently each was dissatisfied with the distribution of authority and responsibility (one having authority in the area of and responsibility for clinical administration and the other authority in the area of and responsibility for teaching).

Residents were supposed to see each patient three times a week fifty minutes a time. I would use my judgment to decide on my own whether it made sense in every case to see a patient three times a week for fifty minutes each time. There was a gentleman foxhunter from the South who was an alcoholic. I thought it would be utterly useless for him to meet fifty minutes three times a week; given his background, cultural presuppositions, and personal style, he would not be able to use the period, end up feeling uncomfortable, and then with no compensating therapeutic gain suffer a drop in self-esteem. So I met with him ten minutes every day, seven days a week. He did fine on that regime, eventually joined AA, and was able to leave the hospital.

On the other hand, there was a young schizophrenic man that I saw with no limit on the amount of time except what my schedule imposed. So I might see him one, two, three hours – and I saw him almost every day for three years. This patient talked to me and taught me more about mental processes, mental illness, and psychotherapy than all my teachers and books. I am in his debt. The Psychiatrist-in-Chief would see the patient with me once a week instead of talking with me about my process notes.

When the Psychiatrist-in-Chief died, which he did during the time I was a resident, I went to see this patient. I started to cry. He held me while I was crying. After an interval, during which I gradually recovered from the death of the Psychiatrist-in-Chief, and once the patient was satisfied that I had recovered, he went berserk. He became extremely psychotic, erupted, became 'violent', had to be put in wet sheet packs. I went to see him while he was in the packs. He would struggle and struggle to get out of them. I sat there. I was not frightened; I knew the patient very well. One day – he was a fairly big man – he got out of the wet sheet packs. As you can imagine, to accomplish this is no simple thing. He stood there naked, grinned at me sheepishly, wrapped the sheets around himself, sat down, and continued to talk to me. He told me later that he was very concerned that I didn't have the strength to deal with him without the Psychiatrist-in-Chief. So he was essentially testing me to see if I could manage his 'craziness'.

One day we were talking in my office. I have a firm rule that my teachers put into my head: 'Never get between an angry patient – or any patient – and the door. Don't do that.' He got up and said, 'I'm leaving.' I said, 'No, you're not.' I got up and stood between him and the door. He sat down and we continued the session. The person who was supervising me at the time said, 'I could never have done that. If I had done that, I would have been so anxious that the patient or I would have jumped out the window. But you apparently were quite comfortable.' I think this supervisor was a good person with whom to work. He didn't say, 'You shouldn't do this. You shouldn't do that.' He tried to understand why it had worked that way rather than the disastrous way everyone would have predicted.

Eventually, I made out a discharge slip, as I was required to do, for this same patient. I wrote, 'Cured.' The medical director called me in and said, 'You cannot write "cured" in a discharge summary. This is a schizophrenic patient. You may write "in remission".' I said, 'I know this man is cured and I'm not going to write falsely on a piece of paper "in remission" when I know he is cured.' Somebody else must have made out the discharge slip because I know I didn't change it. I felt I would have been betraying my patient and expressing a lack of confidence in our work. This man went on to get a Ph.D. As far as I know, and I want to believe, he never had another psychotic episode. Which sometimes happens.

Of course, I did run a risk in taking this stand. Later, a letter was written in answer to an inquiry when I was being considered for a position, 'This man is good but can be very difficult to work with.' I got hired anyway, but it is possible I wouldn't have. You cannot tweak authority's nose without running risks.

There's no such thing as going around saying, 'I'm going to look for some benign authority who will be very nice to me and good to me no matter how skeptical, questioning, and challenging I am.' That takes the risk out of it. Then you're not really dealing in any realistic way with authority.

If you're dealing with someone in authority, that person is going to be something like the medical director. He has a job to do, which is different from yours. He has responsibilities at a different level from you. He has information about situations of which you know very little. He is likely to get annoyed, even mad at you, if you make trouble for him as he tries to take care of the things he is trying to take care of. So you run risks. You balance the risks that you run against the importance to yourself of being true to something in yourself, what you believe, doing the job you have to do (your work with your patient), which is different from the job of the person who works at a higher level than you do, and recognizing that you have information about situations of which that person may know very little. (I assume in all this that you don't have some mindless irresistible impulse to go around tweaking authority's nose for the fun of it.)

Army officer

When I was in the Army, which I entered after my residency, I saw a man in a military prison whom they were about to execute. I fought for a year to keep him from being executed. Essentially, I gave him an extra year of life, possibly to the exasperation of some in the system in which I worked, maybe all the way up to the Department of the Army in Washington. I had discovered an EEG finding that was correlated with assaultive activity. I argued that since it was possible that his behavior resulted from some kind of brain condition he shouldn't be executed. This led to habeas corpus hearings – which I found absolutely absurd. I would keep coming to these hearings. I would keep telling his lawyer, 'Don't ask me whether he knows right from wrong or is insane. These are not questions I can answer.' He kept asking me, 'Does he know right from wrong? Is he insane?' Of course, my answers were of no help to him in these hearings.

Chief of service

After the Army, I became Chief of Service on an inpatient unit in a university department of psychiatry. Although located in a university department, I was not primarily a teacher, although I did teach, gave seminars, supervised trainees. I was primarily a clinical administrator, responsible for a clinical unit and for the patients on that unit. I was anxious. This was my first faculty job and my first job being in charge of anyone or any clinical enterprise.

Here is the moral of this story, and the point I am after in telling all these stories. My whole behavior toward the residents was as if I had never had any of these experiences I had had. I really wanted submissive residents. I wanted them to follow orders. I wanted them to do what I told them to do because I kept having fantasies that they were going to cause me trouble by doing something wrong with one of the patients. I immediately regarded any resident that didn't do what I wanted as a sociopath. (Some of these 'sociopaths' have gone on to become heads of departments.) As far as I was concerned, how they behaved represented a real defect in their characters. I did not hesitate to convey to a resident, 'There's something wrong with you, bud. You can't follow orders. You can't do what I tell you to do.' Some of the residents I apparently worked very well with, but perhaps that was at least in part because they tended to be residents who were more acquiescent, you know, nice people, who would do what you told them to do.

There were a couple of psychoanalysts around this department. They speculated to themselves and to the residents, 'How did Edelson get so fucked up? Something must have gone wrong with his analysis.' Now unless I'm going to come to a similar personal pathology diagnosis (that is, Edelson *really* has trouble with authority), I have to ask myself, 'How weird it is that having had these experiences earlier in my life and having the conviction I had about what led to good learning, I should take this attitude toward trainees once I was responsible and in charge.'

Of course there was bound to be one occurrence or another that seemed to justify the way I treated the residents. I had written a note in the chart about a man who had had an agitated depression, who was recovering. I wrote, 'This man looks like he's much better. But this is the time a person like this is most at risk for suicide. He's been after me for a pass for the weekend. Do not give him a pass.' Of course, the resident on call talked to the patient, talked to the patient's wife, both of whom were insistent, wrote a pass for the weekend and the patient killed himself. Then I could feel perfectly comfortable acting toward residents as I acted, because my worst fears had turned out to be well founded.

What is role here, and what personality? What difference would it make to be able to answer that question? How can the system in which we work change, so that it does not perpetuate this cycle? Or is it in the nature of things, in the very nature of assuming a position carrying responsibility and authority, that this cycle be perpetuated? What do we do in a system that can somehow keep it from happening that all the people we are teaching are going to be horrible imitations of ourselves once they've gotten into the same roles that we're in? I see residents now talking eloquently about how they are treated in ways that are damaging to their learning. They're clear, quite insightful, about this. But observing some of their group behavior convinces me that they're going to teach their residents in exactly the way they've been taught. They will not in fact change their behavior once they get other roles, clinical-administrator roles, Chief of Service roles. They're going to do the same thing I did.

I don't know how to do anything about that. It seems to me that entire systems would have to change. The little bit we can do as teachers is like a drop in the bucket compared to the power of a system and role responsibilities to mold people's behavior and determine how they will behave.

Some thoughts about authority

When I was a student, authority was a source from which I might acquire knowledge and practical wisdom. At the same time, authority threatened to deprive me of my own voice, judgment, my right to make mistakes.

When I became an adult, and at work in my profession, my perspective changed. Now the person who had been given authority by that very act came to represent the task to be achieved. I believed that it was the leader's conception of the work to be done that should guide us. The leader's vision should determine what values or choices we gave priority in doing our work. If not, why had just this individual been appointed or accepted as a leader? A challenge to leadership seemed to me likely to be perceived by both leader and challenger as antitask and an act of sabotage.

What about a bad leader – that is, one who doesn't represent the task, as I understand the task? My attitude tended to be: If I cannot support the person who has been given the authority, then I should either leave the system rather than play a destructive role in it, or be prepared if I take on the leader to be defeated and thrown out of the system.

But, strangely enough, given my identification with authority and these far from 'revolutionary' views about it, in working as a clinician with patients, and as a teacher with trainees, my passion eventually turned out to be to enable these subordinates to empower themselves, to find a voice with which to stand up to and question those in authority – for a long time without realizing that that was what I was about.

When as a psychiatrist I worked to create a therapeutic community in an inpatient setting, the conception that guided me was one of intergroup collaboration, not 'political' ideas about 'sharing power' or 'participatory dem-ocracy'. I saw nurses, psychotherapy staff, administrators, occupational and recreational program directors, *and* patients as groups each with its own and sometimes conflicting perspectives, interests, values, and goals. Ideally, I imagined, in a therapeutic community these groups would organize themselves so that their members, speaking in a community meeting, could represent the group to which they belonged. The objective of the community meeting was to enable these groups to create together a social milieu that would support rather than undermine the therapeutic mission of the hospital. In this meeting, people speaking as representatives of the groups to which they belonged could talk about what problems in living and working in this community existed, work out mutually acceptable policies, negotiate mutually acceptable ways of carrying out these policies, and plan joint goal-seeking activities.

Some thirty years later, I heard from a patient who was in this setting at the same time I was. According to this patient, whatever I thought I was doing, patients perceived me as helping them to deal with the authority structure of the hospital. The patient wrote, 'I had the advantage of [being there] in the sixties when authority and power were being questioned. I had the advantage that you taught and supported busting open secrets and looking at power tools... The success of [the hospital] probably has ... to do with how well it helps to empower the patients, with how well it manages to be a collaborative experience rather than a hierarchic one... When I was there, I felt that the community program and your perspective opened just such a collaborative experience. I deeply appreciated your commitment to trying to understand and share the bigger picture with us. I appreciated that you weren't protecting a power structure that diminished the patients. It was a glimmer into sanity.'

I have some difficulty recognizing this image of myself. Yet at the same time it is familiar and I accept it. Certainly, if that was what I was doing, then I was making trouble for my colleagues and the authority structure of which we were all a part. It's no wonder they treated me with suspicion and opposed me. The wonder is that I did not realize what I was about and so was bewildered and surprised by the opposition.

In my organizational life, I have wanted and do want there to be a hierarchic authority structure, but one that is a tool, a means, a way to organize the efforts of different individuals and groups to achieve shared goals. At the same time, I have wanted and want there to be collaboration among groups both at the same level and at different levels of the hierarchy.

Are these desires unrealistic? Is such a state of affairs possible? Are authority structures – the very nature of authority and people's relation to it – such that my desires contain inherent contradictions impossible to overcome?

I work with those who are relatively powerless: patients; junior faculty or staff with lots of responsibility but little authority; and trainees. First I struggle with the question: 'How can I work with them in a way that enables them to empower themselves in relations with authority, to challenge and question authority when that is necessary to solve a problem or achieve a task?' Then the question 'But how can I tell when I am merely exacerbating personal predispositions to be reactively and mindlessly rebellious?' troubles me; I think a lot about it.

Must followers have the opportunity to influence a broad range of decisions in order to feel committed to and a part of an organization? I feel committed to and part of an organization to the extent it gives me the opportunity, makes it possible for me, to do meaningful work, my work. Of course, what I would like to be able to influence are those conditions and decisions that might constitute, create, or fail to mitigate obstacles to my being able to exercise my competence or to succeed in what I am trying to accomplish. So, the presence or absence of the opportunity to influence decisions that make a difference, that matter, to me and my particular piece of work in the organization, determines my commitment or sense of belonging. I have not been an 'everybody is responsible for everything, everybody does everything, everyone has a finger in every pie, nonhierarchical' person.

I find it useful to differentiate between two sources of power: authority and influence. Formal *authority* goes with a role you occupy, the degree of authority depending on the role. You may have the power to *influence* events and processes, often informally, because of your knowledge, skill, personal characteristics, identity, and so on, somewhat independent of your place in the authority structure.

It is not true that much authority always goes with much influence and conversely that little authority always goes with little influence. Sometimes those with little authority can have great influence in an organization. Think, for example, of the nurse in a psychiatric hospital, who is there interacting with patients hour after hour, or the similar position of the guard in a prison. A discrepancy between authority and influence can pose as great problems for an organization (the kibitzer who influences without the responsibility for consequences that goes with a formal role assignment) as a discrepancy between responsibility and authority poses (trainees who have immense even overwhelming responsibilities and little authority).

A poignant question at this time in my life concerns whether or not an organization is able to make use of senior members, even as it wishes to make way for younger members to move into positions of responsibility and authority. Here the discrepancy between authority and influence can pose a problem.

The senior faculty member in a university department, for example, may have a good deal of knowledge and experience, which may inspire respect, without his necessarily continuing to have administrative authority or responsibility. Suppose someone having authority did want to consult with him. Would she feel free to dissent with him? What if she felt, in view of her understanding of the entire situation in which she exercised authority, that she ought to ignore his proposals or suggestions? Would she feel comfortable doing so? Rather than open that can of worms, she might prefer to avoid consulting with the senior faculty member altogether, maintaining instead a politely distant relation. In that event, both lose, she the opportunity to talk over with someone the various dilemmas that confront her as a leader, he the opportunity to be of some use, to be able to influence to some extent how things go.

CHAPTER 17

Teaching Psychotherapy
A Subversive Activity

Marshall Edelson

It may seem odd to suppose that a psychotherapist's (or psychoanalyst's) effective-ness – indeed, the very process of *becoming* a psychotherapist (or psychoanalyst) – depends in any way on the authority relations in which he or she is embedded, on his or her attitudes toward authority or degree of comfort/ discomfort inhabiting a role that requires the exercise of authority. But as I have reflected on my experiences as a beginner, as a practitioner, and as a teacher of psychotherapy and psychoanalysis, it has increasingly seemed to me that the authority structure in which a trainee learns to do and eventually does practice psychotherapy or psychoanalysis, and the influence of that structure on a trainee's or practitioner's ways of responding to and exercising authority, determine to a far greater degree than is ordinarily appreciated whether or with what difficulty the trainee achieves, or the practitioner possesses, a comfortable identity as psychotherapist or psychoanalyst. Authority structures and their effects on trainees deserve far more scrutiny from both trainees and teachers than they ordinarily receive.

A distinction between two roles

I function as a preceptor rather than as a supervisor in my one-on-one work with a trainee and in my seminars on psychotherapy. The essential distinction between these two roles is that a preceptor is primarily responsible for teaching, for the personal and professional development of a trainee, while the supervisor has clinical-administrative responsibility, and is primarily concerned with monitoring the condition and directing the treatment of a patient with whom a trainee is working. The distinction between these two roles is relevant to a consideration of how I think about authority issues in teaching psychotherapy.

Preceptor

The preceptor has no line position in the organization in which the trainee works, and no authority to tell the trainee what to do or not to do. In fact the preceptor, often a member of the voluntary clinical faculty, may have something to teach the trainee in an area of interest (psychotherapy, group psychotherapy), without necessarily having the specific skills or knowledge required to treat just those kinds of patients that are currently assigned to the trainee in this particular institution. So the preceptor may not be competent to tell the trainee what to do or not to do with such a patient.

Of course, this role-definition has some implications that might trouble a clinical-administrative supervisor. It may mean that the preceptor when in role may neglect to get all kinds of information about diagnosis, the current functioning of the patient, and so on, that would be relevant to the question: 'How is a particular patient doing?'

A preceptor, for example, may not ask a trainee to keep up-to-date by summarizing a number of sessions with a patient or group of patients, and may not even ask a trainee to tell about a patient's pathology, life, or a history of the treatment. For purposes of learning about psychotherapy, preceptor and trainee may instead dwell for an entire hour on a few-minute interaction with a patient, go into detail about some event in a treatment that occurred a long time ago, review a paper together, or discuss the trainee's experiences in the training program or questions about and plans for the future.

Supervisor

This is not the way a clinical-administrative supervisor, primarily responsible for monitoring the care of the patient, would be expected to act. A supervisor, occupying a line position in the institution in which the trainee works, does bear clinical-administrative responsibility for patients being treated in that institution and must have the information and relation with a trainee required to monitor the treatment of those patients. Further, the supervisor is expected to have the specific skills and knowledge required to treat just those kinds of patients for whom the institution is currently providing care. The clinical-administrative supervisor's primary focus is the patient, not the trainee.

We make the distinction between preceptor and supervisor in order to define, clarify, and distinguish tasks. It warns us that if one person attempts to occupy both roles, carry out both tasks, one or the other task may suffer.

Authority relations in teaching

My objective in preceptorial sessions is to enhance the personal and professional development of the trainee. I want the trainee to become able to see that she and I can both imagine more than one way to see or understand a particular event or statement. I want her to become able to tolerate that there are multiple sources of wisdom, not all consistent with each other, and that the most important one is usually her own inner life and life experience. I want her to have the experience of being an active agent, and to have the opportunity to make mistakes. For it is in the consideration of the consequences of such mistakes, in reflecting upon failures, that learning occurs.

The definition of the role of the preceptor makes it possible, in the relationship between preceptor and trainee, to focus on and influence the ways in which the trainee uses, responds to, and takes on authority as he becomes a psychotherapist. I have observed that when clinicians discuss each other's work, their comments rarely convey, 'I recognize myself in you. I have struggled with just what you are struggling with. That is why I have a question about what you said.' More usually, what the comments convey is, 'I think you made a mistake. I would never say anything like that. It is obvious that…' I regard this as a sign that splitting and projection are playing a part in the relation between these clinicians.

The trainee tends to think that all knowledge and competence reside in the preceptor and all ignorance and incompetence in himself. The trainee overvalues and relies too much on external sources of authority (for example, someone else's theory) and correspondingly undervalues and underutilizes internal sources of authority (his own personal experience and nontechnical subjective responses). The trainee assumes that there is at any moment in psychotherapy a right intervention and a wrong intervention; that a particular intervention is either right or wrong; that what is right and what wrong can and should be known *a priori,* that is, before making the intervention; and that a preceptor can know immediately, just by hearing a trainee's intervention and without regard to what follows it, that it is right or wrong according to 'the rules of technique'. All somewhat dubious assumptions.[88]

The competent preceptor vs. the incompetent trainee

I remember, when I was a resident, patients replying to something I said, 'You've just come from your supervisor, haven't you?' I had not made what the supervisor said my own; I was merely parroting it and what I said did not sound to the patient as if it were my voice saying it. I try in my teaching to avoid supporting the tendency any trainee is likely to have, out of anxiety, to swallow what I say whole and to imitate it without reflection or really making it his own. This is not easily achieved.

How can I enable the trainee to empower herself to question or challenge how I perceive and understand what is going on in the story she tells me? I look for teaching strategies that at least make it possible for the trainee to recognize that she knows more about the patient and the psychotherapy she is presenting than I do.

The role-definition of the preceptor enables me to begin my work with trainees by reminding them that, as a preceptor rather than a clinical-administrative supervisor, I do not have the authority to tell them what to do or not to do. I tell them that in my teaching role I will focus in our work on them, their thinking, knowledge, skills, their personal and professional development. We will use our time together considering and talking about whatever is relevant, consistent with that focus.

In searching for the teaching strategy that will set a trainee and me on a more equal footing than is implied by the usual 'teacher knows everything and student knows nothing' split, I ask the trainee, when presenting clinical material, to draw on one session, ideally one that happened some time ago, and to focus in micro-scopic detail on the process, the events in sequence in that session ('the patient said... I thought, felt, said...'). We observe the process, its microdynamics: the perturbations resulting from a particular event, communication, or verbal intervention. We listen for the patient's responses to what he himself has said as well as to what the psychotherapist has said. We bear witness to the patient's struggle to restore an equilibrium after a disturbing event: undoing the event, denying it, criticizing it, regretting and apologizing for it, or distracting attention from it (for example, by changing the subject).

I frequently find myself then in the position of commenting on a single psychotherapy session and usually a piece of that session at that. In this kind of teaching, it doesn't matter if the session is current or old. Indeed, in terms of what I am after, it is perhaps preferable for the trainee not to present what is going on currently in the psychotherapy. Because in presenting what occurred some time ago, the trainee knows, although I do not, what happened later, *after* the session we are discussing. The trainee knows also that she knows more about the patient and the treatment than I do. I only know the one tiny bit. So, the trainee can take with a grain of salt my comments about this one session, suggesting (as such comments tend to do) questions I want us to consider about the possible consequences (good or bad) of various of her interventions. Ideally, although of course it does not always turn out this way, the trainee should, therefore, feel able to question what I say, to be skeptical, to draw on her own experience, and what she has learned from that experience. 'I don't agree with you. My own perception and inclination were instead...' 'You don't know what you're talking about. I know what came after this session. So what you're imagining saying to the patient, I don't agree with that.'

A resident somewhat anxiously said to me, 'Can't we keep up-to-date?' I said, 'It might be better that we're not up-to-date. You are now presenting me with a session that's a month old. We're spending a lot of time on this session. We're saying all sorts of things. You know what's happened in the month since. So you can tell where Edelson's gone off, where he's mistaken in what he thinks is going on with the patient, and where he turned out to have a decent hunch and how his mind worked in arriving at that hunch.'

External vs. internal sources of authority

I imagine out loud what I might say at a certain point in the story, usually before hearing what the trainee went on to say at that point. The trainee has a chance to observe my thought processes, and in particular what his story evokes in me, what comes to my mind as I listen. Theory does not ordinarily come to my mind. I specify what I have seen or heard, how it has made me feel, and what scene or incident it has reminded me of, that might lead me to say just that.

I encourage trainees to let something else besides authoritative theoretical formulas and technical prescriptions come to their minds when they are working. 'Look in yourself for the images, scenes, feelings, fantasies, memories of something else the patient has told you or that has happened previously in therapy, that the patient's communications have evoked, for these are the clues to what story is on a patient's mind that he is either telling or enacting.'

I encourage trainees to stay near to experience in their communications to patients. If they continuously make inferences to thoughts and feelings to which a patient has no access, as they are especially likely to do under the sway of theory, the patient has no choice but to take their word for it. This diminishes and disempowers the patient even as it enhances the power of the psychotherapist. To remain near to experience means to pay close attention to the details (including the mundane details) of what the patient says and does, the stories the patient tells and enacts, in the here-and-now, and to make use of these specific details – rather than timeless universal generalizations or vague attributions of states or traits – in communications to the patient.

Interventions are right or wrong

The trainee and I experiment out loud imagining alternative possible interventions, and the possible functional and dysfunctional consequences of each. We try to be skeptical of each other's certainties, of what seems obvious or self-evident to either of us. We try not to have just one idea, one way of seeing or hearing the material. We generate alternative ways to understand a particular process, a particular sequence of events, a particular similarity or parallel between stories told about different relationships or different realms. We try to discover together what in the immediate context tends to support one alternative against another. (If I assign reading at all, I try to assign readings that challenge each other.)

I don't teach specific techniques or subject matter, the right or wrong thing to say or do. Not what to say, but how to think about what to say. Ways of thinking about problems, not the solutions to these problems. Questions that should be considered, not the answers to these questions. To teach in this way, I have to avoid succumbing to the temptation to think of myself as the one who knows, as the fount of wisdom, as the one who has the answers, who knows what to do. Because the trainee is anxious, and wants me to guide him, and to tell him what is the right thing to do and what the wrong thing, the temptation to grant his wish is great. But I think it should be resisted, and I can resist it successfully, maybe 50 percent of the time.

I say to the trainee, with Lipton,[89] that there is no way to know *a priori* what in a particular instance is the right or wrong thing to say. You can only say to a patient what makes sense or feels right to you at the time. And then, with the curiosity that is at the core of any competent psychotherapist, you conduct a responsible careful inquiry into – which usually means to observe conscientiously and with interest – the impact and fate of what you have said. How did the patient hear it? What did the patient do with it?

We develop at least some preliminary criteria, for example, some kinds of responses a patient might make to some intervention of a psychotherapist, which might lead the latter to consider that she might have been wrong in what she said to the patient. Or at the least off in her timing (that is, in her judgment of what is accessible to the patient and what the patient is ready to use). Or that I might have been wrong in some evaluation of her intervention (made by me without knowledge of the patient's response to it).

In an individual preceptorial or in a seminar, I try to be careful to interfere with a trainee's eagerness to rescue some hypothesis of mine, which given additional information turns out to have been inaccurate. I want trainees to see that I can go astray, especially if I am limited, as one always is, in my access to relevant information. It is true, however, that I am not completely open to criticism. I do seem to have more difficulty really listening to challenges of how I choose to conduct a seminar, a choice I recognize as rooted in my experiences of what has worked and not worked in the past, than I have listening to someone's questioning my ideas about what might be going on in a presented psychotherapy session. But I am not totally inflexible or unhearing when it comes to challenges to the way I organize the work of the seminar. The dissenter just has to work a little harder to get through to me; persistence, at least sometimes, pays off.

Authority relations in the setting in which teaching is going on

I question whether trainees can learn psychotherapy or function as psycho-therapists in a system in which they continually experience themselves as without authority, without choice, and in which they feel required to submit unquestioningly to those who have authority or risk being demeaned or put down in some more or less subtle way. Trainees may feel disempowered or deprofessionalized, as non-physician staff seek to protect patients from their inexperience, respond to their temporary status on a service by diminishing their role, or are suspicious that a resident like other doctors just wants to be the boss over those who remain to struggle hour by hour with problems on the service long after the resident is gone.

Who controls the conditions in which an initial interview occurs?

A resident meets with a patient at admission. During his interview with the patient, the patient's husband and a nurse remain in the room. I ask whether he thought it made for a better interview to have them in the room. He says, 'The husband didn't seem to be doing any harm. The nurse wanted to be present so that the patient would not have to tell her story twice.' It became clear that the resident did not feel that, even in the interest of obtaining more valid data, he might ask to see, much less insist on seeing, the patient alone.

Who controls the conditions in which meetings with patients occur?

A resident is repeatedly late for meetings with patients. The general attitude she encounters is, 'It doesn't matter if a patient is kept waiting a few minutes – unless it's *psychotherapy.*' (What is the perceived status of the patient group in this system?) The resident explains: 'If it's my attending, I don't want to get him mad. If it's my team, well, we have a warm relationship and work well together. I don't want to get up and walk out, because other team members would see me as a doctor who thinks she can do anything she wants. I don't want to negotiate with the team about when the meeting is supposed to and should end so that I can get to my next task on time, because I don't want to be different. Every time I've been different, I've suffered for it.'

Having a choice: to read or not to read

There are ten trainees in a seminar. I have assigned some reading. I forgot to do the reading until the night before the seminar. So I read until late the night before with toothpicks holding my eyes open. I get to the class and four out of the ten people have done the readings. It is very difficult to discuss the material in the reading because that would leave a lot of people out of the discussion. I feel discouraged and annoyed.

Over a period of time in the seminar session, I say some of the following things, 'What's up with you guys? Last week we had a discussion about whether we were going to do this reading or not. You told me you really wanted to read it. You wanted to learn what was in this book. Ordinarily I do not assign books until the fourth year of the residency, in an advanced course in psychotherapy, because earlier it seems to me books are more trouble than they're worth. They're just used as deities telling you what you should do and what you shouldn't do. By the fourth year I figure people are on their way out of the residency. Now you might have some incentive to do some learning on your own, because soon you're going to be on your own, having your own practice, learning what you can from your experiences with your patients. One of the other ways you can learn is to read occasionally.'

One of the residents says, 'I was the only one who read last time. So I thought why should I do this if no one else is going to do it?'

Then someone tells me that in every course, 40 percent of the residents do the reading. 'That's standard procedure.'

I say, 'Well, what is it about this system that we're working in that can lead to such a statistic? That in every seminar 40 percent of the people do the reading.'

There are both residents and psychology fellows in the seminar. (I'm not going to try and identify who's who because the problems they have around an issue like this are very similar.) Various members speak. 'I need more time to think.' 'I am overburdened and have no time to reflect.' 'We have a lot of things to do. We're constantly being told, "Do this. Do that." This is the one time we have a choice. We can either read or not read. We have a real choice.'

That strikes a chord in me, the importance of choice. I've noticed that many trainees don't feel they have many opportunities to make a choice. They don't experience others giving them opportunities to do this or do that – 'It's up to you.' They feel others constantly telling them, 'You can't miss this meeting. You can't miss that meeting. You have to be here. You have to be there. Your clinical responsibilities require it.' I never get a call from anybody in any of my seminars who says something like, 'Dr. Edelson, I'm not going to be in the seminar today because there is something else I would rather do.' No one ever says that, although I am quite sure, knowing the people I'm working with, that many times they would rather be with their patients than attending a seminar. Instead I hear some version of 'I *can't* come to the seminar today'.

My sense of discouragement and annoyance starts to dissipate. I talk at some length with the group about why I assigned the reading and why I assigned three different books. I say, 'I want you to be able to use one book to challenge another book. So that you won't be oversold on any particular point of view. So that you can make a choice based on your experience of what is helpful to you.'

Gradually the discussion comes around to, 'We're immature.' 'Now that we understand why you're assigning the reading, we'll read.'

Someone says, 'I think you should enforce that.' I say, 'How would you suggest that I enforce it?'

I have had a moment when I felt enlightened, that these trainees were actually telling me that they had learned something from me – which was that it was important to use your judgment and make choices. They were able to enact this with me because they felt comfortable with me. I don't want to betray that moment. So I say that actually I feel in a quandary, because anything I do as a result of this discussion will give them permission to read or not to read. That will take all the risk out of making the choice. If I speak, they no longer have to ask, 'Will he be upset? Do we have his permission to make a choice?' I can't think of anything I can say that won't take the risk out of their making their own decision.

One of them then turns to me, and says challengingly, 'Are you punishing us now for not having done the reading by taking up all our time discussing this and not letting us get to a discussion of the clinical material?' The voice of Work. (It is very gratifying when a trainee is able to do something like this.) We turn to the clinical material and have a good discussion.

The two 'supervisors'

A resident tells me the following story. 'I am working with somebody else, a supervisor.' (It's always a supervisor, though the 'supervisor' was actually a preceptor. What is the implication? That this person has authority over the resident, has the right to tell the resident what to do. And this 'supervisor' does indeed go on to fulfill this resident's idea of the role of preceptor by telling the resident what to do.)

The resident reported to the 'supervisor' that he had asked a patient who was speaking very generally, 'Do you have an example?' The 'supervisor' said, 'You shouldn't have said that. That's the wrong thing to say. I don't want you to say that.' The resident got the impression that he wasn't supposed to say that because it wasn't 'psychoanalytic'. (This was weird, because the patient wasn't in psychoanalysis and conditions were not such that a psychoanalytic procedure could be carried out.) So the resident said to the 'supervisor', 'Dr. Edelson said...'

The 'supervisor' said – I am always grateful to my colleagues who are much more tactful than I am – 'Well, Dr. Edelson and I always end in the same place,' perhaps without any first-hand knowledge of how I work, perhaps assuming that, because I'm a psychoanalyst and because I belong to that community, I can be depended on to follow what 'goes' in that community.

In the past I've always been very cautious about commenting on any story I get from residents. I want to stay on good terms with my colleagues. I imagine they'll hear I'm *utzing* the residents and they'll start saying to them, 'You don't want to work with Edelson. There's something off about his work. He's not a proper person to work with.' Or they'll start saying when someone says, 'I want to attend Edelson's seminar,' 'we really need you on the unit.' ('Utzing' is a Yiddish expression meaning 'a mischievous stirring up, provoking'.)

This time I respond to the resident differently. I don't know what kind of difficulty my response might make for someone working with the resident. But I have gotten to a point in my work where I say to myself, 'How can I keep encouraging residents to stand up for what they believe and to express themselves passionately when they're concerned about the care of their patients, if I'm scared to open my mouth because of my fear of making difficulties with my colleagues?

After all, that's the problem for the residents. They're constantly having fantasies that whoever it is will be mad at them. "I'll get a bad letter of recommendation. I'll get a poor reputation in the department."'

At some point I have decided, 'Edelson, you've got to come out in the open. You can't be saying these things to residents and not be willing to take the same risks yourself.' So I am frank with this resident about the 'supervisor's' response. I say, 'What I would say to the 'supervisor' is that there is no *a priori* right or wrong way to do things. We do not know *a priori* that is the right thing to say or the wrong thing to say. Spontaneity is very important. You say what makes sense to you from your understanding of the patient. You can't do anything else but that. What I regard as a psychoanalytic stance is then to be curious about the impact on the patient of what you have said. To follow that and to try and understand it. By following the impact on the patient, you come to the point where you learn something. Later you are able to say to yourself, "I remember one time I said that and what happened after was such-and-such." Not, "I'm not going to say that, because I read in a book that there is a rule against it."'[90]

Secondly, I would say to the 'supervisor' that it is not a teacher's job to tell a trainee what to do and what not to do. That may be the job of a supervisor, someone who has clinical responsibility. A teacher's job is to help a trainee to learn how to think about an intervention, to ask, 'What are the risks I take in saying this? Can I imagine some possible reactions? Some that are functional. Some that are dysfunctional. Which horn of a dilemma do I want to sit on? If I have three or four possible interventions in my head, how do I think about which one fits this patient at this particular point in time, given what is going on right now?'

Then I say what I have never said before. I say, 'If you would like to have the "supervisor" call me, I would be glad to discuss this with him.' I want the resident to feel that I am not just talking. I am willing to back up the resident by getting into a risky discussion with a colleague whom my interference might only annoy.

The resident who stood up for his patients

In Chapter 20, I will tell a story about a resident who was telling me about a group psychotherapy meeting, when I, hitherto silent, suddenly and forcefully listed one after another a number of mistakes he had made. I felt terrible. It seems as if we never stop doing this to people working in a position subordinate to our own. Something about the difference in authority keeps us locked in the same scenario. Much as I've thought this out, I've found myself saying things that others can easily hear or feel as belittling, scolding, or shutting people up – after they have told me, confided in me, what they felt, why they were thinking the way they were. My 'reward' for that confidence is to say something about what's wrong with them. It's very hard not to do this – and under the guise of 'teaching something': 'It's for your own good.' I can think about this day after day and still end up doing it. Again, I wonder if it is intrinsic to an authority relation or something about what kind of person I am: a very painful speculation.

In any event, some time after this painful episode (I am now going to tell the end of this story before telling the beginning in Chapter 20), this resident and I had a discussion about the way he was occupying his role. As far as the psychotherapy group members were concerned, he was a representative of the institution, but he was not taking any responsibility for the policies of the institution, including a new policy setting limits to the time a psychotherapy group could exist. That policy required his announcing to his group that it was being disbanded. In effect, he was also refusing to take responsibility for his patients, who were the particular victims of the new policy. Regardless how wise or necessary the policy was, it was their group that was being disbanded. It did not occur to him to go and raise hell with anybody, 'What do you mean stopping this group! These people need this group.' Although that was the way he felt. So I asked, 'Why didn't you go and protest?'

Here, I felt myself becoming subversive and making trouble for my colleagues. And possibly for the resident. He runs a big risk, getting a reputation as a troublemaker, as someone who acts out and encourages his patients to act out. So I was in conflict, experiencing what we could call a role dilemma.

Is teaching psychotherapy a subversive activity? My goal in teaching residents is to create a relationship in which the resident ends up feeling he can challenge and question me. But then that leads inevitably to an increased ability to challenge and question others, for example, people who are primarily in the patient care system, whose primary responsibility is not teaching – if a choice must be made between which of these two responsibilities will have priority, as in some situations it inevitably must.

What happened was that over time this resident kept on doing yeoman work with this group, gradually stopped being so guarded, got quite involved, related to the patients more actively, got in there with them (which I think is very important, I don't think you can do this work maintaining some kind of aloof 'neutral' stance).

The resident got to the point (I didn't know he was going to do this) where he went to somebody who was part of the patient care system, essentially one of his supervisors (in the sense of 'boss' not 'teacher', a person who could tell him what to do and what not to do in his work with patients). This person said, 'How are things going with your patients?' The resident said, 'Well, if you want to know, where I'm really having trouble is terminating with my group. The group is upset about having the group terminated, and I personally think it's wrong, even though I realize it may be necessary because of resource shortages. At a very gut level, I disagree with the decision and feel that it is wrong to regard these people as expendable just because they are doing somewhat better.' The supervisor said, 'What are you saying!? Do they know how you feel? They're all going to act out!'

The resident immediately began to shrink back, thinking to himself, 'I'm damaging my patients in some way. I'm doing something wrong in my group.'

But – he has my admiration for this – he persisted. 'Why are we painting stairways if we don't have enough money to continue patient care?' The answer he got was, 'You have no understanding what it's like to work around here. We need certain amenities to maintain our morale; otherwise, we get burnt out. Have you talked about this with Dr. Edelson? Oh, I remember he doesn't talk about administrative things.' (!)

The resident's immediate reaction, which is very damaging to the institution I belong to, was to say to himself: 'I'm not going to talk to this person any more, because I just end up feeling scolded, that there's something wrong with me, that I'm doing something bad.' The one who loses by such a development is the administrative leader, who has to know what people are thinking, feeling, what they're doing, in order to be an administrator. You can't be an administrator in the dark. You have to have people willing to come and talk to you. So, if an administrator talks to subordinates in a way that leads them not to talk to her or him anymore, that is a disservice to the institution as an institution.

This resident – a very sturdy guy – got over 'I'm not going to talk anymore,' and was now very concerned about the patients. The patients were saying, 'What are we going to do!? June is coming up and you are telling some of us we have to go to other places and some of us can only have ten minutes every other week in a medication monitoring clinic, and if we aren't on medication we can't come here any more, unless we don't have insurance.' The resident went back to the supervisor and said, 'What am I supposed to tell them? What are they to do if they have psychiatric problems?'

The supervisor said, 'If they're on medication, we'll assign them to medication clinic every other week. If they have no insurance, they can come back here and go to triage. But I'm going to be very upset with you if any of these patients come back here. If they have insurance, they have to go elsewhere. Did you check if they have insurance? What! You didn't check whether each patient in the group has insurance!'

So the resident said, 'You know I have the feeling that no one is taking into consideration my feelings about what's happening to this group. And I'm the group therapist.'

The supervisor said, 'Right! It has nothing to do with your feelings. It's an administrative matter. I want you to tell this group, "What do you think? Here's a schizophrenic out of a job, having hallucinations. Some of you are working. Don't you think that other patients deserve the treatment more than you do?"'

The resident says, 'Yes. They see that. And each one of them is getting sicker and sicker to show me that they deserve the treatment as much as anyone else. I'm having a group now where I'm having individual appointments with almost everyone in the group because everyone is getting very symptomatic and desperate and wanting to have medication.'

A preceptor's dilemmas

I am helping people who are learning psychotherapy to empower themselves so that they can be psychotherapists. That means to be able to stand up to me, criticize me, be skeptical of what I say, to be critical of books and what their authors say they should do and not do, to rely on their own experience.

As I realize that this is what I am trying to bring about, I become somewhat nervous. Residents working with me also start to get more questioning and skeptical in their relation to people in various parts of the department who have authority. I start having visions of my colleagues getting increasingly irritated at what I'm doing. People sometimes seem to think that I'm sitting benignly in my office doing something with trainees that doesn't affect anyone else. In what I have just written, I have come out to reveal that this is not the case.

I don't have any answer to the kind of problems that I have raised in these stories. I don't see any solutions. I am not antiauthoritarian or an anarchist. I believe there should be an authority structure.

I do think authority structures can get overconstraining and inflexible, intolerant of dissent, challenges, questions that make trouble, that make administrative work harder to do. But on the whole, to me an authority structure is a way of organizing and doing a job. I'm all for people having authority and responsibility that are related to task-achievement. I do think that people with different responsibilities will give priority to their own responsibilities and that these priorities sometimes conflict. What often leads to trouble here is that the conflict is personalized and attributed to the difficulty these people have, because of their personality differences, in getting along with each other.

I don't see how I am going to foster the personal and professional development of the trainees I teach, if they cannot learn in their work with me to be passionate about what they believe, to stand up to other people at some risk to themselves for the sake of a patient for whom they care, to be open when they're skeptical, to be questioning when someone tells them to do something.

When they do, they feel good and I feel good; it's clear they are growing professionally. One resident said, after I had discussed some of these matters at a public forum, 'Thank God, the meeting with you was on Friday. I was on duty that weekend. A nurse told me I had to come to the floor and sign something, and I said, "No. I won't do it except under the following conditions." I was very nervous about saying that. I never would have said it if I hadn't heard you talk about this sort of situation.'

But then how can I as a teacher maintain some kind of decent mutually respectful relationship with other people working in the system who have other responsibilities than I, when they could easily view the things I am doing in my teaching as only making trouble for them? Surely, concern with patient care and good teaching cannot be incompatible? I would not like people who are responsible for the clinical care that trainees provide to think I think that they are not able to do any teaching in that situation. I think that there is teaching that can be done. I would prefer it to be the sort of teaching that is not 'this is the thing to do, this is not the thing to do,' but 'how are we going to think about this kind of problem?' That kind of clinical problem-solving might go on all the time.

On the other hand, I realize that, given the preoccupation of delivering care in a situation where there are not lavish resources might put people under considerable pressure. They might let something go for the sake of efficiency or getting something done, where otherwise they might have a more leisurely discussion, encouraging someone to think something out.

But one thing is clear. Teaching psychotherapy is not like teaching surgery. (What follows is a ridiculously oversimplified view of what it takes to learn surgery, but it is a common conception that I will just use to make a point about teaching psychotherapy, which doesn't depend upon the validity of the picture of how surgery is taught.) The cliché about learning and teaching surgery is, 'You watch one, you do one, you teach one.' That might be true where the patient is lying flat and anesthetized. You can just imitate what the person in authority is doing and acquire his skill. The subjectivity of the patient may not be especially important at the moment you are operating. The fact that every patient is different from every other patient, that each patient is always presenting novel experiences and evoking novel responses in you, is not going to trouble you.

But the subjectivity of the patient is at the center of the psychotherapeutic enterprise. It is important, in relating to that patient, to be in touch with that subjectivity and with your own subjectivity, to be in touch with yourself, able to be yourself, even when occupying the role of psychotherapist. You want to be yourself in that role, not just some mechanical rule- governed implementer of that role.

It is no answer for me to have someone say, 'Clinical work and teaching go hand in hand, and it will all work out okay.' That denies what I know: that different tasks, such as monitoring clinical care and teaching, may conflict (that is, may not both be maximizable on the same occasion); that people with different roles will have different priorities, and will do and must do things differently, if they are to achieve the specific tasks for which they are responsible; and that therefore people occupying different roles will inevitably come in conflict with each other in some situations.

It is also the case that there are times when someone goes against authority and it might have a bad ending for the patient. How does the trainee know when to follow what the supervisor says and when to go it on her or his own? Bad things happen. We are dealing with matters of life and death. How do you balance the interests of the learner, including the opportunity to learn from mistakes, and the interests of the patient, for whom mistakes may not be innocuous?

I think that someone who is responsible for patient care has the right to exercise authority in the interests of the patient for whose care they are responsible. I am teaching as a preceptor. If instead I were teaching as a supervisor, as the chief of a unit, for example, I wouldn't now go around harshly calling residents sociopaths when they didn't do what I say, but there would be situations I might say to a resident, 'You can't do that. Just stop it.'

The relaxed exercise of authority is essential for people who have it. It seems to me that would not necessarily be damaging to a resident if it didn't also convey the message that the resident is sick, 'acting out', psychopathic, but simply that in this situation I know more than the resident does and I have responsibility here. I would stop a minute and find out why the resident is proceeding in the way he is, and then I would say something like, 'Okay, I can understand your reasoning but my experience tells me that it is best to do otherwise. And I have the last word on this. I am in charge here. There is, after all, this third party, the patient, and I am not willing to stand by and accept the risks of your way of proceeding.'

I wouldn't like you to think that this doesn't also come up in being a preceptor. I have the experience of sitting in a seminar and having a resident say, 'I hate this patient. I hate this kind of person.' Of course, you have to recognize that you have been able to create a relationship in which a resident feels able to tell you that she is having an 'unacceptable' feeling. It very often turns out that the rejected patient is behaving in a way that offends the values of the trainee, is being exploitative of women, for example, which is something that can get women residents especially very upset. I understand that. On the other hand, I feel strongly that an evaluative judgmental attitude that leads you not to want to work with a patient means you can't even work with the patient to help him change his behavior, should he want to do so, and he may want to do so – behavior that you would actually be glad to see changed. Why not get interested in the patient, try to understand why he does go around exploiting women? I would like to say to that resident, 'Stop that. Putting the patient down. Saying the patient is bad, wicked, and I don't want to work with such people. They're not worthwhile. Because you can't do psychotherapy feeling that way. That means ever more frequently the only people with whom you can do psychotherapy are the people who have your values.' But I don't know how to say that to someone without sounding belittling and attacking. I am also aware that, if I say anything of this sort to the resident, I run the risk of being labeled and talked about as an insensitive 'male authority figure' who doesn't appreciate what women have to go through in our society. I don't have a way out of these difficulties. But I see the dilemma.

One response to this dilemma is to remember that it's easier to accept the advice of someone in authority if you feel that person cares about you and you care about that person. It's very difficult to take advice from people who you feel don't care about what you think or feel. Or don't know you. My question is, 'Is there something about the way we have set things up, the way we work together, and the kind of pressures and conditions that we work under, that fosters the kind of relationships where people can come to the conclusion that we don't care about each other?'

What would it take to change such a system? I think it would take so much that my mind boggles. I can't even imagine how you would go about changing a system in that direction. It's like trying to create a therapeutic community on an inpatient unit. Isn't it essentially impossible?

Perhaps Dan Levinson is right. I am too old and no longer have the strength to tackle such a job. But maybe there is some way I can help those in the next generation who can and I hope will tackle it, and – is it possible? – succeed. Is it possible that a member of an older generation might still make a contribution by using experience and knowledge to collaborate with rebellion to bring about change?

CHAPTER 18

Rebellion

David Berg

One might argue that the question of how to exercise and respond to authority effectively, humanely, and responsibly is *the* central dilemma in organizational or collective life. This formulation seems to reduce organizations to a single dimension. But in fact it is not easy to disentangle the parts played by personality, role, group dynamics, historical identities, and intergroup relations in the unfolding of authority dynamics in organizations.

Managing a business without hierarchy

Is it possible to develop authority structures which encourage those with little or no formal authority to participate in the organization's work even or particularly when it involves challenging the very authority structure of which they are a part? I am reminded of a research experience I had as a graduate student. At that time (the early 1970s), I was interested in studying organizations that, for ideological reasons, had decided to try to organize in other than a traditional hierarchical manner. One of the legacies of the late 1960s was a heightened interest in 'alternative' organizational forms (where 'alternative' meant nonhierarchical).

I approached an organization which was predominantly female and had as one of its stated objectives: trying to manage a business without hierarchy. I spent three months talking to people, observing some of their meetings and the way they did their work. I decided that in order to study this organization on its own terms I needed to make sure that the choice to participate in the research was both public and fully participative. (This decision came from my theoretical approach to organizational diagnosis as well as my compelling sense that this approach would be consistent with the values of the organization as I understood them.)

As I prepared a secret ballot to be distributed to all members of the organization, the most experienced, influential, and powerful members of the organization expressed their interest in the project and counseled me against an organization-wide vote. At the same time the least experienced, low-power employees came to tell me that they had never been involved in an organizational decision-making process before, but that they were going to vote against the project because they did not think it was a good idea.

I came away from this experience with two insights. First, it is very difficult to run an organization, to make decisions, to allocate resources, to apply human energies to the variety of challenges and problems that arise in any organization without some authority structure. If you choose to stay with a formal hierarchy, you struggle with many of the issues concerning the use and abuse of authority that you have been confronting. If you opt for a 'no authority' structure, an informal structure will develop to do the work of the organization, and in this case you will have all the struggles that go with formal hierarchy together with an ever present sense of hypocrisy. In this particular organization, the lower-power employees felt the apparent hypocrisy poignantly, since it had been their expectation that in a nonhierarchical organization they would be invited to participate in a whole host of decisions.

The second insight for me came from my observation that the 'low-power' members of the organization had decided not to go ahead with a project that had provided their only occasion for participation and influence in the organization! The desire to have some influence on your own social system, especially if you *expect* to have influence (based on your experience, training, education, role), is often more powerful than accomplishing a particular immediate task. In this case, the only way the employees who felt disenfranchised could express their desire for a real voice in the organization was to stop a process that had given them a voice. I understood this as an investment. They were giving up the possibility of increased influence on this one decision, in order to make a point about their everyday experience of the organization.

This story is similar to Marshall's story of the trainees who didn't read what they wanted to read, in order to express their everyday experience of 'we have no choice' by making the choice not to read. And his story about the residents who insisted that he, the seminar teacher, allow them to volunteer rather than be chosen by him to present their clinical work, but then – when he accepted their proposal – no one volunteered![91]

Leaders, followers, and rebellion

At the risk of oversimplifying my views, let me suggest that the most critical issue for those *with* authority is how they respond to rebellion, and the most critical issue for those who feel *without* authority is how to initiate and conduct rebellion. I use the word 'rebellion' rather than 'dissent', for rebellion connotes to me 'making a difference', whereas dissent can be acknowledged or tolerated without its making a difference to decisions, at least in the short run (as on the Supreme

Court) – and the short run can last a long time. The reason rebellion is central to my understanding of authority is because it is my way of talking about how people make institutions their own, how they come to have an investment in an organization they did not create but of which they have become a part. It is about feeling a sense of ownership and responsibility for the often large bureaucratic institutions in which many of us spend much of our lives. It perhaps seems odd that I believe such a sense comes in part out of a successful rebellion, successfully handled.

The story of an unsuccessful rebellion

When I was a graduate student in psychology, I took a course in complex organizations. The professor in this course was a tyrant. He lectured interminably, gave spot quizzes, insulted students for asking 'stupid' questions, and was unresponsive to any initiative from the class. Those of us taking the course groused about it on the days between class meetings, complaining bitterly to ourselves about this awful experience. One of us tried to talk to the professor in his office about his experience in the course, but the professor strongly suggested that the student was not approaching the class in the right way.

On the next-to-last day of class, the professor stood in front of the room and read three pages from the introduction of his latest book on organizations. These pages extolled the virtues of designing organizations in such a way as to harness the intrinsic motivations of the individual employees. I could contain myself no longer; so I raised my hand and, when called upon, asked the professor how he reconciled what he had just read with the way he conducted this class.

The room was silent for a brief moment, and then the professor became enraged at me. He said that if I were any kind of man I would have come to speak with him privately about this clearly personal problem. When I tried to say that one of us had tried this approach to no avail and that I believed I spoke for more than myself, he cut me off and yelled that he wanted no more of this discussion. No one else in the room said a word. When the class was over, a number of other students came up to me to thank me for saying what I said and to apologize for not supporting me. I was at the same time proud, ashamed, and infuriated. I had found my voice, but I had publicly humiliated the professor, and been left alone by those who shared similar feelings.

It would be a mistake to see only the extreme dramatic elements in this story. I have never been in a classroom, as a teacher or student, in which there was not some feeling that 'things' would go better if a few changes were made, or if such changes could be discussed. It is not merely that there is no such thing as the perfect classroom. It is, I believe, that a set of relationships constitutes the classroom and the organization. These relationships must be established and then developed. When they involve different levels of authority, one question concerning the relationship is how much influence each will have on the other. Rebellion is the collective expression of that question. How that rebellion is handled is the authority figure's answer.

This story has a postscript. Years later, a graduate student working with me read a chapter I had written many years previously (actually about my aborted research with the 'alternative' organization the story of which I told earlier). What I had written then, given the values and theories she knew I now espoused, surprised and disappointed her. I like and trust this person; yet I could not help feeling hurt, embarrassed, and defensive.

She gave me a way to examine my connection to the 'tyrant' from my graduate school years, for in spite of our differences each of us is engaged in a struggle to live in some accord with our espoused values. Nowhere is this more difficult than when we have power and authority. For the exercise of authority involves not only the powerful person but the perceptions and experience of the relatively powerless as well.

Teachers' responses to challenge

Two more stories from the classroom, a site that often offers a particularly stark presentation of authority dynamics. In the first story, I was taking a class on organizational behavior. My professor viewed organizations as treating adults like children, and so reducing their effectiveness, involvement, and innovativeness. He had developed a coding process for measuring the openness and innovativeness of human interactions as part of his method for studying the impact of certain interventions on interpersonal behavior. For a midterm in the course, the professor assigned a short case and asked us to write a few pages analyzing the situation in the case.

My roommate and I, both taking the course, decided to tape record our discussion of the case and then apply the professor's coding scheme to our own tape. We handed in both the taped discussion and the analysis of the coded data. We were excited about our creativity and, given the values of the professor, sure that he would appreciate our 'innovativeness'. We got an F on the assignment because we had not handed in a paper.

This story does not need a moral, but it too has a postscript, which relates to the question about whether we learn to be 'better' authority figures from our experience of being treated badly by those in authority. Fifteen years after this experience, I taught a class on organizational behavior. One of the students in my class chose to hand in an audio tape instead of a self-analytic paper I had assigned. My reaction was that he was trying to 'get away with something' by handing in an off-the-cuff version of what I had intended to be an in-depth assignment. In fact, I was sure this was his intent. I gave him a barely passing grade and asked him to come talk to me. The upshot of our conversation was that we both stood our ground. He decided to accept the grade, even though I was willing to negotiate some written addendum to the tape.

Was this student trying to slide by on the assignment? Probably. Was he also trying to find out how much I would allow him (and the class) to influence the conditions under which he learned and I taught, how much I was willing to treat him as an informed and potentially creative individual? Probably. Did I respond to both possibilities? I still don't know for sure.

Now, the second story, in which I continue to exhibit my need to satisfy myself that I can trust those with authority to respond nonpunitively to being challenged. In this story, the authority figure's response was different. In a class on group dynamics, we had to write four papers and an analytic book report. By the end of the semester, I did not want to write a fifth paper (the book report); so I conceived a small piece of research. I read Freed Bales' interpersonal coding scheme for groups, collected data from the group I was in, and produced a three-dimensional plexiglas sculpture that represented the relationships in the group according to Bales' coding scheme.[92]

Instead of a paper, I turned in the sculpture. It would have been easy for the professor to hand back the sculpture. After all, how do you give a grade to a sculpture in a social science course? In this case, the professor gave the sculpture an A and to this day both of us remember both the event and the theoretical material on which the sculpture was based.

I am sure that the professor who received the sculpture struggled with the 'assault' on his authority that this 'submission' represented, but his overwhelming response was to the fact that I had made the assignment my own and approached it with a measure of creativity. I felt this statement (both the grade and the obvious pleasure the professor took from my having undertaken such a project in his class) supported my development and my own self-confidence grew as a result.

In this case, there was no downside, no patient at risk, no skill unmastered, no irritated colleagues angry over this professor's relaxed standards. Nonetheless, I suspect it was not easy to take this view of a sculpture. Isn't it the job of an authority figure to uphold standards?

Followership

It is possible for a teacher to see the importance of rebellion and the response to it, to see that a response to it may enable students and colleagues to empower themselves, even to take pleasure in being challenged, but at the same time to mean by rebellion 'intellectual rebellion' or dissent. The tools of 'rebellion' are in this case intellectual tools (for example, the resident who knows details of subsequent events in a patient's psychotherapy the preceptor does not know, and is enabled thereby to challenge the preceptor's interpretation or understanding).

My interest in rebellion and perhaps my choice of the word is rooted in the emotional and relational aspects of this challenge to authority. Rebellion challenges the direction in which a relationship is being taken and the right of one person (the authority) to decide that direction. It is also an expression of the feelings that people have, often ambivalent, about leading and following. In thinking about the question 'how to train a different kind of institutional leader?' I thought of the need to reinvigorate our ideas about followers. I am concerned both with how leaders think about followers and how followers think about themselves.

My fear is that the call for strong leadership is a response to an impoverished view of followership. The term itself, followership, often conjures up images of obedient sheep mindlessly walking one behind the other. In all too many cases, faced with the burdens of leadership and the overwhelming number of tasks required of leaders in large organizations, people with significant authority value obedience more than they might like to admit. (Remember Marshall's attitude when he became the chief of a clinical service toward the residents when they didn't do what he told them to do.) When followers become leaders, and all they know is obedience (a bit of an exaggeration, but only a bit in most organizations), they have a very limited leadership repertoire.

I have asked managers and organizational leaders what they want in a subordinate, a follower. What emerges, in addition to loyalty and competence, is a strong and abiding willingness to speak one's mind even and especially if that mind is in conflict with the leader. No one wants a follower who just goes along in spite of her or his reservations, because this version of obedience jeopardizes the leader and the enterprise.[93] So, if a great many leaders value followers whose strengths complement the leaders' weaknesses, who speak their minds, and who are self-confident, why are there so many instances of leaders who cannot seem to handle these attributes in a follower? And why do we find it hard to handle these attributes in those who are assigned to follow us?

Abusive authority

How do we break the cycle of abusive authority? I must start with the personality or, more accurately from my point of view, the legacy of an individual's experience with authority figures: parents, teachers, bosses, supervisors. I remember Marshall's story of how he used something told to him by a resident who trusted him to criticize the resident and then justified this behavior, which he immediately regretted, with the rationalization, 'It's for your own good.' The phrase reminds me of Alice Miller's work.[94] She contends that authority figures are condemned to treat those in their charge in a way that passes on the abuse they received from parents and elders. This is not an optimistic thesis since parental abuse in reality may be more common than previously suspected, and what the child experiences as some form of parental abuse is probably nearly universal.

I believe that organizational life similarly affects how we fill the role of leader, of psychotherapist, of any position of authority. How others treated Marshall when he was in a subordinate role played a huge part in how he acted when he occupied a role in which he had authority. He observed with distress how easily he became authoritarian in spite of his intense dislike of being treated that way. The implicit belief behind his distress is that bad experiences lead to good intentions and then to good behavior. But, as he experienced, the opposite is what is likely to occur. Abusive authority perpetuates itself and responsible authority likewise.

Most of us have had both kinds of experiences – some good teachers and supervisors and some not so good. Some did not or could not handle rebellion, independence, or creativity within their institutional roles. (I think of Marshall's story about his experience with the Chairman of the Department of Psychiatry when he was a medical student, and with the Clinical Director when he was a resident.) Yet others helped us to trust both our analytic skills and our intuitions, our knowledge and our emotions, so that we can work. (I think of Marshall's story about the Psychiatrist-in-Chief who met his young schizophrenic patient with him, and about the supervisor who understood his action of standing between his patient and the door.) The result of this combination of experiences is that most of us struggle with the exercise of authority when we have it. We may observe with some unhappiness our tendencies toward harshness or unfairness. But at the same time the good experiences may result in our capacity to learn, self-reflection, and our ability to change in our authority relationships.

Dynamics of hierarchical institutions

I want to be clear about one thing, however. Authority figures who are able to engage rather than reject the inevitable rebellion that attends professional growth in a hierarchical social system create conditions for the development of nonabusive leaders. But nonabusive authority relations do not guarantee this outcome. The dynamics of hierarchical institutions stack the deck against collaborative trustful relations among those with differences in authority.

My close friend and colleague Kenwyn Smith studied a number of hierarchical systems and drew a compelling but disturbing picture of their recurring dynamics.[95] His first finding: The position of 'powerlessness' and the vulnerability associated with it produce a deep mistrust and suspicion of 'people at the top' no matter how benign and well-intentioned their actions *really* are. In the one case where I worked with Smith observing behavior in a hierarchical social system, I remember how shocked I was that the low-power group was so mistrustful of an 'elite' for whose noble intentions I had evidence in my research role. It is now difficult for me to imagine overstating the degree to which hierarchy in itself produces mistrust, suspicion, and the attribution of malign intentions.

Second finding: Hierarchical relationships are intrinsically characterized by a distinct unwillingness at all levels to be self-scrutinizing. Smith called this 'dynamic conservatism'. There is a lot of activity, especially at the top of an organization, but very little self- examination. Organizational changes, meetings, personnel shifts, all serve to insulate and seal off the authority structure. The powerless are not terribly interested in examining themselves any more than are the powerful, since this examination itself threatens to increase a group's vulnerability ('show no weakness').

This unwillingness to examine authority relations is a self-sealing process that takes enormous energy to break. Awareness of just how difficult it is to change the social-systemic forces that maintain the authority relations we deplore is cause for distress and discouragement.

But both Marshall and I do have stories about moderately successful attempts to alter relationships between groups in organizations, even groups with different responsibilities and status. Stories about instituting patient–staff community meetings for joint problem-solving. Stories about creating an administrative role dedicated to making sure that the authority structure exposes itself to critical feedback, welcomes it, and is able to listen to it. Stories that we hope will ignite others' commitment to similar undertakings and that now bolster our own.

When leaders make mistakes

We will, however, inevitably make mistakes. There are no perfect organizations, no perfect leadership personalities, no perfect relationships. Even in an 'objectively' perfect world, the differing views of reality born of our group memberships would produce imperfection. So what's to be done about the inevitability of mistakes, especially by those who have institutional authority?

I think the way we respond to our mistakes is probably more important than how frequently we act successfully. This assertion feels related to my statement about the importance of authority's response to rebellion. Only in this case what's at issue is our reaction to our own behavior. Dealing with mistakes is even more difficult when someone with less experience or status points out the error, but this is the circumstance in which a mistake and the way it is handled can make a contribution to the development of positive authority relations. If an authority figure or group denies mistakes, blames them on another person or part of the system, or rationalizes or ignores them, the refusal to examine directly an important recurring part of organizational life cripples the ability of that person or group to function.

Just as important, the subordinate, for example, a trainee or student, now finds herself in a relationship that cannot help but stifle her development. For if a supervisor or teacher can never make or examine a mistake, and *I* as a trainee or student *know* I make mistakes, how can I ever become a supervisor or teacher? Only, of course, if I develop the ability to deny, ignore, not recognize, and never examine whatever mistakes and failures come my way.

The story of a campus strike

I am reminded of that semester during which there was a strike on campus. The university employees who handled all maintenance and food service as well as all the clerical and technical employees walked off the job. In my class on organizational behavior we had many discussions about what to do since picket lines surrounded our building. The class was about equally divided among those who supported the strikers, those who did not, and those who didn't care but resented the disruption. One of our major decisions was whether to hold our class off campus so that a portion of the class would not have to cross the picket lines.

In the midst of this intense and divisive discussion (which mirrored the intensity and divisiveness of the strike itself), I decided to 'teach' the students something about authority figures. After much deliberation, I made the conscious decision to tell the class where my own sentiments were (I supported the strike). I did this to illustrate that authority figures had viewpoints, strong feelings, values, politics, and prejudices, just like everyone else. I wanted to confront the implicit notion that students could only learn from a teacher who was neutral (or who agreed with them); I had observed that students often ignored the values and politics of professors, suspended judgment, in order to prevent their emotional reactions from interfering with their ability to learn. Since teachers, bosses, supervisors, leaders *do* have values and political beliefs, I reasoned it made sense to examine the hypothesis that you can only 'follow' or learn from a neutral authority figure (not often found in nature).

Well, I think I made a mistake. And so did lots of other people, most notably the students in my class. I realized, too late, that my role in the classroom was to help the students learn about what they were experiencing – the tension, divisiveness, distortion, and anger that often accompany a job action. It was my job to enable the kind of exchange from which the class could learn: an open frank discussion, to the extent possible, of the feelings and issues that were affecting our organization and our task. By 'siding' with one of the student factions, I made it impossible for me to do my job. I came to this realization after talking with colleagues about my pain in the classroom and after devoting a class session to working with the students to generate hypotheses to explain our collective distress and tension. The students suggested that my behavior had contributed to the difficult, unproductive atmosphere in the class. To the extent that we were able to 'regroup' that semester, I think it was because we were able to examine my mistakes (as well as theirs).

Part of the story of this mistake was a personal story. In reflecting about why I had made the mistake to begin with, I realized some weeks after that I still reproached myself for not having acted during the 1960s with respect to issues about which I had deep convictions; this time I was determined I was not going to be neutral. This determination led me to believe that I could both reveal a value position on this issue and at the same time avoid being an authority figure influencing the group's consideration of and ultimate stand on the issue. I could not.

The story of the teacher who took a holiday

I also remember a fall course in which I arranged for a colleague to come and teach my class on the Jewish New Year when I did not come to work. At the end of the preceding class, I announced the arrangements and said that I would not be at the next class. A Jewish student asked to speak to me after class and through tears that expressed her fury, and with a few other Jewish students around, she told me how angry she was that I had made arrangements so that I could observe the Jewish High Holy Days, but had left the Jewish students in my class with the dilemma about whether to come to class or 'skip'. Since this was occurring in the first few weeks of their graduate program, many of them experienced this as a tense and unfair choice. That this dilemma was presented to them by a Jewish teacher was especially insulting.

I was crushed. They were right. I was embarrassed and ashamed. It took me a few minutes to realize what I had done and how oblivious I had been to what now seemed so obvious. In hindsight, this event had at least two significant effects. First, I have never done this again, choosing instead to reschedule class or to give an assignment that students can schedule over a period of time during my absence. Second, from that moment forward in the class, I felt that many of the students believed that this was an authority relationship in which they could express a wide range of opinions, emotions, and reactions, without an overriding fear that they would be punished because the instructor, when confronted with anger or blame, needed to find a way to make someone else responsible. My statement that none of us is perfect applies to me, but I think this early mistake contributed to a classroom environment in which it was easier to accept and examine the different experiences of the two 'authority groups' in the classroom.

I think it was Winnicott who said that it is precisely the errors of the parent that allow for the growth of the child.[96] (I find this to be no small comfort as I worry my way through raising my own children.) I would add that the errors of those with authority allow others to identify with them, to envision and enact a relationship with them, a relationship that has a measure of mutuality along with hierarchy. I do not think the leadership of any organization can afford to ignore the information, experience, expertise, and professional development of the rest of the members of the organization. For me this translates into the realization that leaders and teachers influence and are influenced by those with less formal authority, and that organizations involve collaborative relationships that neither obliterate authority differences ('I can't learn [or teach!] unless we are equals') nor demand obedience in the face of these differences ('I can't teach [learn] unless you [I] accept my [your] authority').

Too old for rebellion?

I notice that many of Marshall's and my stories about rebellion date from our years as trainees and graduate students, and that many of our mistakes, and also our insights, occurred later in life as we inhabited authority roles in organizations. I wonder if there is a lesson here. Perhaps, it is too late now for us to be fully engaged in rebellion. We have made and needed to make too many accommodations to the pressures, demands, and opportunities of the 'adult' world. That world, for better or worse, is ours. Perhaps it is those who 'follow' us who, quite naturally, and enabled by our mistakes, must make a relationship with the authority we represent through their rebellion.

We who have authority may still take on the work of changing authority structures in organizations, but our work is not rebellion, rather, collaboration with those of another generation. Our awareness and experience, in collaboration with the potential for rebellion that those who come after us represent, may actually create some movement where neither alone could expect to succeed.

PART 5

Pernicious Processes in Groups

It comes as a great shock around the age of 5, 6, or 7... to see Gary Cooper killing off the Indians and, although you are rooting for Gary Cooper, [to discover] that the Indians are you.

James Baldwin

...The average person is average
the common people is common
the straight people is straight
you gone be the crooked weird
rare intelligent bird creep type
that what you gone be, honey
            you gone look funny
            when they put you in your
            coffin
            like you something
            unright
            like you ain't
worth dying
like every day when they passes out the
honey
you gone get a little vial of fear and
you gone drink it yes you is...

A.R. Ammons

CHAPTER 19

Thrown to the Wolves

Marshall Edelson

Inevitably, the pernicious processes that are part of group and organizational life produce casualties. These processes are destructive of individuals and of the group's or the organization's tasks. It is a leader's job to recognize that such a process is occurring, to refuse the invitation to benefit from it, and to intervene if necessary to thwart it.

I am remembering:

- a leader's *sacrifice* of a subordinate, who was 'thrown to the wolves' (passively or actively offered to other subordinates as a target), in order to protect the leader from dissent or difficulty (though at the cost of unproductive conflict and damaged relations among subordinates)

- a group's or organization's sometimes overtly hostile, sometimes apparently solicitous, *scapegoating* of an individual, who, demeaned and rejected, had become the receptacle of what the other members wanted to disown, what they refused to acknowledge in themselves – and, similarly, an organization's scapegoating of a group

- the *blaming* of an individual in a group or organization, and the similar blaming of a group in an organization, no adequate group-as-a-whole or social-systemic analysis having been made (that is, no attempts to identify the many determinants of or various contributors to a problem having been made), thereby protecting the complicitous, and taking refuge in what seemed simple or obvious rather than struggling with complexity

- and a group's *sacrifice* of one of its members, who had been elected by other members to attack, on their behalf, a leader whom they feared – who had been elected, in other words, 'to bell the cat' – and who, disregarding the risks involved, if indeed aware of them at all, had accepted this assignment.

I am thrown to the wolves

Here is the story of a leader's *sacrifice* of a subordinate, who was 'thrown to the wolves' (passively or actively offered to other subordinates as a target), in order to protect the leader from dissent or difficulty (though at the cost of unproductive conflict and damaged relations among subordinates). I was the sacrificed subordinate. In my first major conscious experience of a pernicious group process leading to a casualty, I was the casualty.

The medical director of a small residential treatment center had invited me to join its staff and do something about the therapeutic community program there. But the egalitarian ethos of that institution made it unsuitable, he implied, to give me any title or position, which would of course have made clear what task he expected me to do. I was to be just another staff member. In fact, it turned out that he had not told anyone why he had asked me to join the staff, apparently feeling that this would imply a criticism and hurt the feelings of those involved in the program.

I was indeed innocent in those days about group and organizational processes, with no sense of what the proper stance and attitudes of a newcomer to such an institution were. Like a lamb to the slaughter, I went full of enthusiasm and ideas about the therapeutic community program, only to find that as I expressed these, I was met with hostility, suspicion, and obstruction. 'We don't do it that way here.' Stupidly, over and over I presented 'brilliant' position papers at staff meetings justifying my proposals for the therapeutic community program. The cleverer my arguments, the worse matters became.

Harmony among staff members was especially valued in this residential treatment center, for they lived as an isolated enclave in a small town, and depended on each other for social as well as work satisfactions. Someone who comes into such an organization and proposes change implies criticism of existing ways of doing things. He will be seen not as enhancing harmony, but as a troublemaker.

It took more than a year of unpleasantness before I was able to bring about the creation of a daily community meeting including patients and all staff. Luck was with me; processes in that meeting led to a real change in the quality of people's lives. A turning point was a discussion that led to the patients actually bringing about a change in the lunch menu to include more hamburgers.[97] The elders of the community ultimately promulgated a statement saying among other things that 'It is now hard to imagine this place without such a community meeting. It has proved its value especially as a place where news is disseminated and destructive rumors can be checked.' However, most of the staff continued to regard me as a difficult person to work with, not a team player, hard to get along with; they speculated about my personality disorders. I felt put in a box from which, no matter what I did or said, I could not escape.

Beginning to understand this group experience

It was an important experience, which came too late, when I subsequently ran across an article by Jules Henry in the journal *Psychiatry*.[98] He described what happens to someone who comes into an organization with an informal understanding of what her or his task is to be, but without explicit delegation of responsibility and authority to carry it out. He seemed to have been eavesdropping on my life, as he described the attitudes of suspicion aroused by every behavior of a person in such a position, and all the sequelae arising from that suspicion.

I thought that the opinions of my colleagues had so damaged my reputation that I would never get a job anywhere else. Fortunately, later on, a chairman of a university department of psychiatry was willing to take a chance on a 'difficult person'; he offered me a position on the faculty, responsible for a teaching program. The painfulness of this whole experience probably had something, although not everything, to do with the fact that my career since leaving that residential treatment center has been in teaching and not in realizing an old dream of creating a therapeutic community.

Having some knowledge of myself, I would not want to deny that my own personality characteristics contributed to my unhappy experience and work difficulties. But the moral of this story for me remains that even when something about an individual seems unquestionably to be causing a problem, it may be worthwhile to change the frame – and ask, '*What is it about the group or organization that encourages and makes use of – exacerbates rather than mitigates – this individual's dysfunctional propensities?*'

Understanding the organizational dynamics underlying this group experience

Usually, the attempt to answer such a question results in becoming aware of how many people at different levels in a hierarchy share some responsibility for what at first seems to be an individual's incompetence, troublesome or obnoxious behavior, or failure. That will include becoming aware also of the way in which leadership 'at the top' functions and what contribution that has made to the problem. What does such leadership want? What are its anxieties, dilemmas, motives? What are its actual though unacknowledged as against its avowed interests? If you want to understand messes at lower levels of a hierarchy, it is always necessary, although obviously also difficult, to look at what is going on at higher levels.

In my story, the medical director preferred not to make explicit the reason he had brought me into the organization. He did not give me a differentiated role. He might have justified this as 'giving the person a chance to get to know the organization and giving the organization a chance to look the person over before committing itself'. But he did not make this justification explicit to me. I, full of ambition and pride in myself and my work, plunged in, without caution, justifying my recklessness, when I thought about it at all, with the idea, 'This is what the medical director secretly and really wants me to do.' So I went ahead and innovated my own role. That stirred up a lot of suspicions and various kinds of fantasies in others about what I was up to. The medical director did not support me as others quarreled with and obstructed me. Rather, he criticized me for my inability to get along with others. I felt abandoned, 'thrown to the wolves'. Feeling that way, I began to withdraw in more or less subtle ways from other staff members, who increasingly felt that I did not care about the their ideas or value their experience.

But, having apparently located the problem in the medical director, or even in the complementary contributions of both the medical director and the newcomer, should we stop our inquiry? Is this all simply a result of their ignorance of what happens in an organization to a newcomer who enters without an explicit role? Is the medical director's wish to avoid trouble, his not wanting to seem to criticize staff members who have been working in the therapeutic community program, simply a quirk, a failure of courage?

Consider the medical director's relations to those above him, the board of trustees, or representatives of the community or other organizations on whose goodwill and respect the residential treatment center depends. (They are sources of patients, of money.) If in our inquiry we keep going up, we might hear that the medical director is under attack from a board member just at the time he recruits the newcomer. The board member has challenged the selection of the newcomer, along with many other decisions the medical director has made, as part of an attempt to discredit him. For the board member and medical director had very different visions of the mission of the residential treatment center.

Knowing this, we might then speculate that the besieged medical director does not want to face challenge from two directions. It is especially important to him to have the support of his staff at this time. So to avoid offending them has priority, as he defends his leadership and vision of the institution from external attack.

Understanding does not mean deciding that it is the medical director, the newcomer, some member of the group that the newcomer joins, or some other group in the organization that is really to blame for 'the problem' – but rather recognizing each one's piece. But neither does understanding mean exonerating any of the participants from responsibility for acquiring a more sophisticated appreciation of organizational processes in order to avoid individual casualties.

A similar analysis of another organization's dynamics

It is years after my trials as a newcomer. I have since reflected on my experiences with authority and as a casualty. I am now talking to a group of residents about their experiences as residents in the Department of Psychiatry in which we work. My aim is to develop a story with them that helps them to understand these experiences, but a story in which there are no villains, a story that *blames no one* for these experiences, a story in which we come to recognize that each actor (individual or collective) responds to different necessities and contributes a different piece.

This is more difficult than it sounds. We all want a world simpler than it is, in which there are heroes and villains, and in which there are no unalterable conditions limiting the actors' actions, no necessities that we cannot ameliorate. We don't want a world in which we are asked to recognize that one way or another we all share responsibility for – we are all implicated in – we all contribute something to – distress, problems, failures in the social systems to which we belong.

The residents tell their own stories full of anger, full of blame for 'the department' and the leader of the residency program. 'No one cares about us. We can't trust anyone to keep their word. We don't get information about schedules, plans, decisions in any predictable way. We have to keep asking, and then someone answers, "I don't know yet." No one seems to be able to make decisions. We can never find out who is supposed to act when there is a problem. Various individual ones of us, acting on our own, have to take care of it; otherwise, nothing happens.'

What is going on in the residents' group?

After some discussion, we begin to notice that a lot of their distress has to do with a sense of how isolated they are in their work. Literally, because it is a big program with many clinical sites, they do not work together. They do not help each other. They compete with each other for desired clinical assignments, fellowships, faculty jobs.

Belonging to the resident group is a negative identity, one to move out of. There is little incentive to identify with this group, or to join with others in it to make joint decisions or to arrive at collective solutions to problems. Residents in their ambitions are identified with the faculty. Above all, they want to be free of 'the group', no matter at what cost to problem-solving, in order for each to be able to wheel and deal as an individual in her or his relations with faculty to get what she or he wants. Many residents do not attend meetings of their own resident association, and seem little interested in resident activities.

This 'individualism' is also expressed in the fact that the residents do not experience themselves as one group. Rather, each year's residents consider themselves as a group different from the other years' groups, with different interests, problems, relation to the faculty. Each group faces its own necessities. Each group insists on having its own representatives in every meeting with the faculty. Each makes its own decisions on matters that concern it. Those in later years do not work with or mentor those in earlier years, but rather are felt by those in earlier years to have the attitude, 'We had to go through all that, struggle with those problems and frustrations. Why shouldn't you?'

In these discussions, then, we come to look at the way in which the residents' personal strivings, wishes to be free of their own group, and their own intergroup relations affect their ability to come together, to make joint decisions, in order to communicate effectively and with one strong voice in their relation to the faculty. This contributes to the difficulty the residents and faculty have in solving problems together.

The structure of the system in which the residents receive their training – the size of the program, the large number of clinical sites to which residents are assigned, the frequency with which they are rotated independently of each other from site to site – exacerbates rather than mitigates their personal dispositions (ambition, competitiveness, individualism). The faculty do not take steps to counter this individualism, this fragmentation of the resident group, by organizing the work of residents in a way that encourages them to form a strong solidary group (for example, assigning a number of residents to work together on a unit, keeping them together over a period of their training, and meeting with each such group to help its members understand the dynamics of their own work group). We may assume that the faculty does not take such steps because faculty members have similar personal dispositions (which are, by and large, supported by the values of the hierarchical, medical, entrepreneurial-research system in which they work). Also, those at upper levels of a hierarchy rarely see any advantage in being confronted by a determined united group of those at lower levels in the hierarchy.

What is going on between clinical institutions in the department?

Moving up and out from the residents' own group, we notice parallels between their individualism and competitiveness and the individualism and competitiveness of the member clinical institutions making up the department. Each one is its own financial center. All except one are embedded in and responsible to leaders in other extra-departmental systems, each with its own sources of funding, budgets, rules, priorities, procedures, staff and faculty, kind of patients, preferred treatment strategies, ideology (veterans administration, the state, a private hospital, a university health service). The leaders of each clinical institution respond to different necessities.

Those leaders in each institution tend to be seen by those in other institutions and by those in the 'center' as having the attitude that, whatever the advantages of recruiting residents to one central prestigeful university program, 'our residents belong to us', and that 'we are the best judges of what training these residents need and the best providers of that training'. Each institution is determined that no decision shall be made by others about the resident program that does not involve it and take into consideration its interests. On the other hand, residents tell stories in which a member of one institution tries to bring about a change in the residents' program by just telling residents to do 'it' (whatever 'it' is), without any consultation with the faculty and staff members of other institutions who would be affected by the residents doing it.

This structure, a federation of institutions each embedded in a different system, a system other than the department, is a social-systemic determinant for what otherwise might be looked at as an expression of the personal traits, as the excessive 'competitiveness' and 'individualism', of the leaders of these institutions. The nature of these inter-institutional relations seems to account for a number of phenomena. One phenomenon is the residents' experience of being 'in the middle' of warring centers of power. A second is the tendency to appoint relatively low-status (junior or part-time) faculty members to the position of Director of the Residency Program, and to be reluctant to give that faculty member, who supposedly 'directs' the residency program, any authority that would enable him to make timely decisions; he must consult with each node of power. (Given that each clinical institution in which residents train has to take different interests into consideration, no institution wants to have to deal with a powerful Director.) This goes a long way toward explaining the long delays before residents get a decision from the Director of Residency Training, and the apparent inability of the Director of the Residency Program, whose decisions may be countered or reversed by powerful others, to make or keep a commitment to the residents. (This inability is usually seen as the result of defects in his personality or character.) A third, expectable phenomenon is the low morale of one Director of the Residency Program after another. He is 'between' residents and faculty, blamed by residents for their frustrations and by faculty for siding and being too soft with, giving in to, the residents.

What is going on in the leadership structure of the department?
Following this analysis, the group and I in our discussion continue to move up the hierarchy. The residents ask, 'Why doesn't the Chairman take a hand? Why doesn't he back up the Director of the Residency Program in his relations with the leaders of clinical institutions when this Director is trying to protect the boundaries of the training enterprise in its relation to the clinical and research enterprises of the department? Why doesn't the chairman devote more time to mediating between clinical institutions when they have differences concerning the training, assignment, and treatment of residents? Why doesn't he do something to mitigate the centrifugal forces and enhance the centripetal forces in the department, to bring people together around common purposes?' (Toward

this end he has in fact made a major perhaps relatively overlooked effort to encourage joint research across clinical institutions.)

But to answer these questions, we have to take into consideration what preoccupies the chairman, what presses on him. What are the necessities to which he responds?

1. The Chairman is largely dependent on the individual clinical institutions for money and space, including money to pay residents. ('He who pays the piper calls the tune.') He is in no position to knock heads together or to make a decision when there is an impasse.

2. The Chairman is likely to give priority in allocating his own attention to the research and clinical enterprises over the educational enterprise, given the relative sizes of the budgets involved, and his perception of the relative importance each has for the reputation of the Department and indeed its survival.

3. Above all, the Chairman, who is on the boundary between the department and its *external* situation, must devote a major part of his time relating to the Dean of the Medical School and the President of the University, and to the agents of change in that external situation, especially when the external situation is changing hugely and rapidly, as it now is – rather than to problems of *internal* integration of the department. Threats and opportunities these days come from outside the department, and problems of internal integration understandably take a back seat. How residents are feeling, while important to the Chairman, cannot compare, with respect to impact on the future of the department, with changes in the discipline of psychiatry, changes in the way clinical care of patients is funded, changes in priorities and the availability of support for research.

So, in this inquiry, moving ever upwards in the hierarchy in our analysis (as in some inquiries, we might move laterally and both up and down in the hierarchy), we reach a similar point and a similar kind of understanding of group experiences.

When I am the leader who sacrifices a subordinate

Much later in my life, when I occupied a relatively high position in a hierarchy, I ducked a challenge from a subordinate on at least one occasion, protecting myself at the expense of a subordinate who took the brunt of the attack which should have gone to and been accepted by me. This was similar to the way the medical director, who many years previously had brought me as a newcomer without a clear role to his residential treatment center, had acted at my expense. (Just what we might expect from the stories in Chapter 16 about how authority figures treat their subordinates as they have been treated.)

Frieda, one of the members of a self-analytic training group, brought the group back to an experience in the previous meeting, when she felt attacked again by Jack, another member, who had energetically and intensely disagreed with something she had proposed. 'I don't understand what happened. Why did he jump on me in that way? That was very upsetting to me, and I thought about it a lot afterwards. This seems to me to have happened before. Is it something about me? Is it because I'm a woman?'

We gradually reconstructed what had happened at that previous meeting. It became clear that if we had not been able to remember the exact events, and more importantly the precise order in which they had occurred, it would have been almost impossible for us to see what led to the event Frieda wanted to understand: Jack's way of disagreeing with her proposal.

In the previous meeting, we had been discussing a way of proceeding with our work. We had all been throwing ideas into the hopper, making a list of things we wanted to keep in mind as we got into the work. After a while, group members had turned to me, the leader, and asked if I would use my notes of the discussion to write up the list, copy it, and distribute it to them. In reply, I had commented on people's wishing to turn to me and have me function as the 'thinking mind' of the group.

Velma, clearly hearing this as a criticism, had burst out, 'That isn't fair! You could have told us at the beginning that we should take notes and write up the list as we went along.'

I had responded, 'If I had done that, I would have been trying to control what happens and what doesn't happen in the group. I would have been making sure that you would not allow yourselves to arrive at a state in which you wanted to depend on me. But I hold myself responsible to create the conditions in which you can learn. How do you learn what it feels like to want to depend on a leader for certain functions if I take actions to prevent you from developing such feelings?'

Velma had subsided, looking down at the table, as if squelched. Then Jack said, semi-admiringly, 'Boy, you sure are a difficult person to disagree with!'

Encouraged by Frieda, the group had tried to mobilize itself to reproduce the list we had been creating in our discussion. She had suggested that, instead of turning to me, members should turn to each other. 'Together, we all have at least some of the points we want to keep in mind in our work. We can put these parts we each have together, and write up the whole list.' But Jack had interrupted this process, objecting strongly to what Frieda was doing that others seemed ready to go along with. He had said somewhat angrily, 'I have the whole list in my head. I don't need it to be written down. I don't need any external help to hold onto what I already have inside myself.'

After making this reconstruction of what had happened in the previous meeting, I offered an interpretation of these events that was intended to answer Frieda's question, 'Why did Jack behave that way toward me?' I said, 'I assume that, just as in a family the younger child watches to see how the parent treats a rebellious older child, learns from it, and behaves accordingly, more circumspectly perhaps, so in a group, members watch to see how a leader deals with dissent and behave accordingly. Jack had heard my response to Velma's objection to what I had said to the group. Responding to her, I had defended myself, explained why I had said what I said, justified it as in the interest of the group. "It was for your own good that I said what I said." I had not accepted Velma's anger at me, inquired about it, asked her to elaborate, or encouraged her to say what it was about what I had said, the way I had said it, or how she had heard it that upset her. Jack had observed the effect of my response on Velma. My "reasonableness" and "reasons" had the effect of putting her in the wrong, silencing her, even perhaps making her feel ashamed of objecting to what I said. Perhaps, Jack had decided then that it didn't pay to tackle or challenge me.

'Frieda's proposal was actually *her* way of disagreeing with what I had said about members' dependence on me. She was saying, "We can do it on our own. We don't need the leader." Jack's disagreeing with *her* proposal was *his* way of disagreeing with me. "I have it in my head. I don't need outside help from anything (or anybody). I don't need to make a list." In this way, indirectly, he had joined with Velma in rejecting what I had said to the group about members depending on me, by rejecting my suggestion about having a list. But he had joined with her safely – that is, without exposing himself to the experience he had seen Velma having – by attacking Frieda, as if, in making her proposal, Frieda had agreed with my comment about the value of a list and dependence on the leader for it. He could not see, because he needed someone beside me to attack in order to express his disagreement with me safely, that Frieda too, although in another way, agreed with Velma and him in rejecting what I had said.'

Following this interpretation, we considered what the moral of this story might be. When a leader suppresses or discourages dissent or challenges to his leadership, is conflict among group members, and perhaps the selection of a particular member as target of the group's wrath, a likely consequence? How much of what goes on among members is a consequence of their relation to the group's leader?

In a meeting months later, Jack presented a situation from his own work setting. During the group's discussion of this 'case', I made several blunt comments, identifying important problems in leadership I thought well illustrated by Jack's participation in the events he described. Since addressing more directly the actions of group members in the situations they presented was a relatively new feature of our group discussions, I asked, at the end of this discussion, how Jack had experienced the comments about his own leadership behavior.

'Fine,' he said. 'I learned a lot from them. I felt comfortable during the discussion.' Then he added with considerable force and feeling, 'But I felt really hurt when Frieda said that, hearing my story, she would not want to work in my institution.' Frieda was taken aback, said that was not what she meant to convey by the comment she had made, and became quite upset about the way in which Jack 'had turned on' her. He was astonished by her response, not having expected his comment to have such an impact.

After the meeting was over, in thinking about it, I remembered the previous interaction involving Jack and Frieda. At our next meeting, I was able to consider with the group whether we now had another example of the same dynamic. For Jack had apparently suppressed any reaction to my comments about his actions. He did not say to me, for example, 'I experienced some of your comments about me as unfair and hurtfully critical. And they seemed to have made other group members see my work setting in an unfavorable light.' Instead any feeling of hurt or resentment he had was directed solely at Frieda.

CHAPTER 20

Scapegoating

Marshall Edelson

Scapegoating is important, ubiquitous, and one of the most pernicious processes in group and organizational life. The typical scenario for the scapegoating of an individual member or a subgroup of a group, or of a group in an organization, unfolds as follows. Members of a group or organization deal with a problem by simplifying it, attributing it to a struggle between two mutually exclusive opposites. It is *either* this *or* that. 'I/We must either be tough or tender, either want to be here or not want to be here, want to do this or not want to do this, either feel this way or feel that way.'

Often, the situation is more complicated. That's really why there is a problem. *Both* this *and* that exist together. But either/or thinking leads members to *split* what actually co-exists. They accept, acknowledge, are willing to own one of the two pieces that issue from the split, while they *reject*, refuse to acknowledge, want to *disown*, the other – some feeling, attitude, belief, or impulse in themselves.

Looking for some person or some group to *blame*, members put (*project*) what is unwanted in themselves into a member, subgroup, or group, already marked in some way as *different* or *other*. That is, they now perceive it to be *there*, outside themselves, where it can be extruded from their group or organization, isolated, 'treated'.

Members remain identified with what of themselves they have projected, and so they become identified with the targets of their projections. (That is why we speak of *projective identification* rather than *projection*.) They not only blame or, trying to help, thereby more or less subtly devalue a particular member; their identification with that member is indicated by how fascinating they find him or her. They dwell upon, come back again and again to, and want to hear all about the scandalous behavior, 'problems', 'difficulties', and 'pain', of those with whom they projectively identify.

Projective identification enters into processes other than scapegoating. Rather than commitment to a task, it is projective identification that may, for example, create bonds among members of a group, defining the group itself, who is in, who is out.[99] Projective identification may also contribute to solving problems by ensuring that a rejected position gets represented, that dissent gets expressed.[100]

Groups turn to scapegoating because it eliminates the need for an adequate group-as- a-whole or social-systemic analysis of what leads to a problem. There is no need to attempt to identify the many determinants of or various contributors to the problem, an always difficult endeavor. This protects the many who are in some way complicitous. Scapegoating offers a refuge from complexity, when what seems the simplest way to understand a problem is chosen. Then the problem has an obvious 'solution'. 'We know – it is clear – what we have to do.' Scapegoating is a way to avoid a struggle with problems that do not admit of any 'easy fix', sometimes of any fix at all.

How groups drive people mad or drive them away

I have had a recurrent experience in groups and organizations. This experience generates a theme that dominates this book. It is a core part of many of the stories I have remembered and told. Reflecting on it has helped me to understand the widespread ambivalence toward groups and organizations I have encountered, which in the beginning motivated my writing this book – made me feel it was necessary to write it.

I am involuntarily caught up in some process. I find myself yielding without reflection and reacting without hesitation to the invitations, perceptions, provocations, and projections of others. Under pressure, I blurt something out, express myself especially energetically or dramatically, say something blunt, challenging, or inciting. I feel overwhelmed by the pressure. I can't stop 'letting go'. I remember it all afterwards. I remember myself losing control. I feel ashamed, as if I had wet my pants. Hating this shame, I do not want to return to the group. I do not want to be in groups because in them I feel somehow dimly something happens to me as an individual, something I don't like.

But loneliness intervenes. Work needs intervene. The desire to participate in groups returns. I realize, when I am in a leadership position, that to try to participate in a way that guarantees I will never again be 'caught' will cut me off from the group. If I am not caught, how will I know what is going on?

Difference

The experience of 'losing myself' begins with difference. The difference between leaders and followers. The difference between members of a group. The difference between a group and other groups. Many stories about group and organizational life have in common the anxieties these differences arouse; the strategies group members use to manage such anxieties; and the consequences for work that strategies whose primary *raison d'être* is reducing anxiety have.

Here then is what I dread about group life. If there is a difference between us (whether we are different persons or different groups), that difference makes you strange to me and me to you. Just because you are different from me in *some* way that I regard as alien, I can reject you as having *nothing to do with me* in *any* way, and just because I am different from you in some way, you can reject me as having nothing to do with you in any way.

Then, if there is something in myself that is different from the rest of me, that I feel doesn't belong in me, you become a container in which I can throw what I want to disown in myself, just by imagining that what I feel to be not-me is in you. You can be the container in which I dispose of my garbage, which has become *nothing-to-do-with-me*. Since what I don't like in myself is now contained in you, I don't like you. Your smell is disgusting to me. I don't want you around. I want to destroy, get rid of, you. Or more subtly I diminish you. *I* do not have the problem you have. I will help you with *your* problem.

But, just as you become the victim of my attempts to get rid of what I cannot bear in myself, so I suffer from your similar attempts to expel your own unwanted self. I become a container in which you can throw what you want to disown in yourself, in which you dispose of your garbage. Since what you don't like in yourself is now contained in me, you don't like me. My smell is disgusting to you. You don't want me around. You want to destroy, get rid of, me. Or you are 'kind', offer to help me with *my* problem. I wince. I think of Thoreau, knowing for a certainty that a man was coming to his house with the conscious design of doing him good, and running for his life, 'as from that dry and parching wind of the African deserts called the simoon, which fills the mouth and nose and ears and eyes with dust till you are suffocated'.[101] I bear the double burden of whatever it is that is apparently wrong with me and my ungracious inability to benefit from your 'help'.

This then is another source of that shame I experience in group life. I am ashamed not only that I lose control of myself but that also I accept being a receptacle for your refuse. I become your accomplice, though I struggle not to be. I am erratic, unreflective, impulsive, vehement, not myself. I am ashamed at this surrender of myself, that I allow myself to correspond to what you want to imagine about me, meet your expectations, fall for your provocations, go along with your attributions, that I fit in with what you need from me, that I permit you to use me, that I take in what you put into me. It is the deepest – a sexual? – shame.

So we fear each other. We imagine attacks, criticism, rejection, injury, condescension. How do we defend ourselves against them?

We see ourselves pictured in another's eye, unrecognizable to ourselves, identity's fragmentation, dissolution. How do we hold onto, restore, regain our selves?

We anticipate and endure stretches of silence. How do we avoid them, break out of them? We are mired in immobility. How do we move?

We might decrease the distance between ourselves, in an attempt to overcome or transcend it. But will an effort to blur difference result in loss of identity?

We might assert difference. We might attempt to protect ourselves against danger by increasing or exaggerating the distance between ourselves, by building the wall higher, by mounting a preemptive strike, attacking, attempting to push away or obliterate the other. But that raises, when we long for harmony, the specter of disagreement, argument, fighting, unpleasantness, and possible shameful or disastrous defeat.

We might instead evade, avoid, ignore, or deny difference, act as if there were no difference to be acknowledged, live in a world without any difference that disturbs. But efforts to avoid conflict are likely to lead to stagnation.

How can we bridge difference? How do we talk across the difference that separates us? How can we create something new out of difference?

Examples of driving a group member mad or out

I have observed a member of a group relations conference become psychotic. The conference staff, upset, discussed what they should do to help the group member, and went over and over whose fault it is that the member became psychotic. This is a disturbing experience for all involved in it. 'Obviously,' I thought, 'better to avoid it if we can.'

Subsequent experiences in other settings paralleled this kind of experience in these conferences. I observed what happened when a member of a psychotherapy group or a patient in a residential treatment center community meeting provocatively violated the norms and challenged the values of the group or treatment center. Other patients reacted to this behavior by seeing and discussing this member as different from themselves (the 'good citizens'), as infuriating, intolerable, hopeless, bad. Embattled, the provocateur went further and further out on a limb, and raising the ante became increasingly isolated. Periodically, other patients, instead of criticizing this 'bad' patient, would ignore or dismiss everything he said, without regard to whatever value it might have, as if all such communications were tainted.

Eventually, he was driven or extruded from the group. His departure would be precipitated by such statements as these. 'I can't participate in these meetings if he is here. I don't feel safe with him around.' Or 'I don't think we can deal with him, control him. He needs another kind of treatment. He will do better in another group/institution.'

Usually, therapists or staff did not even try to interrupt this process. They did not interpret the patients' shared wish to disown and get rid of rebellion in themselves by locating it in the patient who was 'different'. Like the patient members of the group, they too were focused on the one 'problem patient', and experiencing that patient as resistant to all influence. They too were also exasperated, at their wit's end, discouraged. Often, they joined the process and encouraged it, and justified doing so by thinking that 'feedback' from others in the group was just what this patient needed to straighten him out. 'If he knows how others feel about him, that might provide the reality check and incentive he needs to change.'

I also observed what happened when a member of a psychotherapy group or a patient in a community meeting asked the group for help, sometimes just by presenting problems urgently, desperately, despairingly. The other members of the psychotherapy group or community meeting interviewed the distressed patient, gave her advice or reassurance, offered her interpretations. They seemed to mimic behavior with which they were familiar, that of their own psychotherapists. These other members became increasingly concerned about, and concentrated intensely on trying to help, this person who, far from being helped by the solicitude, the suggestions, advice, and interpretations, the expressions of warmth and caring, became increasingly symptomatic, depressed, disorganized, or suicidal. Why?

The implicit message of the helpers was, 'You are the sick one, sicker than any of us. We don't have any of that sickness in us. We don't experience that problem in ourselves or our lives.' The 'good' citizens or helpers in every case seemed to seek out whomever at any one time was their most vulnerable individual, so that by distinguishing themselves from her or him, they could disown their own potential for or experience with badness or sickness, and not have to suffer their own struggle with it. They rarely responded to such an individual by acknowledging, 'At times, I am like that too or want to be. Once, or recently, I had a similar experience, did the same sort of thing, felt the same way.'

Again, usually, therapists or staff did not even try to interrupt this process. They did not interpret the group members' shared wish to disown and get rid of the sickness in themselves. They too were focused on the one 'problem patient', not on the group-as-a-whole. This individual focus, they felt, befitted and was consistent with their own clinical role, as they saw it, outside the meeting. They believed that, if patients benefit when clinicians respond to them in these ways, then patients can help each other by responding to each other in these ways.

So also, in faculty or staff group meetings, in committees, in various kind of task groups, I have seen group members respond in like ways to their perception that one of them was flouting the norms of the group ('bad' behavior) or was exhibiting some personal deficiency or incompetence that was affecting work performance. 'The fault is in that person. He should be dismissed. She has a *personal* problem. She needs counseling. It has nothing to do with us.'

What seems to determine who in every one of these kinds of groups is chosen to be the scapegoat? People are different in a variety of ways. Gender, generation, race, ethnicity, and socioeconomic status are especially important ways of being different. These differences are associated with differences in authority or power.

Those who belong to a gender, generation, racial, ethnic, or socioeconomic identity group that is rated 'low status' are members at special risk – even more so, if they are the only one of 'that kind' in a group, for example, one woman in a group of men, one black in a group of whites, also (involving other kinds of categories) one psychotic patient in a group of 'better functioning' patients, one adolescent struggling to maintain a moral barrier to chaotic impulses in a group of 'sexually liberated' adolescents, one newcomer in a group of 'old-timers'. Because of the difference and the low status associated with it, such 'marked' members are likely to be chosen as 'appropriate' receptacles for what other members devalue, can't stand, and want to get rid of in themselves. For the same reason, they are also likely to accept or confirm what others disown and project onto them by taking it in ('introjecting it') and identifying with it.

In this way, the members at risk become the group's or organization's 'problem members'. They are peripheralized, driven out, or extruded. And they may collaborate in this process. Is it possible that, introjectively identified with other group members, they may accept the projected contents *on behalf of the group*? That they sacrifice themselves in the interest of the desire of *all* its members to get rid of what is bad, devalued, rejected? They and their contributions to the work of the group are lost. Both they and the work of the group become casualties of a pernicious process.

Some ideas about teaching group psychotherapy

'The Story of the Scapegoated Trainee', which follows, illustrates scapegoating. (Its sequel appeared in Chapter 17: 'The resident who stood up for his patients.') This story involves a parallel between what happened between a resident and me in a preceptorial in group psychotherapy and what happened in the psychotherapy group the resident was presenting to me. Before telling this story, and as background for it, I want to describe how I go about teaching group psychotherapy.

If, in teaching a resident about group psychotherapy, I listen only to an account about some 'problem' or focal patient, I may contribute to the scapegoating of that patient. I am certainly hamstrung with respect to my being able to consider other group members' contribution to this apparently individual story. I find that I must ask for details (what were the other characters doing? what preceded these events?) in order to understand the group story.

So my usual way of teaching group psychotherapy is to listen carefully to the trainee's process account of the meeting. A process account is a story of the session that answers the following questions: What happened in what sequence? Who said what to whom? What was going on in the mind of the psychotherapist – at what points? What did the psychotherapist think, feel, remember, imagine – when? What led up to the psychotherapist's interventions? What were the content, the tone, and the nuances of word-choice that made up these interventions? Judging by what followed them, what impact did they have?

Usually, the resident presents me with a mixture of things done and things said, actions as well as the content of what is said, stories enacted in the session and stories told by different patients. I discourage leaping to a conceptual label for the meeting, a categorization of it, a general theme. 'This was a meeting about anger.' 'This was a meeting about dependency.' Instead, the trainee and I try to imagine, in a freewheeling conversation, how one particular event in the meeting led to the telling of a particular story, how one particular story led to another particular story. Paying attention to sequence is very important here.

We then construct a story in which we provide the *links* between events and stories to make one coherent scenario of the meeting. The link is often that one story is a reaction to, an attempt to do something with what has been aroused by, another story. In other words, we infer motivations and motivated mental operations that might lead from one story enacted or told to another.

Or we detect *similarities* among the stories enacted and told, though they belong to different people, have different characters and settings. One story evokes or brings to mind another because they are similar. From these linkages, and from these similarities, we form an idea of what shared problem the group members are struggling with, what shared anxiety they are trying to avoid, and what the joint strategy is they are using to solve that problem or rid themselves of that anxiety.[102] Each member may make a quite different contribution to the carrying out of this strategy.

In order to enable understanding of process, I had been accustomed to using observations of parallel processes in one-on-one teaching of individual psychotherapy. A trainee and I would observe and reflect on similarities between what was happening between the trainee and a patient and what was happening between that trainee and me. David Berg suggested that if I taught group psychotherapy to a *group* of trainees, rather than to a trainee in a one-on-one *dyad*, the trainees and I would have the opportunity to observe and reflect on parallels between processes in the psychotherapy group and processes in the trainee group.

When David and I eventually taught such a group of trainees together, a very lively learning situation resulted.

In this setting, observing parallel processes, I made the same observation that I had made in trying to create a therapeutic community in an inpatient setting.[103] The problems with which groups of 'sick' people (patients) and groups of 'well' people (hospital staff, doctors, nurses, and here trainees) struggle are similar. And some of the solutions they come up with are also similar.

The story of the scapegoated trainee

Some time before I began teaching group psychotherapy in a group, I was meeting as a preceptor in group psychotherapy with one resident; he was giving me an account of a group psychotherapy meeting. The meeting this resident presented to me had begun with Lois, one of the patients in the group, asking about the resident's state of health. (He had recently been out ill.) The resident thought she was trying to establish a special relationship with him, so his response was laconic and guarded. The resident then paused in his account and asked me if I had a comment because I usually talk as we go along. I beckoned him to continue.

He said that John then mentioned that soon the group was to be disbanded. Mary commented somewhat sarcastically that, since the group members were functioning relatively well, the mental health center regarded them as dispensable. The resident reassured the group members that some sort of appropriate treatment would be planned for them, that they would be able to get their medications, and so on.

I was thinking to myself but did not say that this reassurance was likely to lead to suppression of feelings: 'everything will be all right and you are not justified in having the feelings you're having'. The resident again paused in his account, and asked me if I had a comment. I beckoned him to continue.

Adam's troubles took up the rest of the meeting. The resident was much worried about Adam and so had been meeting with him individually. Adam told the group members at some length about his symptoms and, in passing, mentioned a feeling that someone at work had betrayed him. No one noticed that many of the group members were themselves feeling betrayed by the decision to disband their group. Instead they now organized themselves into 'a patient' (Adam) and 'therapists' (the other group members) – a process that the resident and I had observed previously in our preceptorial. As they advised and 'treated' *the* patient Adam as though none of them had any feelings or experiences like his, he became more disturbed.

A member of any group can be driven crazy by everybody in the room agreeing that there is something wrong with him and he needs help. Nobody else has these problems. Everybody else is doing fine. 'What's wrong with you? Just tell us your problems.'

The resident became angry about what was happening to a patient about whom he was very concerned. He made a comment to the group about the process of splitting the group into one patient and eight therapists. Those taking the role of 'therapist' could then separate themselves from the discomfort of having problems or symptoms. The resident exhorted them instead to join up with Adam and share with him their own experiences that were like his. The resident was satisfied with the content of his comment, but the tone, he felt, was angry and accusatory. And, in fact, the patients responded as if he had scolded them. 'We were just trying to be helpful, to be like therapists.'

After the resident finished, I spoke with considerable vehemence, listing one criticism after another. I pointed out that he had not heard Lois (who asked about his health) as representing the shared concern of group members about him. He had not heard Mary (who spoke of the group members as dispensable) as representing the shared indignation of the group members that their valued group was being taken away from them. He had been so overidentified with Adam that he had for a time stopped concerning himself with the distress other group members were having.

The resident's response was a stricken look. I felt terrible. I made some reassuring comment about the value of this learning process: 'It's a very difficult business, learning how to be a psychotherapist.' My apparently kindly comment of course ensured that he would not easily be able to express how upset he was about my landing on him so. I was such a nice guy, so sweet, so helpful. Instead, he made some self-critical comment about his perfectionism.

Now we had two casualties, the patient who had taken on all the resentment at being betrayed in the group so that others could avoid the risks of expressing it, and the resident in the preceptorial. How had this come about?

The resident and I talked about it. We had both observed the first thing I mentioned. Ordinarily I talked along with him and made comments about the process as he presented it to me. Here I saved everything up and then had burst out with it all at the end, and with considerable force in my voice. Why this departure from my usual practice?

Then I became aware that I had become angry myself as I thought about the group being disbanded, presumably because of a shortage of resources. I am not stupid, I understand there is such a thing as a shortage of resources. But I thought that this disbanding had not been done well. There had been no negotiations with the patients, no consultation with them, or sharing with them what the problems of the institution were. Certainly, there was no sense that, as a group, they might offer some useful ideas about how to deal with these problems. The implementation of the policy was left up to the resident, who had not participated in or identified with all the discussions at a higher level that led to the policy. I was swept up into feeling that it was wrong to treat patients this way. Being exactly as timid as the resident was, I became fearful that, if I said anything, it would come out as a criticism of my colleagues, members of a group to which I belonged. I was afraid what I would say would get back to someone that might make life difficult for me. So I held back, with unhappy results for the resident and our joint teaching-learning task.

The process in the group and in the preceptorial was parallel, since the resident too must have felt that he could not listen to the group members' feelings about their group being taken away. He did not feel empowered or encouraged to challenge the administrative decision affecting them. His organizational status supported his reluctance to accept any responsibility for the decision. Hearing what the group members were feeling would mean tolerating his helplessness to do anything about the decision, his reluctance to accept responsibility for it, and his anxiety about blurting out some criticism of his superiors.

The result in both cases was production of a casualty, a patient who was selected because of his individual propensities to represent the group members' anger at being betrayed, and a resident who was left feeling that he was a poor learner.

Blaming a colleague

I have been thinking how easy it is to get mad at someone else in the organization, not part of your group, often but certainly not always an administrator, who seems to be interfering with the work you are trying to do. A supervisor told a resident he knew that the resident had a seminar meeting to go to but continued their session anyway. The resident did not feel he could leave without offending his supervisor. Later, he apologized to me, the seminar teacher, for arriving late, clearly feeling that here too he ran a risk of rejection. In both situations he felt threatened with a bad reputation. The resident had no sense of being empowered to make his own choices and manage his own work schedule. He felt caught between his supervisor and seminar teacher, each of whom seemed to him to be testing to see who was more important to him. Of course, that the resident was so disempowered conflicted with training goals.

But what was going on between the supervisor and seminar teacher? The supervisor was annoyed at the resident's apparent eagerness to leave when they were working together. I was irritated, and blamed the supervisor for interfering with the work of the seminar. Each of us was probably wondering about how much the other valued him and his work. The social-systemic problem of which this incident was a manifestation, and of which the resident and his training were victims, concerned the nature of an intergroup relation, between junior and senior teachers, which these events did not deal with or improve. This is an example of blaming a colleague rather than attempting to address a problem in intergroup relations.

Blaming a group that won't go along

The dynamics of scapegoating a group are identical to the dynamics of scapegoating an individual. What follows is a typical or paradigmatic scenario, which may occur in any kind of organization with some variation in the specifics.

An organization responds to external threat

The story begins when changes in an organization's external situation threaten its survival. The changed circumstances make it more and more difficult for the organization to accomplish its mission.

Leaders of the organization develop a plan for meeting the changed circumstances. The plan involves 'doing things differently'. It challenges entrenched procedures and important values, but members of the organization are urged to 'get on board' and 'go along with it'. Apparently, everyone makes an effort to do so. But obstacles to implementing the plan, sometimes in the form of mysterious glitches, remain.

Assignment of blame

Who is to blame for these continued difficulties? It is easy to answer this question, if there is a pocket of open resistance. One management group, one department, one sector, is identified as 'dragging its heels'. Its members insist on carrying on in the old way, creating a bottleneck for those who want to do things differently. There is someone in that group, often its leader, who has been around a long time, who is perceived as rigid, defiant, not up to it, who must be confronted and, if necessary, gotten rid of.

A 'hero' to the rescue

Someone is introduced by management into this troublesome group, given authority to correct what is wrong, to sweep out the old with a new broom, to deal harshly with recalcitrance. Almost always, there is someone available who accepts this assignment without question, even enthusiastically, with a sense of righteous indignation or mission. (Rarely, the assignment is refused, as in the movie *Patterns*, 1956.) Some see him as the organization's savior, others as management's 'hatchet man'.

He is expected to be strong and decisive, not reflective or inclined to negotiate and compromise. He confronts the recalcitrant leader and group, lays down the law, and, backed by the leaders of the organization, throws his weight around, behavior that inevitably provokes further defensiveness and resistance by those increasingly seen as 'impossible' and '*the* problem' . The outcome is to force them to leave the organization. This is expensive, and usually futile in the long run. Some other group will take their place, adopt their reservations and recalcitrance, so that the opposition to change existing throughout the organization can continue to find expression without risk to any group but the 'chosen' one.

Characteristics of the problem group

Two features are almost always present. One, the identified problem group is a low-status group, whose members, at lower levels of the organization's hierarchy, are different from the members of other groups in the organization. Its members belong to a relatively low-status discipline (for example, social workers in a medical setting) and/or have a low-status group identity (for example, they are mostly women). They carry out a function that is seen as having low priority or as dispensable, or the contribution of which to the overall mission is difficult to define or demonstrate. This group, then, which others devalue anyway, becomes an ideal repository for the rebelliousness, attachment to traditional goals and to old and valued ways of doing things, that others wish to reject in themselves and get rid of (it is dangerous).

The consequences of management's attitude toward dissent

Second, leaders of the organization, beset by a sense of emergency and urgency, presenting plans for dealing with changed conditions in the organization's situation in order to save the organization, in one way or another, more or less subtly, and sometimes even while apparently being willing to hear 'all sides', discourage and suppress expressions of dissent, doubt, and anxiety about the abandonment of old ways of doing things and the apparent sacrifice of values and articles of faith previously held to be sacrosanct. Members of other groups, seeing 'the way the wind is blowing', go along, even convince themselves that they are enthusiastic about new arrangements, procedures, and goals.

But what they do not allow themselves to acknowledge or express incites some in the organization, wittingly or unwittingly, to 'take a stand if no one else is going to'. The resulting more or less articulate opposition to change, while it represents at least some part of that with which everyone in the organization struggles, is disclaimed by others. Those who express it in word or deed are abandoned by others to bear the consequences. 'Too bad they can't get with it. Nothing to do with me. I am squarely behind the leader's efforts to save the organization!'

Using groups as a medium for psychotherapy

Difference is pivotal in our relations with others. Our response to it is intense and complex.

Group psychotherapy as a medium for exploring difference

Psychotherapy groups can be an ideal medium for learning more about the experience of difference, and about how the ways in which we experience and manage differences find expression in our fantasies and actions – in what we want to do with what kind of things or persons under what sort of circumstances. Members of such groups may weave a web of deceptions and secrets meant to mislead. They may defiantly and provocatively exaggerate and flaunt difference. They may react to difference by hiding it behind false personas that proclaim similarity. They may devalue or overvalue those who are different, exoticizing them, or ignoring or denying the difference (living as if it didn't exist).

Can we imagine joining those who are different, instead of avoiding, attacking, or obliterating them? Must we create a world in which they do not exist, a world in which difference does not exist, where nothing reminds us of difference? Must we increase the distance or exaggerate the difference between ourselves and another? Can we attempt to minimize, overcome, or transcend it? Is it possible that we might recognize, accept, even embrace our differences, and so out of them, create *a new reality*?

Intrapersonal and group-as-a-whole processes in psychotherapy groups

We connect intrapersonal processes and group-as-a-whole processes, when we ask, 'What do different group members *do* about intrapersonal states-of-affairs or events?' (These states-of- affairs or events include impulses or wishes, emotions, traits or dispositions to act in certain ways, value-judgments and normative prescriptions and proscriptions.) To answer this question, we may observe and reflect on what happens in psychotherapy groups.

Group members split what seems to be contradictory in themselves. 'I seem to be/feel this way and that way, but I can't be/feel both. It's too difficult, painful, confusing.' They disown one element of such a pair of polar opposites. 'I am not like that. I do not feel that way. It is *not* inside or part of me. It has nothing to do with me.' They project. 'It is not in me. But I sense it around here somewhere. It is in her/him.' They have an uncanny ability to find others who are plausible targets for what they project. A hint, a devalued identity, a shared stereotype, lead them to select just the one among them who will accept or introject what they want to get rid of. 'Yes, I guess I do feel what you accuse me of feeling. I guess I am what you think I am. When you point to my behavior or something I have said, I am convinced that you have proven your opinion of me is right. When I look inside myself, I do find something that seems to correspond to something you have guessed is there. I have to agree with you, although I don't like to.'

So members of a group have similar or complementary attitudes toward particular internal states or events they share. They need each other to deal with these shared states or events. What each member does about them is coordinated with what other members do about them. Members of the group-as-a-whole identify, projectively or introjectively, with each other. 'I identify with you, because you have something of myself (which I don't want in me) in you.' 'I identify with you, because I have something of yourself (which you don't want) in me, and there is some gain for me, and *for all of us*, in accepting that it is in me and nowhere else.'

This 'acting on behalf of all of us, given the circumstances or problem we face as a group', however unwitting, results in bringing about certain ends, a certain kind of situation, for the group-as-a-whole. This situation is brought about by members joining together, each one doing his or her part, cooperating in processes in which different members expel something or take in something. Group members seem to imagine that this collaborative endeavor, if successful, will mitigate particular (unexpressed or unrecognized) anxieties or realize particular (unavowed) wished-for gratifications.

Mitigating these anxieties or realizing these gratifications may have very little to do with the explicit tasks the group exists to accomplish. They are in this sense 'nontask' ends; it is possible that seeking to bring them about may incidentally contribute to or support the accomplishment of the group's explicit tasks. On the other hand, striving to mitigate anxieties or realize gratifications may distract or divert resources away from or otherwise oppose or interfere with the explicit tasks the group exists to accomplish. Then they are, in this sense, 'antitask' ends.

The anxieties are those that group members often feel group life has been especially responsible for arousing, the gratifications those that group members feel group life has seemed especially likely to offer. The processes that come into play in seeking to mitigate some such anxieties or to make some such gratifications available are of a kind especially likely to arouse other anxieties or to result in the production of individual casualties.

Periods when the group gets stuck are especially painful for both psychotherapist and members. Splitting, projection, and introjection are not only experienced as 'solutions', as ways of simplifying an unbearably complex reality, but they are also experienced as self-damaging and therefore dangerous. 'I may think I will enjoy being taken care of by the therapist if I project all competence onto him, but it does not feel good to lose my competence and independence.' 'I may think I can more easily escape or defeat aggression if it exists outside myself, but underneath I feel I have lost something I value as much as I fear it, my own aggression.' 'I may find it delightful to accept your idealized image of me, or gratifying not to struggle any longer against your derogatory stereotype of me, but I do not want to be condemned to live out a false persona.' 'I may accept on behalf of the group that all badness or sickness is in me, so that we may more easily get rid of this bad stuff, but it does feel that I am sacrificing myself for the sake of the group, and I can't help but resent that.'

It is possible that during periods of being stuck, the group members experience an opposition between their yearning to live in the simple, comfortable world brought about by splitting, projection, and introjection, on the one hand, and the fear of these processes, which threaten the loss of valued aspects of themselves, however ambivalently these aspects are regarded, and the imposition of false selves. Group members are stuck in a limbo, both desiring and fearing the unconscious world in which they are simply and undemandingly bonded to one another, at some cost to their self-integrity. At the same time, they both desire and fear the task-related roles that also relate them to each other, that hold out a promise of real achievement, but that make difficult demands on them, demands that are especially intimidating because they open up the possibility of real failure.

Intergroup processes in psychotherapy groups

Processes of splitting, disowning, and projection and introjection, form a large part of what is thought of as 'the unconscious life' of the group-as-a-whole, or play a large part in producing what are felt to be irrational, antitask phenomena in group life.[104] As such, and involving, as such processes do, subtle reciprocal and complementary relations among intrapersonal phenomena (for example, individual dispositions and individual 'valences' or attractions to certain roles) in a group-as-a-whole context, they deserve careful attention from group psychotherapists.

I have observed two other group-as-a-whole strategies that also deserve attention from group psychotherapists: exporting and importing. These are analogues of splitting, disowning, and projection and introjection. But they occur in what is explicitly perceived, sometimes only by the group psychotherapist, sometimes also by the group members, to be an *intergroup* context.

The group members may *export* some unacceptable or anxiety-arousing trait or state. They imagine that it is in another group in their external situation, perhaps in the organization or system in which the group members work, or the society or families to which they belong. The group members help convince each other that what they reject in themselves is 'really' in the other by enacting and telling the relevant stories. That an exporting strategy is being carried out is suggested when group members distance themselves from some 'other' as different and at the same time are obsessively fascinated with this other, who now possesses a lost piece of themselves.

Identity groups (gender, generation, race, ethnicity, and socioeconomic status) exist outside the psychotherapy group. Group members also belong to them, and inevitably represent them in the psychotherapy group. These groups, and members who are seen as representing them, may also become the target of exports. Specific aspects of stereotypes of (beliefs about) such identity groups facilitate the choice of them as targets of particular exports.

Group members may also *import* some trait or state imagined to be characteristic of some other group, including some other group's view of the members of this group, possibly based on the history of experiences members of this group have had with the other group. The members join in imagining that the import is in themselves. They convince each other that it is really in themselves by enacting and telling the relevant stories. That importing is going on is suggested when group members experience that an 'other' is inside of them, that there is something alien or false about what they are saying or doing, that they can't get at what is genuinely themselves. Or when group members accept, and suffer in accepting, a perception of them held by members of another (rival) group. Or when group members refuse to accept what one of them says, 'As a member of a different identity group, I hold a different view or have had different experiences from yours,' and respond to it by denying that any such differences exist, 'No, you are not different. We all think that way.'

The importing strategy is intended to control what is imported by holding it within. Group members engaged in such a strategy are unwilling to risk change, take rigid unbending positions, deny differences, play the same part in a scenario over and over again, rejoicing in the mastery and virtuosity of the performance, while at the same time deploring its emptiness.

In the beginning, group-psychotherapists-in-training find it difficult to grasp that these phenomena actually involve exportation or importation – or projection or introjection – or scapegoating. Among other reasons already mentioned, the group as it convinces itself, convinces the group psychotherapist. 'After all, we all agree that it is so.' We are taught to accept a consensus as validation.

Goals of group psychotherapy

Often, group psychotherapists act as if the primary goal of group psychotherapy were to confront individuals with the social consequences of their individual dispositions and valences, with how others in the group respond to and use or exploit these dispositions and valences, in order to encourage them to abandon or modify aspects of themselves that, for better or worse, they bring to group life. This emphasis may lead to talk of 'gaining interpersonal skills' or 'learning to adjust to others'.

But the goal of group psychotherapy, more deeply and inwardly, may be viewed as having to do with the mitigation of tendencies, shared by group members, to refuse to acknowledge, to disown, or to reject certain experiences, especially certain affective states. These are avoided because, if they were to be experienced, that would lead to unwanted self-characterizations, and so, to one extent or another, to a crippling loss of self-esteem. ('If I, a man, were to take enjoyment in passivity, feel a yearning for someone else's presence or help, or have what I experience as a "soft" feeling, that would be a sign that I am weak or feminine rather than strong and manly, and I would then lose the respect not only of others but of myself.')

The group as a medium for psychotherapy is especially suited to pursuing such themes. For, when scapegoating, for example, makes its appearance, it offers an especially fine opportunity to focus interpretively on such processes as splitting, disowning, and projection and introjection. These processes must necessarily involve members' shared tendencies to reject certain feelings, states, or experiences.

Suppose group members were to be collectively successful in devising and adopting restrictive solutions to shared conflicts between wishes and fears. Such restrictive solutions involve sacrificing wishes to fears and therefore entail disowning, excluding, or getting rid of certain feelings, states, or experiences.

Every member's access to and sense of reality suffers. Every member's access to aspects of self is impaired. The range of what group members allow themselves to think or feel is restricted. Interpretation may call such sacrifices and their costs to group members' attention. The psychotherapist's interpretive activity is intended to mitigate group members' constraints on what each one allows himself to recognize or acknowledge in himself, what each one allows herself to experience.

One of the therapeutic benefits of group psychotherapy is the growing ability of group members to recognize processes such as splitting, disowning part of oneself, projection, introjection, identifications resulting from projection and introjection, and scapegoating – and to resist participating in these processes – to stand against consensus. Only thus, people come to own what is within themselves and to live with it. The payoff: the recovery of lost pieces of the self, and the ability to do without false selves.

Thus, members of a psychotherapy group may come to have more complete access to – and to be more able to express in all its richness, variousness, and many-sidedness – what is within themselves. At a minimum, patients' isolation and sense of being weirdly different from all others – aberrant – may lessen as they participate in a group in which it becomes clear that, whatever the differences among the group members, they do share feelings, problems, wishes, and do join together in carrying out strategies for solving problems and gratifying wishes. They may come to appreciate what their individual contribution is in carrying out these strategies.

Patients, like clinicians, teachers, and administrators, live much of their lives in groups. They also work, play, go to classes, participate on committees, sit with the family around the kitchen table. For them, too, there is some advantage in becoming aware of what can happen to them in groups and organizations, to understand the collective processes by which parts of themselves can be lost, suppressed, or distorted. For them, too, there is something to be gained in coming to understand how they participate in group life, how their own dispositions, the personal scenarios in which they are caught, contribute to the use made of them by others and the use they make of others in collective processes. In the psychotherapy group, they may discover how to reclaim the lost, suppressed, or distorted parts of themselves. They may come to know what it can be like to find one's own voice in a chorus of voices finally singing together clearly and distinctly their different parts.

CHAPTER 21

Individual Frames, Intergroup Scripts, and Scapegoating

David Berg

The story about parallel process in the meeting with the resident and in his psychotherapy group reminds me of Ekstein and Wallerstein's distinction between 'learning problems' (issues of diagnosis and technique in psychotherapy) and 'problems in learning' (disturbances in the teacher–trainee relationship).[105] Problems in learning, they suggest, are often parallel processes, enactments in the teacher–trainee relationship of struggles that exist in the trainee–patient relationship. However, as the story illustrates, efforts to examine and understand parallel process, that is, the problems in learning that teacher and trainee encounter, may free the teacher from blindly and simply re-enacting the trainee's reaction to his patients. Even if the teacher's responses to the trainee parallel those of the resident's to his patients, it is likely to make a difference to learning if teacher and trainee are able to reflect on the parallel process and draw some insights from it.

Changing from an individual to a social frame

We observe over and over that remaining in a psychological-system frame or focusing on an individual in a group setting results in scapegoating. Then what makes it so difficult for us to change our frame?

It takes time and energy to consider the group or organizational context of an individual's behavior. First, we have to let go a bit of our fixed beliefs about that individual. Then, we have to have some idea of what a social-system explanation might look like. Finally, we have to search for additional information to aid us in formulating a differential diagnosis.

Perhaps even more important, a social-system explanation for what appear to be events featuring an individual always expands the set of people who are involved. It increases the number of people who now have some obligation to consider *their* role in bringing about these events. As we consider our own role in such events, we may be asked to examine the groups to which we belong (by birth and acculturation as well as organizational training and assignment) – our relationship to them, and their relationship to other groups in the organization and the larger culture.

Blaming individuals for events that occur in groups or organizations has the advantage of sparing oneself and others in a group or organization the burden of self-analysis. And if I do acknowledge my involvement in a troublesome set of events, my colleagues and peers may isolate me as *the only person* with such feelings and experiences. My acknowledgment does not then produce any social-system awareness. It has merely isolated me and with me the problem.

Intergroup scripts

In most groups, we assign roles to other people in part because of the roles we want to reserve for ourselves and the roles we reject for ourselves (healthy or sick, active or passive, emotional or intellectual, good or bad, angry or conciliatory). Why do groups 'pick' certain individuals to play certain roles, especially the role of scapegoat? All of us have certain 'valences', individual tendencies or psychological predispositions, based on our personal histories and development, that lead us to 'volunteer' for certain roles. But often in groups or larger social systems, our identity group memberships also influence the roles we are 'assigned'.

If members of a group share an image that certain 'kinds' of people are athletic, comical, cheap, or angry, then when these characteristics or emotions are needed to express emerging tensions or anxieties in that group, these members are likely to elect someone among them from the 'appropriate' identity group to play this role. These intergroup 'scripts' are often filled with stereotypes, projected unwanted characteristics, and the legacies of historical events, but when many people in a group share them, they can be powerful determinants of the roles assigned to individual group members.

Gender

Women, for example, are often assigned the 'emotional' role in groups and become the object of the attitudes that we have toward being emotional in a world that values intellect, 'rigor', and control. A lawyer once asked me to do some research on the job of a newspaper reporter. He had the hypothesis that the differences between men and women might lead one sex (men) to be better equipped to be a reporter than the other sex (women). In particular, he wondered whether the 'soft' interpersonal and emotional skills that he believed women possessed more than men might put them at a disadvantage when they needed to be tough and aggressive in an interview or investigation.

There were at least two issues raised by this request. First, the lawyer's hypothesis revealed his intergroup script, which included his image of the differences between men and women. He had ascribed to women a certain facility with emotion and interpersonal relations. Second, he believed that these skills were not appropriate for a particular job or undertaking. Women presumably were not as capable as men in the area of investigative reporting and so one might 'reasonably' expect to find fewer women in these positions on a newspaper.

Why had he ascribed emotional skills to women as a group? Is it because women are better at expressing emotions? Is it because men feel prohibited from certain kinds of emotional expression even when they experience these emotions, and therefore depend on women to do this 'work'? Is it because a man's emotionality is likely to be devalued and cause him to lose status in the eyes of both men and women, while a woman's emotionality fits a shared script about what is acceptable and appropriate?

It turned out that the job of reporting as described in textbooks and by male and female reporters included skills that might be called stereotypically female (empathy, tact, caring, support) as well as skills that might be called stereotypically male (aggressiveness, argumentation, toughness). It was my impression that the lawyer saw the requirements of the reporting job through the lens of his own group (men), and these requirements reflected a shared script, which assigned parts to be played only by men and parts to be played only by women.

Race

The idea of intergroup scripts brings to mind another experience. The first time I was at Howard University, a predominantly black school in Washington, DC, I remember being struck by the lack of friendliness I noticed in the casual contact between students on the campus. When I asked myself why I expected friendliness on this campus when in fact it was not the norm on my campus, I realized that I was generalizing from my observations of the relatively few black students at the predominantly white institution where I worked. I wondered whether my attribution of 'friendliness' to all black people was born of *my* observations of a few black people *living in a white institution.* It seemed obvious upon reflection that connections between the relatively few black people at a white institution could be attributable, in part, to their common predicament.

It is interesting to me that I would never have reflected on these matters if I had not been placed in a context different from my own. As a white person working and living in a white world I had developed certain beliefs about black people which cast them in certain roles in the social settings where blacks and whites were present. I expected blacks to be friendly and to have warm relationships with other black people. My expectations (and I suspect similar ones held by other white people) contributed to constraining the roles the groups to which I belonged 'allowed' black people to play. Like the story of the women whose participation in social systems is constrained when they are cast as the 'emotionally expressive' members so that men can escape the negative consequences of being feeling men, this is a story of unconsciously imposed constraints, here born of racial segregation (an intergroup story) and perhaps my wish for the return of a vanishing sense of community (an individual or group story).

Scapegoating a student

In a school of management, teaching the first few weeks of a first-semester introductory course on *human behavior in organizations* always carries with it the task of dealing with the powerful emotions of adults who are returning to the classroom to begin professional education. They are anxious about how well they will perform, how well they will fit in to what they imagine is the mainstream of their profession, how they will stack up against their comrades, and last but not least how they will cope with the status of being first-year students in their mid-twenties and thirties. The advantage of teaching a course on human behavior is that these feelings and struggles can themselves be treated as substantive material for the course. In fact it has been my experience that to try to ignore these forces dooms such a course to some degree of irrelevancy. But it is not always easy to see these collective concerns and anxieties as the following story illustrates.

In one such class, Sheila, an overweight somewhat older student persisted in challenging any assertions I made and in asking what I experienced as obnoxious questions. Other class members would laugh, giggle, or snicker when she spoke, which suggested that something she was saying expressed something of their own experience, but they also rolled their eyes and 'tuned out' when Sheila persevered. What I noticed most about my own deepening animosity toward Sheila was that the class appeared to share my feelings. We clearly had a problem student in the class, or so it seemed.

My teaching assistant, an African-American doctoral student, also felt a growing animosity toward Sheila, but he felt her isolation as well. He was worried that Sheila would be used to express indirectly the class's discomfort with the student role and anxieties about fitting in.

Sheila's behavior in class seemed to satisfy two collective needs. First, she was able to express the rebellious reactions these adult learners had to being placed in rows, confronted with their lack of knowledge, prodded with daily homework and examinations, and treated (as often as not) like high school seniors. Sheila's overt rebelliousness provided a measure of safety for her classmates who did not have to run the risk of being labeled *a problem student*, with all the possible career risks they imagined went along with such a label. They derived the emotional benefits of her challenging and critical mind without suffering the consequences to which my reactions attest.

Second, because of Sheila's gender and weight, she appeared on the surface to be so unlike the members of the class that they could the more easily disown her feelings and behavior. This difference enabled the scapegoating. Scapegoating only works if the scapegoat can be convincingly disowned, since a person who is seen as representative of a group puts the entire group at risk. It also calmed Sheila's classmates' fears about not fitting in. Sheila's difference and clear non-mainstream appearance and behavior made most of the others in her class feel similar and on track.

The social-system trap was set. If I and my teaching assistant joined in the scapegoating we would not only be contributing to Sheila's isolation, we would also be colluding with the class members' wishes to avoid acknowledging their own anxieties and criticisms of the course. My teaching assistant also warned me that if we participated in scapegoating Sheila, if we treated her rebelliousness as merely a personality characteristic in need of being fixed or removed, we were likely to create a learning environment that stressed obedience and conformity to the mythical mainstream. This kind of learning environment would have been debilitating for the course and our objectives for it. So, we worked hard not to make jokes at Sheila's expense, not to join in the class's giggles or groans when she spoke, and not to dismiss her comments as merely troublesome.

Sheila became a valued member of the class over the course of the semester and the two-year program. It is my belief that our refusal to participate in scapegoating her played a role in enabling classmates to express the ways in which they were similar to Sheila in spite of the desire to see her as 'other'. Had we personalized her reactions to us and the course, and so overlooked what she might have been expressing for her cohort, we would have contributed to her alienation and to our own inability to respond to the anxieties and concerns of incoming students. By treating her as a 'problem individual', we would have sealed ourselves and the class off from examining troubling information about the class and school and from any responsibility for dealing with that information. As authority figures in the class, our struggle to respect Sheila and her experience opened a door through which others could let their thoughts and feelings out, and let Sheila in.

Scapegoating an entrepreneur

I am reminded of another story about scapegoating. An entrepreneurial CEO of a growing company was experiencing problems with the managers who worked for him. Turnover among top managers was very high. As a result, business suffered. The CEO hired a consultant to help him understand (and fix) the problem. Although the CEO had worked well with the management team when the company was small and aspiring, the consultant after interviews with the team concluded that the CEO was a narcissistic person with borderline features. (The consultant was psychoanalytically trained.) The CEO apparently needed to control everything, was defensive and impulsive when criticized, demeaned employees when they made mistakes, and always placed himself in the middle of any discussion or decision. He was variously described as power driven, controlling, unwilling to let go, egomaniacal, alternatingly cruel and cajoling, always playing favorites, and as unsuited for management as he was suited for entrepreneurial creativity.

The consultant's advice to the CEO was to go off and start a new business. This move, the consultant contended, would allow the managers to manage as the company, in its growth, emerged from an entrepreneurial stage to a necessarily more bureaucratic stage. It would also allow the CEO to use his considerable entrepreneurial talents in the creation of a new venture. The CEO responded to this suggestion by saying, 'You're telling me that by my moving ... you're going to isolate the pathogenicity, is that it?' In spite of the consultant's protestations to the contrary, the CEO's comment fit the facts.

It is my experience that, at the time organizations are going through the difficult transition from a family-style business to an organization with a complicated structure, with policies, rules, defined roles, and prescribed procedures, entrepreneurial CEOs are often described with the phrases used to describe this CEO. When *the characters change and the plot remains the same*, I am inclined to think a social-system explanation is likely to prove useful.[106]

It is possible, even likely, that all entrepreneurs share similar personality characteristics. But there is a social-system explanation for the way in which the organization comes to reject personality characteristics that were once valued, or exacerbates characteristics that were once muted or better regulated.

The transition in the organization's life produces a set of tasks that are particularly stressful for everyone in the company. These tasks generate feelings of frustration, anxiety, neediness, helplessness, and confusion. These feelings are conveyed to the CEO, and weigh on him. They call forth her or his particular ways of coping with the difficult job of managing everyone's distress. Members of the organization pressure the CEO to take control, believing that will relieve their distress, even while they indict her or him as she or he tries to comply with that pressure. The actual challenge for the CEO and the organization is to find a way, as the organization moves from one stage to another, for her or him to relinquish control, gradually, carefully, but purposefully. It is this shared organizational task that is ignored in focusing on the CEO's dysfunctional personality.

I cannot be sure what would have happened in this case if the consultant had chosen to focus on this organizational task and the feelings it engendered, rather than the CEO's personal response to them. But it seems obvious that in general it is important to consider social-system perspectives – when the failure to do so may result in removing an individual, which is costly and sometimes not feasible, and in any event likely to leave the real problem unsolved. There *are* consequences of failing to make a social-system diagnosis, not only for the individual who is *mistakenly* identified and scapegoated as the cause of a problem, but also for the clinical, administrative, or teaching task that continues to bear the burden of having the real obstacle go undetected.

Scapegoating an administrator

I have of course also experienced being scapegoated. During my time as a faculty member of a management school, I served in a number of administrative roles, the most demanding of which was the Director of Professional Studies. It was my responsibility to coordinate the professional masters program. The job involved curriculum, scheduling, student support services, transcripts, grades, and a host of program issues.

The three groups – students, faculty and administrators – were all trying to collaborate to produce a high-quality educational experience. All three groups had different ideas about what the essential desirable conditions of a high-quality educational experience were. One job of the Director of Professional Studies, as I saw it, was to keep the various constituencies talking to each other so as to solve problems and seize opportunities.

The job was always time-consuming, often difficult, and a mixture of the very rewarding and immensely distressing. The distress came from my feeling that the people I was trying to help often complained about me. The complaints had the flavor of my having sold out to another constituency at the School. The personal nature of the complaints was upsetting, as was my observation that students, faculty and administrators alike were 'going around me' with problems, questions, and proposals that should have come to me.

The obvious individual explanation is that I was not handling the job as well as I could have. But it is helpful to look at the organizational pattern as well.

I came to realize that a number of group characteristics contributed to my ability to do the job. As a junior faculty member, I was seen as able to identify with the student experience since I had recently been a student myself. As a faculty member who taught in the core curriculum, I was close to the faculty's concerns, attended faculty meetings and struggled with the same need to balance research, teaching and 'citizenship'. As an administrator, I felt a responsibility for the program and had a perspective on it that was informed by a variety of administrative concerns and considerations. These characteristics enabled me to work with and to understand the needs and viewpoints of the three major constituencies of the school. In addition, each of the three groups felt that to some extent I was one of them.

But these same characteristics also made for difficulties at times. For example, my junior faculty status significantly reduced my influence with the senior faculty.

To the extent that I did my job well, I was constantly putting myself in the position of bringing these groups together to solve difficult organizational problems: curriculum needs; minority admission and retention issues; grading and evaluation; perceptions of poor teaching; harassment of various kinds; academic standards; and student participation in school governance. Representatives of the students, faculty and administration would come to me with their side of a conflict or controversy, hoping that I would fashion a solution that represented their interests. Each group had the understandable expectation that I would be especially sympathetic to their point of view. When my actions often forced these groups to work with each other to solve common problems, each group felt betrayed by my apparent refusal to champion their (legitimate) concerns.

I suspect that many administrators have encountered this feeling. I have come to believe that, at a social-system level, this feeling of betrayal may actually be a sign that 'I am doing a good job'. (Is this a possible rationalization for partial success or even failure?) But, although the complaints aimed at me were actually not personal – I was, paradoxically, held in high regard by some, although not all, for the way I handled the job – they were real and painful nevertheless.

The action implications for this social-system interpretation of these complaints centered on what I needed to do in order to function in this role. I needed to maintain constant and candid communication with the parts of the school. I needed to confront the dean's willingness to deal with educational issues that involved my office without my knowledge and/or participation. I needed to accept and understand the emotional demands made on someone in my role. To the extent that I could manage all these requirements, I could do something to avoid becoming a casualty of individual explanations of my behavior by others and to mitigate the distress and self-doubts these aroused in me.

Blaming someone in the organization

The classroom especially is a setting in which my instinctive explanation of events is at the individual level: 'He's just that kind of person.' 'She has that kind of personality.' I am sometimes tempted not only to indict individual members of the class, with the possibility then of contributing to the creation of casualties, but also to blame someone else in the organization for difficulties I encounter in the classroom.

I taught an elective course on organizational diagnosis to advanced graduate students. The course involved classroom work and an extensive field practicum with a real client organization. It was a course that had a reputation for demanding a lot of effort and returning a great deal of learning. The first five weeks were spent in the classroom. The remaining weeks of the course added fieldwork to the normal twice-weekly meetings of the class.

Once, three weeks into the course, I noticed that people were arriving late to class. It was usually the same people although they each gave a different explanation for their lateness. One day fully a third of the class was not present at the starting time and I asked those who were in the room to help me understand what was going on.

The group had been through a course on group dynamics. They understood conscious as well as unconscious aspects of group life, yet they were reticent to offer an explanation. There were some mutterings about the particular individuals who were late, as if their lateness was predictable and due in part to their relative lack of commitment to the course. The truly committed were in the room!

After a few minutes of awkward conversation, the rest of the class arrived in ones and twos. They were all dressed in semiformal clothes, which indicated that they had just attended a job presentation by an organization recruiting on campus. I told them that I had noticed the lateness in the last few weeks and had just asked the class what was going on. The 'latecomers' explained that the Career Development Office had scheduled an important job presentation during class time.

My first reaction was fury. I told the class that such a presentation should not have been scheduled during regular daytime class periods and that I would go talk to the Director of the Career Development Office to make sure this did not happen again. The class knew I was angry at the 'system' for this 'assault' on my course.

At that moment, one of the early arrivers said that the latecomers didn't have to go to the job presentation and that some of those people who came on time wanted to go to the presentation but honored their commitment to the class. The lines were now drawn between the 'committed' and the 'uncommitted'.

For the next few minutes, there was a discussion of commitment – who had it and who did not have it. But then one of the committed group confessed that he too had not wanted to come to class. (None of the latecomers had admitted to not wanting to come to class, but that interpretation of their lateness was implicit in the conversation.) I asked why. He said that he was feeling unprepared to go into the fieldwork part of the course. The idea of working with a live organization, instead of the cases, articles and role playing situations we had worked with in class, was a daunting one.

Soon others from both subgroups were discussing their anxieties about going into the field. It was apparent to the whole class that the latecomers were a little freer than others to represent for everyone in their behavior (albeit unconsciously) the general anxiety about the upcoming fieldwork.

We had successfully struggled through a difficult juncture. My first inclination had been to blame the Career Development Office – to rush upstairs after class and give vent to my anger. In hindsight this would have accomplished very little, since it would not have been directed at the source of the course's problem. The students' initial inclination was to blame each other, to form two opposing subgroups and to use their sophisticated skills of interpretation and data analysis to battle for the explanatory high ground.

What emerged after a member of one group found himself able to recognize aspects of the other faction in his own feelings was much more compelling to all of us. *Both* the committed and the uncommitted shared a common collective reaction to the impending fieldwork. It was this understandable, yet obviously embarrassing, anxiety – not the Career Development Office and not the 'uncommitted' students in our midst – that needed our collective attention.

Splitting in a psychotherapy group

A final story about 'splits' in groups, this time in a psychotherapy group. A group psychotherapist joined his group at the starting time and noticed that only three of the six people in the group were present. He found that the absence of half of the group distracted him, and wondered aloud if other group members had feelings about the fact that a number of people were missing.

Some people expressed disappointment but soon the discussion turned to a discussion of the 'good reasons' the absent members must have had for missing the session. Then one member said, as if to put an end to the conversation, that the group should not waste its time imagining why some people were absent because such talk was merely speculation. This same person encouraged the group members who were present to 'get on' with the session.

The psychotherapist experienced these comments as resistance to the work of exploring the group members' reaction to the absences. He realized that he was angry at the absent members for not showing up and for not calling, and he assumed that group members must also be upset. It was in this context that the psychotherapist continued to work at enabling the group members to express their feelings. They met his next intervention with silence. Finally one of the members stated that she didn't see any point in talking about people who weren't in the room. The psychotherapist felt unable to move the discussion toward a consideration of the phenomenon of the absent members, but now felt responsible for the group's being stuck on this 'non-issue'.

In this example, the split in the group was subtle, between the present members and the absent ones. What was happening in the group was understood as a conversation by the present members about the absent members (how they felt about being left, how they felt about the group in the absence of the others).

Thinking about it this way itself encouraged the present members to disown their connection to the absent ones. Their conversation therefore was likely to have a sterile, blaming quality to it; the absentees were felt to be so unlike those who are present. It became impossible to explore why the absent members might have 'chosen' to miss the group meeting (since 'they' were not present and 'we' who were present couldn't have any reasons for missing the meeting).

The group members were unable to explore feelings about coming to the group meeting (previous events, frustration, fear of conflict) that they all might share, because the split between present and absent members meant that only half the conversation could occur. Indeed the group members felt bored as they talked to themselves about an issue that they experienced as primarily belonging to people who weren't there. If the psychotherapist had been able to imagine that the present members were, in some sense, connected to the absent ones, in spite of what appeared to be a concrete and meaningful difference, he might have chosen to work with the group members to explore the thoughts and feelings they had (or had had) about skipping a group meeting or not coming.

My hunch is that the psychotherapist's initial inability to see a connection between the absent and present members was related to the consequences for *him* of these two different ways of understanding what was going on. Much like the previous example about the 'committed' and 'uncommitted' class members, viewing the absent group members as distinct and different from those present served to make it difficult to examine the ambivalence about commitment that all group members shared, an examination that might have caused the psycho-therapist to feel blamed, inadequate, hurt, incompetent, or unwanted.

CHAPTER 22

Gender

Marshall Edelson

The story about the committed and uncommitted students, who as it turned out were all anxious about the fieldwork, is an example of the part that shared anxieties about the work to be done play in collective phenomena.[107] Because of our interest in the usual sources of anxiety in disturbed individuals, we may forget the anxiety that can be aroused even in well-functioning persons by what sometimes seem to be the impossible challenges of the task they confront together.

In learning how to do psychotherapy, residents face presenting their clinical work in a seminar or to a preceptor. An inpatient staff struggles day after day to treat very ill patients, some of whom may go for long periods without apparent improvement, and some of whom can be uncooperative or even frighteningly belligerent.

People feel anxious about their inability to overcome both real and imagined, and apparently insuperable, obstacles to accomplishing a task – obstacles such as personal limitations, deficits in skill and knowledge, and unfavorable external conditions. Under these circumstances, they may develop a nontask or antitask procedure or way of relating to one another the main purpose of which is to help them defend against, manage, or contain their anxiety.

A trainee anxiously withholds information

A woman resident presented some clinical material in a seminar. She had made an intervention, brief, rather vague, not clearly related to what her patient had been saying, not apparently any kind of interpretation. To my astonishment, the patient responded to this intervention with some deeply felt, insightful comments that were clearly richer in content than what he had been saying before the intervention. After a while, I said to the seminar group, 'There is no point discussing the psychotherapist's intervention in terms of its form, content, or accuracy. It clearly had desirable effects. It's up to us to try to figure out what it was about the intervention that led to such desirable effects. Perhaps the tone...' For some minutes we struggled with this.

Then the presenter said, 'I have to tell you. I edited what I said. Actually what I said was...' It turned out that she had made an interpretation, but not in the form of some inference or generalization about the patient or his psyche. Instead, she had told the patient a brief story, a sort of 'what you have been saying reminds me of...' story. She had described a scene in which a mother comforts a child who has been hurt. It was this story, which she had edited out of her presentation to the seminar, that so affected the patient. The resident told me after the seminar that she was reluctant to share with me or the other group members this spontaneous creative intervention, because she cared deeply about the patient, and did not want this precious exchange with him 'cut up' by comments in the group.

I thought a lot about the way in which values in the social system of which we are members can affect the work in a seminar. We belong to a social system (a university medical school department) that prizes tough-mindedness *over* soft-mindedness; being realistic *over* being imaginative; aggressive achievement, long hours of work, and advancement at any cost *over* pleasure in the arts or 'being with people'; and that prefers – in work with patients – setting limits, not being taken in, maintaining a proper somewhat distant professional stance *over* getting involved (and accepting the risk of becoming overinvolved), caring passionately, developing relationships. It occurred to me that any resident might feel that, in order to win acceptance and succeed, he must show strength. It is not strange, then, that this resident would think it wise to try to hide anything in a response to a patient that others might regard as soft, weak, or undisciplined. But hiding what was said cost something – her, self-recrimination, and all of us, the loss of information we needed for learning.

Gender in a therapeutic community

Many years earlier, some decades ago in fact, at a community meeting in a residential treatment center, a male patient requested help in setting up a tea for a visitor. Grinning, he pointed out, 'Arranging flowers is not a man's job.' A female patient volunteered to help set up tea.

It was announced that someone had taken a poster hung up in the game room off the wall and torn it up. In addition, someone had posted obscenities on the Activities Committee bulletin board. On the bulletin board, a note referred to Small Group X as the 'Smut Group' and the 'Necking Group'. (The patients met in small 'home' groups, which focused on maintaining the motivations needed for participation in the therapeutic community and in various treatment activities including psychotherapy.) The female patients in Small Group X had for some weeks ostracized the male patients in that group, holding separate meetings.

The Pet Committee, which had been organized to deal with the problems arising from the presence of patients' pets, gave its report.[108] Someone asked why the Pet Committee had a closed meeting. It turned out that the meeting had been closed to exclude one male patient the women patients on the committee did not want to have there, 'because he would disrupt the meeting'. Shocked silence greeted this news. The male patient, who was in Small Group X, informed the community that the Pet Committee consisted largely of women from that group. People spoke out about their dislike of using a meeting to deal with an individual this way; they regarded it as devious.

There was a similarity between attitudes toward this man who disrupted and concern about pets who disrupted. This group was preoccupied with inclusion and exclusion. What does this have to do with the treatment center, a social system of which this group is a part? One, membership in this community was based on being 'a sick person', a negative identity. There was a strong desire to split off the sickness and get rid of it, for example, by discharging someone as 'too sick' for this setting, which had no locked units. Second, many patients were disposed to socially deviant behavior. Treatment was the only legitimized mechanism of social control. But the amount of deviance had to be limited, if the community, which eschewed locked doors or physical restraints, was to survive. One way to limit it was to keep 'too much' of it from entering. The other was, if there was 'too much', to get rid of some of it. Keep out or get rid of messy pets!

I encouraged continuing the discussion about men and women by observing, 'Has anyone noticed that recently all the co-chairmen of the community meetings have been women? When the community meeting began, all the co-chairmen chosen were men.' Group members went on to discuss their experience of gender differences in the community. Women were chosen to be co-chairman of the community meeting, after a man had been shamed, accused publicly of being Edelson's stooge.

Who got to be on the community council (a patient-staff 'judicial' committee, which dealt with social problems)? It turned out that one male patient had researched the question. Five of seven on the council were women; five of seven patients referred to the council as social problems were men.

A male patient said, 'Some women in the community are willing to analyze a man and tell him what is wrong with him. They don't want to hear anything back about themselves. So I just forget what they say. Screw it!' A female patient said, 'Women are bitchy and competitive.' Another female patient exclaimed, 'I'm fed up with the passivity and muscle-flexing of men in this community.'

There were many comments about how men do women's work in this community (housekeeping) and women do men's work (carpentry). A female patient said, 'I wouldn't want to be a man in this community.' A male patient said, 'I wouldn't want to be a woman in this community.'

I would never have guessed from some of my difficulties recognizing the importance of identity groups and gender issues in my work as a teacher thirty years later that earlier I had been sensitive to, interested in, and able to help groups discuss feelings and observations about gender. I had forgotten this experience. It is almost as if some competent self had died some thirty years ago, leaving me no memory of it. Later, Dan Levinson and David Berg helped me to resurrect it.

The resurrection

Differences – fault lines, cleavages, that result from or at the least invite splitting – are an important issue in every group and organization. Many stories show how differences, especially (but not only) *gender*, *race*, and *status* differences, get played out in collective processes, some quite destructive. What contributed to my failing to focus in any central way on such phenomena over some period of time?

I was primarily theoretical or analytic in my approach, and interested in work and people's ways of dealing together with the anxieties raised by the particular problems associated with specific tasks and the conditions under which people sought to accomplish them. I tended in my *thinking* to identify with the problems faced by *leaders* of groups or organizations (the people with authority or power), especially the task-oriented leader who was frustrated that members' apparently irrational attitudes or irrelevant concerns often hindered the work. I tended in my *practice* to identify with the problems faced by *members* of groups or organizations, those who felt themselves to be relatively powerless, whom I sought to empower, to give more of a voice (although I did not always think that way about what I was doing). My thinking about identity groups was largely shaped by Merton's discussion of how reference groups affected people's behavior.[109] Going beyond that, taking any more central interest in the dynamics of gender, ethnicity, race, generation, age, professional discipline, and socioeconomic class, I felt might put me in danger of participating in a political process as an advocate rather than dispassionately analyzing social-technical processes as a neutral consultant, and in addition might distract me from what I regarded as a preeminent theme, namely, the anxiety aroused by the challenge of the task itself and how this anxiety was managed.

The group or organization has a task or multiple tasks. Presumably, it is organized to carry out that task or those multiple tasks. Ideally, different subgroups ('task groups') are differentiated to achieve distinctive necessary parts of the task or tasks: for example, production, marketing, and research and development in one kind of system, or clinical treatment, teaching, and research in another.

From a study of Talcott Parsons' work in sociology, and from working with A. K. Rice at Tavistock Group Conferences, I learned a method for detecting what might be responsible for difficulties in carrying out a task. Talking with members of a system and listening to them talk to each other, and consulting such sources as documents, I identified the task(s) that defined the system. Then I would design an ideal-type organization whose parts existed only to carry out those functions necessary for achieving this task. For example, one function was obtaining necessary resources. Another function was establishing and reinforcing norms or rules for behavior (what would count as a desirable arrangement or procedure). Still another was integrating or coordinating the needs and efforts of different task groups. And another was recruiting and maintaining motivational commitments to task-achievement. Relationships among the parts of this ideal-type organization were such that they served only the achievement of the task.

Next I would compare the ideal-type with the actual organization. From the discrepancies between the two, and from an understanding of what motivated those discrepancies, I would come up with a diagnosis of what might be causing the difficulties.

Often, I would discover that what motivated the discrepancies was a problem in accepting or exercising authority or leadership. For example, authority might be diffused among many so that it was difficult to identify any one person as responsible. Or responsibility existed without the needed authority to carry it out. Or someone had a lot of influence over decisions but very little accountability for the consequences of these decisions.

I was curious about what needs, wishes, or anxieties led to dysfunctional arrangements or procedures that seemed to have very little to do with achieving the ostensible task. I was especially interested in the way achieving the task was affected adversely by conflicts among task groups, which competed for limited resources, and differed in their value-preferences and priorities. Such conflicts were of course inevitable, since each task group had as its own specialized goal contributing something distinctive and necessary to the achievement of the overall task. And a lot depended on whether and how these conflicts were resolved.

Then, swapping stories and working with David Berg, I became increasingly aware of the way membership in identity groups (notably, gender, ethnic-racial, generational, socioeconomic, age, or professional-discipline groups), and the conflicts between such groups (usually conflicts between relatively powerful and relatively powerless groups), may adversely influence task-achievement. Over time, I recovered an earlier interest, and became increasingly even more interested, in the effects that gender stereotypes and the effort to impose or escape from them had on group and organizational life. Here, in these conversations with David, influence, contrary to expectations, seems to have flowed from the younger to the older of two generations.

Stereotypes

I began to wonder about the apparently irresistible tendency members of groups had to form crude dichotomous classes, that replace all the complicated things we mean by 'masculine' and 'feminine' and insist instead on attributing to members of these classes grotesquely polarized properties. But actually, for any given characteristic, there was a distribution of it among both men and women. Both men and women were occasionally capable of integrating within themselves apparently incompatible characteristics that they usually tended instead to split between the two gender groups. So, what function did this crudely polarized classifying serve?

I began to struggle, for the most part with little success, to get out of the box 'male authority figure'. David would say to me, 'But, Marshall, you *are* a male authority figure, and you're never going to escape that you are.' My discomfort with this classification of me, and the classification does have a basis in reality, caused problems for me, my students, and the teaching/learning process in which we were engaged.

The story of the 'male authority figure'

A few years ago, I was asked to teach for a few months in a year-long seminar led by a member of the junior faculty who was a woman. From the first day, I had a most uncomfortable experience. Students were silent and unresponsive, when I attempted in ways that on other occasions had been successful to get a discussion going. One woman told me that I was a 'male authority figure' – and therefore had no way of understanding how women went about working with patients.

I had asked the group members to talk about what was important to them in doing their work, and then clumsily enough had gone on to express my reservations about the emphasis by some on the all-importance of 'empathy'. I realized afterwards, too late, that my comments, which arose out of my own theoretical preoccupations, could be taken as a putdown. They were received stonily and would not be forgiven.

I perceived the women as responsible for the class's revolt against my selecting people (as I usually did) to present clinical material for discussion; in my experience leaving it up to volunteers led to problems I would just as soon avoid. Faced with an obdurate determination by the seminar members that presentations should be left to volunteers, I gave in, only to discover that no one in the group – man or woman – was willing to volunteer! The work of the group ground to a halt.

I dreaded going to further sessions. I felt there was no way I could act effectively. I am generally unwilling to make interpretations of group process in a task group. Here, that would have been useless anyway. Members of this group would likely have experienced and responded to an interpretation as a weapon wielded by a male authority figure. In any event, I did not know what interpretation to make. Was I in fact behaving ineptly, awkwardly, or denigratingly in a seminar that had a larger percentage of women than any I had previously taught? Was I behaving in a way – coming in and 'taking over' – that they perceived as demeaning to my co-teacher? Perhaps the most naive, primitive, and self-incriminating feeling I had was the sense of having been deserted and betrayed by the men in the group.

My colleagues on the faculty were in general understanding and supportive, reassuring me that this was an 'unusual' group. (I have heard that about every group in which I have had any difficulty since then, so I don't find it a very reassuring explanation any more.) I had some consultations with David and with Dan Levinson. They both helped me pay attention to the following facts, which of course I had known. The member of the junior faculty with whom I taught was a woman. The other senior male authority figure who had come in for a period to teach with her in this course had had similar difficulties. A woman faculty member who had also come in for a period to teach with her had a fine experience. There were few senior full-time and no tenured faculty women in the department.

I did come to see that it was probable that at least the women group members saw me as displacing a junior woman teacher, who as far as they knew had little power in the system and about as much chance as becoming a tenured faculty member as any of them did. How could they be comfortable, comparing my experience with her inexperience, my status with hers!? The situation was a set-up for me to become the lightning rod for all kinds of feelings about the place of women in the system and perceptions concerning how they were treated.

Having ruled out making any interpretations to the group, I talked the whole matter over in several discussions with my co-teacher, who had invited me to teach with her and who continued to want me to teach with her. What should we do? I suggested that we make use of the dynamic to do some work. She joined me helpfully and enthusiastically in the seminar to set up subgroups by gender. After she presented some clinical material, the subgroups met to discuss how a group of women had heard what had happened in the clinical session and how a group of men had heard it. A secretary in each subgroup reported back to the total group the responses to the clinical material in that subgroup. Then the entire group discussed the reports to see if there were any detectable systematic differences between the responses of the two gender groups. There seemed to be some differences.

The exercise struck me as artificial, and somewhat off the task. I did not feel that much learning of psychotherapy went on. But I was relieved to find a modus vivendi with this group that permitted us to meet together a few more times without overt hatefulness. The co-teacher and I decided to end the seminar a couple of weeks earlier than we had originally planned.

That was the nadir. Things have gotten better since then. In fact, I have never had such a demoralizing experience again, and I hope I never do. But I still have experiences where some – although to be sure not all – women experience me as, if not cruel, certainly indifferent to their personal discomfort when I make comments about clinical material they have presented. One woman, who is a good friend of mine, told me that presenting in an elective seminar of mine at the beginning of her participation in it was like undergoing surgery without anesthesia! Nevertheless she valued what she learned in the seminar, became increasingly comfortable in it, and went on to participate in it for three years. It has taken me some time to realize that such a comment is not necessarily about me or my personal characteristics but something about the task I represent, which I ask the group to work with me to accomplish.

A shift has occurred in how I understand that painful seminar experience. I began to think that perhaps gender and authority issues were not the major causes of difficulties but were instead cover stories for the anxiety about presenting clinical work all group members shared. I notice in retrospect that there were some strains among group members, having to do with painful comparisons and rivalry, which they could ignore if the fight were with 'the male authority figure'.

I have become increasingly aware of the feelings people – men and women – have about presenting their clinical work. I now spend more time addressing these feelings, acknowledging their existence, accepting them, and sharing with the people I teach the similar feelings I have had during my training. I emphasize that in the seminar I am using the material that is presented only to teach something about psychotherapy, not to evaluate the performance of the beginning psychotherapist. The more the presentation gives me a chance to do that, and of course so-called mistakes give me such a chance, the happier I am with it.

Further, I make it clear that I do not intend that group members should monitor or assess the performance of the presenter. Indeed, because of our interest in microdynamics, we confine ourselves to at the most one or two sessions, sometimes to a piece of one session, and limit to a minimum any information about the patient or the previous or subsequent work with the patient. So, I keep reminding the group and the presenter, we cannot realistically make any judgments about the quality of the presenter's clinical work or presenter's interventions.

But the presenter may not feel it that way. For the presenter, whatever I (or group members) say about the material – whether about connections I (or we) imagine seeing, or alternative interventions and their effects I (or we) imagine as possibilities – it somehow becomes an implied criticism in front of other people. It shows something the presenter had not known or addressed. For these ambitious devoted hard-working conscientious competitive people, that was always something they *should* have known.

It is paradoxical that in an educational system, there is such difficulty in really accepting that learning is a process. The focus in everyone's mind always seems to be on the value of *having* knowledge and know-how, and not on the delights of the slow step-by-step slogging-along process of *coming* to know and to know how. Is this something about this particular educational system? Well, it is not exactly common to hear a senior male faculty member talking about what he does not know or wants to learn.

I increasingly identify with both men and women who regard relations as preeminently important, a precondition to learning. Without a relation between a teacher and a trainee that involves mutual affection, caring, and respect, learning may be impossible. I have come to understand that in fact one of the things that makes it possible for students to get through these trying learning experiences is to feel genuinely liked by their teacher. This understanding at least I can act upon, because I am able to recognize (although sometimes belatedly) when I feel constrained or overformal with a woman student, and then to permit myself to lighten up, to become more informal, accessible, and friendly in my manner and tone.

In one seminar, for example, I paused 'in the work' to confide to the group how much I hated presenting clinical material when I was a resident, and to tell some stories about some tricks I used to evade doing so. I could feel the difference this made.

The story of the astonished trainee

My students helped me to break down stereotypes. One woman resident who trusted me enough to talk about these matters with me told me that a male fellow resident had come out of a seminar session with me complaining bitterly about how foolish and inept he felt my comments about the clinical material had made him look. Finding out that he had later signed up for an elective seminar with me astonished her. 'How could you,' she had asked him, 'feeling the way you do about him, go on to want to do further work with him?' I gathered she thought this was some clue about a kind of difference between some men and some women, but to me it emphasized that men and women have very similar anxieties and feelings, however differently some choose to express or conceal them.

Running a tight ship

A difficulty I have gotten into arises from the fact that especially when a seminar gets over a certain size, I run a tight ship. I feel it is important that everyone participate, that everyone have the practice of responding on their feet to clinical material, as indeed everyone will have to do when with patients. So I go around the table calling on people to give everyone that opportunity, permitting of course anyone to pass who chooses to do so. The difficulty arises when someone is embarrassed because they have nothing they can say, or someone has something they are eager to say when I am on the other side of the circle.

I also ask that the presenter not take up the limited time we have defending their interventions in response to comments by group members. For students to be unable to defend themselves against what they experience as misunderstandings of what they were doing, to be shushed, ignored, or prevented from showing what they know, are painful. It is often a woman who is able to represent this pain for the other group members, perhaps just because it has been inflicted upon her in other situations just by virtue of her being a woman. Since women are especially burdened by society's insistence that they prove themselves in an occupational setting, it is understandable then that it is more likely a woman than a man who will protest vigorously about the way I conduct a seminar and keep arguing that, no matter what purpose it serves, I should change it.

And as David has pointed out to me, the meaning of 'being criticized' differs for men and women in this system. 'Being criticized' can be borne by a man, if he sees it as preparing him to move up in the system. 'Being criticized' is often experienced by a woman as her having provided evidence for authority to use to justify preventing her from moving up in the system.

The woman of course expresses for everyone in the seminar the discomfort my way of working evokes in them. When so challenged, I frequently repeat my reasons, based on my conception of the task, for proceeding as I do. (That I continue to respond so suggests that in group settings I may be a relatively slow learner!)

But I have also consulted more with the seminar groups I teach about the problem and with them have developed some ways of more mixing of 'calling on people in turn' with 'free-for-all discussion'. And if a presenter insists on making a self-justifying statement in response to comments about the clinical material, I am now more likely to sit back. In order to take in what my students were telling me, I had to cope with images of myself as callous or sadistic, as obsessive-compulsive or inflexible, and I had to remind myself that I am in general well-thought of as a teacher, that residents – men and women – generously and repeatedly award me best-teacher-of-the-year prizes, that my elective seminars are usually over-subscribed and devotedly attended, and that the atmosphere, on the whole, in many seminar sessions is one of friendship, humor, enthusiastic exchange and serious learning. When how I teach is challenged, I hold on to the comment of more than one trainee, 'This is the most fun I have at work all week!' So buttressed, I am able to listen and learn.

Scapegoating a woman resident

I overheard a discussion about a woman resident. Faculty, in a psychological-explanation frame, were expressing concern about her matter-of-fact condemning comments about patients and wondering how to help her become less moralistic and judgmental.

I realized with a start that, recently in different seminars and preceptorials, I have had several experiences of the same kind with different women residents. (As David would say, 'the presence of "different characters, same plot" suggests that a social-systemic rather than an individual level of analysis might prove useful'.) In each case, the resident seemingly out of the blue made a comment about some patient, which startled me both because it was uttered in a matter-of-fact unselfconscious tone, and because it seemed such a harsh rejecting evaluation of the patient.

I felt an impulse to express my disapproval. But I didn't say anything, in part because I've learned to shut up when something startles me, in part because I didn't know what to make of this behavior even at the level of individual explanation. In my experience, when men residents have made such comments in past years, they have usually sounded half-embarrassed, as though they are thinking themselves that doctors and especially psychiatrists shouldn't judge patients in this way. I was especially puzzled because my fantasy, no doubt also reflecting an unthinking acceptance of stereotypes, had been that the increased presence of women in psychiatry might help to make it a kinder, gentler profession.

It occurred to me that a woman resident might feel that, in order to win acceptance and succeed, she must show that she is strong – for example, by making these 'tough' statements about patients. She may think it wise to try to hide anything in her response to patients that she fears others would regard as soft, weak, or undisciplined.

A man, of course, may have the same concerns, but more typically he might show his tough-mindedness, while at the same time preserving a maternal side, by arguing persistently and rigorously, for example, as one resident did, in favor of a theory emphasizing empathy and the importance of preverbal maternal relationships in a patient's development. In so arguing, he imagined himself opposing what he perceived as my 'traditional' views.

Parallel process in a preceptorial with a woman resident

I was meeting with a woman resident in a preceptorial. She was presenting her work in group psychotherapy. The week previous to the session she was presenting, she had canceled a meeting of the group. She tried with some success to help the group members express their reactions to the cancellation.

At some point I shared the following observations with her. The men in the group were sitting together. The women were sitting together. The men's reactions to the cancellation were stereotypically 'masculine': rational, accepting the 'reasons' for the cancellation. The women's reactions to the cancellation were stereotypically 'feminine': full of feelings, depressed, missing the session. All the members, including the psychotherapist, seemed to accept that men were rational and didn't respond with feelings, and women were not especially rational and full of feelings.

I asked her if it might not be useful to point out to the group members how much they were caught in these stereotypes. 'Don't you think,' I said, 'that this might be affecting not only their lives in the group but their problematic relations with members of the opposite sex about which they have been dropping hints from time to time?'

'After all,' I continued somewhat insistently, 'none of us – they, or you and I – may be able to escape being caught in these stereotypes but at least we can become aware of them and how they affect the way we relate to each other.'

She responded to me, and I could tell immediately that what I had said had come across as a criticism, and that she felt she had to defend herself. 'I understand what you are saying,' she said, in a friendly tone of voice. 'I see what you are pointing out. But I didn't think I could make that kind of comment. It would have upset them, been too much for them, on top of my having canceled their session. I thought it was more important to help them with the feelings they had about my canceling the session than to present them with a new and difficult problem.'

Then came a rare moment! I said, 'Isn't it interesting that you and I have just replayed what we saw happening in your group. I am all masculine, insistent, emphasizing the necessity to keep at the work, to say what must be said. You are all maternal, protecting the group members, aware of what they feel and need.' Her face lit up. She smiled. When we parted, I said, 'This was a good meeting.' She said, 'Especially the last few minutes.'

I thank her for that moment. I hope that David, my younger teacher, and Dan, my older teacher, feel rewarded for their labors with me.

CHAPTER 23

Group Identities

David Berg

The last lines touched me deeply. The work Marshall and I have done together has, indeed, made me feel that I am in a relationship in which the learning and influence flow two ways. This is a satisfying experience in which it is my sense that neither of us must give up who we are, what we think, and what we feel, in order to work and learn together (although, of course, this is an ever present anxiety and challenge).

Part of this satisfaction does come from my awareness that this is not merely a collaborative relationship between two peers, but rather a learning relationship between two generations in which both learn. Often both individuals in such a collaboration are too enmeshed in the historical relationship between generations or between levels of authority to fashion a relationship in which both can learn together, without either denying the differences in age and status or succumbing to the effects of the distribution of power that ordinarily accompanies such differences.

I do believe that Marshall can never shed his 'senior male authority figure' identity. More important, his gender, age, and experience, as well as his place in institutional hierarchies are part of what he brings to our collaboration. As much as he may feel personally indicted when I cast a critical eye on these institutions, it is precisely because *he* has a commitment to them that we can examine them and – in some modest way when possible – strive to change them.

That he, a senior white male, has invited me to labor with him is a powerful intergenerational message: that it is possible to continue learning throughout the life course. Some might argue that the younger generation's satisfaction derives from surpassing (or even displacing) the older generation, from demonstrating that the knowledge of a previous generation is obsolete. But are these greater pleasures than the satisfaction of learning together? Not for me.

From my perspective, the formative discussions that Marshall and I had came during the time he was writing a chapter for the research methods book that Ken

Smith and I were putting together.[110] Since one of the essential points of the book was that our identities (personality as well as group memberships) influence the way we conceive of and conduct research, it was important to me to explain to him the nature of the undertaking to which he was contributing. This explains, in part, the energy I poured into those discussions.

It was clear to me that Marshall was an open-minded scholar, one who was not afraid to learn even at a senior place in his life and career. It was also clear to me that as a psychiatrist who was deeply enmeshed in the debate over the scientific credibility of psychoanalysis, it was difficult for him to accept the arguments I was making about the central role of identity factors in social science research. On those occasions when we shared stories about our work and our struggles at work, I saw much of his experience in his department as a function of age, gender and status, even as he sought to explore personal or interpersonal explanations.

The lens through which I most frequently view organizations has its origins in my experience with organizational diagnosis. During my first attempts at a social-system diagnosis of a human system, I quickly began to realize that how I described an organization depended a great deal on the people in the organization with whom I had talked, what they did, and perhaps most startling how much empathy I had for their story. My reliance on this kind of data seemed to be terribly unscientific.

A dissertation research

In my dissertation research (described in Chapter 10), my analysis of the organization kept changing. When I spoke with psychiatrists, I developed a view of residents and fellows that explained much of what went on in the outpatient department. Then I spoke with the residents and the picture changed. And when I talked to the psychologists on staff (my own group!) an entirely different understanding began to emerge.

My first reaction was to formulate the question in terms of competition: Which of these descriptions of the outpatient department is more accurate? This inevitably led me to ask: More accurate for whom? For the psychiatrists? The residents? Me?

My instinct was to flee from these questions since their existence meant that an analysis of an organization was built upon shifting sands. The more I looked, the more it struck me as right that an understanding of a social system is precisely the fitting together of a puzzle whose pieces are the versions of reality different members supply. The picture on the puzzle, to extend the metaphor, emerges only when the pieces are placed together; no one who possesses only a single piece can see it.

For me this was an important learning about human systems. It is part of the answer to the question posed earlier about why a social-system frame is so hard to adopt. Without fitting the individual pieces together, it is sometimes very difficult to develop a social-system picture. At the same time, the individual (as one of the pieces) cannot see that such a social-system picture exists.

For any individual, a social-system understanding is merely a concept, not something easily felt, touched, or seen, especially not with the emotional intensity with which we experience our individual piece. But once you glimpse the system and its power to explain the relationships among the pieces, it is equally difficult ever again to focus exclusively on the individual.

Over the last few years in our conversations Marshall and I have increasingly sought to develop a social-system understanding of our dilemmas and struggles at work. Even now, however, I sometimes make him 'think like a psychiatrist' by emphasizing the role of hierarchy, gender, or age to an extent that makes him feel that I am 'stretching it'. At those times his comments reinforce the role and power of the individual, a perspective I sometimes lose when I force myself to consider the ways in which individuals express collective dynamics.

Intergroup relations in a seminar facing a threatening task

This struggle reminds me of one of my first teaching experiences in a management school. The introductory course in organizational behavior for masters students had twenty-six two-hour sessions. In 1978 the course included topics such as group decision-making, group problem-solving, leadership, human needs, human learning, adult development, and learning from failure. It also included two classes on intergroup relations and one two-hour session to cover both gender and minority relations in organizations. I acknowledged that these issues were important (and they were interests of mine) but that we had the content of the course (the topics considered of greater significance) to teach as well.

My tune changed in the years that followed as did my definition of content. The last time I taught such a course, twelve of the twenty-four class sessions were explicitly about intergroup relations in organizations and the central theme in the whole course concerned the impact of identity group memberships on team and organization functioning. The shift testified to my increasing belief in the importance of such group memberships and intergroup relations in under-standing organizational life.

Near the end of an experiential group dynamics course in this same school, I asked the class to divide into three project groups, each of which would prepare a presentation to the class during the last three classes of the semester. Over the course of the semester, these folks had gotten to know each other in the context of both the experiential group sessions and the more didactic lecture/theory classes.

The process of forming new project groups was laden with tension, as class members contemplated how to make their feelings about and evaluations of each other known, without hurting others or being unkind. There was much discussion about how to go about this. I had ruled out random assignment on the grounds that this was a course on group dynamics.

We took a preliminary step. I listed the three topics on the board. Anyone could express interest in any or all of the projects. In this way we could see people's interests without anyone having to commit to a topic before they had a chance to see who else was interested in the topic.

I wrote down the name of all those who were interested in each topic. When we were done, and were reflecting on the lists, John, a white male, said that Eric, an Asian American, had not put his name on any list. Eric had been a problematic member throughout the semester, often assuming the role of 'junior consultant' and confronting his fellow students with interpretations of their behavior, but not looking at his own. He also consistently called the other faculty member (not present on this day) to task, but always within the rules of the experiential session.

John now asked Eric for an explanation. Eric replied that he didn't have to give one. Sally, a white female, protested that this was unfair and disruptive. To this Eric replied, 'Learn to live with disappointment.'

The class was on the verge of giving full expression to weeks of frustration with Eric, when Park, a male Korean, observed that Tony, an Italian male, had put himself on all three lists! Tony was well liked in the class. He too had been challenging authority in the course, but not always 'within the rules'.

The observation that Tony had effectively done the same thing as Eric, but that the group members had not noticed it, led to an exploration of a number of social-system questions, none of which had been apparent during the escalating attack and counterattack involving Eric.

Question 1. What was it that both Eric and Tony were doing? It seemed to us that both were expressing the collective displeasure at being forced to acknowledge publicly the private relationships and strong feelings in the room. Both had rebelled at the task, finding different ways to do it. One way was more acceptable to the class – and to the instructor, since I didn't notice Tony's gambit either. The two class members most comfortable with rebellion expressed this desire not to do the work I had set before the class, but it was universally felt.

Question 2. Why hadn't the class noticed Tony's choice, but instead focused on Eric's response? The class was well aware of the role into which Eric had placed himself and been placed. Many in the class feared ending up in a group with Eric, so they had studied the lists to see what Eric had chosen. Since Eric symbolized many people's anxiety over the composition of these new groups, his movements got special attention. Also, having a problem with Eric was familiar, but having a problem with Tony was more unusual. It was extremely difficult to confront having a problem with me.

Question 3. What meaning was there, if any, to the identities of the players in this drama? Was it an accident that Eric was Asian American, that Park, the student who noticed Tony's choices, was Korean? Was it coincidental that, once the observation about Eric had been made, it was a woman who took up the fight? These questions were difficult to answer. They involved a discussion of touchy subjects: who in the class felt able to question or confront; what role the identity of the instructor had in authorizing some students but not others; what role women students played in a course that did not have a woman on the staff; and how nonwhite Americans and foreign nationals experienced events that 'everybody else' took for granted.

In this example too, I am struck by how easy it is to miss the collective or social-system factor in these events. All of us in this course, myself included, found it almost impossible to shift our frame from 'Eric the counterdependent insecure individual' to 'Eric the class representative' – a spokesperson for unacceptable or unconscious anxieties that all of us had in varying degrees.

A female doctoral student's strategy

I was particularly struck by the comment in the story about the trainee who anxiously withheld information that residents may feel that it is necessary to show strength and only strength in their role as physician and psychotherapist. That comment seems applicable to many organizational settings, especially those in which men have defined appropriate behavior (perhaps as a collective defense against the anxiety that attends emotional expression). I have observed countless instances in which men and women feel obliged to present only half of what they thought, felt, or believed, because the suppressed half might be labeled soft or nonrigorous and therefore reflect badly on them.

It seems to me that this has two unfortunate consequences, one individual and one collective. For the individual, she or he becomes increasingly alienated from one whole side of her or his self. One can hold onto parts of the self only for so long that the social world devalues, and then they must be denied (or worse, split off and projected onto others) if one is not to run the risk of being rejected in social and work settings where 'toughness' and 'hardness' are the qualities rewarded. Quite a price to pay for organizational membership; yet it is one that is paid all the time.

At the collective level, we disable organizations from harnessing these 'soft' (or intuitive, expressive) characteristics in the service of the task. If the work of the organization happens to include psychotherapy, the emphasis on strength and toughness makes it extremely difficult to participate in those processes that require an openness to weakness and softness in oneself and in one's patients. If I never learn to treat my feelings as a legitimate source of data about the psychotherapy group with which I am working, choosing instead to rely exclusively on theories and conceptual labels, I am working with a limited set of tools.

Once, while on a university faculty, I was sitting in on a job talk, a presentation of research that took place in the context of a job interview. The presentation was about power in small groups: when groups experienced themselves as powerful and what environmental conditions contributed to this experience. Most of the presentation, by a female doctoral student who was completing her dissertation at a prestigious elite university, involved a high-powered statistical analysis of questionnaire and archival data, most of which supported the research hypotheses (a common occurrence at job talks). After all the numbers were presented, the speaker pointed to the summary finding and said, 'I have confidence in these findings, because I observed each of the groups themselves, and my observations fit with what these data suggest.' When asked why these observations were not part of her data set, the presenter responded that they were not scientific enough (read: tough, rigorous, hard) *and yet they served as the basis for her confidence in the validity of the quantitative findings.*

The moral of this story for me is not that qualitative observations are superior to quantitative survey analysis, but that we are in danger of limiting ourselves and our institutions if we denigrate rather than develop the various sources of our insight, knowledge, and creativity. Perhaps even worse, we participate in a sham when we suggest that our confidence and skill come from only one source, when in fact we draw in practice from many sources. Trainees, staff members, patients, and clients notice this sham, and it has the potential to undermine both the personal development of these members of the organization and the objectives of the organization itself.

White women and minority men elect a course

A story on the theme of 'hard' and 'soft': When I was teaching at a school of management, those of us who taught about human behavior in organizations noticed that we often (although not always) had a disproportionate number of women in our courses on group dynamics and organizational diagnosis. We would occasionally discuss what this meant about us, our courses, and the school.

In one course on organizational diagnosis, I asked the class for its hypotheses about why we were mostly white women and minority men.

- *Hypothesis One* (drowned out by laughter from the class): 'The white men couldn't fit it into their schedules.'

- *Hypothesis Two*: 'None of the finance types would be caught dead taking a "soft" course like this one because of what it would do to their reputation in the school.'

- *Hypothesis Three*: 'This course has a reputation for being a "female" course, one in which it is okay to talk about feelings and relationships, so it attracts people who are interested in those sorts of things as they relate to management and organization.'

- *Hypothesis Four*: 'For white men, the structure and relationships in organizations are not likely to cause them harm or retard their success. It is more likely that the networks and affinities (to say nothing of prejudices and stereotypes) make their success and acceptance easier. But for white women and minority members, this "elective" course is part of a survival kit, a way of understanding organizations – the groups within them and the relationships among these groups – that might help them to survive and even succeed in "traditional" institutions.'

I think the class knew what was going on. Even the joke about the schedules made sense. An advanced finance course was often scheduled at the same time as an advanced course in organizational behavior because no one expected a student to have *both* interests. But the hypotheses also testified to the split within the school, a split between tough and weak, hard and soft, male and female, ideas and feelings, concepts and relationships, numbers and qualitative observations, that placed the former over the latter, and made it almost impossible to imagine (and academically pursue) an integrated education.

Scapegoating a customer relations department in response to anxiety about new technology

A story on the theme of anxiety aroused by changes in the way work is done in a group or organization: In a small private-sector company, it became apparent that a substantial computerization project needed to be undertaken. Each work station would be computerized to the extent possible. A management information system would be created, so that various people within the organization could have access to detailed updated information minute-by-minute.

A computer programmer was hired to begin designing and programming the system. First he worked at computerizing the Account Management Department, showing each individual how 'to make her or his job easier' through the use of the computer work station. But when he began to work with the Customer Relations Department, he met resistance.

The people in this department were uncooperative, uninterested in trying new methods of data input, and adamant in their belief that the new system only meant more work and the hassle of having others looking over their shoulders and second guessing them. Soon the rest of the people in the organization began to complain that if only customer relations would join the computer age, the project could move forward. The customer relations people were described as resistant, insecure, unwilling to learn new things, and ultimately – because of their resistance to necessary change – as unqualified for their jobs.

Then a number of meetings were held with representatives of all the departments in the company to give advice to the computer consultant on how best to design the management information system. Representatives of customer relations participated uncomfortably and defensively in these meetings. They resented the imposition of disruptive changes. They worried about the meddling that would follow the creation of an on-line information system. Again the rest of the organization complained about customer relations.

After many difficult meetings and intensive work on the relationship between the consultant and the Customer Relations Department (described by some as 'starting over'), resistance began to ease. Customer relations employees began trying incremental adjustments to their daily routines. But what surprised the advisory group was that, following these changes in the customer relations group, the Operations Department began to resist the computerization project. The issues they raised were the same as those raised by customer relations: disruption, management intrusiveness. *The characters change; the plot remains the same.*

It finally became apparent to all that members of the Customer Relations Department had not been the problem. The problem was the company's anxiety about a major social and technological change. It turned out on further inquiry that the most important worry about this change was not that it would disrupt work, and not that people might not be able to learn new ways of doing their jobs. Most important was mistrust of management and anxiety about how it might use information to manage and control the organization.

The social-system issue – the impact of new technology on employees, on work procedures, and on managerial behavior – had almost been missed. Isolating the problem in customer relations might have destroyed this department's morale and undermined the competence of each individual member of it, while at the same time major issues and anxieties throughout the company attending this major organizational change would have been ignored.

The risks we run telling these stories

In opening up such subjects as authority, gender, or race relations for discussion, neither Marshall nor I can escape his own identity. So we will inevitably and necessarily portray situations or interpret them through the lenses of our experience as men, as white people, as Jews, and in our separate cases as psychologist and psychiatrist, as associate clinical professor in practice and tenured professor. This increases the odds that the things we write about may be disturbing.

In addition, beginning a discussion about the social-system forces that affect gender relations, race relations, or authority relations is always disturbing. The stage is set for a collective drama in which this collective disturbance will be diminished by isolating it in an individual. For example, to the extent that Marshall discusses his struggles with gender, authority, or race, I anticipate that others may treat him too as if he were the only one with such problems. This could happen in discussions in hallways, private conversations, or comments made to him directly. Just as has on occasion happened to me, his openness could conceivably have the consequence of isolating him as the one who has the problem and with him the disowned problem itself.

Our system is no different from others. It is not immune from the tendency to favor individual over social-system explanations. So it runs the same risks of injury to individuals and inattention to social-system causes of dysfunction. And it lives under the same constraints of time and energy which militate against the emotional, physical and intellectual effort required to look beyond the individual. But we are betting that there is also in the system in which we do our work together a strong desire to grapple with these issues. We are hoping that it may prove to be different in this way from otherwise similar systems.

CHAPTER 24

Belling the Cat

Marshall Edelson

Here is a story about a group's *sacrifice* of one of its members, who had been elected by other members to attack, on their behalf, a leader whom they feared. In other words, this member had been elected to bell the cat – and, disregarding the risks involved, if indeed aware of them at all, had accepted the assignment.

Scene: A group of trainees. Marshall Edelson is addressing the group. 'I have a story this morning. It is long, and not a story I take any pleasure in telling. But I feel bound as your teacher to tell it. When I told it to David, he said that he hoped you would stay with me until its end. He must have imagined you finding it offputting or distressing and wanting to stop it.

'I too hope that you will stay with me to the end, because I tell it in part to give you an example of an *entire process* – all the steps it takes me to arrive at a group-as-a-whole interpretation, and how I go about presenting such an interpretation to a group. The story has many twists and turns; you won't be able to tell how it ends until you hear the last word.

'You remember that from time to time we have spoken of playing with ideas and feelings, just seeing what comes up without too strictly monitoring or censoring what we think, feel, or say. I am going to do that. Then, appropriately, I am in the world of imagination. When I use words like *murder* or later such phrases as *birds of prey*, I consider that what I say, although not literally true, has emotional truth. Some people devalue emotional truth compared to what is literally true, but as clinicians we do not join them. We do not attend primarily to the objective character of events. Instead we tune in to how these events are experienced.

'I want to tell you a story about a murderous assault that has taken place in this group. My detective story focuses on two questions. Who really committed the murderous assault? How was it done – what went into the doing of it?

'David, in talking with me about the story, said that it was not clear to him to what extent the murderous assault about which I am going to tell you was primarily an inevitable outcome of a long history and to what extent it was primarily a response to a recent event that gained its meaning from this long history.

'It is part of the long history of this group that I have felt we do not have a contract, you and I, to learn together. As David put it, you and I have not negotiated any learning contract across the authority boundary; you have not joined me to learn. When I have intervened, to comment on lateness and its possible meaning, or some process going on in the group, or someone's behavior as representative of the feelings or attitudes of others in the group, you have heard me as harsh, critical, chiding, scolding.

'You are embedded in a hierarchical medical system, which I know first-hand. I see you bringing into this group a thousand of what I call "small murders", in which you – as nonphysician staff, as trainees – have felt abused, humiliated, and exploited by those in authority. I would call these *symbolic* murders, but that doesn't fully express what is actually done to and experienced by people when these unnoticed acts are perpetrated.

'So now small murders are what you expect. Abuse, humiliation, and exploitation are what you perceive whenever you relate to someone in authority in the system, whether that is what at a particular moment is going on or is intended. No doubt you are at this moment bracing yourselves for still another verbal slap on the wrist; you are expecting – you are ready to hear this story as – just another scolding, and you might want to interrupt it, to close your ears to it, to leave the room.

'All along I feel you have seen me as another oppressive male authority figure and, like other male authority figures in this system, cruel, demeaning, favoring men who will be promoted and who will inherit authority positions in the system, and having no interest in women who will not. Since the group has treated me as such, and has provoked me to act in a way that confirms this perception of me, I have from time to time acted in a way that you could reasonably take – and that you have taken – selectively, without regard to counterexamples – and that I also at times have taken – as evidence that the perception is generally valid. So, naturally, you have hated me.

'But your fear of authority is such that you have not been able to express this hatred in words. You have been on the whole silent, inexpressive, or placatory. You have given testimony, rather vague testimony, to what you have learned in this group, and have declared that I have been – and acted as if I were – the fount of all this learning. Even when you have permitted yourself some lively exchange with each other, you experienced this as "progress" that would please me. Even when you have felt genuinely that you have learned, you have not been able to express *other* feelings, such as your hatred of me, and of authority in general. From the beginning, and to this day – despite the flickers of sarcasm, mockery, and provocative attack I have called to your attention or which various ones of you have noticed in others – each one of you has denied and disowned any hatred or hostile intent in yourself, but rather has focused on the ways in which you feel yourself the victim of others' aggression.

'To what extent was the murderous assault about which I am going to tell you an outcome of this hatred you have split off from yourselves, and to what extent a more immediate response to a recent "inciting" event? I will now tell you about this recent event and what led up to it.

'Victor, among others, had reported that he could now recognize such a phenomenon as scapegoating when it was occurring but found it difficult to intervene, to use or talk about such an idea in a group. In response, we had arranged that periodically we would spend a meeting using a reading to reflect on our experiences in this group and other groups. In these particular meetings, we would attempt to consolidate what we had learned from these experiences by forming concepts we could use to understand and talk about similar experiences in the future. Consistent with my sense that you have never joined with me across authority lines to learn, you acquiesced to the proposal, but then forgot about it, did not do the reading assignment, were confused about why I assigned the reading, and showed little interest in discussing it.

'David and I then decided to try again. We planned to propose three meetings ago that you read *something we had written about this group*, for discussion two weeks later. We expected that your response to what we had written would help us check our account and our thinking. We hoped that you would join us in formulating for others what we had learned together from our shared experience.

'I left it up to David to use his judgment about when during that meeting he would propose this assignment, suggesting to him that we would need at least a half-hour to discuss your reaction to the proposal. To my discomfort, David, who had already announced he would not be at the next meeting of the group, had not said anything about the proposal by ten minutes before the end of the meeting.

'I felt trapped. I had told him I would leave it up to him. But if we announced it in the last minutes of the meeting, you would have no chance to respond, no chance to let us know whether this was something you wanted to do. So I was forced to become the authority figure that was making and announcing the assignment – and at a time that was apparently too late to hear from you what you thought and felt about it, and so apparently without any regard for what you thought and felt.

'My co-teacher had taken a first step, dissociating himself from me and from the writing we had done together, and turning you against me – "delivering me up to my enemies", so to speak. Younger than I and having less status in the medical system in which we worked (he was not a physician and, a volunteer faculty member, he was not on a tenure ladder), apparently he had some feelings of his own about the authority I represented.

'In his attempts to reconstruct what had led him to do what he had done, David told me about his reluctance to give an experiential learning group an agenda, and about his uneasiness about our reason for deciding that he would make the announcement. That reason was to avoid playing into the group's disposition to see me as the one of us who was the heavy-handed authority that made people do things like study reading assignments; he felt in retrospect our giving him the job of making the proposal was simply an effort to protect me from the group's anger rather than to let it come and deal with it directly. However, it was also true that he did not in talking with me before that meeting give voice to his reservations or refuse the role we had decided upon.

'I finally did go ahead and interrupt the discussion ten minutes before the end of that meeting. Your response to my statement of our proposal was immediate and intense. "You have been writing about us, without telling us!" Some voices, Victor's and Vita's among them, expressed, "You have betrayed us!" "I don't want to read it." "I don't want to see it." Other voices, Olivia's, for instance, expressed, "I'm looking forward to reading it. I want to know what you have written. I am very curious." When I mentioned that there might be some disappointment because a great deal of what we had written concerned our own collaboration, Nora said, "You mean we're not as interesting to you as the many hospital meetings devoted to discussing pets that you reported in great detail in a recent conference!"[111]

'At the next meeting, two meetings ago, David was, as previously announced, not present. Donald did not show up; reportedly, he was having car trouble. Eddie had sent a message saying that he would be late by about forty-five minutes. Victor, the third man in the group, was largely silent in the meeting.

'The group did not bring up the final moments of the previous meeting, and acted as if they had never occurred. Nora led an angry discussion about Eddie's announcement that he had something more important to do, so he would be late to the meeting. Nora connected his announcement, which she experienced as especially provocative, to the group's agreeing to let Clara come late regularly. "If Clara can come late, why can't I? Probably because her lateness was acceptable to us, Eddie felt that it was okay for him to come late. After all, the rest of us have important things to do too." The rage intensified when Eddie came late to the meeting, and left a few minutes later, saying that he did not know if he would return. He did not return. I experienced this as an ever increasing escalation of acting rather than talking in the group, which later I was to feel culminated in the murderous assault.

'The group discussion then focused on exchanges between women group members. There were general lively exchanges in which the women were interested in what they said to each other and felt about each other both in and out of the group meetings. I pointed out again the way in which Olivia, Donna, and Clara became silent when Nora and Vita took over the floor. You all seemed to agree in attributing this recurrent pattern to the fact that Nora and Vita had superior statuses in the system, and that therefore the other three women (Olivia,

Donna, and Clara) felt inferior to and intimidated by them. Clara mentioned in particular her "foreignness" as contributing to her sense of low status. There was a general appreciation that gender differences were not the only thing that influenced people's response to each other, that authority differences were also influential, and that an interaction between authority and gender seemed to be the most influential.

'The women in the group frequently had teased Eddie as sycophantic, "Edelson's boy", "Edelson's ally". He had become especially provocative in recent meetings, taunting the women in turn with their lack of status, and asserting his own access as a male to positions of authority. He declared, for example, that he loved working in the emergency room because he was the boss and instead of being a powerless trainee could order other people around, telling them what to do. David in a subsequent discussion with me identified Eddie's exultation in this role as "identification with the aggressor".

'I was to remember that phrase "identification with the aggressor" when the powerless group members murderously assaulted me. You all had become the ones who could abuse and humiliate me as those in authority had abused and humiliated you.

'I interrupted that meeting to wonder if some of the anger at Eddie belonged to me, reminding you all about the intense reaction to finding out that David and I had been writing about you. David told me after that meeting that he felt that you had experienced this writing as if it were just another example of how those in authority in this system abuse and exploit you. But today none of that rage at me was apparent.

'Donna said almost wearily, "I thought about it after the meeting, and felt that as usual there was nothing I could do about it, so why have any feelings about it. I decided to just forget about it." There was no sign of the rage that I expect to accompany the perception that one is being abused or exploited and the feeling that one is utterly helpless to do anything about it.

'I was left to tell you the story explaining how we had come to do this writing and what I had been able to figure out since the last meeting about why we had not mentioned the writing to you until now. Ordinarily I do not write about an experience while it is occurring, because that might interfere with the functioning of the participants, including myself. So I could imagine not mentioning it because of the possible effect on the work of the group, preferring instead to postpone eliciting your response and collaboration and requesting your consent. This all became complicated by my age and problems with my health. At this age, I have a strong autobiographical impulse, and I did not feel that I could be sure there would be a later time some years hence when I could write about what I found meaningful in my work with you and what I learned from it.

'As I said these words, Vita began to cry and could not speak. Olivia said quietly that it was sad to hear me say this about my health. (There had been previous expressions of concern about my health associated with a brief hospitalization, which had led to my missing a meeting of the group, and group members worrying that they did not know how fragile I was and what the effects of upsetting me might be.) I commented that these feelings were likely to make it even more difficult for group members to express the anger they felt toward me.

'I passed out the readings, saying that I would like them returned the next meeting. Nora, clearly not hearing what I was saying, said, "You're telling us too much. We're not taking it in."

'In the next meeting, the last one we had together before today's, you all seemed to have great difficulty discussing the reading. I started the meeting by reminding you that we had a somewhat different goal in this meeting. We were going to reflect on our experiences and see if we could form concepts that would help us to understand and talk about such processes as scapegoating when we were in groups in which they were occurring, so that we might intervene more effectively.

'There was again the sense of confusion. "When did we decide all this?" "Does that mean it's wrong to comment on our own group process today?" "I don't know what is the right thing to say." "I had reactions to the reading, but I don't know if they fit that goal."

'Donald said he found the reading very exciting, and that he saw the possibility of a new future for psychiatry. No one asked him about this vision of a "new psychiatry".[112] He fell silent, making no effort to discuss the reading further. Eddie, referring to some introductory autobiographical material, talked about his sense of shared ethnicity and childhood experiences with the two teachers. (He told me later that he had not read the main body of the reading, which contained material that was about the group.)

'It seemed that the women were not about to join the authority figure and his followers. They would not discuss the reading or at least if they did, certainly not on the terms dictated by "the men". Olivia, Donna, and Clara spoke of how interested and moved they were by the comments about the teachers' collaboration. Later, encouraged by David, Vita spoke reluctantly about her own background and her allegiances (quite unlike Eddie's), which, she felt, if revealed in the group, would lead to her being labeled an anti-Semite.

'Soon after, Clara was telling me tearfully how much she had learned from me in the group and how important I was to her. David told me after the meeting that he had noticed a few minutes earlier, when I said something about people's uneasiness about ideas, Clara had slapped her wrist in a "you bad children!" gesture. So I now saw her expression of gratitude, however genuine it no doubt also was, as in addition another example of difficulty in owning and expressing the rage that goes with a continuous sense of being scolded, and the need to placate the intimidating authority figure if any of the disclaimed rage does leak out.

'Eddie spoke provocatively of the inability of women to think, their lack of interest in thinking, their interest in feelings instead, and of how they always accused him or any man who tried to work with ideas of avoiding feelings and merely intellectualizing. Nora didn't say much, but her looks suggested that he was filling her up with rage.

'In this meeting, I felt disappointed and alone. Your refusal to discuss what I had written about the ideas David and I had developed together, as though the ideas were without value and I were not part of the group, made me feel very different from other group members in my interests and thinking. Essentially I felt extruded from the group. Remember even those like Eddie and Donald, self-declared allies of mine, did not discuss the ideas in the reading.

'In retrospect, I felt that in that meeting you had all prepared the assault on me that was to come. It was as though I were a member of a herd, being subtly culled from it, isolated, moved off by myself, so that the pack that surrounded me in the growing darkness could move in for the kill.

'It turned out that five group members had not brought the manuscript to the meeting. I said at the end of the meeting that, since the manuscript was filled with highly personal material about myself, was not finished, and I didn't want copies floating around until I decided that it was finished, I would like to have all the copies returned to me that day, put in an envelope and placed in my mailbox. Three group members did so. Two did not: Nora and Vita.

'The next day the "coincidence" struck me – that it should be Nora and Vita who were the ones not to return the manuscript, the two women of whom I had frequently observed that, when either of them spoke at length, the other three women ceased any lively interchange they might have been having and fell silent. I also noticed that I was having one fantasy after another in which I was impotent – helpless to retrieve some important part of myself. I imagined either Nora or Vita saying, "I won't return it and you can't make me!" and the other saying, "I've lost it, you can't blame me for not returning it, there's nothing I can do to get it back to you, I don't know where it is."

'Then I remembered Donna saying with no apparent rage, "No point in feeling anything. There's nothing I can do about it." I realized you were all letting me know how it felt to be abused and humiliated, and to feel helpless to do anything about it. You were letting me know in actions not words because you felt weak, intimidated, and anxious. You communicated what you experienced by evoking it in me.

'By the second day following the meeting, I was feeling a mounting rage. This rage was that rage you had disclaimed and split off from yourselves. Too anxious to express much less to be aware of it, you now filled me up with it.

'I began to have fantasies in which I angrily "discharged" Nora and Vita from the group because of their intolerable "acting-out", because their acting instead of speaking was a violation of an implied contract we had as a group. Then reflecting on these fantasies, in which someone is sent forth from the group, into exile, into the desert, I realized I was participating in my mind in a process of scapegoating. Extrusion from a group, always imagined as a solution to a problem, is a hallmark of scapegoating. So Nora and Vita were being scapegoated. How could I understand that?

'Suddenly I realized that the three women falling silent as Nora or Vita talked was not simply a sign that the three with lesser statuses felt powerless in the presence of the two with greater. Rather I now saw the three as *fascinated* with Nora and Vita. The latter were the two firebrands, the two revolutionaries, the two who could express anger if aroused. The three were studying the two, noting their dispositions, experimenting with what would arouse them. I saw the three in my mind as giant birds of prey, studying their potential victims. For it did not matter to the other group members what risks Nora and Vita ran in expressing feelings and impulses other members in the group were too anxious to acknowledge or express.

'Indeed all the group members had taken note. Each of you did your part to bring the two to a boil. If successful, you could depend on the two to tweak the nose of authority – even to kill off the hated leader. As Nora became ever more enraged, Eddie and Donald teased and denigrated women, flaunted that they, the two men, were the "favorites" and allies of the leader's, and in general acted in a way that could be interpreted as arrogant or contemptuous of others in the group; they played their part. Victor was silent; he played his part. Donna, Olivia, and Clara enacted the low-status women who were being hurt by the men and by the leader. They incited Nora and Vita. Clara slapped the wrist of the naughty child as the leader spoke. Donna said, "There's nothing I can do about it" in a tone that she feels she must suffer it; she cannot even become angry about it. What an incitement to a firebrand or revolutionary! Olivia was silent, was skeptical of the usefulness of a group-as-a-whole perspective, spoke of her resentment about what Eddie was saying. All of you played your parts.

'I don't think of myself in all this as scapegoated. I think of a member as *scapegoated* and a leader as *killed off.*

'How did I come to experience this "innocent" and relatively "trivial" *not returning a manuscript* as a murderous assault? I felt myself becoming increasingly *upset.* I got in touch with both Nora and Vita. Each said they would return the manuscript today, tomorrow. But today passed with no manuscript. Tomorrow came with no manuscript. I noticed that I was worrying about my pulse and blood pressure.

'Then I remembered the discussions in the group about my health, and the worry that *if someone in the group upset me* it might harm me. Anyone who says to a group, "This manuscript is filled with highly personal material about myself, it is not finished, I don't want copies floating around until I decide that it is finished, I would like to have all the copies returned to me today, I would like it put in an envelope, I would like it placed in my mailbox," is saying, "I'm going to be *upset* if the manuscript is not returned to me." Upsetting someone with heart trouble as a means of murder is not unknown – at least in detective stories.

'Five days later, Nora responded to a message from me by saying she had returned it the day before to the receptionist's office, because they had told her I did not like things left in my mailbox. (I still haven't figured that one out.) Nora said earlier in the week she would return it with a note, but when I then retrieved it from the receptionist's office there was no note. Three days after the meeting, I encountered Vita who said she would return the manuscript that afternoon. No manuscript. I received a message from her on the fifth day, after I had left my office, that she would return the manuscript that afternoon. When I returned to my office after a holiday weekend, no manuscript.

'On the eighth day after the meeting, Eddie, who was as far as I could tell unaware of the events following our meeting that I have just recounted, spoke with me about something occurring in the training program. He said that Vita was a *pawn* in what was going on; I was struck by his use of that term, so redolent of a scapegoating process. Also, he said, since their interests conflicted, he was concerned that their relationship, which he valued, would be strained.

'It is my practice, when I see that an individual is colluding with or caught up in what I consider to be a destructive process, in which that individual has been singled out and is being used to represent something for the group, to alert her or him, preferably before I interpret this process in the group. I called Vita on the ninth day following the meeting to tell her that she was the only one who had not returned the manuscript, that I thought the group was using her, and that perhaps she might not want to continue to go along with this. She said she would return the manuscript that afternoon. And so she did. But the manuscript was not in an envelope. I wondered if this was a defiant gesture, a refusal to submit.

'Some work remained for me to do in this *process*, which *began* with my transitorily giving myself up to an intense primitive experience and *then reflecting* upon it in order to *arrive* at some useful *conceptualizations* of it. David helped me do this last piece of work. He asked me, "What's your nickel?" In other words, what disposition in me led me obligingly to lend myself to becoming enraged by these events to a degree I seemed to be colluding with the group to harm myself?

'David told me of an experience in which he had been furious at a group of professors about an injury they had done him. A friend asked him, "What's your nickel? What have you contributed, however minor, to bringing about what they did to you?" David helped me to see – insisted that I see – that the nickel I contributed had to do, as both of us have so often in similar circumstances found it does, with my difficulty in acknowledging my rejection of actions that *I* had perpetrated that were similar to those I now condemned in others.

'I did write about the group without consulting you. I did go along with the idea of using what I had written as the last reading we would study together, with *no reflection* (hallmark of "acting out" or "acting in"), no anticipation of what that would feel like to all of you. I had *suddenly* sprung the fact of this writing on you, with no time to show my interest in consulting with you about the whole enterprise, or letting you know that I was ready for you to have some say in what happened with it. It was easier to reject someone else's *acting rather than talking* than to live with my disquiet about my own substitution of thoughtless action for talk.

'As soon as I was able to accept that I rejected behavior in others that I felt uneasy about in myself, I calmed down. I thought, but was not sure, that I might be able to talk with you about the entire process without recrimination.

'But I do want to make some final comments that are not entirely devoid of reproach and self-recrimination. In my experience group leaders are too slow to acknowledge the hatred as well as other feelings members have toward them and to help them express such feelings in words. The result is that feelings are translated into action. I have not found this to be innocuous.

'*Actions* taken by group members ("acting out" or "acting in") as a result of feelings that have been stirred up do differ from speech. Such actions may at times result in insights. But they also may destroy, or permanently harm, a leader, a member, a work group. Such actions can rupture the boundaries of the work group. If so they may then complicate, often destructively, relations of the group, its members, or its leader to those in the world external to the group. The effects of this kind of action on members, leaders, the relations among members, and the relations between members and leaders are more difficult to dissipate than the effects of speech. For me, such actions are signs of something gone wrong, a soured process, even when something may be learned from them.

'On the other hand, in contrast to that somber assessment, it is interesting that having worked hard with this experience, I now have moments in which I feel somewhat disengaged, in contrast to those moments that were so lacerating and turbulent. The story now strikes me as somewhat silly. I seem to have been silly in the part I played in it.

'Why does the memory of being caught up in strong feelings always seem a shameful one? Don't you too feel a little ridiculous when you reflect on some incident in which you felt furious at being abused, demeaned, humiliated – and then think of others saying, and then join them yourself in saying, "Why get upset about something so trivial, something she/he probably didn't intend? Shouldn't you be more mature, stoical, realistic?"

'This story captures my own experience, whatever was going on with other group members. Suppose you agree that it also captures something of what *really* has happened here. Then I have two questions I would like to discuss with you. The first is: How weak do you really feel you are, that this is the way that you try to recover your dignity?

'The second is: Do you want to join me now in formulating what we learn from such painful group processes, so that we can share with others who also become caught up in them. Here is one possible formulation. Such processes may begin as in this story by members disavowing those feelings that arouse anxiety and projecting them onto a scapegoat. The scapegoat will express them for others in the group, but will also be paid for this service by becoming the object of attack, opprobrium, or implied devaluation or denigration, and may as a consequence one way or another be extruded from the group. Such processes are pernicious because they create individual casualties and because they are costly to the work group.

'May I use this story, with your identities of course appropriately disguised, to help others recognize and understand a group's strong and in part unacknowledged responses to authority – admiration, dependence, and hatred – and the pernicious group processes these responses initiate, especially if they go unacknowledged and unexpressed?'

Subsequent discussions revealed that it was difficult for group members to hear what I said as a description of a *process*, instead defending themselves as if I were still caught up in the feelings and fantasies I described occurring at the *beginning* of the process. Once that became clear, group members began to exchange information that supported that they had all engaged in a process of scapegoating Nora and Vita. For example, Donald gleefully and without elaboration had told Nora, who had been absent at the meeting in which I had given the interpretation, that I had accused her of a murder. He thus incited her to further rage. Now she was indignant about being dealt with unfairly. Both Victor and Eddie did nothing to encourage Vita to turn in the manuscript, Victor in fact egging her on by taking the attitude, 'Oh, this is just one of these personality quirks of Marshall's. Why give into it?'

Nora tearfully protested that she was not the way others in the group saw her. She was *not* a firebrand; she was actually a tender person. Olivia, also tearfully, said, 'I know you *are* a tender person.' Those who had been scapegoated seemed with tears of relief to be reclaiming, and to be given back, their whole, their complex, their true selves. The mood of the group changed. Vita said, 'I feel differently from the way I felt at the beginning of this discussion.'

Producing a casualty or becoming one

What can we do to prevent casualties in the groups in which we are leaders or members? Faced with that question, I am moved to ask myself, 'Well, what *have* I learned from my experiences with casualties? What have I learned from telling and retelling my stories about casualties?'

The tales I have told about casualties have morals. Here they are.

1. I have learned to watch and listen for, and comment on, *either/or thinking* as opposed to *both/and thinking* ('I'm either like this *or* I'm like that; I can't be like this *and* like that.')

2. I have learned to watch and listen for, and comment on, signs of discomfort with, and rejection of one of those polar opposites ('I don't like to think that *that* may be any part of what I'm like or what I think or feel; I don't like how it feels when I experience *that*.')

3. I have learned to watch and listen for, and comment on, signs of the internalization of social *stereotypes* (for example, gender and racial stereotypes), which are an example of and which reinforce either/or thinking.

    (a) Either/or thinking (splitting), (b) disowning aspects of one's self, and (c) believing in stereotypes – all facilitate processes of projective identification (imagining that what you reject in yourself is contained in another) and its counterpart, introjective identification (imagining that you contain what is thrown out by another). These processes lead to the perception of and preoccupation with exaggerated polar differences between members of a group or organization, and that exaggerated polarization facilitates scapegoating (devaluing, isolating, extruding) of a 'problem' individual or group.

4. I have learned to intervene, at least with a comment, *promptly* but not *prematurely* (a fine distinction, and one difficult to put into practice), when scapegoating takes the form of self-righteously, indiscriminately, dogmatically, and without nuance *blaming* an individual or group. Or when scapegoating takes the form (more difficult to recognize as scapegoating) of an obsessive, subtly denigrating, and at the same time self-aggrandizing *solicitude* for or concern about an individual or group.

5. In working with groups, in attempts to understand problems, I have learned to stay as much as possible with a group-as-a-whole or a social-systemic level of analysis to mitigate inclinations to create scapegoats. The disposition to use an intrapersonal or interpersonal (as distinct from a group-as-a-whole social-systemic) level of analysis in diagnosing the cause of problems facilitates blaming 'problem' individuals in a group or organization, or one 'problem' group among many groups in an organization. Problematically, this disposition is especially entrenched among those (members of educational and medical institutions, educators and therapists) whose task is helping to bring about change in *individuals*. They have imported interpersonal paradigms from the dyad. Instead of modeling, 'I have had an experience something like yours and I recognize myself in you,' they model, 'I'll interview you with the idea of helping you. I sympathize with you. You are the one with problems.' (Does this

raise questions about what goes on in many psychotherapy dyads? Do psychotherapists convey, 'I may be able to help you, because I don't have your problem,' rather than 'I may be able to help you, just because I recognize myself in you'?) This entrenchment of a disposition to use an intrapersonal or interpersonal level of analysis, although it no doubt does have utility in some circumstances and for some purposes, may make scapegoating especially likely to occur in educational and medical institutions.

6. I have learned to keep an eye on what is going on at the leader-members boundary. I have learned to encourage conflict, dissent, negotiation across that boundary (easier to state than to do). The leader may suppress, discourage, or evade, and members avoid, conflict or disagreement – or any troublesome or anxiety-provoking communications – across the leader-members boundary. The boundary is then relatively impermeable; leader and members cannot negotiate the differences that the boundary marks. The tensions between leader and members are recreated in or deflected to the relations among the members themselves. The inability to communicate across the leader-member boundary lead to the phenomena I have described as 'leaders throwing members to the wolves', or 'members electing one of themselves to bell the cat'; that is how this inability produces casualties.

I write, 'I have learned…' As is usually the case with difficult learnings, and as many of the stories I tell illustrate, I often seem to forget, when I am caught up in particular processes on particular occasions, I often act as if I have forgotten, these things I feel I have learned.

PART 6

Intergroup Relations

In every organization, groups differ in the amount of power that they have. This may result from their differential access to resources, or from having control over critical information, or from being in a position to influence significantly the destiny of others. Power can also emerge from the perceptions that groups have of each other. A group may achieve power because others are convinced that it will exercise that power in a way that does not undermine the interests of those without power. In some cases, groups will even reject possibilities that would be in their interest, simply because they do not want those who suggested them to have the power resulting from coming up with something that was universally accepted...

When one group has more power than another, the less powerful invariably redefines its condition as absolute powerlessness. This creates the belief that only if the more powerful give up some of their power can the less powerful ever have a chance to improve their situation. In the process, the relatively less powerful group turns a blind eye to the power it does have and defines its condition only in its comparisons with the powerful...

The attempt of the powerless to define its condition exclusively in terms of the powerful is experienced by the powerful as an attempt to seduce it into giving away or letting go of its well-deserved, hard-earned position. This is experienced as an 'assault that must be resisted', setting up the inevitable reactive conflict between those who are conceived of as the 'haves' and the others who are the 'have-nots'. In the extreme form of this, the 'have-nots' become blind to all that they have, and the 'haves' overlook all that they do not have. The attendant polarization leads both to make attributions that intensify the polarization, setting the relations in a permanently conflictual form. The conflict serves well many of the ways each group prefers to relate to those who are different. In particular, conflict with an external group is often used as a way to maintain cohesion. When external conflict exists or can be created, it is easy for a group to generate a convincing rationale for members to put aside the differences that might otherwise fragment it. Then the group can ignore its deviant or convince its warring subgroups to stop their fighting in the service of the group as a whole.

Kenwyn Smith and David Berg

CHAPTER 25

The Search for Community

Marshall Edelson

When mental health professionals interact with patients, each representing their own group, this intergroup interaction occurs in the shadow of stereotypes. The stereotypes result from a process of splitting in which both groups have colluded.

What has been split off in the case of mental health professionals is what they are most anxious about: not knowing something, not knowing how, not knowing what to say, not knowing what to do. If the professionals are to get rid of ignorance and incompetence, some group must be found that will accept these as their own. Here is where patients come in. If *they* can be seen as exemplifying witlessness, then mental health professionals are relieved of their anxieties. 'It is not we who lack knowledge we must have. It is not we who have moments in which we do not know what to do. It is the patients whom we want to help who are confused and helpless, like little children. Compared with them, we are monuments of knowledge and competence.'

Patients, of course, will collude with such a view, because to relieve their anxieties they must believe that somewhere there is someone who understands and knows what to do about their misery and disabilities, someone upon whom they can depend in a world of chaos and darkness. So, in the interest of helping both groups flee from what makes them anxious, patients will give up whatever knowledge and competence they do have in order to create a world in which someone at least is all-knowing, all-wise, all-capable.

It is true that such splitting has its functional effects. It may enable mental health professionals to maintain their confidence in the midst of uncertainty, in the midst of inevitable limitations in knowledge and skill. It may enable patients to maintain their hope in the midst of discouragement and despair. But it also has costs.

Both groups pay a price. Both groups lose a sense of reality. Because mental health professionals must dissociate themselves from patients who now contain what these professionals have tried to split off from themselves, they cannot recognize the something of themselves in patients. So they lose the capacity to use their own experience to understand from inside (rather than merely objectively) the patients with whom they work. They must prevent themselves from acknowledging in their relations with patients their shared humanness.

Similarly, because patients must ignore or conceal whatever islands of knowledge and competence they have in order to accept what professionals want to split off and get rid of, they suffer the indignity of self-derogation. Their self-esteem already eroded by the stigmata of illness and its consequences, they lose in addition whatever knowledge of themselves and the world and whatever competence they still possess that might enable them to work *actively* and *with* mental health professionals to cope with their illness. Both groups, separated by the divide created by their efforts to rid themselves of experiences that make them anxious, must work together handicapped by a view of patients as witless and incompetent, as the necessarily passive and totally dependent recipients of help that exists completely outside themselves.

The stories I tell in this chapter are about such intergroup relations. They are about my past attempts to create in a treatment setting a 'therapeutic community', a community that would be therapeutic just because it was designed to thwart this kind of splitting and to reject the kind of stereotypes and intergroup relations that are its issue. They are about the ways such attempts by me were, naturally enough, resisted at times by both the mental health professionals and the patients with whom I worked.

More particularly, my stories are about work with patients most of whom could afford private psychiatric care in inpatient settings. Not the least of the forgotten virtues of treatment in the time in which these stories are set, when inpatient stays of a year or more were possible and, in the institutions in which I worked, not unusual, was that it permitted us to study intensively, and to learn to cope effectively with, the dynamics of small social systems, and to use such systems as a medium for influencing those who came to us for help. Because these treatment conditions are now rare, these stories may seem to have little to say to those who practice in these times. Nevertheless, I tell them, because I think they do have implications for our work with patients now, in outpatient settings, and in community mental health centers. I also think they have implications for those readers who work in other kinds of organizations altogether, but whose work is also and inevitably affected by the kind of splitting I have just described and by the kind of intergroup relations and conflicts that have their source in such processes.

Therapeutic community

When I worked to create a therapeutic community in an inpatient setting, I imagined different groups in the hospital consulting and collaborating with each other in dealing with the requirements of life in such a setting. Since the role of patient does not entail the total absence of ordinary capacities, patients were to participate as one of the groups, as persons, as citizens of the hospital community. Along with staff, they had a stake in the quality of life in that community. They as well as staff had something to contribute to the solution of problems that arose as patients and staff lived and worked together.

I believed that when people are confident that, if they have wishes, they can bring about changes in the outer world necessary for their wishes to be gratified, at least sometimes, then they also have the confidence they need to look at their inner world, to take an interest in it, and to change their wishes, beliefs, or attitudes, if it seems necessary or desirable to do so. I make no assertion about the causal direction of this relation, just that a sense of power in one's relation to the outer world seems to go together with a sense of power in one's relation to the inner world.

This conviction applies to patients, but equally also to those who are attempting to enable patients to bring about changes in their inner world through psychotherapy. Staff members and trainees, in order to have confidence that they can do their work well must also have confidence that they can affect the world in which they do that work and which impinges on it.

I saw the *therapeutic community meeting* as like a town meeting or as like a problem-solving meeting such as might exist in any organization, rather than as group therapy. This meeting provided patients *and* staff with an opportunity to discover that together they had the power to bring about some changes in the world in which they lived and worked. Together, these groups could create a social milieu that would support rather than undermine the therapeutic mission of the hospital.

Such a perception of the therapeutic community meeting ran counter to the perception of the members of the various groups that participated in it. For them, any meeting in which both mental health professionals and patients met must have as its *raison d'être* the treatment of a powerless group of patients, who needed treatment, by a powerful group of professionals who knew how to treat them.

From the point of view I had adopted, each group in the hospital (nurses, psychotherapy staff, administrators, occupational and recreational program staff, *and* patients) had its own and sometimes conflicting perspectives, interests, values, and goals – as in any organization. So I invited each of these groups to organize itself so that its members, speaking in the community meeting, could represent the group to which they belonged. In this meeting, people speaking as representatives of the groups to which they belonged could communicate what problems in living and working in this community they experienced, work out mutually acceptable policies, negotiate mutually acceptable ways of carrying out these policies, and plan joint goal-seeking activities.

A turning point: The story of the hamburgers

I introduced patient-staff community meetings, first, in a closed inpatient psychiatry unit in a general hospital and, later, in an open hospital (a residential treatment center).

For a long time, those staff members who regarded treatment as the pre-eminent and most valued activity in the hospital insisted on regarding the community meeting as one in which they were present to *treat* patients. Misconstruing the goal of the meeting, which had to do with the state of the hospital as a social system, they behaved inappropriately. For the most part they listened silently. Occasionally, they spoke, focusing on an individual patient and making an interpretation of that individual's psychopathology. They could not imagine any other way to relate to patients. They did not accept the notion that they represented but one group in the hospital, their own, and that in the community meeting it was the relationship between their group and other groups, and among all the groups in the hospital, that was at issue.

Individual psychotherapy was the valued treatment modality on the psychiatry inpatient unit and in the residential treatment center. Any other activity had less status. All members of the meeting, staff and patients, saw things in an individual personality system frame. Eager to do something that was like psychotherapy, they paid attention to the 'sickness' or 'badness' of various incorrigible individuals. 'What do we do about the socially disruptive, rule-breaking, value-challenging behavior of "bad" patients? Do they belong here?' From a group-as-a-whole perspective, many social problems were being 'solved' by scapegoating and extruding individuals.

Meanwhile many tasks that deeply affected life on the inpatient unit or in the residential treatment center were neglected, all of secondary importance next to 'treating' and 'taking care of' individual pathology. These neglected tasks included: providing opportunities and legitimate ways to have fun or gratify wishes; getting information about, understanding, and dealing with the external situation impinging on the group ('What's going on in this place?') and on the unit or hospital ('What kinds of problems is the unit or hospital facing?' 'Can we help?'); finding out what resources were available, and influencing who among the various groups represented in the meeting gets what; creating and maintaining motivational commitments to the mission and values of the unit or hospital. My interventions concentrated on keeping these tasks from disappearing altogether from the meeting's 'agenda'.

In my mind, the first major success of the community meeting in the residential treatment center began on the day patients expressed a discontent with the lunch menus. They permitted themselves to express a wish. They wanted more hamburgers at lunch. Importantly, others took patients' discontent with the lunch menus seriously. By this I mean that neither staff nor other patients dismissed the discontent by interpreting it as an expression of individual 'pathological oral greed'. And the staff did not respond to it by just gratifying the wish for more hamburgers benevolently upon its utterance. Instead, the expression of discontent and the wish led to information-gathering and negotiation with the kitchen staff and administration by representatives of various groups and governance committees, eventually leading to desired changes in the menu. Patients had their first significant experience bringing about change in the setting in which they lived, and doing so by negotiating successfully with other more powerful groups.

The story of snow shoveling

Here is a story about the origin of the idea in me of a therapeutic community.[113] I have mentioned previously the influence that Bronson Alcott's socially oriented approach to teaching had on me as a child. His approach made sense to me and moved me. (But I was also attracted by temperament and character to an ideal represented by the independent, solitary, individualistic Thoreau.)

My story is about an early experience I had shoveling snow with patients that brought home to me that social capacities existed side by side with devastating psychopathology in the same persons. When I was a first-year resident in psychiatry, my wife and I lived on the grounds of the hospital. In a part of the country where snow is a rare event, I woke up one morning to find the hospital grounds buried in snow, no other physician able to get in to work, and myself in charge.

I decided to try to shovel our way out of isolation. I can't quite remember my state of mind at the time. This memory is dreamlike. For some reason, I went to the closed, most disturbed male unit and asked the patients there to help shovel snow.

With the help of the maintenance department, I collected a lot of shovels, went to the unit, and faced a group of catatonic and hebephrenic patients, among others, in various states of agitation, preoccupation, and immobility ('Catatonic' and 'hebephrenic' are terms for manifestations or forms of schizophrenia, not often seen today.) I explained the difficulty the hospital was in, and asked for volunteers to help shovel the snow. As I remember, about ten or twelve out of the twenty volunteered, put on their hats and coats, and marched from the unit. There was no way to provide the maximum nursing coverage deemed necessary when these patients left the closed unit. We only had a few staff members that day available to join us.

We shoveled snow most of the morning. Afterwards, we went to the kitchen together, and had hot chocolate and a pleasant time without incident. During those moments, it would have been difficult to distinguish these patients from those residing on open units. Then we returned to the closed most disturbed male unit. The patients took off their hats and coats and immediately resumed their catatonia and hebephrenia.

The simple but important 'moral' I drew from this story was that behavior can be shaped and influenced by external situations, as well as by the vicissitudes of inner worlds. I also concluded that even the sickest patients have some capacities that illness has not necessarily contaminated. If patients are given the opportunity, they may be able to participate more or less effectively with nonpatients in solving problems arising in the immediate outer world shared by both. The role *patient* does not define all that a person occupying that role can do. It does not exclude the possibility that that person under certain circumstances might effectively occupy other roles as well.

Group relations in a hospital community

Here are two stories about the same 'therapeutic community' – one that had a difficult existence as 'a very different sort of place', an inpatient psychiatry unit that occupied one floor of a general hospital.

Teenagers and older patients

In the community meeting, older patients complained about the intolerably noisy teenagers with whom they were sharing a tiny living space. Gradually, building on what seemed at first to be unrealizable fantasies, we arrived at a consensus; we needed an area for quiet activities. Someone suggested that we move the arts and crafts workshop to another location off the unit, so that we could use that space for a 'quiet lounge'.

At first patients were apathetic. There was no tradition for such changing of the world in which they lived. They distrusted that others in the hospital would actually allow the community to make decisions and bring about changes necessary to make the space available. They assumed that others would do all the work. Members of the staff groups on the unit carried out the negotiations with administrators, professionals, and faculty off-the-unit.

After continued discussions in community meetings, patients ultimately accepted the project of redecorating the area by their own labor within a limited budget. Collaborating with nurses and activities staff, they organized the work, attended auctions, scraped and refinished, built, sewed, and painted. Eventually, the room emerged in an attractive Early American style, with drapes, lamps, sofas, and even a window seat! Materials were chosen so that any current group could make changes from time to time to suit its tastes and needs.

As time went on, 'changing things' became an accepted part of the culture. Debates raged about the position of the television set and the population of the aquarium. Patients painted bureau drawers and painted and decorated their own rooms, according to their own tastes, resulting in shades ranging from deep brown to off-white. Swivel chairs and desks, homemade pipe and stationery racks were in great demand. Patients made variously colored cushions, which appeared on the floors, and a variety of drawings and paintings – from abstracts to nudes and old automobiles – which they hung on the walls.

The teenagers declared that they did not think it fair that the new quiet lounge should only be for the older patients. They began to disrupt quiet card-games, reading, and listening to classical music. Finally, when no one responded in community meetings to their complaints, they took over and barricaded themselves in the quiet lounge. This led to some serious negotiations in the community meeting about how groups with different tastes and interests might share this now highly valued facility.

You cannot assume in an intergroup meeting that the only processes of interest involve strains in the relations among different but monolithically homogeneous groups (patients, nurses, activity staff, psychotherapists). Each group represented in such a meeting has its own subgroups. Strains and differences among these subgroups will affect how a group as a whole (the nurses, for example) perceives and relates to other groups (the doctors, for example) in the meeting. When the nurses were divided on an issue, that division tended to impair their ability to negotiate and collaborate in a relaxed and effective way with other groups. Similarly, when an issue that divided the patients came up, the differences among subgroups of patients led to silence, apathy, withdrawal, or fights with staff groups. (It is also true that conflicts between two groups, especially if not directly expressed, can translate into conflicts among the members of one or the other of these groups.)

A crisis of confidence

In July, on this same inpatient unit, the residents transfer off the unit, and new residents arrive. Every patient at the same time loses his psychotherapist and must relate to a new one.

One particular July, others outside the unit imposed still another change. The Residency Committee of the Department of Psychiatry decided that residents were to be assigned to the outpatient service in the afternoon, and thus would have to confine their activities on the inpatient unit to psychotherapy interviews with patients and attendance at community meetings in the morning. The resident-on-call would answer emergency calls in the afternoons.

Long silences filled community meetings. Five patients became intensely suicidal and had to be constantly attended. Others were on elopement precautions. Patients themselves frequently requested such precautions; then they resisted all efforts by staff to get them off these 'special' statuses. An almost complete breakdown of the activities program occurred because there were not enough staff to accompany patients who needed to be accompanied to activities or to the shop. Activities staff brought supplies from the shop to the unit. Patients made continuous demands for the time of all available staff as well as for medication. Anxious harried new residents, plunged into a situation in which they did not feel at all welcome, supplied abundant amounts of medication. All staff worked many hours overtime and began to show signs of strain and fatigue.

The patients observed these effects, and made one attempt after another to rally. After frenzied preparation, they began projects, only to have them collapse into apathy and disorder. As a result of discussions in the community meeting, where staff and patients were able sometimes to agree to work together to make some project go, staff negotiated with the hospital to allow each patient to paint her or his own room whatever color she or he wanted. Staff and patients planned and attended a theater party together that did something to elevate morale. A 'tranquilizer holiday' was declared over a forty-eight-hour period to show that patients had resources they were not using. Following this, the amount of medication prescribed shrank to its usual size, there were no patients on constant observation, and a period of calm and attempts to keep things going lasted through a week during which I, the Chief of Service, was on vacation. (This was approximately two-to-three years into my first faculty position.)

When I returned, I introduced a new faculty member, a psychiatrist, who, I said, would be working with and helping me on the unit. No comment was made about the newcomer for a week. There were long, intense, stubborn silences in community meetings. Two young patients, who were known for 'acting out', ran away for a couple of hours. Two withdrawn patients had decided not to go on the walk from which the other two had run away. I interpreted this event and the silences as an expression of people's desire to escape from something.

Patients angrily accused me of trying to blame 'the group' and make myself 'lily white'. Some patients, ostensibly trying to help me, made provocative statements about other patients, resulting in even more anger and silence. What discussion there was centered over time around estimating how angry I was becoming in response to events on the unit. A somewhat histrionic patient slapped a somewhat manic patient. Two adolescents broke light bulbs. One planned activity after another collapsed because people refused to attend. Patients broke rules and ignored comments by nurses about this; the nurses increasingly felt impotent and frustrated.

A patient would gather other patients together to do something about the way things were going – usually to do something about some other patient. At the same time, she herself was acting angrily and oppositionally, ignoring bedtime or rules about visiting after evening in another patient's room, not attending activities, coming late to psychotherapy sessions, or encouraging a group of patients to walk out of a group-psychotherapy session.

A patient, who was ordinarily aggressive and competitive, attacked the community as 'inefficiently organized'. He perceived himself as trying to be helpful. It was difficult to find patients willing to orient new patients or show visitors around the unit. A visitor brought to the unit by the Chairman of the

Residency Committee was, as perceived by patients themselves, treated rudely by them.

One patient signed out 'against medical advice', a rare occurrence during an evaluation period that had not happened in almost a year. Two orderlies and a nurse resigned for other jobs. One orderly, who had been an enthusiastic participant in the therapeutic community treatment program, broke a rule as he left and when confronted said, 'I don't care. I'm leaving.' Two residents spoke with the Chairman of the Residency Committee and with me about resigning their posts. Nurses complained about working on community program committees; they felt overworked and that the patients on the committees looked to them to do all the work. The head nurse told me that she felt there was widespread lack of belief in my treatment ideas among the nurses.

The most common comment reported in the nursing notes was about me, to the effect that 'he doesn't care about any of us', and that the treatment program itself, the entire community, was falling apart. The patients in community meetings indulged in orgies of self-blame: 'It's all our fault. We are driving the nurses away because we are so demanding. We desert each other. We let people withdraw. We drive people out of the community by not giving them an example of what the treatment program is really like and what it can do.' No change in what life on the unit was like followed such discussions.

At one community meeting, a patient, having tried to achieve recognition as a powerful leader, felt increasingly isolated from other patients. She challenged me openly. 'Why don't you do something to help? Are you really so impotent? Don't you care?' She turned to the residents. 'How come you don't participate in these discussions? Are you sick, frightened, unsure of your own identities?'

During the ensuing discussion, I wondered aloud that there had been no comment about the new psychiatrist, who had himself said very little during any community meeting. One patient thought the new psychiatrist was smiling contemptuously at the group. Another thought he seemed likable, but there was something malevolent about him. 'I don't see why he's here. I just can't understand what he's doing here.' An aloof patient, whose participation for weeks had been confined to smiling to himself, saying 'oh shit,' or burying his head in his arms, said to me, 'You're just carrying out an experiment on us for the benefit of the residents. You're putting on a show for them.'

I made an interpretation in the form of a story, remembering the events on the unit, and seeing them as following from, and an attempt to flee, the thought that the new staff member had come to replace me. (I think I used the word 'fantasy' not 'thought', which may have been perceived as my denial that there was any plausibility to the thought.) One patient said very quietly, 'Yes.' Another said, 'Oh no! Don't say that. Don't any of you say that.' There was a brief burst of lively discussion.

Silences at community meetings continued; a patient's comment to me punctured one silence. 'I'm still angry about the changes in July. My doctor told me that he could be called for an emergency from an interview with me, but that in the afternoon he could not be called from an outpatient interview for an emergency here. No, don't give me any facts. It's a feeling! You never let us talk about it. You just say we have to accept it.' Other patients made a few unflattering comments about the Chairman of the Residency Committee and the Chairman of the Department.

Following this meeting the staff met. I reviewed all that had happened and my own feelings about these events. I recognized that I had not wanted to be reminded of these feelings, and so I had apparently 'turned off' in subtle ways group members' efforts to express their feelings about the situation.

That night, a nurse and the doctor-on-call met with a patient who could not sleep, discussing the situation on the unit. At the next community meeting, the patient opened the meeting with a moving statement about patients' feelings about the changes in July, that their anger about this had led them to want to destroy the program, and that therefore they had not helped new patients understand the treatment program. The new patients were not 'brought in', and became new sources of chaos. He went on to explain to the new patients present that group members often became angry with me when I made interpretations of what was going on, but gave several vivid examples of how helpful some of these interpretations had been.

I commented that people might have something to blame me for. A patient immediately asked me, 'Are you angry about the changes?' I said, 'Yes.' A lively discussion followed in which I was accused of being either too weak to prevent the change or not caring enough to prevent it. A patient defended my failure to be as powerful as they needed and wanted me to be. 'After all, he's only human.' It was assumed I must be so mad not only about the way the patients had been behaving but at the faculty in the department for wrecking the program that I intended to leave.

There was a discussion about whether the new psychiatrist would be acceptable as a replacement for me. Some said vehemently, 'No! I'll leave.' Others pointed out how helpful the new psychiatrist had been in various committee meetings. There were also fantasies that the new psychiatrist was present for some malevolent purpose – perhaps to represent the Chairman of the Residency Committee. One resident said he thought the new psychiatrist was there to spy on the residents' performance for the Chairman of the Residency Committee, and that this had inhibited his own and others' participation. Other residents said they had not participated in community meetings because they felt they weren't part of the community. When they were on the unit, most of the time they were in individual psychotherapy sessions and felt they didn't know what was going on. Patients in turn said that the residents did not seem familiar with the values of the community; they complied so readily with the patients' wishes for medicine. One patient said that she thought that much of the patients' behavior had been designed to get the residents back on the unit in protest at the change that had taken them off of it.

Group members, both patients and staff, expressed the feeling that the decision of the Residency Committee depreciated the treatment program and revealed others' lack of belief in it. Then those on the unit themselves doubted the value of the treatment program or the point of putting up with the anxiety it inevitably aroused. 'We feel hopeless about the future, and so the work seems futile.'

I notice that this story I have just told is essentially the same story, incredibly enough, that I told about the resident in group psychotherapy who did not stand up for his patients. Separated by thirty years. Different setting. Different cast of characters. I also notice, as I tell this story, and others as well, that what each person/patient contributes to the group process and its outcome tallies with her or his own dispositions, personality, character style, psychopathology.

It is over thirty years ago, and I can't remember the exact sequence of events. But I suspect with something akin to shame that in fact I had already been offered another position. I was thinking of accepting it. I had brought on the new psychiatrist with the conscious idea that he would be available to take my place should I decide to leave. I was not ready or able to talk about any of this to anyone, in part because I was undecided but also in part because I could not manage how guilty I felt about abandoning this community of mine. Yet I was asking others to talk openly about what they thought, felt, imagined, planned, did.

I have noticed recently how important deception is as a plot element in movie after movie, no matter what the genre or decade. I have always been aware of the secrets that seem to be an inescapable feature of family, group, and organizational life. How often I have asked people to tell me and others their secrets, to share secrets in public, so that the leaders or members of a group or organization will have the information they need to understand and solve problems. I, in a leadership position, urge others to provide information. At the same time I withhold information myself. Indeed I unquestioningly reserve the right to tell or not to tell what I choose, and to whom I choose. I live with my own hypocrisy.

Yet what about privacy, and respecting the need for privacy? Another dilemma. Secrets don't come labeled *relevant* or *irrelevant*. How does one distinguish between a purely personal secret – which is no business of a group's as long as it has no relevance to any collective goal, problem, or fear – from what only seems merely personal? An apparently personal secret may be important to an understanding of group or organizational life because it is the result of events or the way things are organized in that life. Or because it represents something shared by others and therefore part of a collective process.

What about the risks to which you expose others in urging them to reveal all in a group situation? Can you guarantee confidentiality, or no reality repercussions, on an inpatient unit, in a residential treatment setting, or in an outpatient psychotherapy group? When I did group psychotherapy in a prison setting, group members told me that there were certain things they would not talk about, although these involved highly relevant aspects of themselves that they would like to change, because if their secrets became known to others in the prison population these others might hurl them off a tier to their death.

Truth-telling can be dangerous, and I have come to respect people's – including patients' – reluctance to engage in it, even when it is necessary to the work we are doing together. I do not think that those in authority should have the right to require disclosure from those less powerful than themselves. When it comes to deciding whether to reveal or keep a secret in a group or organization, shouldn't each person – including each patient – exercise authority over herself or himself? Shouldn't each person – including each patient – making such a decision accept responsibility for anticipating consequences, risks, potential gains, to herself or himself or others, and for thinking out ways of assessing how realistic these fearful or hopeful fantasies are. I try now to confine my expectations of honesty to myself, and let others make their own decisions about how honest to be. When we work together, they have the benefit of my example. Most importantly, they are able to observe the limits of my ability to achieve complete honesty. When my inevitable failures to do so are called to my attention, I try not to deny or rationalize them.

CHAPTER 26

Openness

David Berg

Marshall's scruples about asking others to do something that he himself is unwilling to do, and his reluctance to ask anyone to share emotions and secrets in public, remind me of Clay Alderfer's comment that researchers in the social sciences rarely seem to believe (or acknowledge by their words and behavior) that what we learn about human behavior by studying human beings in laboratories or organizations also applies to researchers![114] It is as if group and intergroup forces, to say nothing of individual conflicts and struggles, play no role in the researcher's life or at least not in her or his research.

Given how patently absurd this is, it is surprising how little discussion occurs in articles and books about the possible impact of the researcher's sex, age, hierarchical status, class, family history, race, ethnicity, and mental health on her research. The literature always gives a well-developed reason, implicit or explicit, for why gatekeepers deem these factors irrelevant to the researcher's 'intellectual' contribution.

So it strikes me as not at all surprising that the psychiatric profession would have developed practices and an associated rationale that prohibit its members from expressing feelings or sharing 'secrets' (what is held to be private), while at the same time exhorting patients for their own good to express feelings and share secrets. I am forced to conclude that there must be something dangerous (to the task? to the profession? to the community? to the distribution of power?) about acknowledging connections between – that something is shared by – researcher and subject, physician and patient. What is this danger? Is it real or imagined? Whom does it protect and what does it support?

Marshall's questions about secrecy that the right to privacy justifies, on the one hand, and disclosures that serve the task (we might say, 'the public good'), on the other, also recall a symposium I attended many years ago on 'Openness'. The first participant, Will Schutz, began by extolling the virtues of openness as a universal good. He argued that the world would be better off if a universal norm of openness existed. Such a norm would result in enhancing relationships, and make information readily available – without the waste that accompanies efforts to discover 'the truth'. He was a compelling speaker. When he was finished, I found myself wishing that we could all make a greater commitment to openness in our relationships.

Next up was Sherman Kingsberry, who took the position that the meaning of openness varies with the interpersonal setting. He gave an example of a person who may be using openness as a way to avoid responsibility for her or his feelings. People can dump anything they like on someone else without having to examine whether their openness was a preemptive emotional strike. Then again, a person may defend a choice not to be open as a choice not to hurt another person, when in fact it may be an effort to protect herself or himself from the openness (hostile thoughts or feelings) of the other.

When Kingsberry was done, I was right with him. Schutz had been too simple. Openness is not merely something to which an individual commits, but it is all tied up in specific interpersonal relationships that make up the individual's life.

Then Kenwyn Smith rose to speak. 'Openness,' he announced, 'is all about power; it has nothing whatever to do with the individual or her or his interpersonal relationships.' 'Consider,' he said, 'the difference between a boss (for this example, male) asking a subordinate (for this example, female) to be open, and the subordinate asking the boss for the same degree of openness. For someone with power, access to information is crucial for the maintenance of that power – or, more benignly regarded, for the performance of his job. So the openness of the subordinate becomes absolutely necessary. The boss may feel a reluctance to *be* open, because sharing information (for example, financial information, long-range plans, ideas) means sharing power and could be disruptive. Besides, such openness is irrelevant to the subordinate's job, right? The subordinate experiences the request for openness as a prelude to exploitation. If the boss knows what I really think or how much I think I can really do, he will punish me or ask me to do 10 percent more. In turn, the subordinate's request for openness (as experienced by her) is a desire to have more certainty and trust in her work environment.'

When Smith was finished, I felt like I had been through the wringer. He was right. Openness had nothing to do with personal or interpersonal processes. It was about power relations across groups.

The moral of the story: whenever you propose an *intergroup* conversation in which you hope for frank and candid talk, be prepared for a very difficult time, for disappointment at least in the short run, and for a long process with lots of ups and downs. An open frank conversation requires groups or their representatives to revisit the history of their relationship, including sources of mistrust. It also requires them to slowly reconstruct through shared experiences a new relationship that can accommodate mutual disclosure.

This is not a matter of technique. The necessary work is nothing short of recreating the relationships among these groups. In some cases, that may not be possible.

CHAPTER 27

The Effects of Intergroup Relations on Collective Problem-Solving

Marshall Edelson

This is a story about a 'therapeutic community' in a residential treatment center as seen through the window of a series of community meetings. In this series of meetings, groups in the community addressed the same problem over many months. The patients lived in a building called the Inn.

The story of pets in the Inn

Vincente Minnelli's underrated movie, *The Cobweb* (1955), tells a story similar to the one I am about to tell. His is about who will select the drapes in a residential treatment center (the head nurse? the business manager? the psychiatrist's wife? the patients?). But the movie focuses on personal and interpersonal stories (troubled marriage, patient disappointed in his psychotherapist), whereas the story I tell about pets in the Inn is an intergroup story.

Other movies that come to mind, because they resonate with the elements in this story that have to do with standing up to authority, are *One Flew Over the Cuckoo's Nest* (1975), which is set in a mental hospital, and in which challenging authority leads to tragic consequences, and *A Few Good Men* (1992). The latter concerns the military as an institution, and it depicts challenging authority as enormously risky – but this second movie has a happy ending.

As you read this story, ask yourself, 'What if Edelson had not identified who made each comment? Could I tell whether a speaker at the community meeting was a member of the patient or of the staff group?' I bet not.

Throughout this story I saw myself not as a group psychotherapist but as consulting with all the groups in the community meeting, as they attempted to relate to each other. My objective: to enable members of *all the groups*, staff and patient, to achieve a sense of efficacy in dealing with their shared life in the hospital.

The homeless dog

It was week 11 (following the inauguration of the community meeting). A dog wandered into the meeting room, which was the living room of the Inn. The dog didn't belong to anyone; it had come in from the world outside. The patient co-chairman of the meeting asked that someone take the dog out. ('Chairman' rather than 'chairperson' was the term used in those days.) There was a chorus of general objections. 'It's not doing any harm! Leave it alone.'

The patient co-chairman appealed to me. (I was the staff co-chairman of the community meeting.) I said I thought it would be a good idea to take the dog out. A patient took it out. I think I gave 'it will distract us from our work' as my reason, and did not mention to the group that I am usually somewhat anxious and uneasy around animals. Professionals are, of course, not supposed to have problems similar to those that patients have.

No one challenged my decision. In this community, direct conflict across the leader-follower boundary was, by mutual agreement, discouraged. Patients did not wish to risk alienating those upon whom they depended. Dissent was expressed indirectly.

A patient mentioned that one patient had been writing bad checks. That patient in response discussed rather matter-of-factly his tangled relationship with his father. Did this story come up just at this point in the meeting because it had to do with a conflict between a father and son?

Then came a series of questions: 'What is this meeting for? Why do there have to be so many of them?' I did not make the interpretation that the group, having stifled any dissent moments before, was now challenging me through these questions. My response to the questions was rather to repeat what I had said previously about the purpose of the meeting. This response probably had the effect of discouraging any more open challenge. Neither I nor anyone else connected my deciding that the dog goes, the subsequent telling of a story about an ambivalent father-son relation and the covert rebelliousness in that relation, and a surge of negative feelings about the meeting. Nor did we discuss what the way we dealt with 'a stranger coming into town' (the probably homeless dog) revealed about the image of the authority structure of the meeting and, by extension, the treatment center (makes all the decisions unilaterally especially about who is in and who is out, inhospitable).

The medical director's memo: 'pets are not allowed in the Inn'

A patient asked what a good meeting would be like. 'Wouldn't it have some humor?' She stated she was afraid to bring something up, because the group might not take it seriously. She then referred to a memo from the medical director that pets were not allowed in the Inn. She said, 'My dog means a great deal to me. My psychotherapist gave it to me before he left. I want to be able to keep the dog with me in the Inn.'

A lively discussion followed. Such liveliness is a frequent result of someone's being able to express a desire directly. But that is a rather infrequent occurrence. Few members of the community, staff or patients, have much confidence that there is any use wanting something that requires a change of some sort in procedures, arrangements, the way things are done in this world. But without the expression of a desire, there can be no exploration of the obstacles to its fulfillment, and therefore no problem-solving. So, in my interventions, I gave priority to trying to help people express what they wanted (and didn't want).

The patient chairman of the patient–staff Community Council said, 'I am going to see the medical director to find out if there is any use in discussing this matter. Can we change the rule? If not, there's no point going on with this.' I wondered aloud if patients felt they had little power to change anything about the treatment center. One staff member supported the owner of the dog. 'I can see how difficult it would be for you to have to give up your dog.' Then he asked others to consider my comment.

But people in general throughout this and following discussions tended to side with fears against the wish. Patients talked about their dislike of animals. The head nurse said such a rule was needed. Someone speculated that zoning laws were the reason for having the rule.

Then, a patient countered by offering to find out just what the zoning laws were (an example of reality testing a fear-inspired objection to a wish), perhaps partly in the hope that the zoning laws would decide the question in favor of the rule. This was an important step in the direction of demonstrating that it was possible to question or challenge authority openly in this meeting, but it was followed immediately by a fearful retraction. Several people mentioned how difficult it would be to take care of animals. A patient said, 'We shouldn't do anything until the medical director says it's okay.'

The medical director had decided not to attend the community meetings. He did not seem to want, and I did not make very energetic efforts to arrange, regular meetings between us, so that I could talk to him about what went on at the meetings. Was this a quasi-fatal flaw in the way the enterprise was set up? I now think so. But I cannot see what in retrospect I could have done about it.

I don't think he liked having his authority questioned. He was an impressive, charismatic, eloquent leader who would appear rarely, mostly when a lot of people were misbehaving, to speak *the word*, invariably inspiring awe and resolutions to do better. He certainly awed me. But I am not at ease with charismatic leadership. It relies on the invocation of commitments through inspiration, rather than through the day-by-day ant work of engaging in a problem-solving process in which many share the credit for the outcome.

I knew what I was going to say might make trouble for him, and that he would not like that. But I went ahead and made the interpretation that group members wanted the medical director to decide the matter. Then they would not have to deal with all the thorny problems involved, with a wish on the one side and all the fears about gratifying the wish on the other. There was an angry chorus: 'No!'

A staff member said, 'If you [the members of this group] were serious about questioning the rule about pets in the Inn, you would agree on a concrete proposal to the medical director. You wouldn't be sending your representative to ask him, "Please, sir, may we have pets?" That might mean one hundred animals overrunning the place. No medical director is going to give a group carte blanche. You would have to come to an agreement among yourselves about how many animals you were prepared to stand. It's clear no pet owner could be responsible twenty-four hours a day. There would need to be agreements about what responsibilities other group members were willing to take.' This staff member had stepped in to thwart a 'let's get rid of the problem by provoking a strong "no" from the medical director' strategy; had given the group a glimpse of what steps or processes a serious attempt to solve a problem might involve; and by implication had suggested that the group might be capable of engaging effectively in such problem-solving.

The medical director's 'inflexible' stand

On Tuesday, the chairman of the Community Council reported on his visit to the medical director. He had asked the medical director, 'Do the patients have any room to maneuver as far as "the administration" was concerned on patients keeping pets in the Inn?' The patient said that 'the administration's' position was inflexible. 'No room to maneuver. No pets at the Inn.' Now, as I write, I hear mythic echoes. 'No room at the Inn.' 'The humble, the outsider, the outcast is not welcome.' 'Go elsewhere.'

The 'administration' – a euphemism for the medical director – had explained that its position was based on anticipating the housekeeping problems that would arise. Also, on the judgment that it was impossible to make an exception. Granting one patient the right to keep a pet would make it impossible to deny the right to others. The situation would quickly get out of hand.

The explanation, whatever its merits, constituted a vote of no confidence in the community's ability to work out a satisfying solution, and suggested that reason and responsibility were possessions of the staff and irrationality and irresponsibility of the patients. Throughout the subsequent meetings devoted to the pet issue, the patients were cast over and over as the group having wishes but lacking the ability to detect the neurotic origins of these wishes or to deal responsibly with the consequences of attempting to gratify them, while the staff was cast over and over as the group having the ability to foresee difficulties and a sense of responsibility, and as conscientiously and selflessly acting in the interests of the patients.

Several patients responded to the medical director's explanation, which by virtue of its very 'reasonableness' was likely to discourage dissent, by a kind of *sotto voce* grumbling. 'What can a patient who wants to keep his dog do now?' 'Board it at a kennel nearby and visit.' 'That doesn't sound like a satisfactory arrangement.' 'That's a silly solution.'

Some patients began to question explicitly the medical director's 'explanation'. 'What are the implications of an inflexible rule?' 'The medical director has not given his real reason for his ruling. There is no state law against having pets in hospitals.' 'The medical director knows very well there are dogs around, since one had visited the small group of which he is a member. Why has he chosen this time to lay down or resurrect the rule about pets?'

Other patients, perhaps alarmed by this risky challenge of authority, rushed in to rescue the medical director, to defend and side with him. 'He knows that dogs bother people. These people don't feel free to say so, because others take a rejection of a pet as a rejection of the pet's owner. He is acting to get people who object to pets, and can't say so, off the hook.' These patients were intervening on behalf of *all* the patients to take back the challenge. But, of course, the groups in the meeting, including the patient group, saw both those who challenged and those who sided with the medical director as acting out of personal motives or character pathology, and then split the patient group into 'bad' patients and 'good' patients — rather than seeing different patients as representing different sides of the ambivalence towards authority that existed in every patient. The director of activities supported this process by casting doubt on the patient who felt so strongly about her own dog's staying and so caused all this trouble. 'She commented recently about another large dog around the Inn that she could understand why anyone would be annoyed having *that* dog around.'

A staff member, trying to remind the group of the costs of merely submitting to authority's decrees, said, 'I am remembering that the patient who raised this issue said that if her dog were forced to go, she would go.' This emboldened another patient to experience and express an identification with the pet-owner. 'Dogs are not the only annoying intruders in the Inn. The presence of outpatients' children annoys some people. I wonder if the presence of my children, when they visit, annoys other patients. I would welcome people letting me know if they feel that way.'

Patients returned hesitantly to talk about the medical director, oscillating rapidly between challenging to siding with or justifying him. 'Is it possible to get the medical director to change his mind?' 'I don't think we should put him on the spot by pursuing the issue further. He had to lay down the law because there has been an increase in the number of dogs highly visible around the Inn.'

Disagreements and conflicts among patients

Turning away from talk about the medical director, with all its difficulties, patients began to interpret the motives and attitudes of individual members of their own group. 'The people who own dogs are not even at this meeting.' 'We ought to discuss the meaning to a person of having a pet at the Inn. It is a public declaration of loneliness.' 'Having a pet is a rejection of human companionship. The people who have pets are rejecting the rest of the community.'

I suggested that making therapy-like interpretations about individuals and their motives in this group might be a way of avoiding a question: 'How was it that whatever the question of patients having pets at the Inn had stirred up had been handled in a way that provoked a statement from "the administration" that the patients could take no action in this matter?'

A patient expressed the community's determination to get rid of this troublesome issue. 'The chairman of the Community Council going to see the medical director has really solved the problem for the group. That settles the matter.'

Responding, I reminded the members of the community that a staff member had pointed out at the last meeting that any administrator faced with the kind of request that the Community Council chairman was going to make would inevitably say 'no'. I directed my subsequent comments largely to the patient group, making it possible for staff to disown their complicity in this process, which stemmed from their own ambivalence to authority, rather than helping everyone to see that all the groups in the community were alike in sharing ambivalence to authority, turning to it, depending on it, rebelling against it, fearing it. I said that, since the members of the (patient) group knew that the medical director would probably say 'no', and did nothing to prevent the Community Council chairman from proceeding, the members of the (patient) group could now grumble rebelliously at the medical director's response while appearing to comply obediently. However, it was my guess that many at the same time felt secretly relieved that, having provoked this response, they were now able to avoid the difficulties of dealing with the wishes and fears members of the (patient) group had about pets. I should have added, 'and able also to avoid the difficulties involved in dealing with authority – the group in the community that possessed power (the staff), and the leader of that group (the medical director)'.

The patient who was chairman of the Community Council became very angry. He said that he had a mandate from the Community Council to see the medical director. Nothing he had heard at the community meeting convinced him he shouldn't act on that mandate. The Community Council was just as important as this meeting! Here he implied that the 'real' issue was that the group was caught between two authority figures, me and the medical director. I would not have heard that, since at that time I was not particularly aware of myself as a person who was an 'authority figure'. So, feeling on the side of 'the patients', I was able to avoid the complex mixture of feelings and different identifications struggling inside of me, and so to experience myself as free of a process that everyone else was caught in. What a delusion!

The patient continued by saying that, besides, the medical director always had the option of asking for a specific and reasonable proposal from the patient group, and saying he would consider such a proposal. Several patients picked up on the last comment, taking it in a somewhat unexpected problem-solving direction. (That the patient's comment enabled them to do so indicated to what an extent the different attitudes existed in everyone, despite the appearance that different patients were on one side or another.) 'What would a reasonable proposal look like?' 'We might suggest building a kennel near the Inn and taking care of the pets there.' 'Since the patients are doing the housekeeping at the Inn, staff concerns about the dogs making messes in the Inn are not as valid as they would be if the housekeeping staff were responsible for cleaning up the messes.' 'We really can't do anything or make any decisions in this community.'

Coming at the question of authority roundabout, and trying to show how the community might deal with problems more effectively, I noted aloud that a sense of futility was the response to any attempt to solve problems in the community meeting. Did members of the community meeting feel futile, because, following discussions in the meeting, they had not yet taken the next step? They did not refer problems that had been fully aired in discussion to the community meeting's action-taking committees (the Community Council, the Activities Committee, the Work Committee) for further consideration and action. Nor did these action-taking groups turn to the community meeting to get the information and consent they needed to make decisions that they and others would take seriously.

There was no response to this 'organization-oriented' comment. Members of the community meeting, faced by me with the possibility that they might indeed have the power to act and the organizational means to exercise that power, began to discuss dogs as child-substitutes. I commented that again we seemed to be turning away from doing something about problems in community living to making therapy-like interpretations.

Staff member: 'This is the one meeting where the patient group as a whole can express what it feels and thinks about a matter.' (I thought to myself that this staff person seems to see the meeting as a patient meeting, not an intergroup meeting, without reflecting that perhaps the staff member had taken a cue from me.) The staff member continued. 'No executive group can take action without knowing from its participation in the community meeting such facts as how many dogs the patients will put up with or how they will arrange cleaning up. Until people begin to say what they think and feel about such matters, no work can be done on the matter.'

The patients, finding it impossible to engage in dissent across the leader-follower boundary, turned against each other. 'I am against pets because they're noisy and messy, just as I'm against people, children, and motorcycles that are noisy and messy.' 'You're hypocritical since you're noisy and messy yourself.' 'Well, I for one am not willing to clean up other people's dogs' messes.'

One patient expressed the willingness of some to face the many-sided complexity of the issue, rather than merely to dismiss it one way or another as impossible or unproblematic. 'I don't want dogs inside the Inn, but that someone would say she will leave if they do not allow her dog to stay bothers me.' I commented, 'There are two problems: Whether to allow pets in the Inn, and how to get rid of those that we don't want.' I added, 'If you take either problem seriously, you may have to face that there are real differences among you. Are we shying away from disagreement and conflict?'

The meeting ended with a discussion of action taken by the medical director in response to a proposal by the patient–staff social-problems council that a patient be discharged. He had placed the patient on probation. If this had been a group psychotherapy rather than an intergroup meeting, in response to the story about a patient facing discharge, I might have interpreted how the groups in the meeting, including the patient group, seemed to be putting the patients' 'messiness' and 'noisiness' into the pets. The pets could then be banished and kept out. I might also have made explicit questions implied by the discussion: 'What and who can we tolerate in this community? What and who do we want to get rid of, discharge, get out of here?' But I did not.

Perhaps there was a cost of not making such interpretations here. This shared, defensive, disowning-and-projecting strategy hampered the group's ability to plan and bring about real change. On the other hand, interpretations directed at this strategy could very well have distracted group members. They might have avoided grappling with the outer world by preoccupying themselves with inner mental processes and making 'interpretations' of members of their own and other groups. Also, unless such group process interpretations were explicitly addressed to members of all the groups present, they could have reinforced the perception that this was 'a patients' meeting', in which patients were treated, rather than a meeting in which different groups came together to solve problems of mutual concern.

Rebellion: rejection of 'the rule'

On Thursday, there was no mention of pets. Friday's meeting began with silence. There were many absences. The patient co-chairman of the community meeting announced that the members of the Community Council had decided that they would not or could not enforce the medical director's rule about pets. It was up to individuals to deal with the rule as they saw fit.

I commented, 'The members of the Community Council have colluded with the rest of us to bring about a convenient arrangement. The medical director was provoked into taking an "inflexible" stand. The members of the community can then collectively disown the part they played in bringing about the decision he apparently made on his own. Each member says, "But the decision has nothing to do with me. I had nothing to do with it." So any individual may accept this *external* decision or not as she or he chooses.'

Patients predictably didn't like what I said. They went on not only to reject the 'rules' but the community in which I was clearly invested as well. 'The Community Council should be expected only to enforce those rules it makes.' 'Rules are foolish.' 'This community, which can't make a rule about pets, is foolish.' 'The medical director would find it inconvenient to hang around the Inn himself, trying to enforce his decision. We don't really have to worry about this any more.'

It was an easy jump from resentment toward me to resentment toward the medical director. Did I make a mistake in not drawing the fire directed to authority on myself more? Would that have brought the feelings toward authority 'here and now' more to the fore? But might it also have distracted the group from confronting the realities of the authority structure of the residential treatment center, and learning how to take steps to deal with it? Would drawing fire on myself have colluded with the fearful insulation of the medical director from the consequences of his own way of exercising authority?

The patients dimly sensed that staff members shared their difficulties but would not be drawn into acknowledging this. 'Nurses are delegated responsibility for enforcing such rules. They are in a difficult position. What do the nurses feel about this question?' Head nurse: 'I personally would enjoy having a few dogs around. Anything that would make this place more like home is welcome.'

This comment seemed to make it possible for patients to speak, but not necessarily in favor of having pets around. They responded as if what the head nurse had said made an undesired state of affairs now more likely to occur. 'I don't want hairs all over.' 'I don't like other people's dogs.' 'Animals are like humans. Janet's dog is being spoiled by being left to run wild.' 'He's not ready to go to college yet.' Laughter.

Gender issues

I said, 'We can't live with the messy lovable little beasts, and we can't live without them.' Later, I made the observation, 'Our discussion has largely centered on mess and discipline. No one has said much about love.' I continued to give priority to wants, which I saw as the best incentives for not giving up, for keeping on with the struggle to solve problems arising in relation to external reality.

A patient responded to what I had said by telling how useful her dog was during periods of withdrawal and depression. 'He continued to make demands upon me according to his own needs. That was comforting. That kept me going.' This, predictably enough, was countered by another patient, who offered her an individual interpretation. 'Your attachment to your dog just serves to justify your neglect of the problem you have relating to people.'

This interpretation didn't sound very friendly. It sounded to me like the voice of authority. Was this the tone patients hear and learn from their psychotherapists? I wouldn't have dared to ask that question aloud in the meeting. Instead I wondered, 'Who, in fact, wants to keep a pet?' A patient replied, 'I want to keep my two dogs.' Another patient said, 'Once I minded your two dogs. But I no longer do.' A patient who rarely spoke in the meeting said, 'I'd like to have a dog too.'

I commented, 'When people can express their wishes directly, it's of great help to us. Recognizing the existence of such wishes gives us an incentive to consider what the actual consequences might be – if they are left unsatisfied and if they are gratified.' In response to the dangers of the direction I was suggesting, and continuing to swing back and forth from one side to another, the same patients who had been concerned about mess, scuffling, and noise expressed these concerns again. Someone again raised the possibility of using a kennel. Someone noted that the patient who had once volunteered to find out about zoning laws had not been heard from since.

I mentioned, 'It's difficult to know how to proceed when we have not heard from so many people in the community about what they think and feel.' One patient directly asked another, 'What do you think?' A third patient objected before the second had a chance to answer. 'People shouldn't be forced to participate.' A male patient said, 'I haven't spoken because it makes no difference to me either way. Too many dogs around the Inn would create a problem.' Another male patient added, 'I wouldn't mind having a few animals, but I think it would be impossible to keep the number to a few.' A female patient said, 'I'm afraid of animals jumping on me, but I don't care because I'm leaving soon anyway.' A patient replied, 'But others might feel as you do.' The head nurse said, 'I'd like to see some pets but I'm concerned about the housekeeping and the matter of putting them out at night. Is there some way to keep the number down?'

In retelling this story, it seems to me now that there were gender differences in the responses. The most vociferous proponents for having pets seem to have been women. This issue does touch on affection, sentiment, dependence – anathema, from the point of view of a stereotype of masculinity. I wonder now if I should have commented on this split. It's interesting to speculate on what the effect of such an intervention might have been.

Further, the last comments made by women patients led to a comment by the head nurse more cautious and qualified than her previous comment. That sequence and the change in the head nurse suggest to me now that fears about physical contact and sexual relations in the group life at the Inn were also in the air. Someone in an untold scenario has an impulse to jump on another who may not welcome the attention; that impulse is then put into beasts. (I knew that patients, nurses, and psychotherapists regarded the sexual aspects of group life as a problem, but could not talk about these worries in the community meeting.)

I don't think I could have made such an interpretation then. It would have threatened too many secrets. The entire group might have backed off not only from this issue but from the meeting itself. But I am not sure about that.

The black cat

Seven weeks went by. There was no further mention of animals until week 18. I was increasingly concerned that the long delays in doing anything to resolve the problems around pets would serve to discourage the groups in the community meeting from believing that they had any power, any realistic ways, of actually doing something about the shared problems they faced in the world they lived in.

Someone asked, 'What shall we do about the black cat roaming around the Inn?' This black cat was 'independent'. It 'didn't belong to anyone'. At least, a patient who was its possible owner was not at the community meeting. 'How can we solve problems in community living when the people involved do not attend the meeting?' 'Why do certain people stay away?'

I suggested, thinking of perplexities shared in previous meetings about what to do about deviance, 'Perhaps people stay away to express for others as well as themselves the wish to be more independent. And maybe we want these "independent" people to stay away. If they came, they might express their rejection of the community and its values, which we, disowning such feelings in ourselves, could not tolerate.'

The iguana

Another twelve weeks passed, during which there was no mention of animals. In the context of a preoccupation with rule-breaking, a breathtakingly fantastic, sad, funny symbolization of deviance or difference and how others in the community responded to it occurred.

A nurse reported that a patient secreted overnight guests in her room and lied to the nurses about this. The nurses felt the patient had made fools of them.

Suddenly, there was a torrent of storytelling, of fantasy, of playfulness. A patient said that he had brought an iguana from home. 'Is there any way I can arrange to keep it? Does the rule about pets apply to iguanas?' Someone, making fun of questions I have asked in the community meeting, asked, 'What is lacking in this community that someone is forced to bring in an iguana to supply it?' Laughter.

'An iguana may grow to six feet.' 'Keep it at the shop.' Shop instructor: 'No. The cage would be too large.' 'Keep it in the bathtub.' 'There is a rule against that.' 'There is no reason to respect any rules; if you want to do something against the rules, you can do it if you don't bring it to public attention.' (This was probably an allusion to the nurse's bringing up rules about patients having others in their rooms at night. The message: Don't tell, and don't get caught.) 'Keep the iguana outside.' 'But it needs a constant temperature of 75 degrees.' There were jokes about the heat in the rooms. 'Keep it in the greenhouse.' 'It isn't hot enough.' 'Something can be rigged up for heat.' 'There isn't enough room.'

'Bring the iguana into the meeting. Let's have a look at it.' The patient brought his iguana into the meeting. 'It's frightening.' 'It looks like a rejected prehistoric creature.' 'It's beautiful.' 'Give it to a member of the nursing staff.' 'I don't want to give it away. I want to keep it.' 'Does it have a name?' 'Puff.'

I made a comment about rules. 'If rules are yes/no, they don't make allowances for individual needs or for differences arising in different situations. Are goldfish, iguanas, dogs, and cats all the same? Do we have to treat each person the same, without regard to specific circumstances, situations, needs?' I wonder now why I became didactic just here, in the midst of this lively discussion? This material cried for participation at the level of fantasy and story.

The almost complete absence of participation by the staff is striking, given the liveliness of the discussion. I think now that this may have been due to the staff's discomfort. Although I was not aware of it then, a number of the jokes seemed to be digs at the staff. Perhaps they were expressions of resentment felt in reaction to the nurse's announcement at the beginning of the meeting.

There were comments by patients about being frightened of reptiles, of not even wanting to pass by a room in which the iguana might be. 'I don't want the iguana here. I'm not alone. Other people are just not speaking up.' 'I'm tired of people who don't speak up always getting their way.' 'What will you do with the iguana if you are not allowed to keep it here?' 'People can eat it.' (I thought about totem animals.) 'I've heard that many people buy baby alligators and flush them down their toilets. Now they have found a good habitat in the sewer system of New York City. I don't believe the story, but one or two sewer men have been reported missing.'

'We have to live by rules. We can't allow one exception because there is then no way of stopping everyone who wants to keep a pet from doing so.' 'You keep your motorcycle in the shop, although that's against the rules. Like everyone else, you want rules with no exceptions, except where you are concerned.' 'Your fear of making an exception is like worrying about crossing the street because you might get hit. No one would ever do anything.'

I suggested that one thing we could do, after sharing our thoughts and feelings about the iguana, was to refer the matter to the activities staff and Community Council. Their members have heard the discussion and could take it into consideration in deciding about what action to take. The iguana was eventually discharged from the hospital.

The patients seemed to have been asking, 'Can you accept what is uncivilized and unsocialized in us – the odd, weird, repulsive, even frightening creatures we sometimes are? Must we be well-behaved pets? If we are not, will you send us away to a closed hospital?'

Animals make a mess

Eight weeks later, someone reported that the cats were making a mess at the shop. Comments were mostly along the lines of 'it would be nice if we could get rid of this or that cat.'

Then, eight-and-a-half months went by with no further discussion of pets or animals at the community meeting, except for a single complaint about a dog. This dog was accused of tearing up papers and contributing to the messiness of the grounds. The owner denied these accusations: 'He used to do that sort of thing, but he doesn't any more.'

I was feeling discouraged, and so were others.

Moving slowly, very slowly, toward action

About forty-five weeks after the issue of pets had first been raised in the community meeting, the patient–staff Community Council, which had both legislative and judiciary functions, found itself faced with vigorous complaints about pets in the Inn from the maintenance staff. Council members debated how to enforce what seemed to be an unenforceable rule. They veered from one course to another. First, they decided to treat patients who kept pets as serious social problems. Then they sought some way to alter the rule about pets, which prohibited them entirely, to something more acceptable to everyone.

The Community Council brought a proposal to the community meeting that pets be allowed in the basement of the Inn. Their owners would be responsible for their behavior and any damage they might do. There were no questions. There was no discussion. The proposal disappeared.

At a subsequent meeting, the Community Council reported that it had decided to evict the cats, but hoped that a way might be found to keep one dog. 'That dog is really no problem. He is clean.' The owners of the cats were resentful.

Back and forth. A patient said, 'The general feeling is that the "no pet" rule is a good one, but some people feel that perhaps it does not have to be a blanket rule. Those who have pets already obviously love them. Understandably, it would be hard for them to give up their pets.' Another patient said, 'We have agreed to stand behind the nurses when they try to enforce rules.' 'But let's agree that no one is going to go around looking for violations.' 'We heard yesterday at the Community Council that hospitals can have pets and still pass inspection.' 'I hope that the

Community Council will be able to work out some policy which will have built-in protection and respect for those who object to pets.' '"No pets" is the only way to protect those who object to pets.'

The patient group continued to be split into those who wanted pets and those who didn't want pets. This process of splitting, which served to maintain the status quo, was probably a response to anxiety about challenging authority. As far as dealing with the problem of relations to authority was concerned, both staff and patients were stuck.

Getting unstuck

A patient who was the owner of a pet: 'Why don't we admit we don't dare challenge the staff because we depend upon them too much?' I wished that I had made that intergroup interpretation, about the relation between a powerless and a powerful group. The conflict between wishes to challenge authority and fears about threats to a relation in which one group feels dependent upon another had resulted in a restrictive solution – forming polarized subgroups *within* the powerless group, so that nothing could happen.

In a subsequent meeting, the owner of the dog, which was, as an exception, going to be allowed to stay, bravely refused to become 'an exception'. She was going to contact someone at another psychiatric hospital to learn something more about their policy regarding pets, and planned to present a new proposal to the community. She got a lot of flak for refusing to accept the easier solution.

Two months passed. Then, Community Council members distributed copies of the new proposal to everyone, after it had been presented to and discussed by the council. Responsibility for implementation would become the Community Council's, helped by a pet committee.

At a subsequent Community Council meeting, its members decided to have the patient-group vote. The vote split evenly pro and con, with a small minority reporting indifference. When a representative of the Community Council reported this outcome at the community meeting, the clinical director said, 'That settles it.' I replied, 'You mean we have agreed to disagree.'

The Community Council chairman reported that not everyone voted, but that only a minority of the patients voted for further consideration of the pet rule. I asked, 'What shall do we do with this minority group of patients – bury them?'

The Community Council chairman: 'The Community Council voted eight to two against reconsideration of the pet rule. However, we didn't want to take the responsibility for killing the whole issue. That is why we passed it on to all the patients for a vote. I myself used to be completely indifferent about the rule, but now I am completely against pets. I am so tired of talking about it.' I: 'Why were the patients asked to vote before hearing and discussing the specific proposal?'

A patient said, 'Everyone should also have a chance to hear what the head nurse said at the Community Council meeting. All of the rooms in the Inn will have to be redecorated if pets are ever allowed. No room can ever have a rug. All rooms will have to be covered with linoleum.' I said, 'I agree that it is important to hear the head nurse's ideas. We can find out what the nurses object to in having pets and what would have to be provided to get them to accept pets. For the same reasons, we should hear from the patients who voted no. Why did they vote no? What are they worried about? What can we think of that might decrease these worries? What would get them to change their minds?' Patient (wryly? sarcastically?): 'Good luck to you.'

I made a long statement. But, as usual in this meeting, my statement was not an 'interpretation of patient psychopathology'. It did not make use of terms from psychoanalytic theory such as 'projective identification' or 'introjective identification'. It did not focus on irrational mental mechanisms, although I did make use of the notion of splitting as a group process. In this statement, I took note of the genius of American political life, which makes it possible for a society to draw together after a conflict over policies or values. 'The Community Council has the job of discovering the kind of consensus that will draw people together and enable all persons concerned to come to terms with a decision. The council seems to have fled from the responsibility to lead, apparently because its members cannot face and deal with their own conflicted feelings about pets. Instead of a thoughtful reasoned decision, the council has come to us with grandmothers' tales meant to frighten children, about linoleum floors and outside inspectors. Have we really tried to hear what the difficulties might be, what the objections are? Do we take them seriously by trying to find some way to meet them? Maybe the split is not between those who say no and those who say yes. The head nurse had once said she would enjoy pets around. Now she opposes having pets around. Maybe the real splits are within ourselves, not the splits between us. I know from many conversations with the staff that many of them have mixed feelings about pets. Without acknowledging and facing these mixed feelings within ourselves, we will never be able to influence each other.'

I notice now, in retelling this story, that I made no mention here about the patients' perception (for which they have some evidence) that the medical director preferred not to have the pet rule changed in any way. The clinical director, no doubt wishing to avoid the medical director's displeasure, worked in the meeting against changing the pet rule. So eventually did the head nurse, although her position when patients had first raised the issue had been quite different.

A patient told me, 'We will never change some people's minds.' I came back with, 'How do you square that prediction with the fact that in part we base our therapeutic work here on the belief that people can change?'

In further discussion, patients told about the anger and fear that led them to vote as they did. The clinical director then said that he agreed that the discussion at the Community Council had been irrational, based largely on a fear of animals. Community council chairman: 'I think we can do better.'

At the next community meeting, there was an uproar about the accusation that there had been cheating during the voting. Following this, the Community Council appointed a committee to study the subject further. I: 'I've caught on. If you want to kill an issue, send it to a committee to study it.'

This is an example of the kind of thing that comes to my mind leading to an intervention. What came to my mind here was not some generalization from organization theory. I remembered experiences I had had in organizations. Specifically I remembered what I had felt when some proposal about which I cared was sent to a committee for further study. My level of frustration, and I supposed that of other group members as well, was high. Throughout these months of discussion of pets, it seemed that nothing would ever lead to resolution, that nothing would come of anything anyone said or did. Patients and staff shared a sense of personal inefficacy with respect to bringing about any change in the real world.

Community council chairman: 'Don't just criticize us. Make another suggestion.' I suggested that the community meeting consider these questions. First, can we, with any sense of comfort, go on at this time to make a change, which the medical director has explicitly opposed, during a period in which he is ill and cannot personally engage in any dialogue about the wisdom of such a change? Second, what about our fear of animals? What does it mean to acquiesce to these fears, or to ignore them? The answers to the question about how we manage fears will influence what kind of community we build.

Some pay-off

The Community Council referred the question to a pet committee, which in the following month issued a report listing the pros and cons of having pets in the Inn. Those interested in having pets reported that a marked lack of interest in the whole subject had developed. A patient: 'I would still like to see the rule changed, but I cannot cope with what I keep hearing. Get the staff to agree first, and then the patients will be able to state how they feel. Get the patients to agree first, and then the administration will be able to state how it feels.' Another patient: 'I suggested that the Community Council go ahead, with an experiment, a one-month trial, and was told this couldn't be. Someone still has fantasies of the place being overrun by dogs.' I: 'Who?' Patient: 'I suppose the medical director.'

As I later did in my teaching, here I was apparently intuitively working to empower those who are relatively powerless. I was trying to help them recognize the impact of authority upon them and to stand up to those who have it. I would not have articulated what I was doing in that way until recently. I seemed to have been largely unaware of what I was doing. It is surprising to me now that I could have forgotten as a teacher that this is the way I used to talk in group situations.

Clinical director: 'It is true he [the medical director] is against pets messing up his house or the Inn, but I know he is willing to listen to any sensible proposals, although there is no guarantee that what the community thinks is sensible will seem so to him.' The Community Council then went on to engage the nurses in a discussion of specific things that might have to be done if there were to be pets in the Inn. It revised and amended the proposal a number of times, building in safeguards to allay the anxieties various people had about what might happen. A patient at a community meeting, after hearing the revised proposal, said, 'At this point, anyone who is still concerned with his fear of animals is talking about pure fantasy.' 'I agree that the proposal meets the objections about fear of pets; it satisfies me completely.' 'Just thinking about what should go into the proposal and feeling that now it might be accepted has been useful to me. If the proposal is accepted, it will enable the pet owners to evaluate the personal meaning of wanting to keep a dog or cat. I am reconsidering my wish to keep my dog. I am thinking of the effect on my ability to spend time with other people and do other things.' I: 'Whatever the outcome of the vote, the work on this proposal reflects a great advance in the community's ability to tackle complicated issues.'

The outcome: too late?

The vote on the pet proposal was held a month later, approximately fifteen months after the issue had first been raised. Patients decorated the Inn with posters, urging votes for and against. For professionalism and humor, the posters against pets had a decided edge. They were signed: CRAP – Committee for the Remedy of Animal Problems. The burden of these posters was that a vote against pets was a vote against odors and messes. Fight crap with CRAP. There was a good deal of banter and an uproar of animal noises during the voting. The final vote was rushed into the community meeting: pro – 18, con – 12, abstentions – 2.

One month later, the Community Council chairman reported at the community meeting that the proposal was on the medical director's desk. 'He's read it. The clinical director and the head nurse want to speak to him about it but they haven't found time for an appointment.' Toward the end of the next month, the medical director suggested minor amendments. During the following month, there was much squabbling as the Community Council tried to incorporate the new amendments. No one seemed interested any longer in working on the proposal. No one, in fact, expressed any interest in having a pet.

At the end of the next month, the Community Council approved the proposal as amended. There was little rejoicing. It was almost as if, after such a long delay, people had forgotten what the whole matter is about. Many new patients, when the result was announced, wanted to know, 'What was that all about?'

The community meeting as an intergroup meeting

I have the feeling that community meetings never really succeeded as *intergroup* meetings. It seemed to me everyone else felt they were there to 'treat', 'control', 'help', and 'interpret' the patients, and the patients came to be 'treated', 'helped', 'controlled', and 'interpreted'.

Most of the discussions were concerned with disturbed or disruptive behavior by one patient or another. The main questions were, 'How can we help this patient? How can we stop this patient from committing these (outrageous/ unacceptable/distressing) actions?' Few in the community meeting were interested in relating problem-phenomena to the way the treatment center was organized, how authority was exercised, or what intergroup relations were like in this organization.

I would have thought that when we discussed having pets in the Inn, someone from the work program might have volunteered to help organize the work that the presence of pets would generate. Or spoken about the implications for the work program of this issue. For example: Would allowing or not allowing pets in the Inn facilitate or hamper people's participation in work, and in what ways?

Nurses might have spoken about the implications of allowing or not allowing pets for interpersonal relations in life at the Inn twenty-four hours a day. What strains might develop? How might patients and nurses help each other deal with these strains? Would the presence of pets make the nurses' work more difficult or offer opportunities for them to do that work? What consequences for interpersonal relations among patients, and intergroup relations between patients and nurses, might arise from favoring the strategy of casting out what is unacceptable in ourselves and finding it in others?

Activities staff might have responded to the wishes being expressed for caring and being cared for. They might have suggested how working with children at the nursery school, an activity sponsored by the center, might help to meet such needs. Would having pets also help gratify such needs? They might have spoken about the implications of having pets around for activities programs and for opportunities for enjoying life at the Inn.

With rare and fitful exceptions, no staff group sought to make use of the meeting as a forum in which its members could speak frankly about their own group or represent their own group. No members of any staff group represented the problems their group had in carrying out its particular responsibilities, its shared anxieties, its collective response to proposals made by others. No staff group participated in the meeting with the expectation that other groups, especially patients, would help, would collaborate with them in coping with these problems.

If that is so, why was it so? I have one thought about it. In my preoccupation with fostering collaboration, I encouraged the formation of patient–staff committees, and the appointment of *patient* and *staff* co-chairmen in the community meeting and in action-taking committees such as the Community Council. I had little awareness of the dynamics that might result when a committee's membership and leadership are divided between a group that is perceived, and perceives itself, as having relatively more power, and a group that is perceived, and perceives itself, as having little or no power.

One result was that the powerless group responded to *intergroup* tensions with an intragroup split, that is, in strains within that group. The patients tended to perceive themselves and others to perceive them as containing a subgroup of 'good' patients who sided with staff and 'bad' patients who rebelled against the staff. The first group scolded the second with a parental voice; the second subgroup ridiculed the first. These intragroup quarrels distracted patients from the problem of questioning and negotiating with authority. Instead they passively submitted to it, or reactively rebelled against it in a way that undermined their own shared interests or goals. So they justified other groups denigrating them or denying authority to them. ('It is clear that patients are too sick, too irrational, too immature.')

Both staff and patients maintained the split. Its consequences were ideal from the point of view of those in authority, if they wanted, for one reason or another, not to be bothered with the troubles a unified patient group might cause them, and ideal from the point of view of patients who are were frightened of challenging authority, especially given their dependence on those who have it.

What would it have taken for the community meeting to have worked better than it did? Someone would have had to meet with each staff group to help it articulate what its goals were, and what it wanted to stand for and achieve in its relations with other groups in joint committees and the community meeting. Someone would have had to help each group authorize its representatives, so that when they participated in these intergroup settings, they felt they could speak for and commit their entire group. I shrink as I think now of the number of meetings that would have been involved.

I think the patients should have had their own meeting. Such a meeting would be devoted to similar attempts at organizing themselves for intergroup meetings. However, I am still nervous about the possibility that the result would have been to heighten what was adversarial rather than what was collaborative in the relations between the groups. Then I think of David Berg's belief that open and freely expressed controversy, especially between groups with different levels of authority, has to precede collaboration.

But how does he know that? Sometimes the more groups realize their irreconcilable interests and differences, once they put these into words, the more they feel that the only thing that will get them what they want is to fight. After all, even when groups share a common interest or value or objective, it is difficult for them to trust each other enough to collaborate in pursuing, realizing, or achieving it. I suppose that one way of articulating part of what being a good leader is all about might be that a good leader helps adversarial groups see what they share or hold in common and give priority to that.

I have still another doubt about my meeting with all these groups separately. What makes me think that a group of nurses, activities staff, or patients could have accepted or trusted me, a psychiatrist, a member of a powerful group, as a consultant to advise them about matters having to do with the interests, values, and concerns of their own group? If I had met with each of these groups, wouldn't I have just moved the scenarios of submission and sabotage observed in the community meeting to another arena? I did try to meet regularly with the nurses, as a matter of fact, and that didn't help much – although it may have helped some – with the problems of their participation in the community meeting I've been discussing. But I didn't know then what I know now; I think I spent a lot of time talking with them about my ideas, perceptions, and purposes rather than inviting them to tell me theirs.

CHAPTER 28

Betweenness

David Berg

The issues raised in the story of pets in the Inn illustrate the swirling collage of individual, group, and intergroup dynamics that constitute organizational life. There are many institutional leaders who would understand the problems encountered in these community meetings as caused by poor clinical practice on the part of a relatively incompetent or misguided individual leader, or as caused by the inability of seriously disturbed patients (sick individuals) to take up organizational roles.

But I am much more apt to see intergroup relations at the heart of stories such as this one. For me, it is a story of intergroup conflict, power, authority, and change, which contains variations on familiar themes. The difficulties others have had and will have with such a story have to do with the difficulty most of us have focusing on intergroup dynamics in interpersonal and group settings. I'd like to speculate on the reasons for this difficulty.

The community meetings in which there was a discussion of whether to try to change the policy concerning pets in the residential treatment center were intergroup events. Both patients and staff struggled (mostly unsuccessfully) to find a different way to relate to each other.

The story reemphasizes the importance of allowing or encouraging groups in conflict to meet by themselves. Then they can, in privacy, articulate their views about the task and the other groups involved, and bring to the surface and struggle with their own internal differences. The patients never met formally without a staff member outside the community meetings and patient–staff committees; in the community meetings, physicians, nurses, and activities staff were always – and purely administrative staff sometimes – present. That put the patient group at a disadvantage in any negotiations. In spite of efforts to provide a setting in which problems could be identified and worked on collaboratively, since neither the patients nor the various staff groups met separately specifically to prepare for these meetings, the structure often simply brought out the tensions in staff–patient relations.

The split in the patient group most likely was an expression of the ambivalent reactions the patients had about the possibility of being in conflict with the staff. Their divisiveness undermined their ability to negotiate on behalf of their own needs. In this case, the choice to focus the community meeting through interpretations on the conflict among its constituent groups was the right one.

In a more general sense, the patients may have been trying to create a new relationship with the staff. In this new relationship, they could ask for what they needed or wanted (instead of mostly being told), and participate with the staff in examining if and how they might be able to get it, and in trying to get it. That new relationship entailed a change on the part of the staff, but just as important, a change in what the patients looked to the staff for. It was necessary then to make interpretations to the community meeting suggesting that the members of the patient group in the community might have to begin to take responsibility for assessing its collective needs, deciding which needs would take precedence over others, and handling the emotions that would accompany such an 'organized' choice. I suspect that the patients had relied on the staff to do this work in the past. That freed them from the discomfort of conflict, disagreement, and disappointment. And the members of the staff had been perfectly willing to play this role, since they were concerned about the patients' (but of course not their own) ability to handle this responsibility and the discomfort that would accompany it.

Alternative interpretations about the members' inner mental processes would have deflected feelings that might have been aroused by the confrontation with intergroup relations the interpretations that were actually given sought to bring about. Individual-psychological interpretations would have moved the discussion into a more comfortable arena, more comfortable because it would not have entailed within-group or between-group conflict, and because it would have put the staff, as mental health professionals treating incompetent patients, back in charge of the community and the community meeting.

In closing, I want to say how much I felt Marshall's 'middleness' in all these stories. He was between the staff and the patients, trying to promote a conversation between the two groups that would ultimately enhance the institution's ability to provide a therapeutic environment for those in treatment. He was 'between' precisely because he could contain within himself both sides: identifications with both groups, both groups' perceptions of the other, point of view, anxieties, and ways of reducing these anxieties. He was torn between his ability to identify with the patients, to see them as human beings capable of work and play, to envision the therapeutic value of their involvement in the decisions and choices that make up community life – and his ability to identify by virtue of education, training, and aspirations with the senior medical administration. His distress was the distress of someone in the middle, unable to get the top to be responsive, to participate fully (in what they would experience as an infringement on and therefore as a diminution of their authority), and similarly unable to get the bottom to realize their potential impact if they could only work within the system.

It's no fun being in the middle. But it is the usual position, carrying similar problems, not only of any member of 'middle management' but of any leader, even a leader who is at the 'top' of an organization. For almost any organization is embedded in a larger organization (as a department of psychiatry is embedded in a medical school which has a dean, and a medical school is embedded in a university which has a provost or president); is responsible to various legitimizing bodies such as a board of trustees; or is subject to financial controls by such a body as a legislature. So any leader is not only 'top' with respect to the member groups constituting her organization, but, as someone in the middle, must mediate between – that is, identify and communicate with, and encourage communication between – those groups and someone that is even more 'top' than she is.[115]

Using Groups to Help People

Unless one understands the character of the helping medium which one is considering using one cannot even begin to make plans and decisions about who is likely to benefit from it and who not, how to plan the effort, and how to proceed while using it... A small face-to-face group, like any other medium for helping people, has its special character, its advantages and limitations, its special opportunities and its potential hazards...

There are times in a group when one can observe the emergence of some shared wish, impulse or hope... If nothing stands against this, that is, if nothing stops it from being expressed openly in the group, then this shared wish, impulse or hope can emerge as a theme for discussion. Often, however, the shared wish or impulse is accompanied by some related shared fear or guilt which is in conflict with the shared wish and fights against its emergence...

The solutions which members find may focus almost entirely on the fears, abandoning for the moment any effort to satisfy the associated shared wish. Or, a solution may simultaneously deal with the fear and allow for some expression or satisfaction of the wish...

At times, in a group, individual tendencies to erect particular defences come together, are mutually reinforced and come to characterize the group as a whole... Another form of group solution consists of collaboratively maintained interactive patterns involving role differentiation. In scapegoating, for example, one person occupies the role of scapegoat while others attack him; in 'playing at therapy', one person assumes the role of the patient or client while others seek to help and advise him. These are two examples of a family of group solutions in which most of the members of the group are protected from self-acknowledgment or self-exposure by depositing risks on to one person in the group.

Dorothy Stock Whitaker

Group Dynamics for Group Psychotherapists

Marshall Edelson

Part 7 is an account of the vicissitudes of my collaboration with David Berg and includes reflections on the nature of the processes that characterize a two-person collaboration when the two persons are male and of different generations. The dynamics of collaboration has been somewhat neglected in our field.

Rather than talking together about experiences we have had separately, here we are working together in teaching group psychotherapy (Chapter 29) and as consultants (Chapter 30). We each contribute our own separate past experiences with groups and organizations to this collaboration; at the same time we struggle with the differences in us these experiences have created.

David makes no separate comments about the stories in Chapters 29 and 30. In previous chapters up to these two final chapters, David has been in a certain role. He has responded to stories I told in which (with at the most one exception) he was not a participant. This mode of presentation was designed to parallel, however inadequately, our conversations at lunch, in which he listened to the stories I brought to him from my past or even as they were unfolding, in which he was not a participant; then he contributed to and acted as a collaborator in my examination and re-examination of these stories. These conversations and examination and re-examination were steps in my 'rediscovering groups' and 'journeying beyond individual psychology'.

In these last two chapters, two things have changed. First, David and I are not simply talking; we are working together. It is no longer a matter of my telling him a story; he is *in* the story, an actor. Second, the last two chapters focus on our collaboration, not in examining and re-examining my experiences at lunch, but in a work situation in which we both have roles, different roles; we are both intervening; we are both experiencing; we have our differences. We face together the difficulties that arise in this kind of collaboration.

A conversation – my telling stories, David responding to them – no longer seemed an appropriate mode for representing this different state of affairs. Rather, it seemed appropriate that instead I should close the account of my autobiographical journey, first, by giving a picture of us actually working together in group situations, and, second, by attempting to convey my vision of the now-and-future role of groups in my own discipline. This close is a way of saying 'and this is where my journey, and the collaboration that has given it wings, has brought me'.

Chapter 29 begins with an account of our work as co-teachers. In our teaching, which occurred in a seminar group, we were now participant-observers together in group processes that before we had shared only in conversation. As we taught, we also bumped up against characteristics of a mental health center, the organization in which the clinicians we taught conducted group psychotherapy. A number of these characteristics seemed to be obstacles either to doing group psychotherapy or learning to do group psychotherapy or both. Experiencing these collisions eventually led us to agree to serve together as consultants to a leadership group in that clinical institution. The leadership group's charge was to develop a proposal for changing the group treatment program. Chapter 30 continues then with an account of this extension of our collaboration, of our work now as consultants to this leadership group, and of the fate of its proposal.

The chapter concludes with a discussion of what we learned from this attempt to introduce a change into an organization – about organizations, and about factors that determine success or failure in attempts to bring about changes in them. The problems involved in bringing about any fundamental change in an organization are daunting. Those we encountered as consultants paralleled in interesting ways the problems I encountered in the community meetings in a residential treatment center (the story told in Chapter 27).

To the extent these chapters focus on our collaboration, they tell a story about a pair or couple, rather than a group or organizational story. The stories of the groups of trainees David and I taught, the story of the group of leaders we served as consultants, and the story of the organization in which we did this work, all remain largely untold. The important characters in those stories appear here only as pale figures who disappear for long stretches, while I tell what happened in the interpersonal story about David and me. I have left it to the reader to see parallels (and differences) between the experiences David and I had in our attempts to collaborate as co-teachers and co-consultants and, on the other hand, the experiences the reader has had in pairs or couples – as a co-therapist, a co-chairperson, in a mentorship, a tutorial, a marriage, or a friendship.

I expect the reader to realize that we have both been changed by this collaboration. I don't want to have to keep repeating defensively, 'That is the way I/he was then. That is not necessarily the way I/he is now. That is what I/he would have done or preferred to do or have happen then. That is not necessarily what I/he would do or prefer to do or have happen now.'

I also expect the reader to assume from a reading of previous chapters that whenever I describe the behavior of individuals in this book, I am doing so because I take this behavior to be an expression of their roles in a group or organization, not of their personalities. I now assume in all my work with groups and organizations that individuals in their behavior in significant part represent, often unwittingly, their groups and organizations, even though others may not recognize or acknowledge, or may deny, that the individual represents them. An individual's behavior is of interest to me in the situations depicted in Part 7 because I see it as a clue to sentiments that members of a group or organization share. (I use the term *sentiments* idiosyncratically here as shorthand for 'thoughts, feelings, beliefs, values, goals, motives, attractions, wishes, fears, and defensive strategies used to deal with conflicts between wishes and fears'.)

In these stories, an individual's behavior tells us something about a group or organization, rather than something about a person. In some cases, the behavior I describe is a manifestation of sentiments people share by virtue of their common commitment to accomplishing a task together. In other cases, the behavior is a manifestation of sentiments people share by virtue of their social identity (gender, age, ethnicity, race, socioeconomic class, profession). Such sentiments may support, contribute to, or oppose task-achievement. In still other cases, the behavior is a manifestation of whatever (possibly idiosyncratic) sentiments people have that leads them (perhaps for different reasons) to join to oppose, to defeat, or to interfere with task-achievement. If I thought that some person's behavior did not represent and was not perceived as representing any group, was in that sense purely personal, or was simply irrelevant to and had no impact on a task a group or organization was trying to achieve, I have not recorded it here.

Three questions about our way of teaching group psychotherapy

In the clinical institution in which David and I taught, teaching of group psychotherapy had previously taken place in pairs. We offered to teach group psychotherapy together, that is, collaboratively, in an ongoing group of eight trainees. The Director of Group Psychotherapy accepted our offer. We anticipated that others might ask three questions about this endeavor.

The first question

Why should you teach group psychotherapy in an ongoing *group* of trainees, rather than in multiple dyads in which each of you separately is a preceptor of one trainee?

PARALLEL PROCESS

We wanted trainees learning group psychotherapy to do so in an ongoing group, to give them the opportunity to observe parallels between processes that occurred in the training or preceptorial group and processes that occurred in their psychotherapy groups. As they presented accounts of psychotherapy-group sessions, and observed what happened in the preceptorial group (for example, as other group members discussed these accounts), we expected they would see thematic and formal affinities in the stories they had told about their psychotherapy groups and the stories preceptorial-group members enacted. Encountering these unexpected correspondences might then move them to reflect upon their experiences in groups.

At the beginning of the preceptorial group, in its first year, some members said they could not come on time, because others expected them to participate in a clinical activity that had priority. David and I debated. Was the system in which we conducted the preceptorial inhospitable to it? Or were these members expressing ambivalence about joining the group? Should we change the time of the meeting of the preceptorial as the members seemed to be requesting? Or should we begin negotiations in an attempt to change the system's demands on these members? Should we bring the topic up in the preceptorial at all? Wouldn't that result in our being seen as demanding, unreasonable, punishing?

As it turned out, we did bring it up, as a boundary issue. The members did begin to attend the preceptorial group on time. They also saw the parallels between their experience in the preceptorial group and their experience as group psychotherapists. Their patients said, 'I can't join your group, because I can't make the time of the meeting.' Their patients came late, or missed meetings, all for 'good reasons'. These psychotherapists-in-training could not decide whether their patients' difficulties in attending were 'realistic', arising from unalterable conditions or a world inhospitable to the therapy enterprise, over which the patients had no control, or instead did reflect the patients' ambivalence about being members of the psychotherapy group. Undecided, without any conviction about either the motives of the patients or the contribution of the external situation, the preceptorial-group members had not felt they could bring up such events for discussion in their psychotherapy groups.

David and I thought that trainees should have an opportunity to experience the same group processes as members that they had encountered in their psychotherapy groups as leaders. It was not long before we heard in the preceptorial group, 'Now I know how my patients feel.' This was an outcome of experiencing what it is like to be in a group, observing parallels between one group and another, and reflecting on these parallels.

Preceptorial-group members sometimes felt they were not getting what they needed from the group. They wanted a one-on-one preceptorial or supervision, with someone whose attention was undividedly directed to their particular experiences, dilemmas, skill-needs, or questions. I found myself fretting about the need I too thought individual members should have an opportunity to meet, a need to focus with someone on the particular interventions they make in their psychotherapy groups, on the context, objectives, and consequences of each intervention. I doubted that we could meet that need in the preceptorial group.

Similarly, patients in the psychotherapy groups felt – and often their psychotherapists also felt – they would do better if they had individual psychotherapy. These patients often presented themselves with emergencies, requiring individual meetings with the group psychotherapist, which the psychotherapist seems more than willing to provide. Did these psychotherapists provide individual meetings, even though this could interfere with the development of the psychotherapy group, because they themselves preferred doing individual psychotherapy? Or did the system have effects here also? The norms of that system held group psychotherapists responsible for every aspect of the care of each individual patient assigned to them. This responsibility was to take precedence over any concern about the group-as-a-whole that might conflict with it. Did the psychotherapists as a consequence feel obligated to attend to the well-being and to respond to the needs of each individual patient, even at the expense of the effectiveness of therapeutic work requiring focusing attention on and directing interventions to the group-as-a-whole?

Preceptorial-group members wondered whether they were learning how to be group psychotherapists in the preceptorial group. Was attendance at the group worthwhile? Weren't other activities more important? Wouldn't they learn more from an individual preceptor? Similarly patients in psychotherapy groups wondered whether they were getting any better. Was the group helping? Was attendance in the group worthwhile? Weren't other activities more important? Wouldn't an individual psychotherapist be of more help?

FINDING A VOICE

We wanted to teach group psychotherapy in a group so that trainees would have a chance to practice alternating between periods of involvement, immersion, almost drowning in a group process, and periods of observing that process, lifting one's head above the water and perhaps speaking about it ('making an interpretation'). We wanted to enable each one of them to be able, to one degree or another, to hold on to their own voices, when the members of the preceptorial group or the patients in their psychotherapy groups, pursuing defensive aims, tried to pressure, persuade, coerce, and seduce them into taking on some role they preferred not to occupy.

CREATING A GROUP CULTURE

Our goal for both our preceptorial group and their psychotherapy groups was the creation of a certain kind of culture. We especially wanted to enable trainees to study and understand the obstacles to creating such a culture.

We had in mind the kind of culture in which people say what is on their minds without censoring it because they reject it in themselves or fear its rejection by others. When through such talk, differences come to light, they do not result automatically in polarization and combat but in reflection. Hearing what others really think and feel extends each member's awareness of all kinds of possibilities of thought, feeling, valuing, and imagining. As a result, group members together are able to hit upon solutions to problems previously unnoticed by or inaccessible to them as individuals. The similarities that also come to light when people speak openly and freely to each other make them aware of what they share, what they have in common. A sense of belonging to a community replaces loneliness and a self-denigrating sense of being different, odd, incompetent, or defective compared to others.

The obstacles we encountered in the preceptorial group to creating such a culture were similar to those the group members encountered when they tried to create such a culture in their psychotherapy groups. Preceptorial-group members seemed uncertain about whether they were participating in a seminar or a psychotherapy group. How personal, how emotional were they expected, permitted, to be? Similarly, patients in psychotherapy groups wondered, 'What are we supposed to talk about here? How much should we reveal about ourselves?'

IMPORTING THE SYSTEM

Finally we thought that if members of a group of trainees shared their experiences doing group psychotherapy, they would more easily understand the impact properties of the system in which they worked had on both themselves as group psychotherapists and on their psychotherapy groups.

We found that a constant theme in both the preceptorial group and the psychotherapy groups was the way in which these groups imported processes from the clinical system to which they belonged: the particular ways the clinical institution categorized people, and people categorized each other; its expectations of how different categories of people (for example, people at different levels of the hierarchy of the institution) should relate to each other; the fears that pervaded it; and the ways of resolving conflicts many who worked in it seemed to prefer.

Over and over, we struggled with these questions. 'Does this difficulty in doing group psychotherapy that our group members describe – for example, getting patients referred to them to join or to remain in their psychotherapy groups – arise because they lack skills connecting with their patients? Shall we concentrate on detecting each one's problems in connecting with patients, and help them with these? That essentially would seem to blame each one of them for the problem, to place it in them.

'But what if it were system characteristics that exploit or aggravate whatever skill-deficits they have? What if the system sets things up in a way that creates obstacles to patients entering or remaining in psychotherapy groups? Then ought we not discuss these system characteristics with the preceptorial-group members, so they might separate out the effects of inexperience and of the setting in which they were learning to do psychotherapy, and reflect on the interaction between the two?' That's what we did. Was this the better strategy?

Pursuing it, we heard, for example, that team leaders gave trainees lists of patients to whom team clinicians had recommended group psychotherapy. They instructed them to call and essentially to pursue these patients until they showed up for a group. This procedure seemed to David and me somehow at odds with what was considered good clinical practice in the community.

We also learned that overloaded clinical teams did not always welcome accepting a new patient for a psychotherapy group for which the clinical team was responsible. Every new patient accepted for a group added to the responsibilities of the clinical team, for the patient then became its patient; it had to take on all aspects of the patient's care.

The second question

Why should you teach group psychotherapy in an ongoing group *together*, that is, *collaboratively*, rather than one of you teaching one group of trainees and the other another group?

We had shared stories over lunch, and we wanted to work together. We needed a medium to make that possible. We thought that together we would come upon some ways of achieving our goals as teachers of group psychotherapy that neither one of us was likely to achieve alone.

From the beginning, we planned to help each other maintain the balance between immersion in and observation of group processes by talking together after the group meetings about how each of us experienced what happened. After each meeting, we reflected upon the differences and similarities in our experiences, and formulated together some conceptualizations that enabled us to hold on to what we had learned that day. Sometimes, we were able to infer together what might be happening in the group by attending to what we thought were probably parallel processes in our own relationship. Though this is difficult to do, it is easier to do with someone else's help and perspective than it is to try alone to infer what might be happening in the group by attending to what is happening in oneself.

From the beginning also, we thought we should meet regularly not only with each other but together with the part-time Director of Group Psychotherapy. We felt that we would need some ongoing sense of the system in which our trainees were doing their work. We also wanted to be able to pass on to someone in that system, who had authority and responsibility, information we might gain from our work with the trainees about characteristics of the system and how these impinged upon their work.

The third question

What happened to the two of you when you taught group psychotherapy in an ongoing group of trainees *collaboratively*?

WORKING TOGETHER

I found that if I became transiently caught up in a group process, I felt freed by David's presence to express, not always 'wisely', how I was feeling then and there. In expressing these feelings, I gave the group members information they needed to understand the problem they were trying to solve, how they were going about solving it, and what price they were paying for resolving it in that way. David provided me with that freedom by being available to comment on the meaning and implications of the feelings I was expressing, and what he had observed had been going on in the group to evoke them. His timely intervention mitigated the tendency of some group members to use my unexpected direct expression of feelings as simply confirming and reinforcing those perceptions and beliefs they already had that were part of what was going on in the life of the group. So we were able to use such occurrences to show the value of paying attention to one's own feelings as clues to what is happening in a group and the possible value at times even of expressing such feelings to give others the information they needed to understand what might be happening in the group.

Sometimes it worked this way, and sometimes it didn't – as when I expressed feelings harshly, resulting in a lingering concern in the group about how hurtful I was capable of being. (My lingering remorse is such that mentioning these 'mistakes' – these failures of sensibility, tact, and nuance – reminds me melodramatically of the hapless psychotherapist in the movie *Color of Night* [1994] whose patient responded to his speaking harshly to her by jumping out of his window.)

David and I did not parcel out these two functions (expression and reflection), or any other two functions, and assign them in advance to each one of us. But, from occasion to occasion, each function would pass from one of us to the other.

DIFFERENCES BETWEEN US

We found that, given the differences in our own backgrounds and the ways we had taught before we taught together, we had to struggle constantly with the different priorities we had and the way they seemed to conflict with each other. I gave a high priority to the trainees finding their voices as group psychotherapists, freeing themselves to say what was on their minds. That meant freeing themselves from spectral authority figures – especially the internalized voices of supervisors, teachers, or the writers of books, rules of technique, theoretical generalizations, or formulas. What they needed instead was to notice what was particular and specific – something remembered, something a patient had once said or done, or something that had happened between patients, some event in a group, some personal experience in the psychotherapist's own life, some image or fantasy or feeling.

One necessary exercise in achieving such freedom called for a group-psychotherapist trainee to present detailed process notes of a group-psychotherapy session – not summaries of it, but who said what and in what sequence, as best the psychotherapist could remember. Having such material, preceptorial-group members would be able to discuss the group psychotherapist's interventions in light of a context: what had been and what was going on now in the psychotherapy group. To what extent the psychotherapist's interventions were responsive to or informed by that context (regardless of whether the content of the intervention referred directly to these happenings) was a topic for discussion. If these interventions did not seem responsive to or informed by the group's process, why not? was a question for discussion. Other group members might inquire, or the psychotherapist remember, what he was thinking, feeling, or imagining before making a vague, general, or formulaic utterance. They could investigate together what might have kept him from noticing, paying attention to, or using what was actually on his mind in what he said. I felt that this kind of practicing, this rehearsing, this imagining what one might say in innumerable specific situations was necessary if trainees were to be able to apply general principles and knowledge in unanticipated and in many ways unique situations. For me, this was how learning to do clinical work, any kind of clinical work, occurred.

In order to make such discussion possible, I favored structuring the meetings of the preceptorial group, assigning presentations in rotation, and primarily (not necessarily exclusively) focusing on the clinical material rather than the group process of the preceptorial group. It was important to me that a meeting of a group I taught be interesting, dramatic, and that participation be lively and full of affect, and I took it as my responsibility to see that it was. I took these characteristics of a meeting as signs that members were involved, held by the group, and learning, and that I was functioning well as a teacher. I tended to wonder what was wrong when meetings were not like this.

David, on the other hand, gave a high priority to helping the preceptorial-group members to experience their own group. He believed that their noticing, inquiring into, reflecting upon, and explaining their experiences in their own group were crucial if they were to function more skillfully not as clinicians in general but specifically as group psychotherapists. This is not to say that he did not see value in presenting and discussing clinical material. He also liked to pass out theoretical papers after a series of sessions devoted to experiencing group processes, in order not only to reflect on but to form conceptualizations based on these experiences. But he saw the primary task of the preceptorial group as giving the trainees a chance to have experiences in a group and to become aware of and to reflect upon those experiences. He believed that accomplishing this task would provide the best foundation for their work as group psychotherapists.

David was patient when meetings were not interesting, dramatic, or lively. He felt that meetings in which the group was stuck were essential in a process of learning, and that learning would follow from them. He was comfortable about observing, doing his work, and waiting. He had a sense of the group as going through phases, getting stuck, working on some idea about the stuckness, and then seeing whether an action based on that idea worked. He was convinced that a group cannot learn an idea or a way to act without experience of it.

For example, he believed the only way people can develop a capacity to manage the tendency to use splitting and scapegoating in response to what one rejects in oneself is to experience being scapegoated or participating in scapegoating another. David would say to me, 'It is having such experiences that opens the door to the use of the kind of guided learning or supervised practicum you favor, in which the focus is on the interventions a group of psychotherapists might consider making when scapegoating appears in the psychotherapy group being presented.

'It is having had such experiences themselves that enables them to consider making an intervention that will broaden participation in order to add to the information group members share: "We're acting as if John (the one being scapegoated) were the only one who has this concern, who feels this way, who has this experience, who looks at things in this way. Is John the only one with this concern? The only one that feels this way?" And to consider also making the intervention that states a conclusion based on that information: "It appears that John is not the only one who has this concern, who feels this way."'

Why is experience (in this case of being scapegoated or participating in scapegoating) necessary to consider making such interventions? David's answer: Because we don't make such interventions without some faith, based on the knowledge that comes from firsthand experience, that it is likely that (in this case) other people do share John's feelings, concerns, way of looking at things, despite their apparent denial or refusal to acknowledge that they do (as evident in their reaction to John).

In this connection, suppose Olivia is late to a meeting, and offers a good reason for being late, involving compelling pressures applied to her by powerful others or conditions over which she has no control. Because we have previously experienced, explored, and reflected on such events in groups of our own, we have faith in our knowledge-based assumption (the knowledge coming from such experience) that 'being late' or 'missing a meeting' is usually motivated, related to feelings about the group or a reaction to something that has happened in the group, and that it is unlikely that only one group member has such feelings – that Olivia's expression of such feelings is an isolated event. Therefore, we have the courage to question unassailable evidence that Olivia 'couldn't help it' – or to resist the consensual judgment that John is evil and deserves what he is getting, that Lisa is bad and the group should extrude her, that Maurice is stupid and others should ignore him, that Tina is sicker than everyone else and others should help her – or to refuse to accept, although it is 'obvious', that Tim is different from the other group members. We are able to say, 'Perhaps Olivia is reacting to what happened in our last meeting by coming late. Is she the only one who had such feelings?' And know that we are likely to hear someone say, 'Well, as a matter of fact, I was thinking on the way here today that there were a lot of things I would rather be doing than to come to this meeting. I toyed with the idea of just not showing up, but I wanted to be a good group member; so I came.'

SOURCES OF THE DIFFERENCES BETWEEN US

The different identity groups to which David and I belonged – for example, our age and status differences – were responsible in part at least for the rationalized differences between us. I found that I was particularly sensitive to moves on David's part that seemed to me to limit my opportunities to share what I knew with the group. I would become irate when David pointed out that, preoccupied with giving my knowledge to others, I had not responded to some trainee's comment, that I hadn't seemed to notice it, that I hadn't focused on people's difficulties saying how they feel or what they are thinking, that I didn't seem to trust what people might come to, working together, without my immediately and at length providing an 'answer'.

I felt I did know, that I had knowledge to offer group members – and I wanted to offer it. I heard them reporting their interventions and the interventions often seemed to me stereotyped ('How did that make you feel?') or disguises for or reflections of their condemnations of patients ('He is manipulative.' 'She is seductive.'). It seemed to me, and I thought of this as a consequence of inexperience, that if there were two ways of understanding what patients were talking about, of understanding the stories patients told, trainees would tend to lean toward the way that put the patient in a somewhat unfavorable light. They usually did not have access to a way of hearing these stories that would make patients truly the hero or heroine of them.

As a result of my own experience I had a different way of listening to patients' stories. I heard them differently. I wanted to tell the group about this way, this difference. I have a lot of confidence in my ability to hear the stories patients tell, and to detect the stories a psychotherapist and patient(s) are enacting. I have a lot of confidence in my ability to see connections stories have to each other, the common threads running through them or what led from one to the other. If someone in the group characterized a story differently, heard another story, or did not hear any story at all, I did not give those impressions the weight I gave to the story I heard or the connections I saw. So trainees often felt when asked to discuss clinical material that they were simply trying to guess what I was thinking. 'Why don't you just tell us what you are thinking, instead of playing games?'

However, I also noticed I did not have the same confidence in my own intuitions when it came to just what interventions I or a trainee might make, given that the patient was telling a certain story, that just these relations between stories existed, or that a particular story was being enacted in the psychotherapeutic situation. Here I felt open to a number of possibilities, and would seriously contemplate and consider what someone else came up with. So it was probably around the question, 'So, then, what intervention might the psychotherapist make?' that I should have concentrated any attempt at back-and-forth exchange between myself and trainees.

I think now in retrospect that a lot of what I was doing in my teaching had pressure behind it, associated with my experiences with illness and my age – the period of life I was traversing. In my sixties, questions about legacies preoccupied me. What legacy would I leave? Would it be valued? Would others give me the opportunity to pass it on? Would they accept it? (To what extent does my preoccupation with a legacy motivate and perhaps at the same time spoil the writing of this book?)

This preoccupation, ironically enough, resulted in my tending at times to pass over, or to pay less attention to, or to apparently devalue trainees' ways of listening to patients. My doing so would lead to drops in their self-esteem. They would feel they had nothing worthwhile to offer, because if they did offer something it would be corrected. ('It wasn't what Dr. Edelson would have thought or said.') I knew they respected me. I also had noticed that at times they also resented my assumption of superior wisdom, because it seemed to imply that I knew everything and they knew nothing. They couldn't or wouldn't tell me about either kind of feeling. Their concern about my experiences with illness played a part in this reluctance; mostly, my age and status held them back, even intimidated them. (David wanted to help them to express this complicated many-sided set of feelings more completely.)

Group members would become silent. Sessions would have periods that were neither lively nor interesting, followed by relief when Dr. Edelson, exasperating David, came to the rescue with some suggestion that provided order or structure.

I began to realize passing on a legacy so preoccupied me that I might create conditions in which it would be difficult for trainees to learn from me. It was possible that I could become ever more 'the old man' who won't shut up in meetings, grand rounds, seminars, but who has desperately to repeat his message over and over. The message is not just *from* his own life experience. It *is* his life experience. His life experience is the legacy he has that he wants to pass on to others. Increasingly, others don't want it. It bores them. They want others, including the old man, to hear and value them. Because of the response he himself provokes, the old man becomes increasingly panicky that no one will listen, no one will take what he has to offer. So he talks, and talks, and talks. Aging can be a cruel process.

I noticed that David, on the other hand, was especially sensitive to moves on my part that seemed to depreciate what he had been saying or the work he was doing with the group. This sensitivity seemed to be the sensitivity that goes along with being younger or having less status. For example, once David was working with the group on their many different feelings about authority, their difficulty expressing these in this group, and their tendency to use him ('Mom') to protect them from me ('Dad'). He told them how they provoked him to say things to me they didn't want to say. At the same time they used him to protect me from them. He says what they want to say tactfully, softening it, or he warns me that something I have said or the way I have said it is open to 'misinterpretation' by group members and invites me to 'clarify' what I had actually intended. David's interpretation about the way the group members perceived us and used us led to feelings of relief and a sense of insight in them – and in me as well.

I then came in with: 'This preoccupation with transferential phenomena, however valuable it is, is itself a retreat from the work of learning to be group psychotherapists, a flight from the pain of facing one's own incompetence, which one must face if one is going to learn.' I went on to assign some readings for the next session.

Prior to the meeting, David and I had discussed this intervention, although we had neglected to agree on a decision about when in the session it would be best to introduce the readings. In retrospect, probably the beginning rather than the end of the session would have been best. David heard the term transferential as dismissive and as placing him in an individual rather than a group frame. He heard the term valuable as protesting too much and signifying the opposite. He became angry.

It is of course interesting that I preceded my interpretation of what the group members were doing with comments about David's work with them. I could just as well have simply made the interpretation that the group members seemed to be having difficulty facing feelings of incompetence that are a necessary concomitant of accepting that they have to learn to be group psychotherapists and have to depend on someone else or take in something from someone else to learn.

Why the prologue? Here, competitiveness rears its head. Of the two teachers, which of us is going to have his way? Who is going to win?

We agreed in our usual post-meeting discussion that a useful interpretation would have been one that integrated our different statements to the group: 'You're having difficulty expressing all of the many feelings you're having about the two of us, because you're afraid that anything you say along these lines will be critical of our competence, and so may incite us in turn to focus on and expose your relative incompetence as group psychotherapists, which you don't want to face.'

THE EFFECT ON US OF BEING IN A COLLABORATION

It became clear to us that our collaboration itself influenced the way each of us felt and acted in the preceptorial group. In our teaching, each by himself, we both tended to bring in all aspects of the learning process, an emphasis on experience, on reflection about experience, on conceptualization, on trying these concepts out in doing some piece of work and seeing how it goes. David, for example, both assigned reading and lectured in his teaching and I was by this time in my seminars relatively comfortably passing back and forth between – that is, integrating – comments about the group process of a seminar and discussion of the clinical material presented by seminar members.

In my own seminars, I was beginning to tell people immediately how I heard what patients were saying, what I made of the stories they told, and then to invite them to discuss my views, their views, the different interventions that might follow from these differences. I wanted to get out of, and was finally succeeding in getting out of, the scenario that started with my inviting their comments and then coming in with what I had been thinking. They would then almost always hear me as saying, 'I am right and you are wrong, so why didn't you think this instead.' They would then view my initial invitation as an entrapment that led to my showing them up.

I discussed this entrapment scenario with David. He suggested I might want to give seminar members some alternative ways of listening to the clinical material, so that my comments did not always carry the meaning for them, 'This is the one right way to hear what the patient said, the one right thing to say to the patient in response.' I developed handouts that seminar members could use in responding to a clinical presentation. The handouts outlined different kinds of interventions, different kinds of observations, and different kinds of inferences a psychotherapist might make. I used these handouts to help trainees expand their repertoire of 'what to notice' and 'what to say'. I also used them to help trainees keep themselves from reporting inferences as observations. I became more comfortable than I had been in a long time using a conceptual framework in my clinical teaching. I found that the conceptual framework I had now designed was near enough to experience to make it relatively resistant to the usages of theory about which I was and am skeptical, those usages involving a defensive reliance on abstraction and ultimately on authority rather than one's own perceptions.

So, in the group-psychotherapy preceptorial, in which David and I were collaborating, teaching together, what led to the splits in functions we had in other situations integrated within ourselves? What led to the assignment of a different function to each of us, and then to competition about which function was more valuable or ascendant?

One factor is perhaps a tendency in a collaboration for one member of the collaboration self-indulgently to devote herself or himself to some favored function, favored perhaps for reasons having to do with group identity (age, status, gender, race, ethnicity, for example), without feeling irresponsible about being one-sided or neglecting other functions. One member of a collaboration moves to an extreme. This move provokes the other – he can be counted on – to make a countermove to the other extreme.

A confusion in us concerning the nature of our working relationship perhaps exacerbated any inclinations we may have had to adopt such irresponsible extremes. Were we truly collaborating? Did we actually coordinate our interventions? Did we decide together what course or strategy to pursue – making executive decisions about schedules, the timing of interventions, readings we would assign – and then subordinate our individual inclinations to this joint product, what we had planned and decided together? I more often felt I was in a relationship in which I was learning from David about working with groups and organizations, consulting him about difficulties I experienced in such settings. Both David and I, for different reasons, seemed to have an image of David as my consultant, not my co-teacher.

But there was something not quite genuine, something ingenuous, something of a *folie à deux*, about this image. For it ignored my own background studying and working with groups and organizations. I had struggled with and been fascinated by group dynamics from the time I was a graduate student in psychology, used social system concepts as I tried to create therapeutic communities in mental hospitals, eventually attended a number of Tavistock group conferences, and ultimately served on the staff and briefly on the board of these conferences. So why the pretense of virginity?

It was not all a charade: As a practicing psychoanalyst, I had not focused on groups and organizations in my daily work for many years. Even though as a teacher I was constantly dealing with group phenomena, I did not so much comment on them as use and accommodate to them. David, on the other hand, was immersed day after day, and had been for years, in his work as a teacher in the area of organizational behavior and as a consultant to groups and organizations. I did learn from him and took pleasure in learning from him.

But to the extent that the image of David as teacher and me as student was overdrawn and that we were enacting something of a charade, it is reasonable to ask, 'What functions does the image of him as primarily a consultant to me, a humble learner, serve?' I think that we exaggerated this image, a case of 'protesting too much', as part of our attempt to cope with the strains that arose from the differences in our age and status. In a sense, I was using a 'feminine' wile, a kind of flattery, to keep David in the relationship, fearing that he might resent my 'masculine' refusal to subordinate myself to the rigors of a true collaboration. Although unhappy with the pretense, to the extent it was a pretense, he may have been willing to go along with it up to a point, because it helped him to deal with his dissatisfaction with a relationship in which he was the younger and the one with the lesser status.

I especially exaggerated this image – as part of my attempt to deal with the fact of my aging and my moving inexorably toward 'outness'. For me, becoming incapable of or losing interest in learning some new body of knowledge or skill was a kind of dying, a sign of impending death. So the sense of learning from David was a way of reassuring myself that I was still very much alive, that my life as a person who enjoyed learning was not over.

In fact, that I did learn from David gave me pleasure, a pleasure I did not want to give up. Therefore, I used the fact that I did learn from him to try to keep him in a relationship whose survival was for me, because of the difference in our age and status, always in doubt. I also used the image to check and keep at a reasonable level my 'masculine' tendencies to throw my weight around, to dominate, to demonstrate my power, to compete with David – which I fantasied, without much evidence, if expressed, would sever our relationship. The more I felt my age as a weakening of my place in the social world, rather than experiencing it as a source of well-earned respect, the stronger these 'masculine' tendencies, now made desperate, became. The more then I had to contain them, and the more I had to use the image of us as consultant ('David') and learner ('me') in order to contain them. So increasingly, this image substituted for an image of us as collaborators and threw us off track in facing the problems we had becoming and acting as collaborators.

THE EFFECT ON US OF THE SYSTEM IN WHICH WE WORKED

We had realized from early on that the problem of the different priorities we represented and were attempting to juggle existed in part because of characteristics of the system in which we worked. There was no general curriculum that addressed knowledge of groups and organizations – and the application of that knowledge in clinical enterprises such as group psychotherapy. In an ideal curriculum, trainees would have begun by learning experientially in a group. Then, through study of the literature, they might learn even more what groups were like, what happened in them, and what vocabularies – not those of individual psychology – were useful in talking about them. A clinical practicum, such as a preceptorial that focused intensely on clinical experiences, ideally would follow this experiential learning. Trainees would have come to such a practicum having had experiences in groups and having acquired the conceptual equipment that now enabled them to comment on their own group process, when it provided a parallel to what was going on in the group psychotherapy being presented, or when it interfered with an attempt to discuss the clinical material. A later seminar would have focused on organizations and the way in which the system in which trainees do their clinical work influences that work.

Somehow we found ourselves struggling to carry out all these tasks in our limited time with the trainees. It is not surprising that we attempted to deal with this impossible complexity by acting as if there were clear-cut competing alternatives.

SPLITTING, PROJECTING, AND COMPETING IN THE COLLABORATION

No matter what the source of the differences between us, or what led us to emphasize or exaggerate these differences, the consequence was a split between 'advocacy of a guided practicum' and 'advocacy of giving primacy to group experience', between 'believing in learning from a teacher' and 'believing in learning from experience'. Having accomplished the split, we now projected an alternative onto each one of us. That is, we agreed covertly that each of us should accept as an assignment taking on the task of representing and fighting for one of these alternatives. So the problem became a simple one, compared to the difficulties in pursuing the integration of different functions, and the difficulties in working out joint plans and decisions to which we would both subordinate our individual inclinations. The problem now became: Which one of us is going to win, to defeat the other, to have his way?

But a cornerstone of our method of teaching group psychotherapy depended on experiencing, observing, and reflecting upon parallels between processes in psychotherapy groups and processes in the preceptorial group. So we needed immersion in and attention to both kinds of processes. Nothing could happen until we accepted that both of us wanted to achieve both what I 'stood for' and what David 'stood for'. Our task was to find, if possible, a way of doing that.

Early on, in one of our post-meeting discussions, I, enamored of rational means, such as 'division of labor', and exasperated by how things were going, said to David, 'This is not working. Why don't we just divide up these two tasks? I'll discuss the clinical material. You can discuss our group process. I'll leave that to you and you can leave the clinical discussion to me.' David said quietly, 'That would be to give up on our collaboration.' I saw that that was true.

On another occasion, I exploded, 'I can't stand this endless group process shit! I don't feel I'm myself. It's when we discuss clinical material that I have something to say.' David said, 'Okay, Marshall, let's do it the way you want to do it. It's your course. It's your system. I'm not really a member of it. I don't want to be responsible for you not being yourself.' I replied, 'Now it is you that wants to give up on our collaboration.' And David saw that that was true.

David contended that it is natural to want to pull out of collaborative relationships. Each feels, at different points, that the collaboration is obliterating his individuality, silencing the very voice that has the potential to make a contribution. To withdraw, to pull out, threatens the collaboration and the relationship that makes it possible. But to stay in and express this 'hostility', this anger at being obliterated, likewise runs the risk of tearing the collaboration apart.

In one post-meeting discussion, I said reproachfully, 'David, I felt you cut my legs off from under me!' At another time, David said angrily, 'Marshall, don't you ever again belittle me by that kind of sarcastic "joking" reference to what I've said! "As David would say..."'

WHAT HOLDS A COLLABORATION TOGETHER, MAKES IT WORK?

What binds a collaborative relationship at these times? What makes possible the continuation of a relationship in the face of forces pulling it apart?

In each case, we found it was likely that one of us had no awareness of how the other experienced what he had said or how he had said it. In each case, we tried not simply to defend ourselves but instead to join in a 'good faith' attempt to figure out what was going on that led one of us to behave in a way that the other experienced as noxious. Once we understood, there seemed to be no carryover, no holding of grudges, no worries it would happen again. But of course it did happen again.

We began to resist any attempt by one of us or by group members to give us pre-assigned competing mutually exclusive roles. Our aim was that each of us was to feel free to intervene in any way, to make any contribution to the discussion he felt inclined to make. David might hold something back, deferring to my status, or feeling that we were doing this work in my bailiwick and that he, David, was an outsider, a guest. During post-meeting discussions, I would then ask David, 'Well, why didn't you say that, if that was what was going on in your mind?' David would say to me, 'You are oblivious of – you deny – the effect you have on me and on the group simply by virtue of your identity as a senior white male tenured professor.'

We would try to address these observations and questions. We worked together to free ourselves from worry about each other's reactions. We found that (David's) tendencies to overemphasize or (mine) to deny differences in our statuses often led to these worries, so we tried to correct for these tendencies. Instead, we wanted simply to be aware of these differences in status so that we could tell when they made a difference and what kind of difference. Based on our experiences with each other over time, we began to assume that, if one of us spoke, he could depend on the other to respond in whatever way made sense to him. On the whole it was likely, more often than not, that what one of us said would provide support for or contribute to what the other was trying to achieve.

We had no fixed paradigm for how we were to function together in the group. The result was that we often surprised each other by saying the unexpected. The 'clinician' would make comments on group process and the 'group process expert' would comment on clinical material.

From my interactions with David, I began to realize how complex a creature collaboration is. David: 'Each of us brings to it different views, passions, competencies, needs, commitments, ideas, and experiences. A collaboration ebbs and flows, involves risks and failures as well as gains and successes, frustrations and satisfactions, moments of collapse and moments of maturity, intimacy and betrayal, commitment and withdrawal, differences that separate and alienate along with differences that stimulate creativity and originality. The relationship between a collaborating pair is paradoxical, for the creativity of the collaboration is founded upon the willingness of each to assert strongly his individuality, his individual views, needs, feelings.'

Sometimes I am unregenerate. Then this is my picture of myself. I like to depend on my own judgment even if I turn out to be wrong. I don't like depending on someone else when I have a vision, which drives me to realize it. I don't like someone else's inclinations, dispositions, opinions holding me up. I don't like compromises. I'd rather make an imperfect product that is my own than a perfect one sired by someone else. I thrill to a performance by a soloist whose aria soars, although the mastery of a great quartet – its members' sensitivity to and melding of each others' slightest nuances or subtlest intonations, the selfless subordination to a great end they all display – also awes and excites me. The most exhilarating experience for me is coming up with something 'on my own' even if this 'on my own' is an illusion. And yet, and yet, and yet... I take great satisfaction when a group comes together as a team, an ensemble, in which I feel I have a part to play.

You can imagine my difficulty, if my conception of David's and my collaboration remains dominated by a fantasy about marriage. It is hard for me in a relationship with a man to be comfortable with such a fantasy. As David and I create something together, and that's what collaboration seems to be about, the questions that come to my mind, if I let myself go a bit, are some version of 'Who is inseminating whom?' 'Who bears the child?' 'Who in pain and labor delivers it?' I imagine the one that is heavy with child, feeling the full responsibility of carrying it, at times resenting the 'male' other, who having planted his seed is now free to go about his business or pleasure. I imagine the 'male' envying and yet also wanting to support the feminine 'other', in whom the seed grows and takes on life. 'Who gets the credit?' 'Whom does the child look like?' 'Whose child is it anyway?' 'Ours.' 'Indeed. In what sense, ours!?' 'Who takes the responsibility for bringing up, nourishing, staying with this child, until it can stand on its own?'

Still and all (it seems there is no end to my ambivalence), it is a good experience when two people who care about each other share the child they have brought into the world and with the help of others raised.

At times, I would become aware of a risk. Our attention to our own collaboration, to the satisfactions and difficulties of our own relationship, our interest – competitive or not – in what each of us had to say and in responding to each other in the teaching session threatened at times to preoccupy us at the expense of attention to the group-as-a-whole and the problems with which it was struggling.

I found myself remembering that, when as a teacher of group psychotherapy I met with a pair of co-therapists, it was sometimes very difficult to discuss anything about the psychotherapy group. In any discussion of a group-psychotherapy session, the way in which one therapist felt the other interfered, got in the way, went her or his own way, sooner or later claimed our attention. The co-therapists' rivalry, and their search for some way of supporting each other's work, compellingly distracted them from the task of the group.

In addition, David and I made no attempt to conceal our differences from the group. Frequently we would respond to each other during a preceptorial session. This collaboration was public. Our exchanges fascinated group members, and stirred up feelings in them. One feeling was, 'It helps me to see how the two of you work together, talk to each other.' But the public disclosure also created distress, a feeling that, since *we* did not seem to be together, *they* were not safe. Our dilemma was that we knew that they knew we must disagree about some things. If we suppressed our disagreements in public, we would be inviting the group to idealize us or our relationship, to deny whatever tensions our differences created in them, and to work these tensions out on the patients they treated or to blame each other as their source.

In all this, again the marriage fantasy haunts me uncomfortably. Now a family, parents and siblings, peoples it. The siblings have passions and fantasies of their own. They want the relationship between 'Mom' and 'Dad' to be strong and dependable. They are curious about their doings. They are capable of playing off one against the other, inviting arguments, provoking one to protect them from the other, or seeing to it that one protects the other from them.

Seeking a structure for teaching group psychotherapy in a group

In the first year we taught together, we sought a structure that would satisfy both of us. To satisfy me, we began with a rotation of clinical presentations. To satisfy David, we suggested that in each case the presenter become the leader of the group discussion. The presenter as leader was to begin the detailed account of a meeting of a psychotherapy group by declaring his preferences. Did he want members of the preceptorial group to interrupt the account? Would he rather they wait for him to pause and ask for discussion at various points in the presentation? We commented, when presenters avoided making any statement of how they wanted to conduct the discussion, that they showed they were reluctant to behave as leaders. They felt brutally criticized.

The group discussed the role of leader and why members wanted to avoid occupying it. Fear of, placating, pleasing, resisting, and resenting authority was a constant theme. We tried a series of 'experiments', each time inviting the group to observe and discuss how a particular way of doing the work was going. We invited the members to negotiate changes with us when they felt dissatisfied.

By the end of that first year, we had arrived at the following procedure and role-assignments. A presenter would have two consecutive meetings in which to present. At the beginning of each meeting, an observer was selected to observe how the group was functioning. During the first forty-five minutes of each session, the presenter read process notes to the group, and the members, sometimes invited by the presenter, and sometimes interrupting, made comments. Ideally, in their comments they emphasized similar experiences or problems that they had encountered in their own psychotherapy groups. They avoided evaluations of the presenter's interventions or suggestions to the presenter how to do group psychotherapy. In the second forty-five minutes of each session, the observer began the discussion by sharing her perceptions of the group's functioning during the first half of the session. In particular, the observer noted how the group may have departed from these ideals. In the discussion that followed, the group sought to understand why such departures may have occurred, and to become aware of and to make explicit parallels between the group process in this session and the group process in the psychotherapy group that had been presented.

How did this structure work?

Here is an example of such a parallel between group process in the preceptorial group and group process in a psychotherapy group. It involves scapegoating in different groups. In a psychotherapy group presented by a preceptorial group member, a patient volunteers to talk about a problem. Other group members respond by making 'helpful' suggestions, interpretations, corrections. The volunteer seems to feel increasingly 'the sick one', while the other members, disclaiming any such 'sickness' in themselves, pride themselves on their helpfulness, competence, and wisdom. In the preceptorial group, a presenter offers the group an account of a group-psychotherapy session, perhaps mainly wanting the other members to appreciate this piece of clinical work. But the presenter finds group members have all kinds of suggestions, interpretations, corrections – and begins to feel that others regard him as having a problem that apparently none of them has, or that they have all solved. At the same time, the other group members experience themselves as helpful, competent, and knowledgeable. For the duration of that kind of discussion, they are unaware of their own anxieties as beginners about how competent they are.

Here is an example of another such parallel, involving splitting leaders in different groups. The co-teachers of the preceptorial group are split: the insider and the outsider, the comparatively good and the comparatively bad one, the soft and the hard-assed one, 'Mom' and 'Dad'. At the same time, the group members remain unaware of tensions between the men and the women in the group. A staff person and a new resident, who are co-therapists, experience a similar split in patients' views of them in a psychotherapy group.

Changes in the co-teachers

From this first year of working with David, I gained more confidence that, if the co-teacher leaders refrained from immediately offering structures for work, the group would still 'get there'. Group members would be more likely wholeheartedly to use a structure that emerged after they had a chance to discuss their expectations and anxieties.

During the same time, David was rethinking his inclination to discourage group members from depending on the co-teachers. In one of the post-meeting discussions, I said, 'I've been thinking that dependency is a different problem in a medical system from what it might be in a business. My experience as a clinical teacher is that beginning psychotherapists fear, and are reluctant to allow, patients' becoming dependent on them. Patients are similarly counterdependent. When a worried psychotherapist sees a patient as "too" dependent, as she often does, her patient is usually actively evoking that worry in her to create distance between himself and her – because, no matter what the surface appearance is, he is judging his own dependent tendencies even more harshly than she is.

'This is not merely a psychological phenomenon. The economic need in the current system to get patients out of the hospital and out of treatment as rapidly as possible encourages and exacerbates it.

'Furthermore, medical training keeps emphasizing the importance of independent functioning, relying on your own judgment, making your own decisions even in the presence of the insecurity engendered by insufficient knowledge. Trainees often end up like hyper-independent street children who have learned that they must take care of themselves; they cannot depend on anyone else. Their independence is hypertrophied; they cannot ask for help without feeling a loss of self-esteem.

'I've been wondering if we should allow people in our group to become aware of their counterdependency and make it easier for them to permit themselves some experiences with feelings of dependency.' David replied, 'Over the last week, I've been thinking the same thing.'

Nevertheless, this continued to be a live issue, and one of the most troubling, in our relationship; events stirred it up again and again. Though I felt David's concern that people in general and so these group members too were likely to feel powerless and to be oversubmissive and overdependent in relations to authority, I was inclined to focus in my observations and interpretations on instances in which I experienced these particular group members as rejecting, disowning, and avoiding experiences of feeling dependent (for example, by picking a fight with an authority figure or constructing an image of an authority figure as distant, forbidding, punishing).

David would accuse me from time to time of teaching too much, offering suggestions or formulating a topic for reflection and conceptualization in such detail and in a way that was too much mine when we had created a structure for a reflection-and-conceptualization session that involved group members taking over responsibility for it (in this case, he experienced himself as protecting a boundary we had established), offering interpretations prematurely rather than letting group members struggle with an unpleasant state-of-affairs – and so encouraging group members to rely on me. I would accuse him from time to time of being too detached and withdrawn, too impersonal, too stingy with his comments, leaving the group too much and too long on its own, and expecting them to take leadership, devise ways of proceeding, and solve problems for which they did not have the knowledge, when he knew, counterdependent as they were, that they would not allow themselves to experience or recognize their need for help much less to ask for help. I felt that thereby he set up situations in which they would inevitably fail, and likely have to face then interpretations of their failure that they would experience as esteem-lowering criticisms.

That I had experienced medical training first-hand, and that we were teaching in a medical setting with which I was familiar, influenced me. That he had taught in a school of organization and management, that in his teaching he usually had two sessions a week (rather than the one session a week we had) and so was able to alternate experiential and reflection-conceptualization sessions throughout the year, that he dealt with many nonmedical organizations in his practice whose members had very different attitudes toward dependency or for whom dependency was not a central issue (for both professionals and patients in a medical setting, it was a central issue), influenced him.

An emerging structure

In planning the second year of the preceptorial group, David and I agreed to devote a number of sessions at the beginning to the process of 'becoming a group', discussing how it felt to be a group psychotherapist and how it felt to be a member of the preceptorial group, what expectations people brought to the preceptorial group and what fears they had about their performance as group psychotherapists.

We gradually began to explore how the group members imagined using the preceptorial group to learn to do group psychotherapy. A split developed between new members and old members, who then competed with each other. Members suggested that instead of preparing detailed process notes, they simply spontaneously offer vignettes in an ongoing discussion.

I interpreted this emphasis on 'spontaneity' as, paradoxically enough, an attempt to avoid exposure to what they felt would be devastating criticisms of their interventions. If they selected a particular isolated vignette, which made the point they wanted to make, they remained in tight control of what they presented and what it meant. But suppose they presented detailed process notes, not attempting to select – according to some agenda they would like to see pursued – bits from all they remembered, but instead reporting a sequence of 'he said' and 'then I said' and 'then he responded', and 'this is what was going on inside of me at that moment'. Then they would have much less control over what exchange or series of exchanges out of all these exchanges, what utterances or actions, someone might choose for discussion. They would have much less control over what others might then see in that material, or do with it, and would have to face the surprising ways others might relate it to the context in which it had occurred.

A method of proceeding evolved. Over a period of two meetings, a member presented detailed process notes. At particular points, the presenter invited group members to comment, or accepted their interruptions. Observations of parallels between what was happening in the preceptorial group and what was happening in the psychotherapy group were high-priority contributions to the discussion and could come at any time.

The major problem was that we rarely got through more than a small amount of the material that the presenter had worked hard to prepare. 'Why should I prepare pages of notes, if the discussion is going to take off from the first few minutes of my group-psychotherapy session, or concentrate on one or two episodes in that session!?' Apparently a felt imbalance between attention to clinical material and to the interventions of the group psychotherapist, on the one hand, and attention to the process of the preceptorial group, on the other, continued. 'The presenter never gets to finish!' 'The presenter never got to the "moment", the "event", or the "problem" about which she or he was most eager to hear group members' comments!' Group members acted as if, in presenting their own therapy group, they were parents telling other parents about their own child.

The co-teachers attempted to share a different image of the presenter's role. The meeting did not belong to the presenter. We had not designed it to provide the only or the major opportunity the presenter would have to learn something about group psychotherapy. The group's task was not to 'evaluate' or 'help' the presenter. That conception of the task was a symptom of the way in which 'focus on the individual and on individual pathology' rather than on 'the group-as-a-whole' continued to dominate. It was also an expression of competitive trends in the group.

Instead, the task of every meeting was to provide an opportunity for all members to learn something about group psychotherapy. The presentation was a means to that end. The presenter's role was to offer some clinical material to the group to take off from. It was a gift to the group. Group members would make use of this gift by contributing their own memories. They would tell stories of experiences they had had as members or leaders of groups, including their experiences as group psychotherapists, which the presenter's account had evoked. Instead of each group member talking to the presenter, or to one of the teachers, group members would talk to each other.

Together they would put together their various experiences. Together they would reflect on what pattern the various experiences made. Together they would attempt to conceptualize what they had experienced and observed in such a discussion. We expected that the participation of group members in such a process would add to their competence and knowledge as group psychotherapists.

What prevented the group members from accepting such an image of the presenter's role? They participated in a medical system, which had taught them to focus on individual patients and their illnesses; encouraged them to compete with each other for opportunities, positions, and rank; and exposed them on clinical rounds, when they 'presented', to shame – public evaluations of their clinical performance, their competence, their ability to acquire and to remember necessary information here and now.

Group members did not share our image of the presenter's role. Perhaps it was at such odds with the norms of the system in which the group members work, and with their previous education, that their sharing it with us is an impossible goal.

A story of the group's response to a new proposal

Increasingly, members reported feeling 'changed' by their experiences in the preceptorial group. For example, they were now intuitively able to recognize when a process of scapegoating was occurring in one of their psychotherapy groups. But they still could not talk to the psychotherapy group about what was happening. The words would not come. The ideas did not seem to have consolidated to the point they could use them.

David and I responded to preceptorial-group members' desire to be able to articulate such process observations in their psychotherapy groups, to be able to tell stories about scapegoating, for example, in these groups, by developing a plan in a post-meeting discussion. In a subsequent meeting, I presented our plan. We suggested that the preceptorial group give up rotating assignments to present clinical material. Instead it could leave it up to its members to bring in material about their psychotherapy groups for discussion. The material could still, but would not necessarily, take the form of previously prepared detailed process notes. The group would have such discussions over a specified number of meetings, all the while paying attention to group processes in the preceptorial group. Then periodically, perhaps once a month, being able now to feel and to see what is going on, the group members might read something together that would help them formulate concepts that articulate their experiences, observations, and reflections. These newly acquired conceptual tools might then enable them, in their work as group psychotherapists, to put into words and to talk about what they, having experienced in the preceptorial group, would now be able to observe in their psychotherapy groups.

The group was apparently enthusiastic about this proposal. The members organized themselves to order copies of Dorothy Stock Whitaker's *Using Groups to Help People.*[116] Holidays led to a three-week hiatus during which we read some chapters, and then had a meeting in which we discussed them. One theme in that discussion was the sense of being coerced, and the collusive defenses against the dangers of expressing this sense of coercion (silence, talking outside of the group instead of inside the group, avoiding the group).

The next meeting, David was absent. (He had previously announced he would be.) Early in the meeting, I announced the assignments for the meeting at the end of the month. Melissa: 'What do we do in between, for the next three meetings?' When I didn't answer this question, there was a discussion about the mechanics of getting the book.

Then Nancy announced she would be leaving the group in two weeks; her boss had told her not to make such an announcement until arrangements for a new position were completed. Charles pointed out that this 'holding back' was characteristic of the group. 'We don't share things. We don't explore things.' Bernard: 'I don't think that's why we're here, to share personal things.' Melissa and Minerva both made comments in response to Bernard that Nancy's going would affect everyone in the group. They would miss her. Minerva (to Nancy), 'I have lots of feelings about your leaving.' Melissa: 'I'm going to miss you.' Bernard: 'I don't feel that way. I know groups change and that there's nothing we can do about it.' Lana was incredulous at this. Charles and Tom both commented that the group would miss Nancy's role. Tom: 'I like the idea of figuring out what role Nancy has played in the group.' Minerva: 'Why?' Melissa (to Nancy): 'I have very much appreciated your willingness to raise difficult issues.' I noticed but did not comment at that time on the differences in the way men and the way women responded to Nancy's announcement.

Charles announced that he also had been holding back telling the group he would be away next meeting. Putting this together with the increased number of people who had started coming late to the meeting, I said these events reminded me of the saying about deserting a ship in difficulty. Nancy: 'Now we're rats!' Minerva: 'I like to think we're the crew.' I made the following interpretation. They were emphasizing their sense of being depicted as rats, and their indignation about this comparison, in order to evade the image of a sinking ship. Melissa (to me): 'Why do you think the ship is sinking?' Tom ('joking'): 'Actually, it's getting lighter all the time.' Minerva: 'I'm going on vacation soon and will also be away.'

I wondered aloud: 'Did anyone else feel that the men in the group responded differently from the women to Nancy's announcement that she was leaving?' A chorus of 'No!' Melissa: 'You can tell us your thoughts. You haven't answered either of my questions. Why are we waiting three weeks to discuss the assignment? Why do you think the ship is sinking? What is the gender difference you noticed?' I: 'There was another question as well Melissa: 'I don't remember.' I: '"What are we going to do during the next three meetings?"'

Charles: 'We don't answer the questions.' Lana: 'We don't know the answers. Why are we waiting three weeks?' I: 'I'm the only one who remembers the plan we made together?' Melissa: 'I was away when you made the plan.' Tom: 'I don't remember how long it was going to take to get the book.' Melissa: 'What was the plan?' Charles: 'It was something about bringing in material from our own groups.' Nancy: 'I remember that, but I don't remember how long we were going to do that.' Charles: 'I can't remember what he said.' Theresa (somewhat sarcastically): 'He changed the "master plan".'

People tried to remember when this change took place. I had a strong sense of blankness, confusion, absence. I wondered briefly if I was mistaken in believing that we had discussed the plan with the group, and that they had assented to it enthusiastically. Then I began to remember vividly snatches of that discussion. The group atmosphere seemed incredible to me. I had a strong impulse to tell them the whole story. But I remembered conversations with David about how important it was that they have such experiences. I remembered my patients letting me know how important it was to them that I could bear it when they were in an awful state or being awful – that at such a time I could remain quietly with them without anxiously trying to get them out of a state painful to us both. I did not tell them the story.

Minerva: 'I feel overwhelmed! The ship is sinking. Please, someone, remember the plan!' Melissa: 'I can't tolerate ambiguity.' Tom (wistfully): 'I wish David were here.' Melissa: 'Maybe he would tell us.' Tom: 'I feel punished by Marshall for not remembering.' Charles: 'The group irritates me.' I: 'I experience Charles as taking David's place and protecting me from the group by imitating me – enacting the image of me as critical of the group – and so deflecting the group's attack onto himself.' Long silence.

Melissa: 'I wonder why that comment made us quiet? It's hard to respond to it.' Theresa: 'Charles, did you agree with it?' Charles: 'I like it when affect in the group is high. I try to provoke it. Is it that I don't want to criticize Marshall?' Theresa: 'Are you running interference for Marshall?' Charles: 'Am I pissed off? I would like Marshall to answer the questions.'

I commented on a split in the group between those who wanted me to answer the questions and those who felt something was amiss with the group. Theresa: 'This is a change. Usually when David isn't here, you become the good guy. Today you're the bad guy, the punishing wounding father.'

There was some confusion expressed about the timing of the assignment, its being announced by me just on the day that David was away. Minerva: 'Was David here when we made this plan?' Gradually, people began to remember snippets of the discussion we had had about 'the plan'. Nancy: 'I'm positive we recapped it when I returned from being away.' Tom: 'I remember it had something to do with our not presenting our groups any more. We were going to talk about the issues. We were all going to volunteer vignettes.' Then immediately there was a discussion of ordering the books, the cost, how we would arrange to pay for them. Minerva: 'How was it decided what chapter we would read next?' I commented, 'As Tom started to remember, group members, instead of associating to what he was saying or being reminded of anything by it, turned to discussing the arrangements for the book.' Nancy: 'I remember that we were going to bring in clinical material and read something that related to it.'

At this point, I discussed how a group can pass on functions like memory to a leader, then feel dependent on the leader to exercise those functions, and feel frustrated if the leader didn't. I also commented that, having divested themselves of functions like memory, they had appeared almost mentally ill, unable to remember, confused, staring in different directions off into space. So, in their psychotherapy groups, if their patients acted in the same way, that would tempt them to attribute it to the patients' pathology, rather than lead them to realize a process such as we had just been experiencing was going on in the group.

Tom and Theresa began to tell stories of how their patients divest themselves of functions all the time and expect the doctors to perform them. 'They will never remember when they need a new prescription. They expect us to remember it.'

I commented that the group members not only pass things on to me to do, but do this to others in the group. I referred to the earlier discussion of Nancy's toughness and how members will miss it. Tom: 'Right. If she raises difficult issues, then I don't have to.' I: 'And Nancy can accept that assignment from the group or refuse to accept it.'

Melissa: 'Who decided on the date for discussing the reading?' Nancy: 'Maybe we did.' Melissa (looking at my notebook): 'No, we didn't. I don't have it written down.' I (amidst laughter): 'You want to share notebooks.' Melissa: 'You assigned the reading today.' I: 'You felt that I assigned you reading you didn't want to do.'

Over the next exchanges, I interpreted the group's 'amnesia' as a solution to the conflict between a wish to learn and a fear that a sequence of events might unfold, in which their teacher coerced them, they expressed resentment about this felt coercion, they rebelled against it, and finally he punished them for that. The group's solution was all on the side of the fear; it helped them to rebel against coercion without expressing resentment and facing the danger of retaliation. The solution didn't help them at all to fulfill their wish to learn, because it required them to sacrifice for safety's sake functions they needed in order to learn.

Melissa: 'I don't understand assigning reading for a meeting three weeks away without any explanation.' Nancy: 'The explanation is in the plan we're all forgetting.' Minerva: 'I don't like this experience. When I am the psychotherapist in my psychotherapy group, I like to be clear. I like to use logic and reason, to be clever.'

I: 'The problem is, the smarter the psychotherapist gets, the dumber the patients become.' Minerva: 'I feel my clarity and reason are defenses against being overwhelmed.' I: 'It's almost intolerable to sit with the sense of madness and dysfunction, nobody talking, nobody remembering, everyone confused, everyone mad at you for not helping to dispel this terrible state of affairs. We are all tempted to accede to the pressures on us to stop the discomfort.' Nancy: 'People are taught to be that way in groups. I sit in a group with the Head of the Clinic, and I think, "I don't have to remember this. He'll remember it and send out a memo. That's his job."' I made some comment on the loss to the work of the group when a leader has followers who disavow competence. Nancy: 'I act that way, because I don't feel I have any power.'

I: 'Was the flurry of announcements about people being away and the "amnesia" due to fear or resentment? I have the sense you continue to struggle with the fear that if you present your clinical work, you will be forced to confront your own incompetence. I don't think you are so afraid of what I will think about your work or what others will think of it. I think that each one of you feels overwhelmed and dismayed that you are not as competent as you feel you ought to be to do the work that you are doing with patients that need you.' Silence. No one said anything in response to this interpretation, but I felt that it had been heard.

Melissa: 'I didn't like not being consulted.' Nancy: 'I wanted to do the reading.' Charles: 'I'm pissed about the entire session. Marshall came up with the idea, spelt it out. He did it for us.' Theresa: 'We struggled the entire session with this.' Nancy: 'I hate this. After this, I'm going to write everything down.'

I did succumb, and reminded people that they had been dissatisfied with the last assignment because it didn't bear a close enough relation to where they were with their groups. They then recalled their comments and recognized that the assignment today had been in response to the dissatisfaction they had expressed. Tom and Theresa returned to the parallel they observed in how members in their group acted as they had in this meeting. Theresa imitated their patients talking to them. '"Dr. Smith, I have a problem doing such and such right now. Would you do it?"'

Charles (provocatively): 'We're being good little dogs in here. Reach for it, a little higher, a little higher.' I (quoting the first part of a famous line from the movie *Tea and Sympathy* [1956]): '"When you speak of this some day, and you will" – remember that it was Nancy who spoke of rats and Charles of dogs, not I.' Burst of laughter.

Minerva makes a somewhat sarcastic comment about Charles's picking up a paper I had dropped. I used this as an example of some feeling between the men and women in the group. I described the women as responding to Nancy's leaving by expressing feelings toward her, and the men as responding with more intellectual interests, such as the problem the group is having, or figuring out roles.

Tom: 'I'm going to say something to Marshall I'm afraid to say. It's hard to be critical of him. He's the leader and I feel like a piss-ass little kid. You say we divest ourselves of our memory. We also don't want to be in that position. We fight against it. We want to be group leaders. I think you act in ways that invite us to depend on you. You're coy about giving information, implying that you have it. You don't answer questions. But you do remind us. You do structure things.'

I: 'It wouldn't surprise me. As much as anyone, I find it difficult to tolerate periods of confusion, ambiguity, "amnesia".'

Melissa: 'I feel we're being infantilized. Marshall is holding up biscuits, tidbits.' Tom: 'He's holding them too high. We can't reach them.'

Melissa referred to Charles as the favorite son. Theresa: 'But Bernard actually has more time with Marshall, takes more of his courses.' There was much laughter. In the midst of the general hilarity, Tom said to Melissa: 'It's your job, it's a woman's job, to make Marshall some soup.' Nancy said drily, ironically, 'Of course, there are no gender issues in this group, just as – according to my patients – there are none in my psychotherapy group.'

CHAPTER 30

The Now-and-Future Role of Groups in Psychiatry

Marshall Edelson

As David and I discussed together, and with the Director of Group Psychotherapy, the work we were doing with the trainees, we became clearer about the way in which the structure of the program affected what group psychotherapist trainees were able to do and to learn. Out of those discussions came a request from a recently appointed Associate Director for Program Development, which the Director of the Outpatient Division enthusiastically endorsed, that David and I serve as consultants to a small group of leaders from the Outpatient Division as they tried to formulate a proposal for a new group program.

A case study: the development of a proposal for a new group program

In our role as teachers of group psychotherapy, David and I became increasingly aware of the trainees' problems in doing and learning to do group psychotherapy. We chose not to view these problems as primarily expressions of the trainees' inexperience or ignorance, but rather as expressions of properties of the system in which they did their clinical work and tried to learn how to do it better. We now brought these problems to the attention of this group of leaders, who in their roles were in a position to do something about the system itself. As we explored these problems with the group of leaders, together we uncovered and became aware of still other problems.

Problems

We had heard from trainees that they found it difficult to begin new groups, and difficult as well to replace members who leave a group with new members. Trainees had described procedures the system employed ('the lists of "bad" leads') that contributed to these difficulties – and how the clinical team structure may also have contributed to them.

The trainees who were assigned to us seemed to have little knowledge of groups. They did not seem to be able to apply whatever knowledge of groups they did have to the psychotherapy groups with which they worked. They focused on each individual group member as if they were doing individual psychotherapy in an aggregate. Their main talk was about the pathology of various members of their groups and the particular difficulties each of these individual patients presented.

Trainees found that others throughout the system tended to devalue group psychotherapy. They encountered widespread skepticism at all levels in the organization about the efficacy of group psychotherapy. Their teachers and the people with whom they worked seemed unable to articulate just what group psychotherapy might accomplish, and how it accomplished whatever it might accomplish. Adequate distinctions between treatment goals and processes, on the one hand, and rehabilitative goals and processes, on the other, were indiscernible to the trainees as they participated in the system. There was no basic research on group psychotherapy, and no ongoing collection of data about patients, group psychotherapists, or the clinical enterprise ('action research') that might provide information administrators of the group treatment program needed.

Dynamics of the leadership group

The group of leaders meeting with us reviewed these problems. They became increasingly invested in, challenged by, and excited by the prospect of bringing about a change in the system. They worked hard to formulate a proposal for a group program in the Outpatient Division designed to resolve these problems and others that had come to light in our discussions.

A major goal of our work as consultants was to encourage the leaders consulting us to express, in the leadership planning group itself, their doubts, skepticism, opposition, or ambivalence about the ideas emerging in their discussions with each other. We wanted also to encourage them to explore in this group strains in the relationships among them, especially as these strains flared up in response to the ideas they were discussing. We were only partly successful. The prediction, emphasized especially by David, was that what went unexpressed here would infect the way these leaders participated in presenting the proposal to, and discussing it with, others, and eventually how they would participate in implementing it (if there was a decision to implement it).

The group, in formulating the proposal, apparently agreed with me that it should be responsive to one of the charges to this university-based, state-supported institution – to develop innovative approaches to meeting the needs of its patient population that would be exportable to other institutions in the state. However, this group's members in their roles did not function on the boundary between the organization and the state; so understandably they were not wholeheartedly, unambivalently committed to this end.

Group members anticipated that, if the changes they proposed were truly innovative, others in the Outpatient Division would perceive them as radical. They assumed that their colleagues would respond to a perception of radical change with opposition, confusion, and various other forms of distress. They did not guess that others might evade that perception altogether, that they might greet the proposal, as they eventually did, with 'acceptance', and merely assimilate it as a new way of talking about what they were already doing – and therefore as not demanding any real change of them. 'Perhaps,' people were to say, 'this proposal is much ado about nothing.'

Most early discussions and drafts of the proposal emphasized the radicalness of the changes proposed, and anticipated and attempted to respond to opposition to such changes. But then something interesting happened, the sort of thing that makes possible some learning about organizations and processes of change in organizations. Ostensibly out of worry about the anticipated opposition, group members softened the final proposal. They avoided specifying details, especially those concerning changes in authority relations, as well as unfamiliar or controversial ideas or themes, such as rehabilitation. They did not share or discuss the final proposal with their two consultants before presenting it. Reportedly, when group members did present the proposal, no one of them challenged – instead they agreed reassuringly with – the reaction of their colleagues that 'this is just what we are already doing, and no real change is involved.'

Various group members that had developed the proposal, and the Director of the Outpatient Division, expressed pleasant surprise that there was no opposition to the proposal – even from those whose known ideological stance would have almost certainly led them to oppose it. Should this have surprised the group members and Director?

In retrospect, we can speculate that it was leaving one fundamental question unanswered during the group's work that determined the shape the final proposal took – how to change authority relations in the organization so that its authority structure reflected the task-analysis that underlay the proposal. That this problem remained unsolved, was in some sense 'too hot to handle', might have been a key factor in the group members' reluctance to discuss the final proposal with their consultants. That may also account for presenting it to – and discussing it with – others in the organization evasively.

The proposal

What was this proposal? People in the leadership group had become enthusiastic about it, committed to the ideals it espoused, excited by the vision it represented;

they worked devotedly and creatively together to develop it. Then why in the end were they hesitant about stepping forward to espouse it, much less to put themselves forward as leading it, or even as leading the effort of winning acceptance for it, in its undiluted form? The emerging proposal had eight essential, distinctive, and interrelated components.

1. The dominant theme for the entire Outpatient Division should be using groups to help people – not just patients but the people who work here as well, not just groups for treatment but also the groups in which we work together (how do we make these the kind of groups that help people do their jobs?).

2. The 'default' treatment – to which staff in the Outpatient Division would assign patients requiring problem-focused active treatment or rehabilitation (as distinct from 'case management') – should be one in which a group is the medium or agent of treatment, unless in a particular case such an assignment was contraindicated. Staff assign patients to other forms of treatment such as individual psychotherapy and chemotherapy if assignment to a group is contraindicated, or when it seems that one (or more) of these other treatments is required to support or enhance group treatment or to enable a patient who otherwise cannot participate in group treatment to do so. (The sense of 'default' in the idea 'a default therapy' is familiar to those who work with computers. A default setting is any selection among alternatives that the computer makes automatically unless the user specifies a different selection.)

3. Work with patients in the Outpatient Division should focus on capacities rather than exclusively on incapacities or pathology. Such a focus is the hallmark of an enterprise that gives rehabilitation a high priority. Therapy groups are intended to be curative, to bring about a more or less lasting remission, to modify or permanently change some self-destrucive pattern that cuts across many areas of a patient's life, or more usually to solve in a more or less definitive way some circumscribed particular problem in living with which a patient is struggling. Rehabilitation groups, in contrast to therapy groups, are intended to maintain or even enhance a level of functioning in a patient with a permanent disability, to prevent deterioration, to help a patient to adapt to (and that includes finding ways of compensating for) a permanent handicap, to integrate the patient with others in a social setting, or to forestall the adoption of or building an identity exclusively around a 'sick role'. An important means to these ends is to focus on, enhance, and when possible expand those aspects (interests, goals, talents, capacities) of the patient that are not necessarily implicated in or compromised by his or her handicap.

   It is most likely that therapy groups achieve their aims primarily through talk, while rehabilitation group achieve their aims primarily through activity, but exceptions to this correlation may be found among both kinds of groups. Activities include 'projects', 'recreational and social activities', 'educational activities', 'skill acquisition', 'running a business together', 'taking trips', etc. (Talking as part of planning such activities together, and talking about experiences together afterwards, may, of course, be an important aspect of these activities.) The term *group psychotherapy* is reserved for the first kind of group, and *activity group treatment* for the second kind of group. In this system of classification which distinguishes between the goal (therapy or rehabilitation) and the means for reaching it (talking or activity), psychotherapy (that is, talking) groups may have primarily either therapy or rehabilitative goals, and similarly activity groups may have primarily either therapy or rehabilitative goals.

4. Staff assign every patient receiving continuing care in the Outpatient Division to a Clinical Team, and within the Clinical Team, to a Home Group, whose primary functions are not treatment but rather case management. Case management includes embedding a patient in a social nexus, as well as assessing ongoingly a patient's current needs, problems, and capacities, and subsequently referring the patient for whatever treatment might at a particular time be indicated. If treatment is indicated, the Home Group Leader also decides, based on her assessment, whether to refer a patient to a problem-focused therapy group or a rehabilitation group (the default choices), or decides that referral to a group is contraindicated, and decides as well whether to refer the patient to other modalities of treatment in addition to or instead of a treatment group.

    This kind of assessment and decision may well be done better in a group over a more or less brief period of time than in one or two one-on-one interviews. In the Home Group, the leader can carry out an assessment of the patient's potential for making use of active-treatment or rehabilitation resources, based on information obtained not just in listening to what the patient says but from a broader field, watching the patient in action responding to and interacting with a variety of others – much as Bion assessed potential for leadership by observing men participating in an unstructured group rather than by interviewing or testing them.[117]

5. The task-analysis on which the proposal is based implies changes in the administrative structure of the Outpatient Division, and therefore changes in authority relations. Clinical Teams (responsible for case management) and all Treatment Programs, including the Therapy and Rehabilitation Group Programs, should be administratively separated. Treatment resources should not be located *within* each team, but should be available to all teams.

6. The group program (including those groups responsible for case management and those responsible for therapy or rehabilitation) should have a full-time Director of Group Programs.

7. The Director of Group Programs should provide appropriate training for those who use groups to achieve management, treatment, and rehabilitation ends.

8. Those responsible for groups and group programs should have information – a database developed by an action research enterprise. This database should contain information organized in such a way that it can be used to answer ongoing questions raised by those who must make decisions as they work with groups and administer group programs.

Belling the cat

What follows is a snapshot of a moment in the history of this small group of leaders. One member forgot our meeting and scheduled something else that overlapped it. Another, on hearing of this, scheduled something else, taking it for granted (without consulting the group) that the time of the meeting had now become available as open time. Following a series of last-minute phone calls, we ended up having the meeting.

Comments made toward the end of this meeting suggested that group members had assumed on their way to the meeting that it would be our last. This assumption was impressively bizarre. Clearly, no one who saw herself as a leader of this enterprise, who had read the reports and studied the list of problems we had already generated, would have accepted such a limitation on our deliberations. She, feeling in the position of leader, would have made the judgment, 'This is preposterous! At the least, as soon as I get to the meeting, I will have to raise a question about it.'

During the meeting, group members discussed their own relationships. Did they really intend to work together in the area of rehabilitation as well as group psychotherapy? Did each of them actually have a real commitment to the role of rehabilitation in the group program? It was clear from the discussion that a number of group members did not feel that they had the knowledge and skills to run a group program that included rehabilitation groups as a central and not peripheral part of the enterprise.

I said that I didn't believe that the events around scheduling the meeting, the assumption that it would be our last meeting, and the discussions we had during the meeting, simply implied ambivalence about taking leadership in the group program, about the group program itself, or about participating in this particular committee – or merely expressed the doubt and distrust charging relationships between committee members. I said I believed rather that these events represented a response to a specific, immediate, and pressing problem. I gave this interpretation, an answer to the question, 'Where are we now?'

'Looking at the list of problems we have identified, and the kinds of solutions we have imagined, it is clear that no minor tinkering with the present program will suffice. Since the problems have to do, among other things, for example, with widespread beliefs about treatment and mission, and with the nature of organizational structures and leadership, anything we propose will be radical. That is, anything we propose will require major changes that will strain the system.

'It is easy to imagine that such a proposal will arouse intense reactions at every level of the system. As a committee, then, right now we face a problem of this kind: "Who is going to bell the cat?" Which of us is going to lead the effort to win acceptance for the proposal and shepherd its implementation if it is accepted? Not without some reason based upon experiences in the system, we are imagining that that person will inevitably become the focus of intense, and in many cases the victim of unpleasant, at times perhaps even cruel, reactions at every level of the system. As I look at what's been happening in this meeting, I imagine members of this committee responding to the question "Who will do it?" by saying, "Not me." "Not me. I am in too vulnerable a position in the system. I do not have the necessary clout. I do not want to create strains in my relationships with others. I have my job/my promotion to worry about." "Not me. Given where I am in the hierarchy, I do not have the status." David: "Not me. I am only peripherally a member of this system. I am a volunteer. I don't really belong." Marshall: "Not me. I do not have any line position in the system and therefore no role in which I have authority giving me the right to take such action."

'What has happened in the group today says, "I am not going to take on the role of leader in this committee." That is also a way of saying, in answer to the question "Who's going to lead when it comes to introducing this proposal into the system?": "It's not going to be me."

'If all this is true, how do we imagine proceeding – and what do we imagine is going to happen, following our coming up with our radical proposal?'

David emphasized that to understand an organization, and therefore to understand what might be an obstacle to, and what might facilitate, change, those who want to bring it about must talk with people at all levels of the hierarchy and in all groups in the organization. Of the two of us, he had been the one most attentive to, and the one most likely to remind the group of, the question of how leaders should introduce any proposal for change into an organization. He felt that a proposal was likely to lead to meaningful change only to the extent that leaders involved people at all levels of the hierarchy in considering and developing it; the idea is for them to feel they have had a hand in it. Leaders must encourage people in an organization to disagree openly about proposed changes with those who have power and authority. Only if leaders invite their subordinates to disagree openly, and to participate in a process in which everyone thrashes out disagreements rather than suppresses or overrides them, will members of an organization be likely to commit themselves to whatever changes ultimately occur.

However, pragmatic considerations weighed heavily on the leaders in our group. 'We have to think of what is practical.' 'We are under pressure.' 'We have to get something going to meet the problems we face now.' These considerations and pressures, and perhaps also anticipating that opposition would be unpleasant and difficult to manage, tended to distract them from wrestling with questions about how to introduce the changes they were concerned with bringing about. In fact, as I have previously mentioned, the decision to go ahead and present the proposal, and to what groups to present it, occurred without any consultation with the two consultants.

Steps in a process of change

A major question was what priority to give these various components, should the organization decide to accept the proposal.

1. Initial consideration suggested that, with regard to timing, we should start with a full-time Director of Group Programs in place. It would be best for the Director not to be in a hurry, not to be under pressure to prove himself or the value of what he was doing. It would be best for the Director to have the attitude, 'No major change ever takes less than five years to bring about.' We needed a director then who was ready to commit himself, a significant piece of a career, to bringing this change about.

2. Then, as a second step, the Director should proceed with the development of a training program. Depending on what was feasible, she might begin in selected sectors or units in the organization to develop a cadre of skilled clinicians who were able to use groups to help people.

3. Further consideration suggested that – rather than changing everything at once – the Director should proceed initially in a limited way, using pilot tryouts of components of the proposal with selected groups of patients and clinicians, and assessing each step of the way. This leader should watch for each opportunity to demonstrate the value of the developing program (the 'hamburger principle', illustrated by a story in Chapter 25) – and then take the next step.

Fate of the proposal

But events did not unfold in this way. Why not? The group of leaders was sincerely committed to the proposal. They brought idealism to developing it. The

Director of the Outpatient Division showed a positive and benevolent interest in it.

In our attempt to understand the consultation and organizational processes determining the fate of the proposal, we want to pay attention to the form it finally took, how it was presented, what response it received. We want to assess whether resources turned out to be available and whether conditions existed that were necessary or that favored its implementation.

In the final proposal prepared by members of the leadership group and presented to the Director of the Outpatient Division and to groups in that division, using groups to help people was not identified as a dominant theme. The idea that group treatment is to be the default treatment was either lost or at best expressed in a subdued inconspicuous way. There was one passing allusion to rehabilitation; it was mentioned without discussion or elaboration toward the very end of the document. The claim that a full-time Director of Group Programs was required was conspicuously absent. The relation between the Clinical Team structure and the Therapy and Rehabilitation Group Programs was not treated as problematic. So, in the proposal as presented, Home Groups became treatment rather than management groups, and at the same time (anomalously, from the point of view of task-analysis) became the responsibility of the Clinical Team Leaders rather than a Director of Group Programs. (The creation of Home Groups was the one component of the proposal that was eventually – within two years – partially realized, and received enthusiastically by many staff and patients.)

Few details were specified in the presentation that might have stirred opposition. For example, no mention was made of the probability that if the Home Groups were to fulfill their function, they would have to meet more frequently than the bi-weekly groups that were presently in place on the Clinical Teams. These current bi-weekly groups reportedly were accepted in discussion as essentially equivalent to the proposed Home Groups. In general, the differences between what now existed and what was being proposed for the future were played down or blurred.

People are not likely to make sense of a proposal, or will see no reason to accept it, if they do not share the perception that a problem exists that the proposal is intended to do something about. But there had been in the presentation no explication of the problems that motivated the proposal.

If people do not have a chance to disagree, to raise questions, to object, then these unaddressed and unexpressed disagreements, questions, objections will go underground and affect the implementation of the proposal. But anything that might have evoked controversy had been omitted from the presentation.

Why did this process – this softening, these omissions and deemphases – occur? Does this cautious but self-defeating strategy tell us something about the motives or personalities of the people who adopted it? (Caution: Watch out for scapegoating here!) Is the strategy a clue to some flaw in the proposal itself, some issue that is fudged, something contradictory or inconsistent, in it? Is the strategy a response to, or encouraged by, characteristics of the organization? Did we as consultants fall down on the job in some way?

What we learned from this case study about organizations and about bringing about change in an organization

The consultants had not been successful in helping the leaders who had developed the proposal express and work through their differences before it was presented. After the presentation, one leadership group member expressed dissatisfaction with the final formulation of the proposal, because it lacked emphasis on rehabilitation: 'Particularly for patients with serious and prolonged disorders and disabilities, it may make more sense to conceptualize the core work of mental health care as the ongoing *rehabilitative* enterprise in which patients build a productive life for themselves on the basis of their existing strengths and despite, and within the limits imposed by, their disabilities. In the process of acquiring and maintaining stable housing, taking care of daily needs, developing meaningful relationships and participating in meaningful activities, it is quite possible that more complicated (that is, psychological) issues may arise that will require focused psychotherapeutic work. But this work can be conceptualized as "supportive" of the ongoing rehabilitative work rather than vice versa, and will be goal-directed and time-limited so as not to foster dependency on individual clinicians or [groups] focused on problems, pathology and problematic personal identities.'

The consultants had also not been successful in focusing the planning group on the problem, much mentioned by David, of how best to go about introducing a change into an organization. The group had avoided grappling with this issue. They agreed that they continuously felt under pressure from the Director of the Outpatient Division to move more rapidly to present the proposal to him and then in various settings chosen by him. But we do not know to what extent such pressure actually existed. No group member, as far as I know, and neither one of the consultants, spoke to him about these problems, or presented him with any ideas about how the group wanted to deal with them. Could the consultants have been more helpful to the group in enabling them to manage differently the expectations they thought they faced? I am inclined to think so.

One implication of adopting using groups to help people as a primary theme would seem to be that the director of the entire clinical program should be a 'group' person. This is the same sort of reasoning that leads an organization to choose a marketing person, or a research and development person, or a finance person, as its leader, depending on its analysis of the kinds of problems it faces or the kinds of solutions it plans to employ. If groups are the default medium or agent of treatment, then the Director of Group Programs de facto is the Clinical

Director. Team Leaders, responsible for case management and the Home Groups, and the Directors of the Active-Group-Treatment and Rehabilitation-Group Programs, as well as Directors of Individual Psychotherapy and Pharmacotherapy (treatment resources available to members of groups), are all responsible to the Director of Group Programs.

The consultants also failed to help the group face this implication and its consequences, which were not represented at all in the final proposal. In general, the consultants failed to help the leadership group think through what innovations in authority structure and relations followed from the analysis of tasks and the relations among them that underlay the proposal. I especially had urged the leadership group to avoid rigging a jerry-built authority structure or set of authority relations that simply accommodated to the capacities or wishes of particular available persons or existing resources, but instead to attempt to design an adequate task-oriented authority structure. But I had not followed through with any sustained effort to enable the group to work on the question of what authority structure or relations would be appropriate to the proposed group program.

It would appear that the consultants were reluctant themselves to experience the unpleasant interpersonal encounters with members of the leadership group that were likely to be associated with such work. This group included current leaders in the present group treatment program, whom the proposal would affect. We knew the people involved too well and in too many other roles. As teachers of a group preceptorial, we met regularly with the current part-time Director of Group Psychotherapy. One leadership group member was also a member of the group preceptorial in which we were co-teachers. Another member met regularly with me, his mentor and advisor.

David and I probably didn't even want to imagine the strains on the system that would arise as new demands, changes in status, and questions like 'Where do I belong in this new setup, if at all?' confronted people. Much less, did we want to anticipate the possible response of the Director of the Outpatient Division to being saddled with the difficulties involved in dealing with these strains, and in finding the resources needed to implement the proposed program and the persons who could fill the positions it called for.

It was not only the case that the two of us were involved in too many ways with the cast of characters. In addition, just as in our collaboration around teaching, here again we were confused about our roles in this collaboration around consulting. David could function as a consultant. It was his role in his work in his practice outside the university. He was in many ways something of an 'outsider'. At least, there was no reason to suppose that he had any major personal or role-driven stake, when acting as a consultant to this group, in the group's product taking one form rather than another. He encouraged the group to clarify who was giving the group its charge, and exactly what that charge was.

David was concerned when he observed how much I initiated, how much I drove the process. He wanted to get the group members to take responsibility for their work. He faced them over and over with the question, 'Do you really want to do this? Are you committed to it? Who do you imagine actually doing this or that?' He feared that to the extent I drove the process and the group members felt on the periphery of this planning endeavor, they would not be able to take any proposal that resulted anywhere.

I did not believe that the problem was that members of the leadership group did not buy into what they perceived as 'my' vision. There were meetings in which I felt the group was inspired, in which every group member was plunging in, putting something into the pot, and ideas were boiling up, ideas that no one of us might have come to on their own. I responded to David's cautions with, 'If we merely listen to what in the beginning they have to say and suggest, won't we just end where we are now? How can people embedded in a system, who have a stake in current arrangements, who are fearful about how any changes in current arrangements might affect them, come up by themselves with a vision of something really new?'

So, while David could function as a consultant, supported by his 'outness', and his own practice, his daily work as a consultant with other groups and organizations, it was otherwise with me. I was a senior tenured faculty member in the Department of Psychiatry. Others experienced me as – and I was – an 'insider'. I was a member of other groups, such as the tenured faculty group, and in contact with other faculty members, including the Department Chairman, the Associate Chairman for Education, and the Director of the Residency Program. From discussions with them, as well as from participating in the department for many years, including for an extended time as Director of Education, I was aware of the problems and goals of leaders in the department who functioned in arenas outside the one occupied by this particular group to which I was nominally a consultant.

For example, I was acutely aware that one of the charges to this university-based, state-supported clinical institution was to develop innovative approaches to meeting the needs of its patient population that could be exported to other institutions in the state. Its degree of success in fulfilling this charge most likely would influence the relation between the state and not only this particular clinical institution but the Department of Psychiatry to which it belonged. I saw no particular sign that the Director of the Outpatient Division and his Associate Director for Program Development hoped or expected that the proposal developed by this group of leaders should or would contribute to the success of the clinical institution in fulfilling this charge. Such a hope or expectation was not part of the charge to the group. However, I kept bringing it up in my discussions with the group. I cared very much as a senior faculty member that the work of the group should have this result.

So, as a responsible member of the senior faculty, unlike David, I, of course, had a role-driven stake in the outcome of this group's work as it might affect not only the Outpatient Division or the clinical institution of which it was a part but also the Department of Psychiatry to which the clinical institution belonged. I had no line position in the organization either of the clinical institution in which the Outpatient Division was located or in the department. I had no authority derived from such a line position. My role was essentially (and, as I see it now, unavoidably) that of a senior faculty advisor, who inevitably then would attempt to advise and influence. No doubt my past as well as present experience, my relationships and discussions with other senior figures, and my role as a senior faculty member and teacher in the department, affected what advice I gave and in what directions my influence was exerted. On the other hand, in my role as an advisor, I was clear that I had no line authority, no right to insist that others follow my advice, and no reason to expect that in every instant I would successfully influence the work of the group in which I had a role best described as senior faculty advisor rather than consultant.

The Director of the Outpatient Division was certainly aware that he was relating to a senior faculty advisor and not to a consultant. He was careful to stipulate, in supporting the arrangement in which David and I served as consultants to this leadership group, that it was to be understood that he was not bound to agree with or to implement what the group came up with. He made it clear that he expected there would be no hard feelings if he decided not to implement the proposal or any part of it; he had responsibilities for the entire division and would have to act on any concerns he might have about how the proposal might impinge on or compromise other goals or arrangements of the division. The specter of the butting-in senior faculty member certainly loomed, even though the Director of the Division felt secure enough, and was willing, to take a chance on me.

If from the beginning David and I had been clear about my role, we might not have failed in the ways mentioned above. I might have been clearer why I was in the group and what behaviors were appropriate to my role in the group. I might have functioned more confidently in the light of that understanding. David might then have been freed up to behave very differently from me, and vice versa, without either of us feeling that we were somehow not collaborating well as two co-consultants.

The moral of the story

The authority structure of an organization (or a program or subsystem of an organization), and the authority relations that authority structure depicts – and so the definition, distribution, and assignment of responsibilities as well as the delegation of authority to carry out these responsibilities – should ideally reflect or parallel a task-analysis. The task-analysis motivates the choice of authority structure.

Such a task-analysis includes these steps: (1) explicating goals or missions – and the values implied when we assign priorities to goals or missions; (2) delineating the tasks or functions we must carry out to achieve these goals or missions and to realize these values; and (3) also delineating the relations among these tasks or functions, especially relations of supraordination, subordination, and coordination.

The leader of an organization should design an authority structure (and the authority relations it depicts) that is based on a task-analysis. Ideally, she should not settle instead for an authority structure or set of authority relations that she has designed primarily to fit the capacities, or to accommodate to the wishes, of particular available persons, or to adapt to existing resources. At least, the leader should not do so without realizing and accepting the possibly deleterious effects such a choice is likely to have on attempts to achieve goals or missions or realize values – and the potential such effects have to bring about deteriorating morale and quality of working life for those who participate in the system. If the leader decides to settle for something other than the ideal, it should be with the determination that there will be no scapegoating of individuals or groups in the organization, no blaming them for the strains, failures, interpersonal difficulties, and demoralization that are likely to result.

If the leadership planning group and the two of us had done the work of devising an authority structure based on the task-analysis in the proposal, then the proposal might have had a very different fate. If the authority structure implied by the task-analysis that underlay the new program had been presented as part of the proposal, it is unlikely that there would have been 'no opposition'. It is more likely that the leadership group developing the proposal, instead of having presented it, would still be arguing about it among themselves.

This proposal, set afloat in this organization at a particular moment in time, may not have been destined to stay afloat. It may not have been in the stars for it to be implemented. Two things suggested that it would not be, despite the idealism, enthusiasm, and collective effort that went into its making.

One, a cadre of people with the range of specialized skills needed to use groups in a variety of ways to help people and to teach these skills to others did not exist in the organization. No one responded to the proposal by suggesting a way to bring such a cadre into being, and no one volunteered to become a part of it.

Two, although there were those who liked the ideas and were willing to support them, no one stepped forward and said, 'This is me. I take this vision for my own. This is what I want to devote a chunk of my career, of my life, to realize.'

But I did not feel estranged from the leadership group or the organization when its members did not share in all particulars my image of its mission or take on as their own all of a vision that happens to be important to me. I did not think the members of the leadership group or the Director of the Outpatient Division should feel badly if it turned out that the proposal presented then did not fly. When resources and conditions are not available, and it is not in the cards to acquire the resources or do anything about the conditions, you have to be able to say, 'Not now. Not yet. Perhaps later. Perhaps something more important, more do-able has the floor right now.'

Psychiatry's identity crisis: if psychiatrists are to be leaders...

Where is psychiatry going? What is it? Psychiatry, changing rapidly in response to societal forces, has its own identity crisis. Trying to solve this crisis by securing a medical identity, it has been supine before the advance of managed care. Does it risk losing all it knows about the importance of dependable human relationships, the importance then of developing bonds between human beings, and so, of course, the importance of having enough time in alleviating emotional distress? If psychiatry bases itself on knowledge of neuroscience, will it cease to have a reason for being? Could it be replaced by, become a branch of, neurology? If it turns from human relationships and language to chemotherapeutic agents as primary in the treatment of mental illness, does it abdicate responsibility to other mental health disciplines for the care of those with emotional problems, character disorders, problems in living? What is psychiatry's relation to other mental health disciplines? Can it argue for administrative hegemony (for privileged access to leadership roles on treatment teams, for example) on the ground that it alone is capable of integrating a vast array of treatments and knowledge of both body and mind – without taking more interest in group and organizational dynamics in its clinical work, in its teaching, and in its research, than it now does?

The boundary between psychiatry and the social sciences is now relatively neglected and impermeable. Will it ever open again? If the mission of psychiatry – as of medicine in general – continues to include the rehabilitation of chronically ill patients (and not just the eradication of symptoms or the cure of illness), then knowledge from the social sciences, and especially knowledge of the dynamics of social relations in interpersonal dyads, within and between groups, and within and between organizations, will remain an indispensable resource.

We must have knowledge from the social sciences so long as there are organizations whose inputs and outputs, the objects of its processes of conversion, are recalcitrantly human. These 'human materials', unlike those that enter into the making of an automobile, interact with and affect those whose work it is to admit ill persons, disabled persons, and persons who lack knowledge, and produce well persons, rehabilitated persons, and inquiring persons. Working in such organizations as these (which are in crucial ways unlike those that convert inanimate materials), we must recognize and recruit – and like it or not we also do react to – the motives of those we process. We must find ways to get them to join us. We require their active cooperation. We must manage the motives and feelings, the anxieties and passions, they stir in us. We must get and use knowledge of the dynamics of social relations in interpersonal dyads, relations within and between groups, and within and between organizations – or we fail.

In conclusion: what the stories in this book make me want

Here is my image of one best-of-all-possible-worlds.

As a psychotherapist and psychoanalyst, I would like to see individual stories that are full of *conversations between different internal voices* become as popular as interpersonal stories.

As a group member, leader, or consultant, I would like to be able to tell *group stories* powerful enough to drown out *individual stories of blame*. I would like to tell stories about either/or thinking, splitting, self-disowning, projection, and scapegoating (whether marked by relentless attack or obsessive solicitude) that are so vivid and compelling that anyone who had heard them would, remembering them, immediately recognize 'I am participating in that kind of scenario!' and, breaking out of it, improvise new lines.

As a psychiatrist, I would like to see professional groups *give back at least some of the excess competence* they have accepted from those with whom they work, and at the same time their clients take back whatever competence they had given away at some cost to themselves.

And, finally, as a person interested in the study of groups and organizations, I would like those who study groups and organizations to show at least as much interest in the problems, the anxieties, the conflicts, that emanate from the *demands of work*, the conditions in which it must be done, and the stringencies of media and materials we use – as in the problems, anxieties, and conflicts that arise from the social, the fact of simply belonging to a group, any group. I would like them to show as much interest in the joy and terror of transforming and making as in the joy and terror of belonging and interacting.

Notes

1.   I will alternate use of 'him' or 'her' as generic pronouns to avoid the awkwardness of 'him or her'.
2.   See note 1.
3.   In three recent papers of mine (Edelson 1992a, 1992b, 1993), I have considered the implications of a focus on narrative for, respectively, psychoanalytic theory, psychotherapy research, and teaching psychotherapy. Material from Edelson (1993) – revised, in somewhat different form, and supplemented – appears here in Chapters 1–3.
4.   I shall not present evidence for this claim. It has been well-argued by cognitive scientists: e.g., Schank (1982, 1990); Schank and Abelson (1977). For a different view, arguing for 'rule-based mental models' in processes of inference, learning, and discovery, see Holland *et al.* (1989).
5.   Luborsky (1984); Luborsky and Crits-Christoph (1990).
6.   Schafer (1992).
7.   Freud (1900); Edelson (1972).
8.   Richards (1929).
9.   Edelson (1998).
10.   Holland (1968, 1973, 1988).
11.   Rapaport (1960).
12.   Murray (1938).
13.   Stephenson (1953).
14.   Stein (1948).
15.   Edelson (1975).
16.   Lipton (1977).
17.   Edelson (1991); Hopkins (1988).
18.   Edelson (1988, 1989).
19.   Stoller (1985, pp.105–106).
20.   Arlow (1969a, 1969b).
21.   Schafer (1968).
22.   Reik (1941).
23.   Stoller (1985).
24.   Fodor (1975, 1981, 1983, 1987, 1990).
25.   Edelson (1991); Hopkins (1988).
26.   Wollheim (1969, 1974, 1979).
27.   Schank (1982, 1990); Schank and Abelson (1977).
28.   Lakoff and Johnson (1980); Johnson (1987): Lakoff (1987).
29.   Lakoff (1987, pp.380–415).
30.   de Sousa (1987, pp.181–184).
31.   Bordwell (1985a, 1985b).
32.   Fenichel (1941, pp.42–43).
33.   Schafer (1976, 1983).
34.   Levenson (1988).

35. Shapiro (1989).
36. Kris (1982).
37. Edelson (1998).
38. Vendler (1995, Introduction, pp.1–8).
39. Shapiro (1989).
40. Pulver (1987, pp.147–165).
41. Edelson (1998).
42. There are many other details to consider in constructing the story or stories most on the patient's mind in these particular sessions (Edelson, 1998; Pulver 1987).
43. Sawyer and Weingarten (1990).
44. I discuss the fallacies associated with looking for confirming rather than disconfirming instances and with leaping from contiguity or sequence to causal connection in Edelson (1984, 1988).
45. Bordwell and Thompson (1993) have distinguished these kinds of meaning.
46. Breuer and Freud (1955, pp.160–161).
47. Those, for example, of E. Durkheim, M. Weber, T. Parsons, R. Merton, and A. K. Rice.
48. Ezriel (1952); Sutherland (1952); Whitaker and Lieberman (1964).
49. Smith and Berg (1987).
50. Wells (1985).
51. See Chapter 20.
52. Bion (1959).
53. Wells (1980, pp.176–177).
54. Bordwell (1985b).
55. Alderfer (1987).
56. Alderfer and Smith (1982).
57. See Chapter 10.
58. Suggested by Marshall Edelson, reflecting on his own work as a clinician.
59. See also the discussion in Chapter 20 of the use of a group as a medium to achieve psychotherapeutic goals.
60. See 'A similar analysis of another organization's dynamics,' in Chapter 19, 'Thrown to the Wolves' for an example of social-structural contributions to this kind of outcome for anyone occupying the role of Director of the Residency Program in a university department of psychiatry.
61. Redl (1958).
62. See, for example, Staiger (1995, especially Introduction, pp.1–14).
63. See Chapter 12.
64. Smith and Berg (1987).
65. Holland (1968, 1973, 1988).
66. Lopate (1995).
67. Major influences on my thinking about the aims of different mental processes and about relative autonomy include: S. Freud's 1911 essay 'Formulations on the two principles of mental functioning'; and D. Rapaport's essays on ego autonomy (1951, 1957).
68. Madsen (1990, p.111).
69. Bordwell (1985a).
70. Perkins (1972, p.156).
71. Crisp (1989, p.184).
72. Greene (1994); Simon (1982).
73. Basinger, (1993, pp.6–7, 505–506).
74. Perkins (1972, p.137).
75. Crisp (1989, p.126).

76. Crisp (1989, pp.8–9).

77. I owe this way of looking at *Pretty Woman* to David Berg, personal communication.

78. See Chapter 20.

79. Long after finishing this book, I came across the following passage in which Booth (1988, pp.13–14) makes a distinction (between 'aesthetic transactions' and 'efferent transactions'), which he attributes to Louise Rosenblatt: 'For some readers, fiction even of the least didactic kind will be read "efferently"– that is, in the search either for some practical guidance, or for some special wisdom, or for some other useful "carry-over" into non-fictional life. For some other readers, even the most aggressively didactic authors can be turned into an aesthetic transaction, just as time can occasionally transform a work like *Gulliver's Travels*, originally loaded with didactic freight, into a children's story, read for the sheer fun of the fantastic adventure.'

80. These were discussed in Part 2.

81. Whitaker and Lieberman (1964).

82. Bion (1959).

83. Namjoshi (1994).

84. See Part 6.

85. Redl (1958) discusses how what kinds of relations exist among members of a class depends on the kind of teacher they have.

86. Hill (1958).

87. Casement (1991).

88. The arguments for the dubiousness of these assumptions are given by Lipton (1977).

89. Lipton (1977).

90. Lipton's (1977) discussion of this point is the best one I know.

91. The second of these two stories appears in Chapter 22: 'The Male Authority Figure.'

92. Bales (1950).

93. Berg (1998).

94. Miller (1984).

95. Smith (1982).

96. Winnicott (1965).

97. See Chapter 25.

98. Henry (1954).

99. Wells (1980).

100. David Berg makes this point in Chapter 5.

101. Thoreau (1937).

102. Whitaker and Lieberman (1964).

103. See Part 6.

104. Wells (1980).

105. Ekstein and Wallerstein (1958).

106. Wells (1980).

107. Jaques (1955) and Lyth (1988, 1989) discuss the ways in which social institutions provide ways to manage anxiety. See especially Lyth's 'The functioning of social systems as a defence against anxiety' (1961); 'Staff support systems: task and anti-task in adolescent institutions' (1979); 'A psychoanalytic perspective on social institutions' (1986).

108. For a story about these problems, see Chapter 27.

109. Merton (1968, pp.279–440).

110. Berg and Smith (1988).

111. See Chapter 27.

112. See Chapter 30.

113. These stories, and those stories about therapeutic communities and community meetings that follow, are told in greater detail and embedded in different theoretical contexts, along with other stories, in Edelson (1964, 1970a, 1970b). My reflections about these stories, and the morals I draw from them, are different now from what they were when I wrote those books.

114. Alderfer (1988).

115. Smith (1982).

116. Whitaker, D. (1985).

117. Bion (1959).

References

Alderfer, C.P. (1987) 'An intergroup perspective on group dynamics.' In J. Lorsch (ed.) *Handbook of organizational behavior.* Englewood Cliffs, NJ: Prentice-Hall, 190–222.

Alderfer, C.P. (1988) 'Taking ourselves seriously as researchers.' In D.N. Berg and K.K. Smith (eds), *The Self in Social Inquiry.*

Alderfer, C.P. and Smith, K.K. (1982) 'Studying intergroup relations embedded in organizations.' *Administrative Sciences Quarterly* 27, 35–65.

Arlow, J. (1969a) 'Unconscious fantasy and disturbances of conscious experience.' *Psychoanalytic Quarterly* 38, 1–27.

Arlow, J. (1969b) 'Fantasy, memory, and reality testing.' *Psychoanalytic Quarterly*, 38, 28–51.

Bales, R. (1950) *Interaction Process Analysis: A Method for the Study of Small Groups.* Reading, MA: Addison-Wesley.

Basinger, J. (1993) *A Woman's View: How Hollywood Spoke to Women, 1930–1960.* New York: Alfred A. Knopf.

Berg, D.N. (1998). 'Resurrecting the muse: followership in organizations.' In E.B. Klein, F. Gabelnick and P. Herr (eds) *The Psychodynamics of Leadership.* Madison, CT: Psychosocial Press.

Berg, D.N. and Smith, K.K. (eds) (1988) *The Self in Social Inquiry.* Newbury Park, CA: Sage.

Bion, W. (1959) *Experiences in Groups and Other Papers.* New York: Basic Books, 1961.

Booth, W. (1988) *The Company We Keep: An Ethics of Fiction.* Berkeley, CA: University of California Press.

Bordwell, D. (1985a) *Narration in the Fiction Film.* Madison, WI: The University of Wisconsin Press.

Bordwell, D. (1985b) 'The classical Hollywood style, 1917–60.' In David Bordwell, Janet Staiger and Kristin Thompson *The Classical Hollywood Cinema: Film Style and Mode of Production to 1960.* New York: Columbia University Press, 1–84.

Bordwell, D and Thompson, K. (1993) *Film Art: An Introduction.* Fourth edition. New York: McGraw-Hill.

Breuer, J. and Freud, S. (1955) 'Studies on hysteria, 1893–1895.' In *S.E.*, Vol. 2, ed. J. Strachey. London: Hogarth Press.

Casement, P. (1991) *Learning from the Patient.* New York: Guilford Press.

Crisp, Q. (1989) *How to Go to the Movies.* New York: St. Martin's Press.

de Sousa, R. (1987) *The Rationality of Emotion.* Cambridge, MA: MIT Press.

Edelson, M. (1964) *Ego Psychology, Group Dynamics and the Therapeutic Community.* New York: Grune and Stratton.

Edelson, M. (1970a) *Sociotherapy and Psychotherapy.* Chicago: University of Chicago Press.

Edelson, M. (1970b) *The Practice of Sociotherapy: A Case Study.* New Haven, CT: Yale University Press.

Edelson, M. (1972) 'Language and Dreams: *The Interpretation of Dreams* Revisited.' In R. Eissler *et al.* (eds) *Psychoanalytic Study of the Child.* New York: Quadrangle Books 27, 203–282.

Edelson, M. (1975) *Language and Interpretation in Psychoanalysis.* Chicago: University of Chicago Press, paperback reprint, 1984.

Edelson, M. (1984) *Hypothesis and Evidence in Psychoanalysis.* Chicago: University of Chicago Press.

Edelson, M. (1988) *Psychoanalysis: A Theory in Crisis.* Chicago: University of Chicago Press, paperback edition, 1990.

Edelson, M. (1989) 'The nature of psychoanalytic theory: implications for psychoanalytic research.' *Psychoanalytic Inquiry*, 9, 169–92.

Edelson, M. (1991) 'Review of Clark, Peter and Wright, Crispin (eds), *Mind, Psychoanalysis and Science.' Psychoanalytic Quarterly*, 60, 1, 101–108.

Edelson, M. (1992a) 'Telling and enacting stories in psychoanalysis.' In J. Barron, M. Eagle, and D. Wolitzky (eds) *Interface of Psychoanalysis and Psychology.* Washington, D.C.: American Psychological Association Press, 99–124.

Edelson, M. (1992b) 'Can psychotherapy research answer this psychotherapist's questions?' *Contemporary Psychoanalysis*, 28, 118–151.

Edelson, M. (1993) 'Telling and enacting stories in psychoanalysis and psychotherapy: implications for teaching psychotherapy.' In A. Solnit, P. Neubauer, S. Abrams, and A. S. Dowling (eds) *The Psychoanalytic Study of the Child*, Vol. 48. New Haven, CT.: Yale University Press, 293–325.

Edelson, M. (1998). 'What is this movie doing in this psychoanalytic session?' and 'Response' *Journal of Clinical Psychoanalysis*, 7,1, 5–47, 79–93.

Ekstein, R. and Wallerstein, R. (1958) *The Teaching and Learning of Psychotherapy.* New York: International Universities Press.

Ezriel, H. (1952) 'Notes on psychoanalytic group therapy: II. Interpretation and research.' *Psychiatry* 15, 119–26.

Fenichel, O. (1941) *Problems of Psychoanalytic Technique.* New York: The Psychoanalytic Quarterly.

Fodor, J. (1975) *The Language of Thought.* New York: Crowell. Harvard University Press reprint, 1979.

Fodor, J. (1981) *Representations.* Cambridge, MA: MIT Press.

Fodor, J. (1983) *The Modularity of Mind.* Cambridge, MA: MIT Press.

Fodor, J. (1987) *Psychosemantics.* Cambridge, MA: MIT Press.

Fodor, J. (1990) *A Theory of Content.* Cambridge, MA: MIT Press.

Freud, S. (1900) 'The interpretation of dreams.' *Standard Edition*, Vols 4 and 5. London: Hogarth Press.

Freud, S. (1911) 'Formulations on the two principles of mental functioning.' *Standard Edition*, Vol. 12. London: Hogarth Press, 1958, 218–226.

Greene, G. (1994) *The Graham Greene Film Reader.* ed. David Parkinson. New York: Applause Books.

Henry, J. (1954) 'The formal social structure of a psychiatric hospital.' *Psychiatry* 17, 139–151.

Hill, L. (1958) 'On being rather than doing in psychotherapy.' *The International Journal of Group Psychotherapy*, 8, 115–122.

Holland, J., Holyoak, K., Nisbett, R. and Thagard, P. (1989) *Induction: Processes of Inference, Learning, and Discovery.* Cambridge, MA: MIT Press.

Holland, N. (1968) *The Dynamics of Literary Response.* New York: Columbia University Press, 1989 edition.

Holland, N. (1973) *Poems in Persons.* New York: Columbia University Press, 1989 edition.

Holland, N. (1988) *The Brain of Robert Frost.* New York: Routledge.

Hopkins, J. (1988) 'Epistemology and depth psychology: critical notes on *The Foundations of Psychoanalysis.*' In P. Clark and C. Wright (eds) *Mind, Psychoanalysis and Science.* New York: Basil Blackwell 33–60.

Jaques, E. (1955) 'Social systems as a defense against persecutory and depressive anxiety.' In M. Klein, P. Herman, and R. E. Money-Kyrle (eds) *New directions in psychoanalysis.* London: Tavistock.

Johnson, M. (1987) *The Body in the Mind: The Bodily Basis of Meaning, Imagination, and Reason.* Chicago: University of Chicago Press.

Kris, A. (1982) *Free Association: Method and Process.* New Haven, CT: Yale University Press.

Lakoff, G. (1987) *Women, Fire, and Dangerous Things: What Categories Reveal about the Mind.* Chicago: University of Chicago Press.

Lakoff, G. and Johnson, M. (1980) *Metaphors We Live By.* Chicago: University of Chicago Press.

Levenson, E. (1988) 'The pursuit of the particular.' *Contemporary Psychoanalysis,* 24, 1–16.

Lipton, S. (1977) 'The advantages of Freud's technique as shown in his analysis of the Rat Man.' *International Journal of Psychoanalysis,* 58, 255–273.

Lopate, P. (1995) 'It's not heroes who have bad grammar; it's films.' *The New York Times,* Sunday, June 18.

Luborsky, L. (1984) *Principles of Psychoanalytic Psychotherapy: A Manual for Supportive-Expressive Treatment.* New York: Basic Books, Inc.

Luborsky, L. and Crits-Christoph, P. (1990) *Understanding Transference: The CCRT Method.* New York: Basic Books, Inc.

Lyth, I. Menzies (1988). *Containing Anxiety in Institutions: Selected Essays,* Vol. I. London: Free Association Books.

Lyth, I. Menzies (1989) *The Dynamics of the Social: Selected Essays,* Vol. II. London: Free Association Books.

Madsen, R. (1990) *Working Cinema: Learning from the Masters.* Belmont, CA: Wadsworth Publishing Company.

Merton, R. (1968) *Social Theory and Social Structure.* New York: The Free Press, 1968 enlarged edition.

Miller, A. (1984) *For Your Own Good.* New York: Farrar, Straus, Giroux.

Murray, H. (1938) *Explorations in Personality.* New York: Oxford University Press.

Namjoshi, S. (1994) 'Excerpt from "The Ubiquitous Lout," in *St. Suniti and the Dragon.*' London: Virago Press Ltd. Cited by Marina Warner, (1995) *Six Myths of Our Time: Little Angels, Little Monsters, Beautiful Beasts, and More.* New York: Vintage Books.

Perkins, V. F. (1972) *Film as Film.* New York: Penguin Paperback.

Pulver, S. (1987) 'How theory shapes technique: perspectives on a clinical study.' *Psychoanalytic Inquiry,* 7, 2, 141–299.

Rapaport, D. (1951) 'The autonomy of the ego.' In M. Gill (ed.), *The Collected Papers of David Rapaport.* New York: Basic Books, Inc., 1967, 357–367.

Rapaport, D. (1957) 'The theory of ego autonomy: a generalization.' In M. Gill (ed.) *The Collected Papers of David Rapaport.* New York: Basic Books, Inc., 1967, 722–744.

Rapaport, D. (1960) 'On the psychoanalytic theory of motivation.' In M. Gill (ed.) *The Collected Papers of David Rapaport.* New York: Basic Books, Inc., 1967, 853–915.

Redl, F. (1958) 'Group emotion and leadership.' *Psychiatry,* 5, 573–596.

Reik, T. (1941) *Masochism in Modern Man.* New York: Farrar, Straus.

Richards, I.A. (1929) *Practical Criticism.* New York: Harcourt, Brace, and World.

Sawyer, T. and Weingarten, A. (1990) *Plots Unlimited.* Malibu, CA: Ashleywilde, Inc.

Schafer, R. (1968) 'The mechanisms of defence.' *International Journal of Psychoanalysis,* 8, 175–202.

Schafer, R. (1976) *A New Language for Psychoanalysis.* New Haven, CT: Yale University Press.

Schafer, R. (1983) *The Analytic Stance.* New York: Basic Books, Inc.

Schafer, R. (1992) *Retelling a Life: Narration and Dialogue in Psychoanalysis.* New York: Basic Books.

Schank, R. (1982) *Dynamic Memory.* New York: Cambridge University Press.

Schank, R. (1990) *Tell Me a Story.* New York: Charles Scribner's Sons.

Schank, R. and Abelson, R. (1977) *Scripts Plans Goals and Understanding.* Hillsdale, NJ: Lawrence Erlbaum.

Shapiro, D. (1989) *Psychotherapy of Neurotic Character.* New York: Basic Books

Simon, J. (1982) *Reverse Angle: A Decade of American Films.* New York: Clarkson N. Potter, Inc.

Smith, K. K. (1982) *Groups in Conflict.* Dubuque, Iowa: Kendall-Hunt.

Smith, K. K. and Berg, D. N. (1987) *Paradoxes of Group Life.* San Francisco, California: Jossey-Bass.

Staiger, J. (ed.) (1995) *The Studio System.* New Brunswick, NJ: Rutgers University Press.

Stein, M. (1948) *The Thematic Apperception Test: An Introductory Manual for its Clinical Use with Adult Males.* Cambridge, MA: Addison-Wesley Press.

Stephenson, W. (1953) *The Study of Behavior.* Chicago: University of Chicago Press.

Stoller, R. (1985) *Observing the Erotic Imagination.* New Haven, CT. Yale University Press.

Sutherland, J. D. (1952) 'Notes on psychoanalytic group therapy. I. Therapy and training.' *Psychiatry* 15, 111–117.

Thoreau, H. D. (1937) *Walden.* New York: Modern Library.

Vendler, H. (1995) *Soul Says: On Recent Poetry,* Cambridge, MA: Harvard University Press.

Wells, L. (1980) 'The group-as-a-whole: a systemic socio-analytic perspective on interpersonal and group relations.' In C.P. Alderfer and C.L. Cooper (eds) *Advances in Experiential Social Processes.* New York: John Wiley and Sons, 1980, 165–199.

Wells, L. (1985) 'The group-as-a-whole perspective and its theoretical roots.' In A. Colman and M. Geller (eds) *Group Relations Reader 2.* Washington, D.C.: A. K. Rice Institute, 109–126.

Whitaker, D.S. (1985) *Using Groups to Help People.* London: Routledge and Kegan Paul.

Whitaker, D.S. and Lieberman, M. (1964) *Psychotherapy through the Group Process.* New York: Atherton Press.

Winnicott, D. W. (1965) *Maturational Processes and the Facilitating Environment.* London: Hogarth Press.

Wollheim, R. (1969) 'The mind and the mind's image of itself.' *On Art and the Mind.* Cambridge, MA: Harvard University Press, 1974, 31–53.

Wollheim, R. (1974) 'Identification and imagination.' In R. Wollheim (ed.) *Freud: A Collection of Critical Essays.* New York: Anchor Press paperback, 172–195.

Wollheim, R. (1979) 'Wish-fulfilment.' In R. Harrison (ed.) *Rational Action.* Cambridge: Cambridge University Press, 47–60.

Subject Index

Author Index